# ArtScroll Series®

Rabbi Nosson Scherman / Rabbi Meir Zlotowitz

*General Editors*

THE FRIEDMAN EDITION

# RAV NOSSON TZVI

The Beloved Rosh Yeshiva of Mir
From his mother's heart and through the eyes of a talmid

## REBBETZIN SARA FINKEL
### AND RABBI YEHUDA HEIMOWITZ

Published by
Mesorah Publications, ltd

FIRST EDITION
First Impression … March 2012
Second Impression … April 2012
Third Impression … July 2012


Published and Distributed by
**MESORAH PUBLICATIONS, LTD.**
4401 Second Avenue / Brooklyn, N.Y 11232

Distributed in Europe by
**LEHMANNS**
Unit E, Viking Business Park
Rolling Mill Road
Jarow, Tyne & Wear, NE32 3DP
England

Distributed in Australia and New Zealand
by **GOLDS WORLDS OF JUDAICA**
3-13 William Street
Balaclava, Melbourne 3183
Victoria, Australia

Distributed in Israel by
**SIFRIATI / A. GITLER — BOOKS**
6 Hayarkon Street
Bnei Brak 51127

Distributed in South Africa by
**KOLLEL BOOKSHOP**
Ivy Common
105 William Road
Norwood 2192, Johannesburg, South Africa

**ARTSCROLL SERIES®**
**RAV NOSSON TZVI**
© Copyright 2012, by MESORAH PUBLICATIONS, Ltd.
4401 Second Avenue / Brooklyn, N.Y. 11232 / (718) 921-9000 / www.artscroll.com

ISBN 10: 1-4226-1193-0 / ISBN 13: 978-1-4226-1193-7


Typography by CompuScribe at ArtScroll Studios, Ltd.
Printed in the United States of America by Noble Book Press Corp.
Bound by Sefercraft, Quality Bookbinders, Ltd., Brooklyn N.Y. 11232

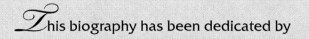*This* biography has been dedicated by

## Hershey and Raisy Friedman and Family
### of Montreal, Canada

as a tribute to the Rosh Hayeshiva *zt"l* for his incredible accomplishments of expanding and building Yeshivas Mir Yerushalayim into the fortress of Torah that it is today.

He touched the hearts and souls of thousands of Yidden in Klal Yisrael with his special warmth, respect, and outstanding מידות טובות.  His home and heart was always open for all members of עם ישראל.

May this book serve as an ongoing inspiration for us all to emulate his noble דרך החיים and be a זכות for his pure נשמה.

## זכרו הטהור חקוק בלבנו לנצח

## ת.נ.צ.ב.ה.

## Approbation of the Rosh Yeshiva
## Harav Eliezer Yehuda Finkel *shlita*

ישיבת מיר ירושלים

YESHIVAS MIR YERUSHALAYIM

Founded in Mir 1817. In Jerusalem 1944
RABBI E.Y. FINKEL
DEAN

עי"ר 580037638

בס"ד נוסדה במיר בשנת תקע"ז. בירושלים בשנת תש"ד
הרב א.י. פינקל
ראש הישיבה

בס"ד

ח"י לחודש אשר נהפך התשע"ב

שמועה טובה תדשן עצם הנני בזה להביע הכרת הטוב לזקנתי מורתי שתחי' על
אשר זכתה לערך על המוגמר, ולהנציח בזה את זכרו הטהור של אאמו"ר זצוק"ל
הכ"מ, ובודאי דברי זקנתי תלמידי"א אינם צריכים חיזוק, אך יש בזה הכרת טובה בשם
המשפחה שהרבה טרחות טרחה ע"י, יהי' שתראה ברכה מרובה בעמלה ורוב נחת
מכל יוצ"ח מתוך בריות גופא ונהורא מעליא לאורך ימים ושנים דשנים ורעננים.
התגלה והברכה להרה"ג יהודה הימנוביץ שליט"א שקרב אל המלאכה והפלי'א
לעשות בזמן קצר חיבור נאה לוקט את הרבים, ושמעתי שיש בו דברים מועילים
ומוסר השכל ללמוד מדרכיו וארחותיו של אאמו"ר זצוק"ל. שיזכה להגדיל תורה
שיהגו רבים לאורו. וכן אפריון נמטייה להוצאת ספרים "ארטסקול" אשר היוו
אכסניא ליצירה זו וטרחו להוציאן בכלי מפואר ולשכללו ולהביאן אל המוגמר.
ברכה מיוחדת להגעיד המפואר מורם מעם ומוקיר תורה הרה"ח ר' חיים הערש
פריעדמאן הי"ו ממונטריאל קנדה, אשר נשא לבו לשאת את עול המלאכה הזו
ולהיות שותף להנעצת שמו של אאמו"ר זצוק"ל הכ"מ. שיראו הוא ונ"ב החשובה
מרת רייזל תחי' העומדת לימינו בצדקת פזרונו, שיחיו ברכה מרובה במעשה ידיהם
ויזכו להרבות פעלים לתורה, ויאריך ה' ימיהם ושנותיהם בנעימים מתוך נחת עדנים
ובריות גופא ונהורא מעליא דשנים ורעננים יהיו עד ביאת ינון בקרוב.

ישיבת מיר ירושלים
## YESHIVAS MIR YERUSHALAYIM

Founded in Mir 1817. In Jerusalem 1944     עייר 580037638     בסייד נוסדה במיר בשנת תקעייז. בירושלים בשנת תשייד
RABBI E.Y. FINKEL     הרב א.י. פינקל
DEAN     ראש הישיבה

17 Adar 5772

Rabbi Yehuda Heimowitz, as a loyal talmid of the Yeshiva and of the Rosh H'Yeshiva Rav Nosson Zvi ZT"L for thirteen years, began his work with a clear perception of the essence of the personality he so exquisitely brought to light. In that aspect, he is truly a befitting co-author with the esteemed mother of the Rosh H'Yeshiva, Rebbetzin Sara Finkel, who likewise used her blessed talents to celebrate the special person that her son was.

The work of a biographer begins, much like that of a sculptor, after the raw material has been set before him. The painstaking and persistent chiseling, inch by inch, is what brings forth the true form of the personality he is portraying. Smoothening rough edges and polishing to a shine are imperative for the biographer as well.

Remaining faithful to the art of writing and yet completing this work within the time constraint that was given is truly amazing. Perhaps what made it possible is what the authors have in common with the multitudes of Klal Yisroel – love for Rav Nosson Zvi.

It was a pleasure to work together and it is our hope that "Rav Nosson Zvi", like in his lifetime, will be marbeh kvod shomayim.

**Harav Binyomin Carlebach**             **Harav Nachman Levovitz**

רח. בית ישראל 3 ת.ד. 5022 ירושלים 91050 טל. 02-5410999 פקס. 02-5323446 עייר 580037638 ● 5880037638 Fax. 02-5323446 ● Jerusalem 91050 Tel. 02-5410999 Fax. 02-5323446 3 Beth Israel St. P.O.B 5022 Jerusalem 91050 Tel. 02-5410999 Fax. 02-5323446

# TABLE OF CONTENTS

# ᏰOOK 2

Partner / "Don't Take Away My Baby" / Incentives / Friday
and Shabbos / Until the Very End / $400 for One Seder /
Today's Battlefield /Celebrating Torah / Combating Bitul
Torah / The Call / No Hafganos / The Kitchen Is Always
Open / Shabbos Getaways

---

**PHOTO CREDITS:**

Agudath Israel Archives
R' Yehuda Baum
Shlomo Zalman Englander
R' Yosef Ettlinger
Finkel Family Albums
Rav Gedalya and Rebbetzin Mimi Finkel
Rebbetzin Sara Finkel
Yossi Finkel
Yinon Fuchs / Mishpacha Magazine
Hazricha B'Paasei Kedem, reprinted
with permission of Mishor Publications

Rav Refoel Katz
Rebbetzin Tzivia Levinson
R' Beinish Mandel
Mir Archives
R' A.J. Rowe
Chaim Schvarcz / Kuvien Images
Mrs. Tzivia Solomon
Nachum Chaim Srebro
Mrs. Mindy Stern

# ᏐUBLISHER'S ᏐREFACE

ᏐT IS A PRIVILEGE TO PRESENT THIS WORK TO THE PUBlic. The *gaon* Harav Nosson Tzvi Finkel זצ"ל was unique, and at the same time he was proof that everyone can aspire to the heights and reach them. His story will be especially meaningful to young people who may feel that they lack the background or ability to make great strides in Torah and service to *Klal Yisrael*.

He grew up in Chicago long before higher Torah education and years in a *kollel* became givens in America. He received a fine Jewish education by the standards of the day, but he was hardly on the fast track to attain one of the very highest positions in the world of Torah. Would anyone have predicted that he would become the Rosh Yeshiva of the Mirrer Yeshiva of Jerusalem and the builder of the world's largest Torah center? Surely that was an unreachable fantasy!

Yet that is what he accomplished.

That he was able to do so is a tribute to his parents; to his iron will to grow and excel in Torah and service of Hashem; to the vision of his two great mentors, the *geonim* Harav Eliezer Yehudah and Harav Beinush Finkel זצ"ל; and to the *siyata d'Shmaya* that he richly earned. That he achieved so much in defiance of the Parkinson's disease that would have completely hobbled lesser people makes him all the more a remarkable and truly inspirational role model.

It is said that the Vilna Gaon declared, "If you *vill nohr* (only want it enough), every one of you can become a *gaon*." Rav Nosson Tzvi was living proof of how great a Jew can become if he wants it enough and applies himself to it unstintingly.

No one can read this book without marveling at the Rosh Yeshiva as a servant of Hashem and of *Klal Yisrael*; as a loyal son, husband, and father; as a wise and loving mentor to thousands upon thousands of *talmidim*, as a man who lived for others; and as a tenacious warrior against a debilitating disease.

**Rebbetzin Sara Finkel** תחיה, a woman of outstanding accomplishment in her own right, has performed a great service by writing so skillfully and movingly about her revered son. She gives us insights that only a mother could share, and in doing so she makes us feel and understand the Rosh Yeshiva in ways that would be impossible without her. Every reader of her masterful biography will be grateful.

Book 2 of this volume was written by **Rabbi Yehuda Heimowitz**, a *talmid* of the Rosh Yeshiva. He interviewed many scores of people, from family, to colleagues, to *talmidim*, to ordinary people. The Finkel family and Roshei Yeshiva of the Mir gave him their full cooperation, and shared memories, impressions, photographs, and documents. That Rabbi Heimowitz could assimilate and organize such a wealth of material in such a short time and write it so well is extraordinary.

In addition to the story of Rav Nosson Tzvi, this volume also presents the history of the Mirrer Yeshiva, the oldest continuously functioning yeshiva in the world, from its founding in the 19th century. It also introduces us to the Rosh Yeshiva's namesake and ancestor, Rav Nosson Tzvi Finkel זצ"ל, the Alter of Slabodka; Rav Leizer Yudel Finkel זצ"ל, the Mirrer Rosh Yeshiva, great-uncle of Rav Nosson Tzvi and the one who first foresaw and developed his potential; and Rav Beinush Finkel זצ"ל, the Mirrer Rosh Yeshiva, father-in-law of Rav Nosson Tzvi, and one of the hidden giants of his time.

We are grateful to **Rav Binyamin Carlebach**, a Rosh Yeshiva in the Mir and a very close colleague of the Rosh Yeshiva, for envisioning this volume, helping bring it to fruition, cooperating in every possible way, and for giving us the honor of publishing it.

Rebbetzin Finkel and Rabbi Heimowitz have done justice to their subject, and that is an astoundingly great feat. Every reader of this magnificent portrait will share our gratitude to them. We pray that this volume will help further the goals to which Rav Nosson Tzvi devoted his life: to imbue love of Torah and aspiration for greatness.

Rabbi Meir Zlotowitz / Rabbi Nosson Scherman

Adar 5772 / March 2012

# ACKNOWLEDGMENTS

I T IS WITH GREAT HUMILITY THAT I EXPRESS MY GRATI-
tude to the *Ribono shel Olam* for giving me the ability, especially at this trying time, to share with my readers memories,
thoughts, and feelings that I experienced throughout the years relating
to my late beloved son, Rav Nosson Tzvi *zt"l*.

I wish to acknowledge with the utmost reverence and respect the
memory of my esteemed late husband, R' Eliyahu Meir Finkel *zt"l*. I am
deeply grateful for his devotion and I cherish his memory.

To Miriam Zakon, chief editor of this work: It has, indeed, been a
great pleasure for me to work with her. I found that she excelled in the
editing as well as in organizing my manuscript. I am grateful to her for
her patience and sensitivity.

My deep appreciation to my beloved son, Rav Gedalya *shlita*, for the
help he has given me during the writing of these memoirs, for sharing
some of his *divrei Torah* with me, as well as for his continued encouragement and support, especially at this particular time.

To my beloved daughter-in-law Leah, for her loyal friendship from
the very beginning of our relationship, as well as her selfless devotion
to me throughout the years, in so many ways.

To my beloved daughter-in-law Mimi, for her devoted friendship
and being available whenever I need her. Thank you Mimi for checking

over the manuscript, translating when necessary, as well as helping to procure information.

My deep appreciation to Rabbi Binyamim Carlebach and Rabbi Nachman Levovitz for their unswerving devotion to my late son, Rav Nosson Tzvi zt"l, in his efforts on behalf of the Yeshiva. Their devoted efforts on behalf of Yeshivas Mir have been extraordinary.

Many thanks to Aviva Durrant for the help she has given to me so graciously. I appreciate your efficient outlining of the manuscript and helping me with the typing, as well as making useful suggestions.

My profound gratitude to Mr. and Mrs. Hershey Friedman for their significant dedication of this book.

My deep appreciation to my grandchildren, who provided me with some of the interesting stories they heard at the *shivah* or which they themselves experienced with their late father, Rav Nosson Tzvi zt"l. I also thank them for allowing me to take this special time away from them to prepare this work, saying,"Bubby, when are you finishing the book already; we're waiting for you."

I want to thank all those who provided me with stories that they experienced with my son. Many of them I found to be very moving and made me even more aware of the special dimension he engendered.

I am grateful to Rabbi Yechezkel Leiman of Lakewood, New Jersey for the inspiring letters he sent me concerning his relationship with my son during the time he was learning in the Mir Yeshiva.

My deep appreciation to Rabbi Nosson Scherman, to Rabbi Meir Zlotowitz, and to Mr. Shmuel Blitz of ArtScroll Publishers, for accepting so readily the publishing of this work.

I wish to acknowledge  Rabbi Binyamin Ginsberg for some of his ideas on tefillah.  I would also like to thank Rav Aaron Lopiansky for reading over my manuscript and commenting on it favorably.

My heartfelt thanks to the kind and generous people who have helped my late son Rav Nosson Tzvi zt"l in his efforts on behalf of Yeshivas Mir. Words fail me to adequately express my deep appreciation to each one of you who have shown devoted friendship to him, and support for this holy institution, thereby making my son's task lighter. He has often mentioned your names to me with much fondness and admiration.

Rebbetzin Sara Finkel

Adar 5772

# CACKNOWLEDGMENTS

I N A SENSE, THIS BOOK CLOSES A CIRCLE.
Approximately six years before Rav Nosson Tzvi passed away, I was faced with a dilemma of whether to stay in Eretz Yisrael and pursue a part-time career writing for the Torah world, or move away from Eretz Yisrael to accept an offer from one of several Kollelim in the Diaspora, which would have allowed me to remain in full-time Torah study.

I went to consult with the Rosh Yeshiva, explaining that I felt very comfortable in Eretz Yisrael and I wanted to stay – but perhaps the opportunity to study Torah full-time overrode that consideration?

The Rosh Yeshiva smiled warmly and issued a characteristic answer: "Stay in Eretz Yisrael, and remain in full-time learning."

I smiled back, and answered, *"Im ein kemach, ein Torah"* (If there is no flour, there is no Torah; *Avos* 3:17).

"In that case," the Rosh Yeshiva replied, "stay here and write."

But to say that this book closes a circle because I owe the Rosh Yeshiva my writing career would be a severe understatement.

Like some other Mirrer *talmidim* of this generation, I came to the yeshiva assuming that I would spend a year there, two at most, and then return to the United States to complete the college degree I had begun before coming to Eretz Yisrael.

Within a month of my joining the Mir, I knew for certain that this was my home. It took just one Elul *zman* for me to grow to love everything about the yeshiva – the style of learning, the warmth of the *hanhalah*, the camaraderie among the *talmidim*, and the tangible feeling of *kedushah* that permeates the Holy City in general, and the Mir in particular.

Thirteen years later, I am still at home in the Mir. The credit for this, as you will read in this book, belongs to Rav Nosson Tzvi. It was he who fostered the atmosphere of warmth, it was he who created programs to spur the *talmidim* to learn with diligence and with a set goal of completing a *masechta* each *zman*, and it was his interest in connecting with each *talmid* that made me and so many others feel that the Mir is truly our home.

And so this book closes another circle: a debt of gratitude to the Rosh Yeshiva for making me love learning and providing me with a home in which to grow in Torah and *avodah*.

I am forever grateful to the *Ribbono shel Olam* for enabling me to join the Mir and to have a personal connection with the Rosh Yeshiva. This connection will *iy"H* continue to shape me and my family even as we try to come to terms with the loss of Rav Nosson Tzvi's influence in our lives.

The decision to take a break from my pursuit of a career was made with the guidance of *mori v'rabi* Rav Chaim Kitevits of Yeshiva U'Mesivta Rabbeinu Chaim Berlin, who continues to guide me in every step I take and cares for me like a father. May he be *zocheh* to continue to disseminate Torah amidst good health *ad mei'ah v'esrim shanah*.

Upon arriving in Mir, apart from the relationship forged with the Rosh Yeshiva, most *talmidim* connect with other *hanhalah* members with whom they feel a natural bond. In my case, I connected first with Rav Elya Baruch Finkel *zt"l*, whose radiance and good humor I miss until today. He had a way of endearing the Torah upon the hearts of every *talmid*, and anyone who learned in his *shiur* will never forget the utter joy on his face when he resolved a difficult *sugya*.

Another bond I still cherish is the one I formed with the *mashgiach*, Rav Aharon Chodosh, a few months after arriving in Mir. Aside from our weekly *chavrusashaft*, the *mashgiach* often hosted me at Shabbos *seudos* and has taken an interest in my life in every step of the way since. The *mashgiach* also spared a few hours of his busy schedule to share his memories of the Rosh Yeshiva and the history of the Mir, where he has served on the *hanhalah* for over fifty years. May Hashem grant him the energy to continue his *avodas hakodesh*.

During my last *zman* as a *bachur*, I approached Rav Binyamin Carlebach and asked him if I could learn *mussar* with him *b'chavrusa*. My bond with him began with those sessions learning *Chovos Halevavos*, and has since grown.

Rav Binyamin has been the visionary and guiding force behind this book. As the Rosh Yeshiva's closest ally in fundraising and running the yeshiva, Rav Binyamin's memories serve as one of the most crucial components of this book, and he graciously gave hours upon hours of his time to share those memories.

Rav Binyamin also read the entire manuscript, commenting and correcting when necessary – along with offering the encouragement and *tefillos* to see it through to completion.

Rebbetzin Bat Tzion Carlebach runs many aspects of the yeshiva from behind the scenes, and her input and sharp recall of the process of the yeshiva's expansion added an extra dimension to the book.

May they be *zocheh* to continue in their tireless and selfless efforts on behalf of yeshiva *ad bi'as go'el tzedek*.

I humbly acknowledge the involvement of Rebbetzin Finkel, the Rosh Yeshiva's wife, who put aside her personal grief and not only consented to this project, but also provided guidance and shared some family pictures for the book.

An additional *yasher koach* is due to Rav Nosson Tzvi's sons – the current Rosh Yeshiva, Rav Eliezer Yehuda *shlit"a*, for his encouragement as the book took shape, and Rav Yosef Shmaryahu and Rav Shaya Finkel, who welcomed me into their homes and shared their personal recollections with me.

Rav Menachem Zaretsky: thank you for all of your time and assistance.

I am grateful to Rebbetzin Sara Finkel, for entrusting me with the task of eternalizing her son from the perspective of a *talmid*. Her encouragement was a comforting backdrop in these frenetic few months. As the author of Book 1 of this volume, she beautifully portrays the Rosh Yeshiva as no one else could. May she see only *nachas* from her entire family.

An extra measure of gratitude is owed to Rav Nosson Tzvi's brother, Rav Gedalya Finkel, who took the time to review each page of the manuscript and offer many valuable additions. I thank his wife, Rebbetzin Mimi Finkel, for facilitating many aspects of the publication.

In an interview, R' Mendy Horowitz, a longtime *talmid* and Brooklyn host of the Rosh Yeshiva, shared an amazing memory. He recalled that at the end of a day of fundraising, they would often review how much they had accomplished that day and conclude that it was physically impossible to have done so much in one day (see p. 371).

This book merited a similar "*kefitzas haderech.*" The decision to have this biography ready in time for the Mir Dinner was reached in late December 2011. In the less than three months that have passed since that decision, over fifty people graciously provided interviews for the book, scores of people sent material and pictures, and several others set aside large chunks of time to review and comment on the manuscript.

Yet there is no way to explain how this book came into being in so short a time without acknowledging the merit – and the lessons – of the Rosh Yeshiva. Most Americans arriving in Mir are accustomed to learning a total of 10-15 *blatt* in a *zman*, and are often shell-shocked upon hearing that they are expected to master an entire *masechta* in one *zman*. But the Rosh Yeshiva taught us that when one sets lofty goals, he can merit the *siyata d'Shmaya* to attain them. I experienced this phenomenon throughout the writing of this book.

There were times when the merit of the Rosh Yeshiva shone through in an incredible way. Several times, I felt that I was missing a story or a fact that was crucial for the chapter I was writing. On the very day I was at an impasse, I'd meet someone in the yeshiva dining room or in a hallway and ask him for his memories – and the person invariably provided me with a story that filled the gap. As was the case with everything else about Rav Nosson Tzvi's life, the book *Rav Nosson Tzvi* was accompanied by remarkable *siyata d'Shmaya*.

I would like to thank the Rosh Yeshiva's brothers-in-law, Rav Nachman Levovitz and Rav Aharon Lopiansky, as well as *hanhalah* members Rav Avraham Shmuelevitz and Rav Tzvi Partzovitz, for sharing their thoughts and memories of the Rosh Yeshiva.

Rav Yosef Elefant and Rav Refoel Katz, two of the key figures in the success of the Beis Yeshaya building, each spent several hours sharing their unique perspectives of the Rosh Yeshiva with me.

An additional resource that made this book possible were the recordings of nearly 200 *hespedim* delivered in the Mir and around the world. Though I didn't merit to interview all of the *maspidim*, I am grateful for the opportunity to eternalize their thoughts and stories in writing.

I have been fortunate to know the staff of the American office of the Mir for many years, and specifically the person who leads the massive undertaking, R' Mordechai Grunwald. R' Mordechai, thank you for your friendship and for your considerable assistance in making this book happen.

I would also like to thank R' Chanoch Zundel Hershkowitz and Miss Nechama Goldwag of the Mir office for dropping everything on several occasions to provide material for the book.

Everyone is astounded by the *chessed* factories in and around Mir, most of which are due in great measure to the dedication of four people: R' Zevy Chodosh, R' Shaya Ehrentreu, R' Asher Eisenberg, and R' Eli Landesman. I have treasured their friendship for many years, and they were of invaluable assistance, providing me with a wealth of background material and pictures.

Special thanks is due to R' Yehuda Neuhaus both for taking the time to share his memories of his unique relationship with the Rosh Yeshiva and for coordinating the effort to gather pictures in the last stages of producing this volume.

A common denominator between all of the people who were influenced by the Rosh Yeshiva is the gracious manner in which they interact with others. I was astounded time after time at how everyone who knew Rav Nosson Tzvi would bend their schedules to make time to be interviewed for the book. I am grateful to the following people for their contributions to the book (listed alphabetically):

Mr. Shael Bellows, Rav Avrohom Cheshin, Eli Fogel, R' Moshe Dovid Fox, Mr. Gary Fragin, Mr. Greg Fragin, Mr. Hershey Friedman, R' Yitzchok Gerstel, R' Ari Gottesman, R' Yitzchak Grant, Rav Moshe Meir Heizler, R' Moshe Helberg, Shlomo Hirschey, R' Mendy Horowitz, R' Yitzchok Kalifon, Rav Daniel Lehrfield, Rebbetzin Tzivia Levinson, R' Mordechai Linzer, R' Beinish Mandel, Mrs. Rikki Munk, R' Zalman Rosental, R' A. J. Rowe, R' Eli Schneider, R' Yankel Schwartz, R' Nochum Stilerman, R' Uri Talesnick, R' Meir Wahrsager, Rabbi Harvey Well, R' Shmuli Wolman, R' Chaim Yarmish, and Zion the barber.

It has been a true honor to have two of the foremost writers in the Torah world, Rabbis Nosson Scherman and Yonoson Rosenblum, serve as my mentors for the last six years.

I am extremely grateful to Rabbi Scherman for serving as my guide on all writing-related matters since I first got to know him. In the last two weeks, Rabbi Scherman set aside time to edit every page I wrote in this biography. Though he wouldn't forgive me for writing what he would consider excessive praise, I will say that it is a pleasure to watch – and learn from – a maestro at work.

R' Yonoson has always been kind enough to share his constructive criticism, whether in projects I did as his protégé or in my current role as editor of his weekly *Mishpacha* column. All frum biographers measure themselves against R' Yonoson, and at the very beginning of this project, he sat with me and magnanimously shared his tricks of the trade.

This is the tenth book I am publishing, either as writer or editor, with the ArtScroll/Mesorah staff. The level of professionalism and *mentchlichkeit* of the team Rabbi Meir Zlotowitz has put together astounds me anew every time we produce a book. It is truly a pleasure to work with each one of them.

This project has been guided from its very inception by Shmuel Blitz. That we were able to produce a full-length biography by this deadline is in no small measure due to his steady input and guidance.

In a turn of *hashgachah*, an old neighbor of mine from Boro Park, Mrs. Miriam Zakon, served as the editor overseeing this project. Her guidance, editing, and most of all, encouragement, kept this book moving along through many endless nights of work.

As this project took shape, Mendy Herzberg and I communicated by phone and email daily at first, then hourly, and at the end, practically every few minutes. Thank you, Mendy, for being unflappable under the most intense pressure, and for keeping the smile on all of our faces.

The complex and painstaking job of designing this book chapter by chapter was handled with aplomb by Miss Devorah Bloch, whose talent as a graphic artist jumps off every page in the book. Thank you for working all those overtime hours on *Motza'ei Shabbasos* and Sundays to complete this book in time.

Eli Kroen – they say you can't judge a book by its cover. I can only hope that this book stands up to the breathtaking cover you created.

Mrs. Mindy Stern undertook to proofread this project despite other important obligations. I appreciate her sound judgment and easy manner in dealing with the fine details that make a good book great. Her modesty, generosity, and dedication are astounding. She was assisted by Mrs. Faigy Weinbaum and Mrs. Frumie Eisner.

Although I did not work with them personally, I am well aware that R' Sheah Brander has set the standard of excellence that will distinguish the final product, and that R' Gedaliah Zlotowitz is a key component in all the superlative work of ArtScroll / Mesorah.

Avrohom Biderman has always been a close friend and ally, and I appreciate the time he took to provide guidance when we needed him –

despite numerous other projects he was involved in during the bulk of the production time of this book.

The idea that I would be *zocheh* to write the biography of the Rosh Yeshiva began to germinate because my employer, R' Eli Paley of *Mishpacha* magazine, asked me to produce a special supplement on the day of Rav Nosson Tzvi's *petirah*. I appreciate his friendship and the easy manner with which he treats all of his employees.

"*Knei lecha chaver*" – I am fortunate to have acquired a friend who is worth much more than money can buy: Rabbi Yisroel Besser, a colleague on the editorial board of *Mishpacha*. I am forever indebted to him for his help in many aspects of producing this book, and specifically for sharing a wealth of material on Rav Nosson Tzvi.

I am deeply grateful to the managing editor at Mishpacha, Mrs. Shoshana Friedman, who has left an indelible mark on my writing style through her incisive comments and editing of my articles for the magazine. Special thanks is also due to her husband, R' Yossi Friedman, a *talmid chacham* of note who has been a friend of mine in the Mir for the last twelve years.

I would also like to express my appreciation and admiration for the rest of my colleagues on *Mishpacha*'s editorial board, R' Binyamin Rose, R' Eytan Kobre, and Mrs. Rochel Ginsberg.

*Acharon, acharon chaviv* – my family.

To my parents, R' Meir Zev and Mrs. Dina Heimowitz: Words cannot describe all the gratitude I owe you for everything you have done for us over the years, and especially for convincing me to come to Eretz Yisrael to begin with and for supporting us in our decision to remain here.

To my in-laws, R' Hershel and Mrs. Esther Gerstel: Thank you for enabling us to return to Eretz Yisrael and the Mir after our wedding, and for your continuous encouragement on all fronts.

To all our grandparents and siblings: We appreciate your steady love and support, even from afar.

May you all continue to see *nachas* from our family and from all of your children and grandchildren, in good health and prosperity.

While speaking at a *siyum* held in his home by one of the *maggidei shiur* in the Mir, Rav Nosson Tzvi made a point of thanking the *maggid shiur's* wife for all that she did to free him to learn and teach Torah. After he spoke, the *maggid shiur* approached him and said, "The Rosh

Yeshiva should know that I wasn't remiss in not thanking my wife – she specifically told me that she doesn't want me to thank her publicly."

"I know," replied Rav Nosson Tzvi, "and that's why *I* thanked her."

If Rav Nosson Tzvi would be writing acknowledgments for this book, he would undoubtedly take the opportunity to thank my wife Malky for all that she has done to make this project a reality, from taking on far more of the burden of the household than usual to her direct input in editing each chapter. Her imprint is on every page of this volume (aside from these few paragraphs).

I can only pray that the spirit of the Rosh Yeshiva that has permeated our household during the last few months, when almost all conversation in the house centered around this book, should continue to rest on our home, and that we should merit to raise a family that would make him proud.

At a *hesped* in Toronto for Rav Nosson Tzvi, my dear friend Rabbi Yisroel Besser shared a beautiful thought. Many people noted that the Rosh Yeshiva shares a *yahrtzeit* with Rochel Imeinu, about whom the prophet states, "*Rochel mevakah al baneha ki einenu* – Rochel cries for her children, for *he* is not there" (*Yirmiyahu* 31:14). Shouldn't it say that she cries for her children for *they* are not there?

R' Yisroel cited a parable of a family that makes a birthday party for their mother. When she arrives, she sees that only eleven of her twelve children are there. Her joy is not diminished by only one-twelfth because of that child's absence; she can't fully enjoy the time with the rest of the children either because that one child is missing.

The Rosh Yeshiva loved each *talmid* so much, explained R' Yisroel, that if even one *talmid* wasn't happy or wasn't successful in learning, he couldn't fully enjoy the success of the thousands of others.

Rosh Yeshiva, as the humble *shaliach tzibbur* to perpetuate your legacy, I pray that you should be a *meilitz yosher* for your own family, for the broader Mirrer family, and for each member of *Klal Yisrael*, whom you loved so dearly, so that you can truly enjoy your rightful place in Gan Eden when you see each one of us thriving.

Rabbi Yehuda Heimowitz

Yerushalayim, 19 Adar, 5772

# BOOK 1:

# RAV NOSSON TZVI

## FROM HIS MOTHER'S HEART

Rebbetzin Sara Finkel

# ꟽNTRODUCTION

ꟷHE FIRST EREV SHABBOS AFTER I HAD SAT
shivah for my son Rav Nosson Tzvi zt"l was not easy for me.
As I walked up the few steps into his house about an hour
before licht bentchen, as usual I entered the living room where I always
found my son, and where I would greet him upon my arrival. But,
alas, he wasn't there. I looked at the table where he usually sat learning, often preparing his shiur for the coming week, but he wasn't there.
Then I turned to look at the sofa where he sometimes would be resting
or talking to a visitor from abroad; he wasn't there either. Although I
realized he wouldn't be at any of these places, I still felt compelled to
look where I had always found him — and I suddenly faced the reality
that his place was empty. During Kiddush, which I had heard him recite
so many Shabbosim, he was not at his place at the head of the table, and
I could not hear him recite Kiddush, enunciating each syllable, each
word, so distinctly. I then realized that this was something I had to face,
something I had to accept, though it was not easy for me to visualize it
... as a reality.

This Friday, Erev Shabbos, as I write these memories, it is my turn to
go there again. Though I find it very pleasant to spend Shabbos with my
wonderful daughter-in-law, Rebbetzin Leah Finkel, and her children,
my grandchildren, and their little ones, I must admit it's not easy; not
easy to see that my beloved son, Rav Nosson Tzvi zt"l, is not there ...

In recalling our recent personal tragedy, I found that so many mourned the loss of my revered son, Rav Nosson Tzvi Finkel *zt"l*. In addition to the countless number of people throughout Israel, many men and women came from abroad during the *shivah* to personally convey their condolences, flying in from the United States, Belgium, England, and other countries.

The yeshivas and seminaries here in Jerusalem were closed on the day of the funeral and the students were instructed to go to the *levayah*. Nearly all the *chareidi* newspapers and magazines had wide coverage of the tragic event. Numerous publications were devoted to the funeral and the *shivah*, and to the life and manifold accomplishments of Rav Nosson Tzvi *zt"l*.

It was reported that over 100,000 attended the funeral, where *hespedim* were delivered by roshei yeshiva and members of the family. Thousands came to convey their condolences when I sat *shivah* together with Rav Nosson Tzvi's esteemed rebbetzin, my beloved daughter-in-law, Rebbetzin Leah Finkel; her children; and my son Rav Gedalya. During the time we sat *shivah*, women told me that there were long lines outside my son's home waiting to get in. Women approached us, many with tears in their eyes, others crying softly yet incessantly, while sharing their husband's and their own personal experiences with Rav Nosson Tzvi. They told stories of how he helped them personally and how he played a major role in changing their lives in a truly significant way. One woman told me her family did not make any major decision before consulting with Rav Nosson Tzvi. Other women told me stories of how their lives were improved because of his invaluable advice as well as his *berachos*.

*Hespedim* were given throughout Jerusalem each day of the *shivah* and continued here and abroad during the month of *sheloshim*. Many of them were given by my grandsons, who hold positions in Mir. A huge crowd of women and Bais Yaakov students gathered in the Tamir Hall to hear moving *hespedim*.

I sometimes wondered how I had the strength to endure the great tragedy that had fallen upon me and upon our family, and I ultimately realized that the relative composure I experienced under such trying circumstances all came from Above. Hashem, in His infinite graciousness to me at this critical period in my life — for a mother to lose a beloved child, one of such stature and achievement, who touched the lives of countless others — gave me the strength and calm to endure that which

He sent to me, and to be able to maintain it in the face of the many who came to console me with broken hearts and tears literally flowing from their eyes. They came not only when we were sitting *shivah*, but for weeks afterward, when I was already back in my own home.

After a number of days I thought I would write out the stories that I had heard from so many others, as well as the thoughts that entered my mind about my precious son, as a method of catharsis, in order to somewhat relieve the pain that I felt at the great loss I had just endured. I found that writing could be a source of therapy, a source of healing.

As I was about to begin to write these memoirs of my son, Rav Nosson Tzvi *zt"l*, I wondered if it was the right thing for me to do. I consulted with my grandson Shaya, who is a *meishiv* in the Friedman Building of the Mir Yeshiva. His answer was, "Bubby, it would be a *kiddush Hashem* for you to write about Abba's life. It's another way of perpetuating Abba's name and it is important for people to learn from the many great things Abba achieved, as well as the warm, embracing relationship he had with countless people all over the world. Yes, Bubby, all over the world," he reiterated. "There is so much that Abba left behind to learn from; the world needs to read about it, over and over again. Besides, the Chazon Ish said that the best *mussar sefer* is stories about *gedolei Yisrael*. Go ahead, Bubby, write about Abba, write it, it will be a *zechus* for all of the family."

# CHAPTER ONE
# BEGINNINGS

**M**Y HUSBAND, R' ELIYAHU MEIR FINKEL *ZT"L*, came to Israel a few years before his bar mitzvah with his parents and his older brother, Rav Eliezer Menachem *zt"l*. They came from Minsk, then home to the Slabodka Yeshiva, where my husband's

**My Husband** grandfather, the first Rav Nosson Tzvi *zt"l*, was Rosh Yeshiva. My husband's father, Rav Avraham Shmuel Finkel *zt"l*, became a *mashgiach* at Chevron Yeshiva. His mother, Rebbetzin Golda *a"h*, was the daughter of the distinguished Rabbi Yehuda Hachanachi, who was the Rav of Chechenoftze. She came from an illustrious lineage, the descendant of seventeen generations of *rabbanim*.

My husband celebrated his bar mitzvah in Yerushalayim in the year 1928. That same year, after his bar mitzvah,

Rabbi Yehuda Hachanachi,
Rav Nosson Tzvi's
great-grandfather

My in-laws, Rav Avraham Shmuel and Rebbetzin Golda Finkel

there were vicious riots in the city of Chevron, and many students of Chevron Yeshiva were savagely slaughtered by the Arabs. Rav Moshe Mordechai Epstein, the Rosh Yeshiva of Chevron Yeshiva at that time, quickly hid young Eliyahu Meir under the sofa in his room, in order to save his life. My late husband told me that he was so frightened he actually said *vidui* and asked Rav Epstein for *mechilah*, in anticipation of what he thought would inevitably happen to him.

My husband eventually attended Yeshivas Chevron in Yerushalayim, where it moved after the murderous riots. He received *semichah* from Rav Isser Zalman Meltzer, Rav Eliyahu Rom, and Rav Yechezkel Sarne. Shortly after my husband was awarded his *semichah*, Rav Samuel Sar, the head of Yeshiva University, which was known as Yeshiva College at that time, came to visit

My husband, Eliyahu Meir Finkel, at his bar mitzvah in Yerushalayim. This actually was a postcard that was sent to Rav Leizer Yudel Finkel, thanking him for his bar mitzvah gift.

Chevron Yeshiva for the purpose of selecting a group of students to come to his yeshiva in New York in order to be *mashpia,* that is, to have a favorable influence on the student body of Yeshiva College. R' Eliyahu Meir was among those chosen, and he traveled to New York in the year 1938, where he enrolled in that yeshiva to continue his learning.

Rav Samuel Sar

## My Childhood

I GREW UP IN A FAMILY WHERE I saw a lot of *chessed. Hachnasas orchim* was an everyday affair, and as a youngster I always saw guests in our home. My father was a *shochet.* My parents, R' Shmuel and Kreindel Leah Rosenblum, were very giving people. I recall many *rabbanim* coming to our front door, with some of them staying several days. I also saw different kinds of people — a man with crutches, a hungry family — and my mother always served them a good meal. I also saw my mother constantly preparing packages to send to Eretz Yisrael because of the dire poverty that existed there during that era.

I recall the *chagim* in my home so many years ago. Pesach was a special *Yom Tov* for us children. I can still see the Pesach Seder in my mind's eye, my father lifting the *kos* of wine in his hand. As he recited the *Kiddush* there were tears of joy in his eyes, and a faint smile on his lips, as if he

My parents, R' Shmuel and Kreindel Leah Rosenblum, with their infant son, Aaron

actually were experiencing *Yetzias Mitzrayim.* He recited each word so distinctly and clearly that not only was I able to hear him pronounce each syllable, but also he somehow conveyed to us the feeling, the thought that we Yidden are free. I felt at that very moment as if we had just come out of Mitzrayim. Yes, as I look back now, Pesach was indeed a time to commemorate and to celebrate the freedom of *Am Yisrael.*

My mother *a"h* was from Gerrer Chassidic lineage; her father, Yitzchak Meir Lubling *zt"l,* was a *lamdan* in Bedzin, Poland. My family immigrated to America a few years after World War I. My mother had great *emunah.* Whenever some misfortune or something unpleasant occurred, she always said to us children in Yiddish, *"Danken Gott for deim —* Thank G-d for this." She would never allow us to complain. Another expression she used was *"Kik arup —* Look down," there are always people who have it worse. These words of hers remain with me even today, and I often repeat them to my adult grandchildren. As I remember the environment in which I grew up I think of my son Rav Nosson Tzvi *zt"l,* who always had this same attitude — no matter what came his way, he pushed on — and I wonder if this was a reflection of his grandmother's legacy.

I grew up at a time when Bais Yaakov was yet not established in most of America — especially in St. Paul, Minnesota where my family lived. But my father sent me to Hebrew School, which took place after public school for less than two hours each day. I continued on to Hebrew High School, which was out of the area in which we lived, but I gladly traveled there by streetcars; motorized buses were a relatively new invention and had not yet reached my hometown!

Even after I was married and my older son, Nosson Tzvi, was born, I was eager to continue my Jewish studies. I had this urge to learn that continues on until today, so many years later. I found out that there were evening classes being given for teenage girls, and although I was no longer a teenager I was permitted to sign up. It was a class on *hashkafah* based on the Rambam and *Sefer HaKuzari,* which I attended after feeding little Nosson Tzvi supper and tucking him into bed.

IN 1940 A SIGNIFICANT OCCURRENCE TOOK PLACE, WHICH MADE a great impact on my life and ultimately led to my marriage into an

**My Marriage** illustrious Torah family. It was Friday night, *leil Shabbos,* following *Maariv* in the shul where my father davened, and where he served as president. All the men had already left the shul except for one distinguished-looking rabbi, a newcomer to our city, who remained. My father said, "Come, you will spend Shabbos with us," and he took him to our home.

I was sitting across from this rabbi at the Shabbos table when he suddenly said in Yiddish that his feet were hurting him. I immediately got up from my seat, went into my father's bedroom to get his slippers, and brought them to the rabbi. I said to him, "Here, put on these slippers and your feet will feel better." After Shabbos the same rabbi asked me directions to a place he was going to visit. Somehow, the directions I gave him were not clear to him, so I put on my coat and walked with him toward his destination. Much later it occurred to me that he was testing me. *Baruch Hashem* I passed both tests. I told a friend once about this, and she said it reminded her of the tests Rivkah Imeinu passed when Eliezer approached her when looking for a *shidduch* for Yitzchak Avinu.

After spending some time as a guest in our home, often asking me questions, the distinguished rabbi ultimately spoke to my father about his son, Eliyahu Meir Finkel. He told my father a number of things about his family — that his son came from a lineage of seventeen generations of rabbis, etc. (In his humility he did not speak about his own *yichus*; he spoke only of his wife's.) My parents went to my grandmother, my father's mother, who was a very wise woman, and told her what he had said. My grandmother declared, "It seems too good to be true." She had always wished I would marry into a family that had strong Torah values. I recall that one time my Bubby came to me and said if I would marry a boy who was committed to Torah learning and mitzvahs she would give me $200, a tidy sum about 70 years ago. It could have been her life's savings.

I subsequently met Eliyahu Meir and found him to be a very fine person, highly intelligent and with refined character. But we were from completely different backgrounds. Eliyahu Meir was born in Europe and had lived in Eretz Yisrael most of his life and I was an American girl. These countries had completely different cultures. When I returned home from the meeting and my older brother asked me, "Sara, how did it go?" I answered him, "The girl who marries this fine young man will be a lucky girl, but I am not sure he is for me." Well, Hashem had His plans, and ultimately, after more meetings with Eliyahu Meir, *baruch Hashem* I turned out to be that "lucky girl"!

I LEARNED FROM MY HUSBAND ABOUT THE *GADOL* WHO became my grandfather when I married into the Finkel family, and I

## Rav Nosson Tzvi zt"l, the Alter of Slabodka

wondered to myself how I had merited to become the granddaughter of such a great man — someone who had so much influence in molding the characters of the Torah leaders of today.

My son Rav Nosson Tzvi's great-grandfather and namesake, Rav Nosson Tzvi Finkel *zt"l*, was known as the Alter of Slabodka. He was born in the town of Rasein in the year 1849 to Rav Moshe Finkel. He was orphaned as a young child, and raised by a relative in Vilna who inspired him to grow in the Torah lifestyle. By the time he reached the age of 15 he already was known as a Torah scholar. He married Gittel, the daughter of Rav Meir Bahes, who was the son-in-law of the Rabbi of Kelm. Rav Bahes supported them so that Rav Nosson Tzvi could continue learning uninterruptedly.

The Alter of Slabodka spent his lifetime spreading Torah. He substantially increased the number of yeshivas in Lithuania, each one headed by a *talmid muvhak*, a star pupil. As a spiritual heir of Rav Yisrael Salant, the innovator of the principles of *mussar*, the Alter spread the learning of *mussar* throughout the many yeshivas that he established. His flawless character

The Alter of Slabodka, whose name Rav Nosson Tzvi bore

traits as well as his genuinely outstanding personality were a true example of the *mussar* principles that he instilled within his *talmidim*.

In his approach to ethical teachings the Alter emphasized the towering qualities of the individual, rather than pointing out the flaws of man, for the purpose of curbing the evil inclination, the *yetzer hara*. By contrast, the yeshivas of Novaradok felt that identifying and focusing on the shortcomings of the individual was the effective path to self-improvement. The Alter followed the principle of dwelling on the positive attributes and values of his students, thereby instilling within them the desire to reach higher both spiritually and ethically.

The Alter himself was a man of great stature, who possessed outstanding refinement of character. He put much emphasis on broadening his students' minds and was opposed to pettiness. His motto was:

Be wise and good. He taught that a person should constantly reach higher and higher in perfecting himself in *middos, yiras Shamayim*, breadth and depth of Torah knowledge, as well as in his awareness of the needs of others, spiritual as well as material. The Alter of Slabodka molded the character of his disciples by instilling in them the values as taught by our Sages, "The soul is insatiable because it is Divine."

Many years later, as I thought about the Alter's "*derech*" in cultivating his students — who became such Torah leaders of stature — I was inspired by his unique educational methods, and I tried to incorporate them in raising my children. As they were growing up I always tried to point out to Nosson Tzvi and Gedalya the good things they accomplished, recognizing their positive behavior when the opportunity arose and trying not to unnecessarily rebuke them.

My son followed in his great-grandfather's footsteps, and he encouraged and strengthened the study of *mussar* in the Yeshiva, considering it an integral part of the learning. The students at Mir learn *mussar* each day, and a *mussar shmuess* is given in the Mirrer Yeshiva regularly by Reb Aryeh Finkel.

MY OLDEST SON, NOSSON TZVI, WAS BORN IN THE SPRING, ON the 6th day of Adar, 5703 (March 12, 1943) in Mt. Sinai Hospital, which

### Rav Nosson Tzvi's Birth

was on the west side of Chicago, Illinois. In those days it was customary for women who gave birth to remain in the hospital for a period of 10 days. Can you imagine! Only after the fourth day were we even permitted to sit up. Nosson Tzvi's *bris*, therefore, took place in the hospital, attended by a number of prominent rabbis from Chicago.

I saw, as he was growing up, that he did things in an orderly and disciplined fashion. When I went shopping with little Nosson Tzvi I would leave him in the carriage without strapping him in, and mind you he sat quietly by himself, not even attempting to climb out from his carriage,

Young Nosson Tzvi and his father

quite unlike many other impatient toddlers. When he was already in school his book bag was always in perfect order.

NOSSON TZVI AND HIS YOUNGER BROTHER, GEDALYA, GREW up in our warm and loving home imbued with Torah and its values. My
**A Warm Childhood Home** children were nourished with affection as well as recognition for the things they did well. Whenever I returned home from running errands, as soon as I entered my house my little sons hurriedly ran toward me. Then we got on to discussing the kinds of things that interested and involved our two boys: how they spent the day, how things were in school, what they learned, who they played with, what games they played. We talked with one another, we laughed with one another, we simply shared so many things.[1]

This same feeling of closeness carried over in my relationship with my grandchildren and great-grandchildren today.

Little Nosson Tzvi was an obedient child, a good boy. I can hardly recall him giving us trouble. I remember an incident when he was about 4 years old. Someone gave him chocolate. Since it was close to dinnertime I said to him with a smile, "Darling, save the chocolate until after supper, because if you eat it now it will spoil your appetite." He immediately put the chocolate in his pocket. My aunt, who was with us at the time, remarked, "This is really unusual for a 4-year-old. Most children that age would rebel if they were not allowed to eat the chocolate immediately."

Young Nosson Tzvi

At the age of 5 he was among the first students in the Central Park Hebrew Day School, which was later renamed Arie Crown Day School.

_____

1. For Rebbetzin Finkel's insights into parenting, see p. 71.

Going to PTA meetings was always a pleasure, hearing a good report about him.

Although at his *bris* he was given the name Nosson Tzvi, for his illustrious great-grandfather, he was known as Nathan in school, and his family and friends called him Natie until he went to Eretz Yisrael. He had many friends and he was well liked by them. As a matter of fact, when he returned to Israel the second time, after he finished high school, a group of students accompanied him to the airport, and I saw that they had tears in their eyes, saddened by his departure from his hometown.

Although the Torah world in those days was much smaller, our family merited having many roshei yeshiva visiting our Chicago home through the years. Among those that I remember so clearly were Rav Aron Kotler and his son, Rav Shneur Kotler; Rav Shmuel Greineman; Rav Mordechai Shulman, Rosh Yeshiva of Slabodka in Bnei Brak; Rav Moshe Chevroni, Rosh Yeshiva of Chevron Yeshiva; Rav Yosef Farber, Rosh Yeshiva of Heichal Hatalmud in Tel Aviv, and many others. We considered it a great honor to have these prominent *gedolei Torah* in our home. Some of them stayed a week or even longer, and others came for a brief visit.

I clearly recall the time Rav Leizer Yudel, my husband's uncle and the Rosh Yeshiva of Mir, came to Chicago and visited our home. Rav Beinush, the previous Rosh Yeshiva of Mir and my daughter-in-law Leah's father, was a guest in our home for over a week. We really felt privileged, and I still remember his warmth, wisdom, and *simchah*. One Friday afternoon Reb Beinush and my husband went to meet a philanthropist who lived quite a distance from our home. There were some unexpected delays and as they were driving back they saw that Shabbos was approaching. My husband parked the car, hid the contribution to the yeshiva and the car keys in the car, and they walked back to our home, almost a 2-hour walk. At the close of Shabbos, when they went to the car, they found everything intact.

I also particularly recall the visit of the Ponovezher Rav, Rav Yosef Shlomo Kahaneman, to Chicago almost 50 years ago. I still remember the following experience, which made a marked impression, even today. We had the honor of having the Ponovezher Rav at our home for dinner. I considered it a great *kavod*; after all, this was the Rosh Yeshiva of Ponovezh Yeshiva in Bnei Brak!

Everyone was sitting comfortably at my dining-room table, even though it was a weekday. When I brought in a platter of food I pro-

Ponovezher Rav             R' Eliyahu Meir Finkel

ceeded to set it down on the table in front of him. It was an honor that I wanted to extend to the Ponovezher Rav. I felt it was only right to serve him first.

Before I had a chance to put the platter of food down in front of him, he extended his hand and pointed his finger toward my husband, saying, "*Baal habayis rishon* — the master of the house should be served first." This really impressed me. Today, when I am invited to the home of my grandchildren for Shabbos and they want to extend me the honor of serving me first, I relate this experience that I had with the Ponovezher Rav so many years ago, and I tell my dear grandchildren, "Always serve your husband first." Even though I know they are well aware of this, I want to emphasize to them the importance of giving honor to their husbands, to be witnessed by their toddlers and growing children. I also consider it a lesson in *shalom bayis*.

Throughout my sons' youthful years, my husband encouraged both Nosson Tzvi and Gedalya to advance in learning Torah. Rav Yehoshua Levinson *zt"l* was hired to teach Nosson Tzvi and Gedalya at home after school, which was not a common practice in those days.

Years later, when they were already in Yerushalayim and learning in Mir, my husband helped them financially for a time, rather than having them take their stipends from the Yeshiva. My husband was also always eager to hear *divrei Torah* from our growing grandchildren. In his later years, whenever any of our grandchildren came over he asked them to say a *dvar Torah*. He would say, "*Nu, lomen heren a shtikel Torah fun dir.*"

My husband was active in the community. He was among the first organizers of Agudas Yisrael in Chicago, where he served as vice president. He was also among the organizers of Telshe Yeshiva in Chicago, and sat on their board. He truly honored and supported numerous *talmidei chachamim* and Torah institutions.

## Nosson Tzvi's Bar Mitzvah

YOUNG NOSSON TZVI'S BAR MITZVAH WAS HELD IN THE SHUL that my husband founded, Kehilas Jacob-Beth Shmuel, which bears the name of my father and father-in-law. (Both were named Shmuel. Our shul merged with another called Kehilas Jacob, and it was agreed to call it Kehilas Jacob-Beth Shmuel.) As a matter of fact, when the shul was founded, the *minyanim* were initially held in our home. It was only later that a group got together to erect the shul building in our neighborhood. Rabbi David Silver, the shul's *baal korei*, was a good friend of ours, and he taught Nosson Tzvi his *haftorah* as well as the *parashah,*

At Nosson Tzvi's bar mitzvah. L-to-R: My son Gedalya; Rav Mordechai Shulman; my husband, R' Eliyahu Meir; and the "bar mitzvah boy," who made us all so proud!

which he read beautifully and distinctly. I stood with pride as I witnessed my older son enter the obligation to perform the mitzvahs.

The bar mitzvah was attended by friends and relatives. The dinner celebration was held in the Sheridan Plaza Hotel in Chicago. Among the distinguished guests was Rav Mordechai Shulman *zt"l*, Rosh Yeshiva of Slabodka Yeshiva in Bnei Brak. He came to Chicago quite frequently and we were privileged to have Rav Shulman stay in our home whenever he visited Chicago.

# CHAPTER TWO
# A YOUNG BOY IN THE MIR

**O**N THE YEAR 1957, BEFORE ROSH HASHANAH, MY HUS-
band and I took a trip to Eretz Yisrael. We took along Nosson
Tzvi, who was 14 years old at the time. We traveled by boat,
cabin class, to Paris, then we flew to the Holy Land by plane. Young
Nosson Tzvi was just as eager as we were to visit Eretz Yisrael — to see

**Leaving Young
Nosson Tzvi in
Eretz Yisrael**
the holy sights, to visit family, and to simply
bask in the *kedushah* of the land of our forefathers. We left our younger son Gedalya with my
mother.

For me, coming to Israel was a completely new experience. As we
visited my husband's uncles, aunts, and cousins, I felt like a bride
meeting my husband's family for the first time — and a very illustrious
family they were. Among them were his cousins: Rav Leizer Placinsky,
a prominent Rosh Yeshiva; Rav Eliezer Goldshmidt, a *dayan* in Tel Aviv;
Rav Simcha Zissel Broide, Rosh Yeshiva of Chevron when it moved to
Yerushalayim; Rav Dovid Finkel, the son of R' Moshe Finkel, my father-
in-law's twin brother (Rav Dovid Finkel is survived by his wife Chana
Finkel, who lives in the Mattesdorf area today); and especially Rav
Leizer Yudel Finkel *zt"l*, my husband's revered and beloved uncle who

Rav Leizer Yudel Finkel, "the Uncle"

headed the Mir Yeshiva in Poland and reestablished it in Jerusalem in 1944. I say "especially," because my husband was very close to his saintly uncle, whom we visited frequently during this eventful visit to the Holy Land.

I remember that during that visit we spent Shabbos with our cousins in Bnei Brak, Rav Mordechai Shulman, Rosh Yeshiva of Slabodka Yeshiva, and his Rebbetzin, Chaya Miriam Shulman. One of the things that stands out in my mind is meeting Rebbetzin Shulman's mother, Rebbetzin Guttel Sher, the daughter of the Alter of Slabodka and rebbetzin of Rav Isaac Sher. Rebbetzin Sher was bedridden because she had suffered a stroke not long before. I remember so clearly standing at her bedside. She raised her hand and stroked my cheek while repeating just one word: "Fine, fine, fine." She was unable to speak clearly because of the stroke. I understood this as her way of indicating her approval of me — her approval of her nephew's American wife.

It was the day before Rosh Hashanah during that fateful first visit to Eretz Yisrael. I recall the Uncle (that's how my husband referred to him), Rav Leizer Yudel, summoning me to his room to speak with me concerning a serious decision I had to make. He asked me in Yiddish to leave my son Nosson Tzvi in Eretz Yisrael to study in his Yeshiva, the Mir. Before uttering a reply I thought to myself, *What, leave my son, at the tender age of 14, across the ocean, thousands of miles away from home without his parents and his younger brother? How could I possibly do such a thing?* When I hesitated he added, with a warm smile on his face and a twinkle in his eye, *"Du darfst hobben em unter dine fachtug?* — Do you need him attached to your apron strings?" To which I answered in Yiddish, the language I learned from my parents as a youngster growing up in St. Paul, "I will have to think about it." I repeated, "I will think it over," and I thought to myself, *How can I leave him behind?*

On the second day of Rosh Hashanah after *Shacharis,* following the reading in *Parashas Vayeira* that narrates the moving story of *Akeidas Yitzchak,* it was customary for the family to congregate for *Kiddush* in the apartment of Rav Chaim Shmuelevitz *zt"l* and his family. Their daughter Rivkah, who was unmarried at that time and is today known as Rebbetzin Ezrachi, was a teacher in seminary then. She reviewed the *parashah* again in English. When I heard her repeat once again the story of *Akeidas Yitzchak,* I thought to myself, *If our patriarch, Avraham Avinu, was willing to bring such a korban, to make such a profound sacrifice, why am I hesitating?* It was precisely at that moment that I made my decision, which I later related to "the Uncle," Rav Leizer Yudel: "I will permit Nosson Tzvi to remain in Eretz Yisrael." I somehow felt at the time that I was giving him to the world; what a thought for a young Jewish mother.

My beloved son Nosson Tzvi *zt"l* came into the Mir, into the world of Torah learning, at the reading of *Parashas Vayeira* on Rosh Hashanah, and he left this world, and the Mir, also during the week of *Parashas Vayeira.* I often wonder what significance this amazing occurence might have. Certainly, it cannot be a mere coincidence. (Speaking of the word coincidence, I recall walking through Meah Shearim with my beloved *mechutenesteh,* Rebbetzin Esther Finkel. I used the word *"bemikreh,"* which means coincidence. To which she said to me "Nothing is *bemikreh* — nothing is coincidence — everything is *min haShamayim.*")

OUR SON WAS GIVEN THE ROOM ADJOINING THAT OF HIS uncle, the Rosh Yeshiva. Once, in the middle of the night, Nosson Tzvi

## In the Room Next to "the Uncle"

observed his uncle extend his arms and embrace the Gemaras on the bookshelf in his room and then kiss them one by one, saying, *"Dos iz mein* (This is mine)"; certainly an unforgettable lesson in *ahavas haTorah.*

His uncle arranged the most learned *chavrusas* to learn with young Nosson Tzvi: Rav Chaim Kamiel, who subsequently became Rosh Yeshiva in Ofakim; Rav Yehoshua Kurlansky, an accomplished *talmid chacham*; and Rav Yosef Stern, who was chosen because in addition to the fact that he was a *talmid chacham,* he was also fluent in English. Rav Kamiel, especially, made a marked contribution to what Nosson Tzvi achieved in learning in his early years.

The families of Rav Moshe Finkel, Rav Chaim Shmuelevitz, and

Rav Chaim Shmuelevitz                    Rav Nochum Partzovitz

Rav Nochum Partzovitz all lived in the same compound, in apartments adjoining the Yeshiva. Having an American boy among his Yerushalmi family was quite a delight. Rav Elya Boruch Finkel *zt"l*'s younger sister Leah Breskin recalls what excitement it brought to all the family, especially the children, to have a cousin from America come to Mir to live in their midst. Sometimes, of course, his American ways were puzzling. Rebbetzin Miriam Broide, the rebbetzin of Rav Simche Zissel Broide, told how Rav Leizer Yudel, the "Uncle," in his eagerness to please Nosson Tzvi, asked an American *bachur* what he thought an American boy would enjoy eating the most. The *bachur* immediately answered, "A steak." Rebbetzin Broide then called the butcher and asked, in *Ivrit*, "*Mah zeh steak*? — What is steak?"

My cousin Rebbetzin Rivka Ezrachi recalls that when Nosson Tzvi was 15 years old, before Pesach, when all the rebbetzins were busy cleaning, the young children were interfering with their work and making a rumpus. Young Nosson Tzvi organized a game where he sent them on errands in order to get them out of the house so the women could do their work. When the children returned from their errands — which kept them out of the house for over an hour — he awarded each one with a prize, which made them very happy and proved to be a great incentive for them to go out on "errands" again. Rebbetzin Ezrachi told me that even at a young age Rav Nosson Tzvi understood the needs of the children, and as he grew up it became clear that he understood the needs of the *bachurim*, his students.

Rav Leizer Yudel acquired a great fondness for his American-born great-nephews, Nosson Tzvi and Gedalya. It was the custom of the Rosh Yeshiva's daughter, Rebbetzin Miriam Shmuelevitz, to leave her father a serving of her home-baked cake with which he could refresh himself after his early-morning davening. Each morning he left half of it for his young American great-nephew, Nosson Tzvi. A few years later my younger son, Rav Gedalya, came to Yerushalayim. Remembering his first night there, he told me, "You know, Mom, when I was 10 years old we arrived from the United States late in the evening. I was told to sleep in the Uncle's apartment. It was Rav Leizer Yudel's custom to go to sleep early and to rise early in the morning. He was already sleeping when I came. I went to bed and had a good night's sleep. When I woke up early in the morning, I opened my eyes and I saw hovering over me a short, elderly man — he was 85 years old at the time — with a glowing white beard. He said to me, 'I want to embrace you, I want to embrace you — have you washed *nagel vasser*?' This was an expression of his love that I remember until this very day, more than 50 years later."

I sometimes wondered if the warmth and affection that Rav Leizer Yudel showed to his great-nephew was something that rubbed off, because later my son, the Rosh Yeshiva, Rav Nosson Tzvi, was famous for his love for his students. After thinking about it, though, I came to realize that this was Nosson Tzvi's inborn characteristic. He simply loved his fellow man, and especially his *talmidim*. He personified what our *chachamim* teach, "*Ve'ahavta l'rei'acha kamocha*, You shall love your fellow man as yourself." I think that Nosson Tzvi loved others even more than he loved himself, because he constantly gave so much of himself to others.

AFTER SPENDING EIGHT MONTHS IN ISRAEL UNDER THE GUID-ance of his esteemed Uncle, Nosson Tzvi returned to Chicago, where he was born and grew up, just before he turned 15. It was obvious that he

**Back to Chicago** had matured and had become stronger in Torah learning, in *hashkafah*, and in his desire to continue his *derech* in his learning. (I recall receiving an aerogramme: "You cannot imagine, Mom and Dad, what a great love I have to learn Torah, to advance in Torah.") He subsequently continued his studies in Chicago Jewish Academy until he graduated when he was 17.

A student in his high school who worked together with Nosson Tzvi on a project to send funds to the poor in Eretz Yisrael told me, "Nosson

Rav Nosson Tzvi's yearbook picture

Tzvi and I were in charge of this project, where we worked closely for over two months. I still recall how easy it was to work with him. He had endless patience, enthusiasm, and stamina. He was very organized and encouraged all the students who participated. His criticism was always made in a positive way without hurting anyone. These characteristics were emphasized over the years and made him so beloved by all who came into contact with him ... And in the end our class pulled in the largest amount of money!"

He was popular in his school, with many friends. In checking with one of these high school friends, who currently resides in Eretz Yisrael, I received the following moving letter:

*[Rav Nosson Tzvi] and I were in the same grade throughout all of high school. But it was really only in eleventh grade that we*

## My Friend, the Rosh Yeshiva

*became good friends. My memories of him were very positive. He was tall, a most imposing figure. He was soft-spoken, kind, and never had a mean word to say about anyone ...*

*We were very close during those years. We were in the same shiur and often learned together. We would often spend Shabbosos at his home. Our conversations would extend far into the night.*

*The qualities that he [Rav Nosson Tzvi zt"l] possessed as a Rosh Yeshiva were already apparent at that time [in high school] but who would have thought he would become "HaRav HaGaon, Rav Nosson Tzvi, Rosh Yeshiva of Mir"?*

*After high school, we both came to Eretz Yisrael to learn, Natie to the Mir and I to another yeshiva. And though we were in different yeshivos, I spent many Shabbosos and Yamim Tovim at the Mir, which was always exciting. I remember one* particular Shabbos which I spent at the Mir. When I got there Erev Shabbos, Natie took me to meet the Rosh Yeshiva, HaRav HaGaon Rav Leizer Yudel. That was quite an experience and we spent a few amazing minutes together. Indeed, I remember that on Shabbos the rosh yeshiva looked preoccupied and I asked Natie why he looked so reflective. He told me that the rosh yeshiva was wondering whether to give me an aliyah since I didn't have a hat. In the end he decided in the affirmative.

I remember that night, that year, and those experiences with Natie as if they were yesterday.

The next time I saw Natie, it was no longer Natie, but Nosson Tzvi. He had recently gotten married, and was back in Chicago, visiting his parents. He and his wife came over to our apartment one evening and we had a great time talking and reminiscing. The rebbetzin was a wonderful match for Nosson Tzvi. But I knew things were going to be different when Nosson Tzvi wouldn't eat anything. He and his wife would just drink the water. Even so, the evening flowed. It was just like I had seen him before, without any hesitation in the conversation. He now wore a suit, but his middos were the same and that wonderful smile of his was evident in everything we talked about.

The next time I saw Nosson Tzvi it was now "Rav Nosson Tzvi." We had kept up a kesher over the years, but at best it was sporadic. In 1991, my son Ranan was learning in Israel and I wanted him to meet Rav Nosson Tzvi. We went to him in the Bucharian neighborhood, where he greeted us like old and dear friends. It didn't take long to feel welcomed and comfortable and the rebbetzin was a wonderful hostess. Rav Nosson Tzvi gave my son a test on the masechta in Bava Kamma that he was learning and he knew everything except the name of the perek. My son was impressed that I had such an important friend, and I was impressed and glad that our friendship was strong and secure.

The last time I saw Rav Nosson Tzvi zt"l, it was now "HaRav HaGaon Rav Nosson Tzvi."

It was last Pesach. I went with my brother to visit him on Chol HaMoed, in his home across from Mir. My friend had changed. His speech was hardly audible, and you could see the effects of so many years of Parkinson's. But in all of the important ways, he was the same. Sweet, accepting, respectful (he stood up when his cousin Reb Aryeh walked in), and with the fantastic smile on his lips. I gave him a kiss and reflected on 50 years of friendship. He had a sefer in front of him, his Pesachim shiurim. I told his gabbai, Rav Zaretsky, that I wanted a copy of the sefer and after a few smiles, winks, and nods I got it, which I cherish.

This wasn't a time to talk about old times. This was a time to marvel at the gadlus that sat before us. Who would have believed that he would become the rosh hayeshiva, and yet who could not see the Torah u'gedulah b'makom echod, Torah and greatness in one man.

When we got up to go, I gave him another kiss and he held my hand forcefully in his. It was clear that during all of the years, whether I saw him or not, our relationship had remained strong and intact.

On the way out, we talked to his mother, Rebbetzin Sara Finkel, and to his wife, Rebbetzin Leah. In many ways HaGaon Rav Nosson Tzvi zt"l exhibited the middos, the characteristics, of his mother, who was always an eishes chayil. And as for the rebbetzin — if my friend became a rosh yeshiva I believe that she certainly had a big part in that.

One last word — the Rosh HaYeshiva always knew who he was. He knew where he came from and he never denied his history. He knew that the past helped make him the gadol that he was, and that's why we, he and I, would always be able to share a common past. I loved him dearly, and I always will.

# CHAPTER THREE
# RETURN TO THE MIR: MY SON GROWS UP

FTER GRADUATION IN 1960, NOSSON TZVI WAS eager to return to Eretz Yisrael, but we, his parents, hesitated. We wanted him to remain at home; we wanted him to be with us in Chicago, and to continue learning here. To no avail: he was determined to return to Eretz Yisrael. We pondered the question and discussed it with some of his rebbis. Rabbi Meir Getzel Kagan, his rebbi in his yeshiva in Chicago, encouraged us to let him return to Eretz Yisrael. He said he felt that it was important, especially since this was the wish of Rav Leizer Yudel. Rabbi Meir Getzel Kagan

Standing (L to R): R' Yitzchak Ezrachi, R' Aryeh Finkel, R' Aharon Chodosh
Seated (L to R): R' Refoel Shmuelevitz, R' Nosson Tzvi, R' Chaim Zev Finkel (Rav Beinush's older brother)

R' Eliyahu Meir Finkel, Rav Nosson Tzvi's father,
at the Kosel with Rav Chaim Shmuelevitz

had been one of the students from Mir, Poland who subsequently went to Shanghai during the war, before immigrating to the United States.

And so young Nosson Tzvi returned to Eretz Yisrael and continued to learn in Yeshivas Mir. His goal, at age 21, was "learning, learning, learning." Our contact at that time was by and large through aerogrammes, the main method of correspondence during those years. Telephone calls took several hours to go through and were expensive.

Rav Avraham Shmuelevitz told me that when Nosson Tzvi was in Israel as a *bachur*, he had a lot of contact with his cousins, Meir and Avraham Shmuelevitz and Rav Elya Boruch Finkel, *zt"l*. Nosson Tzvi had his *leil Shabbos seudah* together with Rav Leizer Yudel. His younger cousin Avraham joined them in order to have a *mezuman*. Rav Avraham told me that he remembers Nosson Tzvi giving a lengthy Torah discourse at the table, which lasted about an hour. He said that he observed that even as a teenager Rav Nosson Tzvi had excellent *middos*. He was very sensitive to other people's feelings, he appeared to be in control of every situation, and he showed much kindness and consideration to others. When he first came to the Mir as a *bachur*, Rav Nosson Tzvi shared a room with Rav Refoel Shmuelevitz, Rav Chaim's oldest son, who now is among the roshei yeshiva of Mir.

BEGINNING IN THE EARLY 1960'S, MY HUSBAND AND I CAME frequently to Eretz Yisrael and stayed from Rosh Hashanah through

**Encounters in Eretz Yisrael**

Succos to spend time with our son. At the same time, we enjoyed the privilege of davening in Mir on the *Yamim Noraim* and visiting with the various members of our family.

I will long remember the impression that Rav Leizer Yudel made on me at that time. He made me feel as if I were one of his daughters. I recall one time when I wanted to discuss something with him. I stood at the entrance to his room, waiting to be summoned by him. As he looked up and saw me standing there, he beckoned to me, and then, with a warm smile on his face, he said to me, *"Kum arein, kum arein, farvus shteist du?* — Come in, come in, why are you standing there?"* Each year when we visited Israel during the *Yamim Noraim*, he presented me with a gift that his daughter Rebbetzin Miriam, the wife of Rav Chaim Shmuelevitz *zt"l*, purchased for me at his request, gifts that I cherish even today.

### Gedalya's Bar Mitzvah

MY SON GEDALYA'S BAR MITZVAH, HELD IN ERETZ YISRAEL, was a memorable affair. Guests from opposite ends of the spectrum attended. The bar-mitzvah celebration took place in Goldshmidt's Restaurant on Yaffa Road, since catering halls were not popular at that time. Rav Moshe Finkel was master of ceremonies. Gracing the head table was Rav Leizer Yudel. Also sitting at the dais were Rav Yechezkel Sarne, Rosh Yeshiva

Rav Aryeh Levin, "the *tzaddik* of Yerushalayim," wishes Gedalya mazal tov at his bar mitzvah

Rav Leizer Yudel at Gedalya's bar mitzvah. Behind them (L to R): Rav Moshe Chevroni
(partially obscured), Rav Meir Chodosh, Rav Yosef Farber

of Chevron; Rav Chaim Shmuelevitz; my husband, Eliyahu Meir Finkel;
Rav Moshe Chevroni; Rav Meir Chadash; Rav Aryeh Levin, the "*tzaddik*
of Jerusalem" — and the famed Israeli politician Abba Eban, who was
Minister of Education at the time. Our connection with him was that his
sister was married to my brother David. The master of ceremonies introduced the final speaker, Abba Eban, as the Minister of Education. I still
remember his opening remarks: "I am not here as a representative of the
government, I am here as a member of the family."

My son Rav Gedalya recently told me this story about his bar mitzvah.
Nosson Tzvi, who was 19, wrote his brother's bar-mitzvah *derashah*.
Rav Leizer Yudel was sitting next to his great-nephew, the bar-mitzvah
boy, and it was time for him to say his *derashah*. After he had recited
the *derashah* for several minutes, the guests began to sing him down,
a common custom in Israel. Gedalya proceeded to sit down on his
chair when he felt a hand pushing him back up. It was "the Uncle,"
who wanted him to continue his *derashah,* because to Rav Leizer Yudel
nothing was as enjoyable as hearing *divrei Torah*. None of those present
were aware that it was the Mirrer Rosh Yeshiva who was responsible
for Gedalya standing up again. Everyone stopped singing, thinking that
Gedalya simply wanted to continue his *derashah*. Gedalya continued to
speak; then after a few minutes, again the guests in the hall began to sing
him down. Again, Rav Leizer Yudel extended his bony fingers upward,
making it impossible for Gedalya to sit down. Once more Gedalya was

forced to get up and once again the guests grew quiet. This continued a few more times. Rav Leizer Yudel's great *ahavas Torah* eventually was carried over by both his great nephews — Rav Nosson Tzvi and Rav Gedalya, the grandsons of Rav Leizer Yudel's brother, Rav Avraham Shmuel *zt"l*.

## Nosson Tzvi's Marriage to Leah Finkel

NOSSON TZVI CONTINUED LEARNING DILIGENTLY IN YESHIVAS Mir. It was the year 1964 when the issue of marriage came up. Rav Leizer Yudel, the Uncle, called for me to come to Eretz Yisrael concerning a *shidduch* for Nosson Tzvi. It appeared that he wanted Nosson Tzvi's mother's approval.

At R' Nosson Tzvi's vort. (L to R): Rav Chaim Shmuelevitz; Rav Nosson Tzvi's future father-in-law, Rav Beinush Finkel; Rav Nosson Tzvi's father, R' Eliyahu Meir Finkel; Rav Leizer Yudel; the *chassan*, Nosson Tzvi

The *chassan*, Nosson Tzvi, greets his future father-in-law, Rav Beinush, at his *vort*

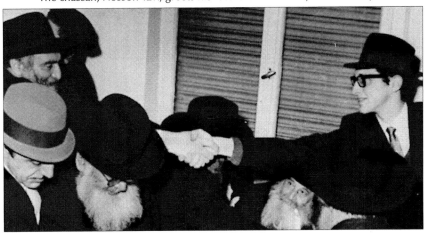

When the idea of finding a *shidduch* for Nosson Tzvi was first broached, Rav Leizer Yudel called the *menahelet* of the Bais Yaakov Seminary and requested, "Please send me your finest student." Rebbetzin Rachel Sarne, wife of Rav Chaim Sarne *zt"l* and daughter-in-law of Rav Yechzkel Sarne *zt"l*, the late Rosh Yeshiva of Chevron, also came with some relevant suggestions for *shidduchim*.

The following Shabbos, I saw Rav Leizer Yudel pacing the floor back and forth in the living room of his apartment, which adjoined the Mir Yeshiva. With his index finger pointing upwards he was repeatedly exclaiming excitedly in Yiddish, *"Vos tu ich, ich vill em far zichr, ich vill em far mihr. Er hot nisht kein feller, er hot nish kein feller.* — What am I doing, I want him for myself. [That is, for one of his granddaughters.] He has no faults."

Not long afterward the *shidduch* between Nosson Tzvi and Rav Beinush's oldest daughter, Rav Leizer Yudel's granddaughter, Leah Finkel, became a reality.

As I came to know Rebbetzin Leah I found her to be a true *eishes chayil* to her husband, as well as an extremely devoted daughter-in-law. I deeply cherish our friendship and our relationship. Rebbetzin Leah comes from an impressive lineage. Her mother, Rebbetzin Esther Finkel, helped many people through the years obtain proper medical care through her contacts with top physicians. Both the Chazon Ish and the Steipler Rav were her great-uncles from her mother's side. Rav Shmuel Greineman was her maternal grandfather and, of course, Rav Leizer Yudel was her paternal grandfather. However, Rebbetzin Leah

Nosson Tzvi at his *chasunah*

has *yichus atzmah,* for the countless acts of *gemillus chessed* she performs each day.

Rav Nosson Tzvi's constant learning brought her much joy and she did everything possible to help him in every way, especially not to distract him from his learning. She accompanied him on his trips abroad and to the various cities he visited here in Eretz Yisrael. Their home is a center of *hachnasas orchim,* and when I spend Shabbos there I always see guests around the table. Many women consult her with problems and she is happy to help them or to offer a good word to lift their spirits.

## Memories of Nosson Tzvi's Wedding

NOSSON TZVI AND LEAH WERE MARRIED IN THE PORAT Yosef Yeshiva in 1964. Rav Leizer Yudel was the *mesader kiddushin* and the Ponovezher Rav was given the *kavod* of reciting all the *berachos.*

There were hardly any catering halls or suitable hotels in which to hold weddings during that era. Besides the many invited guests who attended, there was a special table where poor people sat in order to eat a good meal. This was the practice at every Finkel *simchah.* Others in need roamed around the wedding hall asking for *tzedakah,* and were made welcome.

The following day a number of guests complained of an upset stomach, which we found out later was due to the chopped liver that was served as a first course. In spite of this my *mechutan,* Rav Beinush, hired the same caterer for his next daughter's wedding, which took place shortly after this one, so that the incident would not leave the man with a bad reputation. I thought that was very commendable, but this was the way of the Finkel family, always performing acts of *chessed* in so many different forms.

Rav Beinush, my daughter-in-law's father and my husband's first cousin, was a real *tzaddik.* As I got to know him I used to harbor the thought that he was one of the "lamed-vuv-niks," because of his admirable character traits. He became the Rosh Yeshiva of Mir after his father, Rav Leizer Yudel. Just one story to show what a man he was: On the way to the airport on one of our trips back to the United States, we stopped off in Bnei Brak where Rav Beinush lived (this was before he became Rosh Yeshiva). My husband left him a gift of cash. Our taxi was driving away from his house, when his young daughter ran toward the car shouting, "*Rega rega, rega* — Just a minute!" — which was a common expression used in Israel. My husband rolled down the window and Rav Beinush's daughter handed him a matchbox. My husband, who was a smoker in those days, assumed he had forgotten the matchbox. Later, when he opened it to light a cigarette, he found the money he had left for Rav Beinush, who refused to accept monetary gifts for himself.

Rav Beinush was a great man, and unusually humble. Once, he realized that his next door neighbor's water system was not working, and they did not have water running through their faucet. Rav Beinush climbed up on the roof, filled up a tub with water, and poured the water down the neighbor's pipes so they would have water until the system was repaired.

Rav Nosson Tzvi had a close *kesher* with his in-laws, and visited them frequently. After Rav Beinush's *petirah*, Rav Nosson Tzvi would always go to his mother-in-law's home to bid her farewell before his many trips abroad.

WHEN GEDALYA COMPLETED HIS HIGH SCHOOL STUDIES AT Beis Medrash L'Torah, he joined his brother in Eretz Yisrael to learn

**Gedalya Joins His Brother in Eretz Yisrael**

in Mir. As a *bachur* Gedalya came to learn in Mir in the year 1967, at the age of 17. After a period of time learning in Mir he returned to Chicago for two years, becoming *chavrusa* for a year with Rabbi Yaakov Perlow *shlita*, who would later become the Novominsker Rebbe.

Gedalya subsequently returned to Mir in Yerushalayim, where he learned with *hasmadah*. A few years later, Batzion Carlebach, Rebbetzin Leah's sister and the wife of Rav Binyamin Carlebach, suggested Gedalya as a *shidduch* for her sister-in-law, Miriam Carlebach, a very special person and an exemplary teacher. Gedalya and Miriam were subsequently married at a truly elegant wedding in Brooklyn, New York. Rabbi Schneur Kotler *zt"l* was *mesader kiddushin*. Today Rav Gedalya is a *maggid shiur* in the Mir Yeshiva in Yerushalayim. He instills in his *talmidim* a great *ahavas Torah* and helps them acquire greater depth in their learning. Like his older brother, Rav Gedalya is very devoted to me, and he comes to visit me almost every day on his way home from the Yeshiva.

BEFORE HE BECAME ROSH YESHIVA, RAV NOSSON TZVI GAVE *shiurim* in Mir. I recall a moving incident one Simchas Torah. I was standing in the *ezras nashim* of the Yeshiva, upstairs. As I looked down at the *hakafos*, with large numbers of yeshiva students dancing around

### Rav Nosson Tzvi as a Maggid Shiur

the *bimah,* my eye suddenly caught Rav Nosson Tzvi holding the Sefer Torah. He was a young man then, and as he encircled the *bimah* with the other prominent *maggidei shiur* and roshei yeshiva my heart swelled with the kind of emotion only a mother can experience.

At this time he was learning *yom v'lailah,* day and night, learning constantly, not only preparing his *shiurim,* but also simply learning for the sake of learning, *lishmah.* He learned *b'chavrusa* as well as by himself. He had a powerful drive to forge ahead in Torah learning.

We recently found a ten-page handwritten letter that Rav Nosson Tzvi wrote to his brother, Rav Gedalya, when Gedalya was a *chassan.* The first few paragraphs give a picture of how much he was putting into his learning at that time:

*You'll really excuse my not writing sooner. I haven't even written home in a while as I am very busy with my chaburos. I have never been so much on the run. I have a lot of work. You'll excuse me writing about myself, you asked what's new.*

*I learn with Rav Chaim Kamiel all morning, [perek] Chezkas Habatim. Then at 2:30 – 4:00 I have a chaburah every day, where between you and me I have to say a shiur five times a week, which needs a lot of preparing… It is baruch Hashem going extremely well. Everyone speaks up, which I like a lot, and it is very leibedik. And we go through a lot of things, as you know how I learn. We are holding at daled amud beis.*

*Then in the afternoon I learn with Bodenstein and then, from 8:15 – 9:30 I have another chaburah four times a week …*

*They are very good boys, and we are going according to Rav Nochum's [Partzovitz] shiur, which, as you know, is pretty fast. Meaning, that I can't say s'tam pshat, but I have to say a piece of Torah just about every day. I have to say new stuff as the boys are real good and they all know Rav Nochum's shiur well. So I have to say something Rav Nochum didn't say ... This really keeps me working as I have to keep up to Rav Nochum's shiur.*

*That's enough about myself, and a bit of an excuse why I didn't write. Now what's with you? ...*

## We Make Aliyah

MY HUSBAND AND I MADE *ALIYAH* TO ERETZ YISRAEL IN THE year 1973. We moved into our apartment in the Pinsker Building, in the Talbieh neighborhood bordering Rechavia. The building was occupied mostly by Americans, which made it easier for us to adjust to life in Israel, which was quite different from living in Chicago. There was the language, the shopping; it was not long after the war and many things were still scarce. I remember cocoa was hard to find and I wanted to bake my favorite recipe, brownies. Coffee was scarce. I recall friends from Chicago who came on a trip to Israel and brought me a can of coffee. Living in America I would have considered it a strange gift to receive from someone, but at this particular time I relished it, especially since my husband enjoyed a good cup of coffee and I liked to serve it to my Israeli guests, especially during the cold winter months.

After we had arrived in Israel and settled into our apartment in the Pinsker Building, relatives who lived on the other side of town came to visit us: our younger cousins, many students and *avreichim* in the Yeshiva. Rav Aryeh Finkel, who is currently the Rosh Yeshiva of Mir Brachfeld, used to come to our home to learn with my husband every day. After a while they continued to learn together in the Mir, so my husband drove each morning to learn with him there in Yeshiva. They also learned together in the evening.

Our sons and daughters-in-law came frequently with their young children to spend Shabbos with us. Today, my grandchildren still talk about the fun they had visiting us on those Shabbosim in the Pinsker Building. One of my granddaughters, who is now the mother of a growing family, once said to me, "Bubby, will you be *moichel* me? — Will you forgive me?" "For what?" I asked. "One day, when I was little," she went on, "when we were visiting you in Pinsker, I took some of your brownies from the freezer while you were sleeping." We certainly had a hearty laugh from that.

I remember that first Yom Kippur, we were davening in the shul on the ground floor of the building. Suddenly a number of the men raced out in the middle of davening to join the ranks of the fighters battling in what would become known as the Yom Kippur War. Whenever there was a siren, we rushed to the bomb shelter, which was just below the shul.

We remained living in the Pinsker Building for 20 years. As a result of my husband's illness we moved to another apartment in the area called Gush Shemonim in order to be closer to our children. Another reason we moved was because it would be much closer for Rav Nosson Tzvi, who was already suffering from Parkinson's disease. We didn't want him to have to make the long trek to Rechavia on Friday morning, when he came regularly to join us for breakfast. However, he never even suggested the move; I felt it was the right thing to do to make his life easier.

# CHAPTER FOUR

# MY SON, THE ROSH YESHIVA

THE SON-IN-LAW OF RAV MATTIS KATZ TOLD ME THE following story, which he heard from his father-in-law, who was my husband's *chavrusa* for many years. Rav Nosson Tzvi was an 18-year-old *bachur* in the Mir. The Rosh Yeshiva, Rav Leizer Yudel, told Rav Mattis, who was learning in Mir at the time, that Rav Nosson Tzvi had "a good head" and that when he reached the age of 30 he would become Rosh Yeshiva.

A few years later Rav Mattis went to Rav Nochum Partzovitz, one of the roshei yeshiva, and asked him, "How old is Rav Nosson Tzvi?" Surprised by the question, Rav Nochum asked him why he wanted to know. He answered by telling him what Rav Leizer Yudel had said. Rav Nochum answered, "It's true, because even at that time, as a *bachur*, Rav Nosson Tzvi was already looking out for the needs of the Yeshiva."

What was life like for a rosh yeshiva? Often, when I visited Rav Nosson Tzvi and Rebbetzin Leah at their home I saw lines of people waiting to consult him. They came to question him concerning issues they were facing, they came to get a *berachah* from him or for him to cut a snip of hair — an *upsherin* — from a little boy's curly locks when he reached the age of 3. There were those who came to ask his advice or merely to unburden themselves — and he listened so attentively. I often saw that his listening was a great service, a comfort to these broken people. They came from all stripes and colors, so to speak. He was always eager to help where he was able.

Everywhere the Rosh Yeshiva went, people of all ages ran to greet him. Whenever we went to a *simchah* — a wedding, a bar mitzvah, a *bris* — Rav Nosson

Rav Refoel Katz brings his son to the Rosh Yeshiva for his "upsherin"

Tzvi and Rebbetzin Leah always picked me up to take me there with them. As the car came to a halt I would see people rushing to his side of the car to greet him or ask for a *berachah*.

MY SON RAV GEDALYA RECENTLY SPOKE TO ME VERY MOVINGLY and insightfully about his brother's strengths and remarkable success.

**Thinking Big**  "The Rosh Yeshiva, Rav Nosson Tzvi *zt"l*, was aware at a young age that an important technique to grow in learning was by imposing obligations, commitments, and incentives to one's growth. For example, by joining a *chaburah*, a group in which you have to say your own *chiddushei Torah* to the other members of the group. Another technique is by committing yourself to writing *chidushei Torah*. Rav Nosson Tzvi himself started to do this at a young age, thereby furthering his growth in learning. With the passing of years he implemented this technique with his students. He gave cash prizes — as did

Rav Nosson Tzvi with his brother Rav Gedalya at a simchah

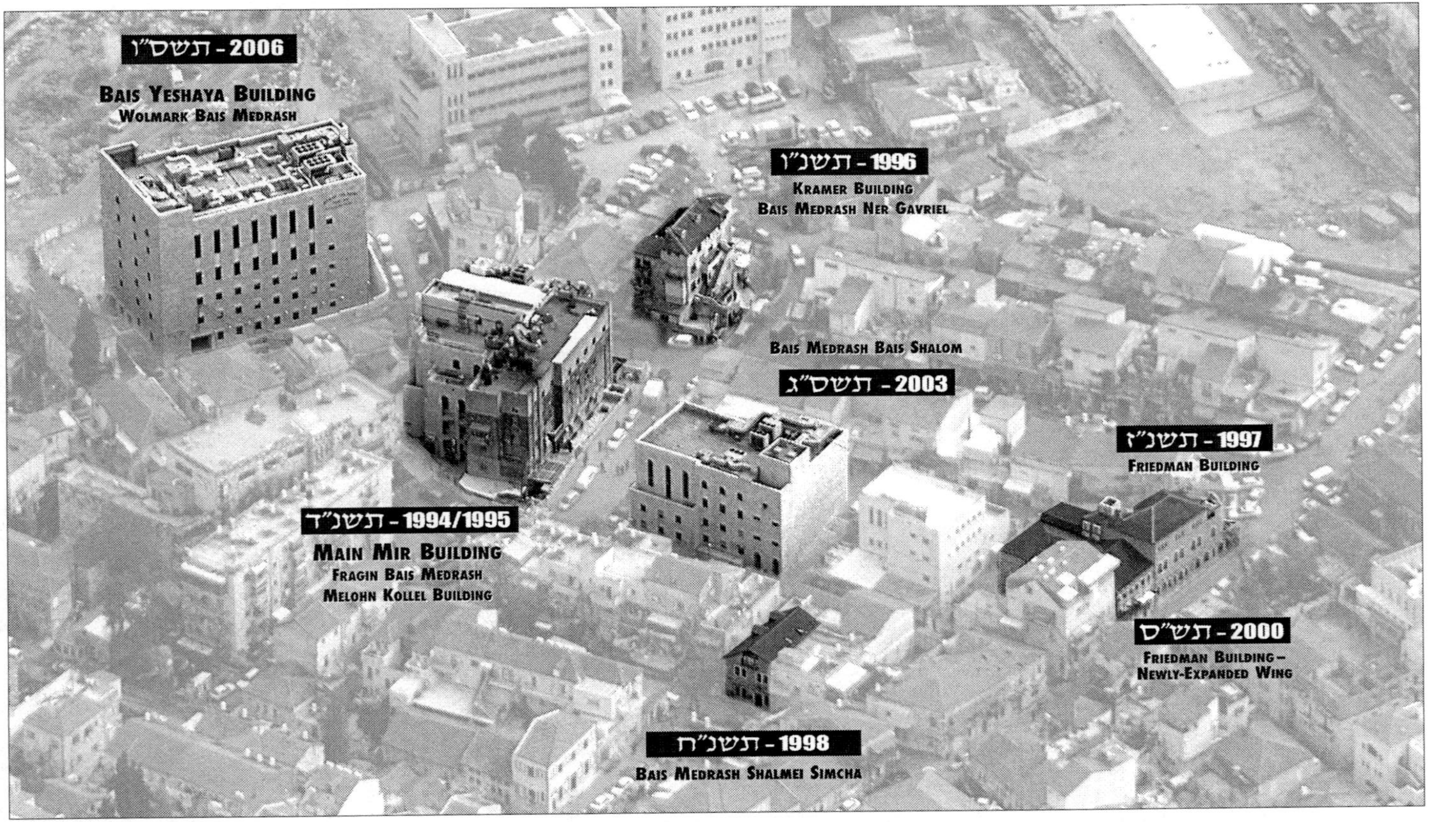

תשס"ו - 2006
Bais Yeshaya Building
Wolmark Bais Medrash

תשנ"ד - 1994/1995
Main Mir Building
Fragin Bais Medrash
Melohn Kollel Building

תשנ"ו - 1996
Kramer Building
Bais Medrash Ner Gavriel

תשנ"ח - 1998
Bais Medrash Shalmei Simcha

תשס"ג - 2003
Bais Medrash Bais Shalom

תש"ס - 2000
Friedman Building –
Newly-Expanded Wing

תשנ"ז - 1997
Friedman Building

When you "think big": The Yeshiva's enormous growth

his great-uncle, Rav Leizer Yudel — as incentives to his students to complete *masechtos* and to write *chiddushei Torah*, with people contributing funds for this purpose."

Rav Gedalya continues: "Nosson Tzvi was a big thinker. He always talked in big terms and had big projects in learning as well as big goals in learning, and in time he had big projects for the Yeshiva. For example: A number of years ago he asked me after Rosh Hashanah davening, 'Do you know what I was thinking about today? I was looking out of the window from

Rav Nosson Tzvi in the Beis Yisrael neighborhood, where the Mir would see phenomenal growth in the decades to come

my seat in the *beis midrash* and I saw across the street a plot of land that had a small building on it. I said to myself, looking at that plot of land — I am going to build a big building for the Yeshiva there one day.' A few years later the tremendous Beis Yeshayah building was built, consisting of two large *batei midrash*, two floors of dormitories, and the biggest lunch room (*cheder ochel*) the Yeshiva has."

Indeed, Rav Nosson Tzvi thought big. "It's only because he thought big that he achieved big." Rav Gedalya says that he considers this a valuable lesson in life. Though the *baalei mussar* say: One should go step by step in *avodas Hashem* because if one jumps too high at one time he might fall, but Rav Gedalya adds, "at the same time one should always shoot for a **big goal,** because only if you shoot for a **big goal** will you in the end accomplish **big;** if your goal is small you will accomplish small."

I RECALL ON ONE FRIDAY MORNING VISIT, WHEN RAV NOSSON Tzvi was in his 40's, we were sitting at the table together at breakfast

### Rav Nosson Tzvi's Mission Despite Parkinson's

and I noticed his hand trembling. I said to him, "Why are you shaking?" There was no response. A short time after that Rebbetzin Leah, my devoted daughter-in-law, and I went with him to a top neurologist in Hadassah Hospital,

Rav Binyamin Carlebach

who diagnosed his condition as Parkinson's disease. It was the first time I really knew of that illness, since no one in either of our families had it. ·

After some years the symptoms of the disease seemed to accelerate, but that did not hamper him from continuing his sacred work — giving *shiurim* regularly, receiving the long lines of people waiting for *berachos* and advice, testing and meeting with *bachurim* who wanted acceptance into the Yeshiva, attending the annual festive dinner in New York on behalf of Mir, as well as flying to various countries to raise badly needed funds to maintain the Yeshiva. It especially bothered him when he did not have sufficient funds for the monthly stipends of the *avreichim*, since for many it was their only source of income.

Even in recent years, when his shaking became more intensified and his stamina weakened, he still traveled for the benefit of the Yeshiva. Not long ago he and Rebbetzin Leah flew as far as Panama, Argentina, Brazil, England, and New York. I remember that several years ago they flew with his entourage to his hometown of Chicago, where he was received with open arms by former classmates. They greeted him with the words, *"A gadol returns to his roots."*

*Baruch Hashem* he invariably met with success in these places. His brother-in-law, Rav Binyamin Carlebach, usually accompanied him on these trips on behalf of the Mir Yeshiva and was a big asset in assisting the Yeshiva. The two felt a profound respect and esteem for each other. And of course, Rav Binyamin is a *talmid chacham* of stature, and among the roshei yeshiva of Mir.

Rav Nosson Tzvi accomplished so much every day of his life. How did he do it, with such a severe disability? It seems to me that a person's *neshamah* knows what it needs to do, and Rav Nosson Tzvi simply did what his *neshamah* directed him to do. He was more soul than body. Where did that power come from? I believe it was his unbounded love and honor for Torah learning. The Torah is the only means by which a person can aspire to the level of a *malach*, an angel. Angels always accomplish their mission, and so did my son, the Rosh Yeshiva.

IT SEEMED TO ME THAT BRACHFELD WAS RAV NOSSON TZVI'S pet project. (The official name of this branch of Mir is Yeshivas Mir in

## Mir Brachfeld

Modiin Ilit, but most people refer to it as Mir Brachfeld, after the name of the person who built it.) He traveled there twice a week to give *shiurim* to the students, to learn with them and to spend time with them, inspiring them, building them up with his encouragement, as well as by example. He built Brachfeld from scratch, both materially as well as spiritually.

Yossi and Ruchi Stern are prominent members of the Mir Yeshiva family. Rav Nosson Tzvi *zt"l* and his Rebbetzin always cherished their friendship with the Sterns. They provided the major funding to build Mir Brachfeld as well as Beis Yeshayah. Both of them are magnificent buildings. Reb Yossi wanted to glorify this *"beis Hashem,"* choosing the elegant appointments by himself. Mir Brachfeld was endowed in memory of Yossi Stern's father, Eliyahu Yehoshua, and Beis Yeshayah was endowed in memory of Ruchie's father, Yeshayah Weiss. The Mir Brachfeld today stands as a majestic edifice; the Torah learning within its buildings, however, is even more majestic. Today it houses about 700 *bachurim, kein yirbu,* all top-level students.

The story of how Mir Brachfeld was established is one I would like to share with you. My grandson Rav Yosef, Rav Nosson Tzvi's son, came to visit me in my home one afternoon during *bein hazmanim.* He sat across from me at my dining-room table and told me that at the request of his Abba, Rav Nosson Tzvi, he was going to Bnei Brak and other places to find *bachurim* in order to start a new Yeshiva in Brachfeld, an area in Modi'in Illit. I said to him, "Yosef, why do you have to run around like that? Why don't you simply put an ad in the newspaper and the boys will come to you." "Oh no, Bubby," he answered in *Ivrit* — the language I use to speak with my grandchildren — "we are not looking for average boys, not run of the mill teenagers. Abba's idea is to find *bachurim* who are on a higher level in learning and have top *middos.*" He referred to them as *bachurim b'ramah* (on a high level); they were needed in order to start a yeshiva of the highest caliber. And so it was: Before long Brachfeld became known for its select students who learned with great *hasmadah,* as well as its elite staff of *mashgichim, maggidei shiur, and meishivim.*

Brachfeld building

I spent the Shabbos just before he was *niftar* together with Rav Nosson Tzvi *zt"l* and my daughter-in-law Rebbetzin Leah at Mir Brachfeld. As we were sitting having our *leil Shabbat* dinner I saw that Nosson Tzvi's condition had deteriorated considerably. It pained me so much to see him suffering. I asked him if there was some way I could help. He smiled at me in sort of an acknowledgment; nevertheless, he continued his demanding schedule for the day. He just didn't give up. He gave his usual *shiur* to the students and was up in time for *Shacharis* with the yeshiva. Even during *shalishudis* he was with the students, giving a *shmuess* and exchanging *divrei Torah*.

I recently returned to Mir Brachfeld for a *hachnasas Sefer Torah*. A beautiful new Sefer Torah had been generously donated in memory of Rav Nosson Tzvi *zt"l* to Mir Brachfeld by a family from Brazil, where my son had visited about 2 years ago. I was sitting in the *ezras nashim* with my cousin Rabbanit Shifra Nebenzahl, Rebbetzin of Rav Avigdor Nebenzahl, who was Chief Rabbi of the Old City of Jerusalem. We were viewing the dancing and the excitement, and Shifra said to me in *Ivrit*, "*Aht Yodaat*, Sara, you know, we see a beautiful new Sefer Torah, a magnificent Sefer Torah, but it cannot replace the Sefer Torah we just lost — Rav Nosson Tzvi *zt"l*."

### Remembering a Very Special Visit

A GROUP OF YOUNG CHILDREN WHO WERE SICK OR HANDI-capped came from the United States about half a year ago, on a trip sponsored by Chai Lifeline, to see my son Rav Nosson Tzvi and to receive from him a *berachah* as well as words of *chizuk*. Many of their mothers accompanied them, with their broken hearts so apparent on their faces. I was told that this meeting with my son was the highlight of their trip to Eretz Yisrael. The Rosh Yeshiva clasped the hands of each one of the handicapped youngsters warmly while expressing to them his sincere wishes for a *refuah sheleimah*.

Today, about six weeks after Rav Nosson Tzvi's *petirah*, one of their volunteer counselors came to my home with her mother to share their memories with me. They brought with them quite a number of pictures of the youngsters. You can see Rav Nosson Tzvi showing each child so much warmth. The counselor said to me that both the children and their mothers could clearly see that the Rosh Yeshiva felt the pain of each one of these youngsters as he gave them a *berachah*.

I found the pictures of Rav Nosson Tzvi greeting every child so

A memorable visit for Chai Lifeline youngsters

warmly very heartening and moving — so real. I felt as if I were sitting in front of him watching him speak to each of these handicapped children as if they were his own, with so much patience, so much interest. My reaction was, may his *berachos* to these handicapped young people be fulfilled and may they recover to become strong, healthy individuals.

One of the counselors in the group, a young girl, approached the Rosh Yeshiva for a *berachah* for a *shidduch*. Rav Nosson Tzvi *bentched* her, and shortly after the trip she became a *kallah*. It seems that someone so involved in Torah, and who loves Torah so much, which was manifested in both his teaching and constant learning, has a special power and a special mission.

As I was looking at these pictures I thought of times gone by when I would show my son pictures of him that were sent to me — pictures of Rav Nosson Tzvi with a group in Panama, or in a shul in Argentina, or at a gathering with rabbis in Brazil, London, or Baltimore. (All these trips were for the purpose of Rav Nosson Tzvi's strengthening and disseminating Torah.) I still recall the pleasure it gave me to be able to sit with my son and show him these pictures. I felt that I was, in some measure, sharing with him the many trips he made to faraway places. Now, as I viewed the photos of these children, and saw how photogenic my dear son was — and how he clasped the hands of these crippled children with so much love apparent in his warm smile, reflecting the feeling in his heart — a fleeting thought entered my mind: *Oh, I want to show these pictures to Nosson Tzvi, I want to show them to him when he comes.* And then the thought suddenly left me just as quickly as it had entered my mind, and I began to face reality again ... reality .... realizing that I cannot do that .... I will not be able to share these precious moments with him again — never, not ever ... how very sad, very sad indeed.

A day before this meeting a family came to my home. One of their daughters was disabled from birth. They came to ask me for a *berachah* for a *refuah* for their daughter, a lovely girl of marriageable age. I suggested that she should recite *Tehillim* each day to be followed by a *tefillah* for her recovery. I then suggested to her mother that she recite a special *berachah* for her daughter at *licht bentching* and also when giving *tzedakah*. I went on to express my wish that she should find her true *zivug* within the year. As they left my house I bid them farewell with a warm and heartfelt *berachah*. As they were leaving I thought to myself — this is what my son Nosson Tzvi would have done.

I believe it was Rav Nosson Tzvi's *ahavas Torah and ahavas ha'brios*, as well as his *hasmadah*, his diligence in all that he did, both teaching and learning, that were to a large extent responsible for his success. I think because of this he had *siyata d'Shmaya*, help from Above. He was able to connect with so many people on a deep level because of his determination and strong will as well as his sincere love for them. He was always ready to give of himself — to share with others that with which he was endowed or had acquired.

# CHAPTER FIVE

# BREAKFAST AT MOM'S PLACE

OR MORE THAN 30 YEARS RAV NOSSON TZVI ZT"L and Rav Gedalya came on Friday morning to our home, where we had breakfast together. Even after my husband passed away, about 15 years ago, they continued coming each and every Friday morning about 8:30. After davening I watched for them through my kitchen window. Rain or shine they came. It hardly mattered what came up, they were here. If Rav Nosson Tzvi had a *bris* — where he invariably was *sandek* — he would come to have breakfast with me either before or immediately following the *bris*.

Toward the end I saw that it was not so easy for Rav Nosson Tzvi to travel to my home and climb up the flight of steps, so I said to him, "Don't come, I'll come to you." Nevertheless he kept coming; each Friday morning like clockwork, he was here. We sat together, schmoozing, remembering the past and exchanging conversation about the happenings of the past week. It was also an opportunity for me to consult with him on questions that came up.

Yehuda Lang, a Mir *talmid*, was a great help to the Rosh Yeshiva, devotedly accompanying him to some of the various places he had to go. I still recall Yehuda coming with my son to my home on Friday mornings. Although my apartment is a mere one and a half flights up and the elevator stops one flight up, that half flight of stairs was at times difficult for Rav Nosson Tzvi to climb by himself. I can still envision Yehuda helping him up and then onward to my apartment, to the dining room where the table was laden with some of the breakfast delicacies my son enjoyed, which I was so happy to prepare.

Rav Nosson Tzvi *zt"l* as well as Rav Gedalya excelled in the mitzvah of *kibbud av va'eim*. In the early years when we davened in Mir on Rosh Hashanah, both of my sons came upstairs together toward the women's gallery at Mir. They stood just outside of where the women were davening and summoned me out. Then, with a warm smile, they both expressed to me their wishes for a good year, for a *"Shanah tovah,* Mommy!" I felt so moved by their gesture.

I also very much enjoy the close relationship I have with both of my daughters-in-law, keeping in touch each day by phone as well as when they come over to visit. Like Rebbetzin Leah, Mimi, Rav Gedalya's Rebbetzin, is also an exemplary person. Her *hachnasas orchim* is unmatched. I spend alternate Shabbosim with them, and always enjoy seeing the many guests around their table.

One Friday morning at our pleasant weekly breakfast, which both of us looked forward to, I recall sitting together with Rav Nosson Tzvi. It was the day that my second cookbook, *Simply Delicious,* came out. He looked it over carefully, and then turned to me with a big smile on his face and said, "Mom, you're okay." That was his way of expressing his approval when I accomplished something significant: "Mom, you're okay." I can still hear him saying it and somehow I still see that broad smile on his face. I can't deny that it gave me a good feeling to have his approval on something I had achieved.

At our Friday morning breakfasts Rav Nosson Tzvi would share with me and my son Rav Gedalya some of his experiences of that week — the people he met, the *gedolim* who had visited, others who came to consult with him. It was especially interesting to hear about some of his experiences during his travels abroad, about the friendships he formed and the generosity he witnessed. I recall the visit he told us about, that he had with a wealthy philanthropist. It was not so long ago, during the global financial meltdown. It generally was his practice not to ask for funds directly. His mere presence made people understand that his travels were on behalf of the Yeshiva. While they were sitting together this wealthy man said to him, "It's a little hard for me now." To which the Rosh Yeshiva answered him, "I understand, it is hard for me also." Upon hearing this, the philanthropist paused for a moment and then wrote out a sizeable check to the Yeshiva.

It was truly a very special experience for our little family to be together, which all of us felt so deeply. Rav Nosson Tzvi talked about the colorful people he had met that past week, about the strides my adult grandchildren, his children, were making in teaching and learning, in their productive roles in spreading Torah values in the various institutions of Jewish education. I saw the pride he felt in his grandson who had just finished learning Mishnayos; he told me about the one who already knew all of the *aleph-beis*; about their *teudot*, their excellent report cards, etc. etc.

The young woman who lives with me and is a very devoted member of my household told me that when Rav Nosson Tzvi came to my apartment on Friday mornings, she observed that he felt like he was coming home — to a warm environment that made him feel calm — away from all of his responsibilities, away from the Yeshiva, which, of course, he also loved. She said he always seemed so relaxed on those wonderful Friday mornings.

### Breakfast at Mom's Place ... Continues

ONE FRIDAY MORNING, A FEW WEEKS AFTER WE SAT *SHIVAH*, when I had already returned to my home, the new rosh yeshiva, Rav Nosson Tzvi's oldest son, Rav Eliezer Yehuda, who is my oldest grandson, came to my apartment with some of my other grandsons for breakfast, emulating their revered father, Rav Nosson Tzvi *zt"l*. They did not want me to be alone Friday morning. They wanted to continue one of the traditions their Abba had maintained in the *kibbud eim* he showed to his mother, their grandmother. They now have been coming every Friday morning, in the hope of emulating this gesture of their departed father.

Each one of them has a special place in my heart; needless to say they are very dear to me. They help to fill a part of the gap, but it is only a part of what is so significantly missing, because that which is gone can, unfortunately, never be replaced.

# CHAPTER SIX
# FROM HIS FAMILY'S HEARTS

E ACH TIME THAT RAV NOSSON TZVI *ZT"L* LEFT THE house, he was always careful to bid "shalom" to the rebbetzin. Once, he had already left home with Rav Yehuda Neuhaus, who used to accompany him to davening on weekdays, when

**A Family Man**

he suddenly said, "I must go back, I forgot something at home." Rav Neuhaus escorted him back. Rav Nosson Tzvi entered the house, said good-bye to the rebbetzin, and left again.

My grandson Rav Chaim, who comes to visit me regularly, told me that whenever his father gave a *shiur* at the Yeshiva completing a *masechta*, he always made a *siyum* in their home, in the presence of his family, his growing children, and with the *talmidim* who were learning that *masechta*. Chaim told me that this made a profound impression on him not only as a youngster but throughout the years. Following this example, Chaim told me that last week he made a *siyum* in his home for his 10-year-old son who had completed a section of Mishnayos in *cheder*.

On Seder night Rav Nosson Tzvi made a point of telling each of his grandchildren where to sit, always as close to him as possible. Indeed,

Rav Nosson Tzvi in his *succah* with family and friends. Seated at right is Rav Nachman Levovitz; at the left is Rav Binyamin Carlebach. Rav Yehuda Yurman, a close *talmid*, is standing.

he saw to it that the Seder be specifically geared toward his children and young grandchildren. He made a point of asking every grandchild questions relating to the Seder. He made the youngsters at the Seder, as well as the guests who were always present, experience the feeling of *Yetzias Mitzrayim*.

My granddaughter shared with me her memory of her children's visit to their Saba, Rav Nosson Tzvi, a day or two before Succos. The children brought decorations, which they eagerly put up in their Saba's *succah*. Their Saba, Rav Nosson Tzvi, praised them so lovingly, telling them how beautiful and appropriate each decoration was, and thanking them with his famous warm smile. That was his way, to acknowledge wholeheartedly what his children and grandchildren did for him.

I would like to continue with a collection of stories of Rav Nosson Tzvi *zt"l* that I heard from our family members.

One of my grandsons told me: During the Gulf War a loud siren went off. Everyone ran to their sealed rooms. Abba left home to go to the

## From Rav Nosson Tzvi zt"l's Children: Our Abba

Yeshiva in order to be with his students. "I want to be with my boys in time of crisis," someone heard him say.

My granddaughter tells me that her Abba was very interested in everything that concerned his children, even as they became adults. Besides their welfare, he always asked about everything that concerned them. She said to me, "He not only asked about things from the outside but was interested in that which was inside each of us, our feelings and our aspirations; he even asked about our friends." When she went to bed at night she was able to sleep well hearing her Abba learning in the living room. She went on to say that during the time we were sitting *shivah* so many women came to her and each one felt that her family had a special *kesher* with Rav Nosson Tzvi; each said that she felt the Rosh Yeshiva loved her husband the best.

Another of my grandsons told me the following:

A *chavrusa* of mine, a serious and dedicated *yungerman,* once told me, "As a teenager I related more to the national religious movement. I was not sure that I would continue in yeshiva or go into the army. I was at a *beis midrash* where there was a *yeshivas bein hazmanim* of Ohr Elchanan Yeshiva and Rav Nosson Tzvi *zt"l* came to speak to the *bachurim.* I watched him as he came in — in such a weakened condition. He said only one sentence. '*Ashreichem hamachzikim b'Toras Moshe* (Fortunate you are who hold onto the Torah of Moshe).' These few words, as well as his warm smile, impressed me and convinced me that Torah is the only thing in life. My doubts were solved and I continued in yeshiva."

My granddaughter, the wife of one of Rav Nosson Tzvi's sons, came to my home after we finished sitting *shivah.* She quoted her husband: "Abba learned Torah continuously. I remember a day before Shavuos when everybody goes to rest because it is customary to learn throughout the night on Shavuos. Abba said he was unable to go rest because it was a day before *Kabbalas HaTorah.* 'How can I rest on such a day?' Subsequently, he sat and learned throughout the night and of course, as a result he became fatigued the next day, but again he repeated, 'How can I go to bed on this day when it is the day of *Kabbalas HaTorah?* I cannot rest on this memorable day.' On Motza'ei Shavuos, when he finally went to retire for the night, there was a knock on the door, and lo and behold it was another *avreich* who asked to learn with Abba *zt"l.* The member of the family who answered the door told the young man that the Rosh Yeshiva was extremely tired and it would be difficult for him to learn then. When Abba *zt"l* heard that he said, 'We never send a *chavrusa* away.' He let him in and they sat and learned until it was almost dawn."

Rav Eliezer Yehuda, *shlita,* the new Rosh Yeshiva, told this story in his *hesped* for his father: Rav Kreiswirth *zt"l,* who at the time was an elderly Rosh Yeshiva, went to visit Rav Nosson Tzvi. While he was there he asked him for a *berachah.* Later, Rav Kreiswirth was asked, "Why do you go to him when he is so much younger than you?" To which he answered, "A Rosh Yeshiva who has several thousand students and knows them all by name — it is my duty to visit him." When they related this episode to Rav Nosson Tzvi he responded, "I don't know if I know them all by name, but one thing I do know — I love all of them."

The Rosh Yeshiva himself showed how much satisfaction one can derive from spiritual achievement. In one of the *shmuessen* that he gave in the Yeshiva he told the *bachurim*, "I have a lot of troubles, a lot of suffering, and I can stand everything. One thing that really bothers me, though, is *bitul Torah*." On the other hand there wasn't any happier person than he was when he saw people learning. His joy and delight during *siyum* celebrations in the Yeshiva was extraordinary. Very often when he spoke at the *siyum* he announced a *mivtza*, a project, a special program for the following *zman*. He used to promise some extra hundred *shekels* for *avreichim* who would be careful to come on time, write *chaburos*, or be tested on certain pages in Gemara. His announcements were spontaneous. He didn't plan them in advance and when he made them he didn't know where he was going to get the money. But his ambition to spread Torah was extremely strong. (His great uncle Rav Leizer Yudel had the same practice of giving extra monies to *avreichim* who excelled in learning.)

This morning one of my grandsons talked with me about the relationship that he had with his late father. "Abba never talked down to me as a *yungerman*. He always made me feel that I was on the same level as he, even though Abba was a truly great person." I thought to myself, *What a legacy my son Rav Nosson Tzvi zt"l left to his children. They saw him as a great individual, a great person, yet at the same time he left them with the feeling that they were not a bit less than he — their towering Abba.* I think of boys with fathers who are great achievers, and because of that, the sons have the feeling that they will never be able to reach such a high level, and often they sort of give up. My grandchildren of course showed their father the proper respect due a parent; at the same time, because of the way he related to them, his children felt they could, ultimately, reach his lofty heights. I think this is something for parents to think about in their *chinuch habanim*.

His son Rav Yosef told me about his father's love for Torah:

"Abba's favorite *pasuk* was: מָה אָהַבְתִּי תוֹרָתֶךָ כָּל הַיּוֹם הִיא שִׂיחָתִי — *Oh how I love Your Torah; all day long it is my conversation.* This *pasuk* accompanied him his entire life.

"I love all of them": Hundreds of Rav Nosson Tzvi's *talmidim*

"Let me describe what it means to learn Torah all day continuously.

"On the day of the wedding of one of my sisters, the photographer came to the house to take pictures of the *kallah* and the entire family. There was nowhere for Abba *zt"l* to learn, so he moved into the kitchen and learned there together with his *chavrusa* until it was time for the *chuppah*. As the family was leaving to go to the *chasunah*, they knocked on the kitchen door. Only then did Abba get up and leave with them.

"Another episode took place during a trip to the United States. It was on a long night flight when usually everyone is sleeping and the airplane is totally dark. Every so often, I would go to check to see how he was feeling and if he needed anything. At one point, I came and asked him if he needed anything, and he motioned with his hand that I should return a little bit later, but he didn't speak at all. I returned a little while later, and his face was shining with happiness. I asked him what had happened. He told me with a smile that he had just finished preparing a Gemara *shiur*! Just imagine the concentration required to prepare the *shiur* in flight.

"In his youth, Abba *zt"l* sat and learned with his Rebbi, Rav Chaim Kamiel *zt"l*. On the same bench sat the great *gaon*, the Rosh Yeshiva Rav Nochum Partzovitz *zt"l*. Rav Nochum was an expert in the entire *Shas*, so the *talmidim* were constantly coming to ask him questions. The questions were very interesting, touching on all areas of *Shas*, and naturally those around would stop to listen to the give and take. But Abba would not turn his head at all; he was deep in his own learning without any interruptions.

"The last Shabbos of his life, he was in Mir Brachfeld. During the meal, he didn't feel well and his breathing was heavier than usual. After the meal he went to rest, but he wasn't able to relax. After an hour, he got out of bed and sat down to learn. He prepared an entire *shiur*, and learned *Chumash* with *Rashi*. Only then, after learning for a few hours straight, was he able to go to sleep calmly."

MY GREAT-GRANDSON YERUCHAM FINKEL, RAV NOSSON Tzvi's grandson, told me that this last Shavuos Rav Nosson Tzvi asked

**From Rav Nosson Tzvi's Grandchildren: Our Saba**

him to learn with him during the night. Rav Nosson Tzvi always sought the opportunity to learn with his grandchildren. Yerucham thought that his Saba would learn with him an hour or maybe two hours and then Yerucham would let his Saba rest, and he would go to the Yeshiva to continue learning. After the *seudah*, which took quite a while since they had important guests from America, Rav Nosson Tzvi sat by the table and started learning with his grandson. After learning for about an hour and a half, together delving into the Gemara, Rav Nosson Tzvi asked his grandson to help him recline on the sofa since he was tired. Yerucham helped him to lie down and rest, then got ready to leave. Rav Nosson Tzvi called him back to continue learning with him while he was in a reclining position. Yeruchem sat on a chair next to his grandfather and they continued learning. From time to time the rebbetzin interrupted them and begged Rav Nosson Tzvi to go to bed, as it was already the middle of the night. However, he refused and he continued learning with Yerucham. At about 3 o'clock in the morning his eyes closed and it appeared as if he had fallen asleep, but Yerucham kept reading the Gemara and explaining. After nearly half an hour, seeing his grandfather's eyes closed, he decided to leave. When he nearly reached the door his Saba called him back and said to him, "Please bring the Maharsha from the bookcase." They were discussing the *sugya* they were currently learning and the Rosh Yeshiva had a question about it. He wanted to find the answer in the Maharsha, as tired as he was. It appeared that he was not really sleeping because his mind was constantly working. They continued until *vasikin*, when they proceeded to daven.

Yerucham's younger brother, Dudie, told me that when he came home from *cheder* and went to visit his Saba, Rav Nosson Tzvi would ask him to review the Mishnah or the Gemara he had learned that day. Even though his Saba would sit quietly, and Dudie thought he had dozed off, Dudie said, "Whenever I made a mistake or missed something important Saba was still able to hear it, and he would tell me, 'Please repeat it correctly.'" It seemed that nothing really went over the Rosh Yeshiva's head. His mind was constantly delving in learning, whether it was obvious or not.

My granddaughter, who came to visit me this afternoon a mere two weeks after her own little Nosson Tzvi was born, reminded me of Purim at Rav Nosson Tzvi's, her father-in-law's home. The *talmidim* of the Mir came to the Rosh Yeshiva's home for a *berachah*. It made a very powerful impression on her, seeing how he showed each of them so much warmth, giving each *bachur* a kiss and a blessing — even those who came in drunk. Occasionally one of the *talmidim* became boisterous and did not behave, but Rav Nosson Tzvi still treated him with warmth, compassion, and respect.

One Succos 8 years ago, my grandson Nusi was there when a widowed mother came to visit Rav Nosson Tzvi with her 7-year-old son, who told him over a Mishnah. Rav Nosson Tzvi gave the boy 20 *shekels* for this and told him he would give him 20 *shekels* every month if he prepared a new Mishnah. He added that the boy should call him every month on the phone to tell over the Mishnah to him. "I will learn with you on the telephone," he told the fatherless boy.

# CHAPTER SEVEN
# THE SHIVAH AND BEYOND

ELLING STORIES OF *TZADDIKIM* WHO HAVE ALREADY reached the world of eternity is an aspect of *avodas Hashem*. These stories further our service to Hashem by encouraging us to try and emulate the deeds of these *tzaddikim*, by learning about their behavior, their piety, their character traits, as well as their Divine service to the *Ribono shel Olam*. Here are a collection of stories we heard about Rav Nosson Tzvi *zt"l*, both at the *shivah* and during the visits people made to my home afterward.

SOMEONE TOLD ME THAT SINCE THE DAYS OF RABBI AKIVA'S 24,000 students, there hasn't been a Rosh Yeshiva with so many *talmidim*; it is

**His Ahavas Yisrael** estimated that Rav Nosson Tzvi has had, over the years, 25,000 students. And like Rabbi Akiva, Rav Nosson Tzvi lived by the Torah principle: *Ve'ahavta l'rei'acha ka'mocha* — You shall love your fellow man as yourself. Each student in the Yeshiva had a special relationship with the Rosh Yeshiva even if he did not learn directly with him. After he passed away there was a special *chaburah* in Brachfeld. After the *chaburah*, it was decided that each participant would tell a special story about his relationship with Rav Nosson Tzvi. Amazingly, each and every student had something to say about his loving relationship with my son.

A moment of happiness with his beloved *talmidim*

It was with this love that he inspired thousands of men to reach heights they never dreamed possible. It did not matter where they were from, their family connections, or what their I.Q. was; Rav Nosson Tzvi was ready to help each student reach his potential.

The following was conveyed to me by a friend of Rav Nosson Tzvi. "I never really learned in the Mir Yeshiva, but through amazing *siyata d'Shmaya* I was *zocheh* to spend a great deal of time personally with the Rosh Yeshiva, Rav Nosson Tzvi *zt"l*. I am so grateful for this *zechus*. My children ask me why I consider HaRav Nosson Tzvi to be my Rosh Yeshiva, why I consider him to be my rebbi, and why pictures of him are on the walls of my home, if I never learned in the Mir. My answer is simple. I felt that he loved me more than any rebbi or rosh yeshiva I ever had. When my father passed away the greatest *nechamah* I had was the call I received from the Rosh Yeshiva, who cried with me over my loss. I knew he was feeling my pain wholeheartedly and that he wished he could be here with me to hold my hand."

Once when there was a heavy snowstorm, which is rare in Israel, Rav Nosson Tzvi was advised by his students not to go out because they felt it would be dangerous. He answered that when there is snow the *bachurim* are very much *b'simchah*, "and I enjoy seeing the students happy." He proceeded to go to the Yeshiva, which was quite a distance from his home, to join the *bachurim* in spite of the slippery, snow-covered ground. One of my grandsons, upon hearing this story, explained

Chapter Seven: The Shivah and Beyond □ 85

that Rav Nosson Tzvi, his Abba, never missed *Shacharis* in the Yeshiva, and he gave this reason for going out in a snowstorm because he didn't want to boast about that.

The following story is from a woman who lives in Har Nof who came to visit me:

"My two older sons were part of the pioneer group that learned in the yeshiva in Brachfeld and were *zocheh* to be very close to the Rosh Yeshiva *zt"l*. My husband and I were at a wedding where the Rosh Yeshiva was the *mesader kiddushin*. After the *chuppah* my husband brought me over to meet the Rosh Yeshiva and I introduced myself as the mother of my two special sons. The Rosh Yeshiva turned to me and said, 'You are a very, very rich lady.' Needless to say, I burst into tears from feelings of such *hakaros hatov* to the Almighty that my sons had the *zechus* to grow under the influence and guidance of the Rosh Yeshiva, Rav Nosson Tzvi."

ONE SUCCOS RAV YEHOSHUA SOLOMON CAME TO VISIT RAV Nosson Tzvi while he was sitting in his *succah*. He found Rav Nosson

**His Ahavas Torah**
Tzvi in a weakened condition and he thought he should leave. Nevertheless, Rav Solomon told him a *dvar Torah*. And after he heard the *dvar Torah*, Rav Nosson Tzvi suddenly had additional strength and he felt all his energy return.

Heard from Rav Don Segal: "He [Rav Nosson Tzvi] walked into a *beis midrash* in Lakewood, N.J. and when he saw all the students learning, he was overtaken with joy and it was so apparent through the perpetual smile on his face. It showed real *ahavas Torah*, revealed in the joy he felt when he saw people learning in other yeshivas in other parts of the world as well, not only in Mir. We learn from this to have joy in another's Torah study." Someone else told me: "A few years ago there was a *Siyum HaShas* in Binyanei Ha'umah for the English-speaking Torah world. It was a long night with many speeches and *divrei Torah*. The one that is repeated very often in our home, to my children and grandchildren, is the following: It took the Rosh Yeshiva *zt"l* a few minutes to get up to the podium. The entire audience waited in silence to hear his words of inspiration. When the Rosh Yeshiva *zt"l* finally got up to the microphone, he said one sentence, which says it all, 'YOU HAVE TO MAKE TORAH SWEET TO YOUR CHILDREN.' "

Rav Nosson Tzvi was in America and he visited a known philanthropist. He was thirsty but when he lifted the glass to drink, his hand began to tremble. Seeing this the philanthropist started to cry. Rav Nosson Tzvi told him, "I love Torah. I learn because I love the Torah. Hashem sent me this illness in order that I will learn Torah in spite of my illness, so that I will learn Torah with *mesirus nefesh, l'sheim Shamayim*."

IT APPEARS TO ME THAT THE GREATEST AND THE MOST SIG-nificant legacy my son left behind, in addition, of course, to his love for

**His Warmth to Others**

Torah that he disseminated so widely, was his love for others, the genuine love he felt and showed to his *talmidim* as well as to the countless others who crossed his path. For example, two *avreichim* came to my home today to discuss certain matters with me. The topic they primarily spoke about, so genuinely and with such great fervor that I saw and felt they were speaking from their heart, was the love they received from their Rosh Yeshiva, Rav Nosson Tzvi *zt"l*. One of the *avreichim*, who has been in Mir for 18 years, told me that when he came to Mir as a *bachur* at the age of 18 from a yeshiva in New York, he came to Rav Nosson Tzvi to register, hoping to be accepted. He told the Rosh Yeshiva that he had not prepared a *dvar Torah* to give him. The Rosh Yeshiva answered, "Don't worry, now you owe me a *chov* (a debt) that you can repay. After you prepare the *dvar Torah* bring it to me." The *bachur* answered, "But I soon have to go back to the States for my sister's wedding." The Rosh Yeshiva said to him, "Go to your sister's wedding, go *gezunter heit*, but after the wedding come back; I will be waiting for you." The *avreich* added: "You cannot imagine what that experience did for me. I came as a young boy to meet this great Rosh Yeshiva, almost trembling with fear — I wondered if I would even be accepted — I did not even prepare a *dvar Torah*, which is customarily required, and he put me so much at ease." This *avreich* related this story to me as if he were experiencing it now, with so much authentic feeling. It appeared to me as if he were energized just by recalling this encounter. When he was about to leave, I told him that I was moved by his experience and I might want to include it in the memoirs I was currently writing, and I might need to contact him to see if I remembered everything he told me. To which he answered, "You can call me anytime, anytime throughout the 24 hours of the day, I will be happy to talk with you." And I thought to myself, *to talk to me about my beloved son, about his Rosh Yeshiva zt"l*.

The Rosh Yeshiva had extended an invitation to the entire student body of the Yeshiva to attend his granddaughter's wedding. A young *avreich* came to the wedding and the Rosh Yeshiva in his *simchah* greeted the *avreich* with a warm embrace. It made the *avreich* feel so good, so welcome. He went on to say that until today he remembers it. It made him feel so important, it *mamash* elevated him.

Rav Yitzchak Grant told me the following story: An American young man who was not observant came to Israel with a program and someone took him to Rav Nosson Tzvi for a *berachah*. As he got the *berachah* he was so impressed with the Rosh Yeshiva, with his warmth and the depth that he conveyed, that he decided to become *frum* and start learning in a yeshiva. Since he was returning to America he enrolled in a yeshiva there and started to dress as a yeshiva *bachur,* instead of in jeans as before. After two years he came back to Israel and went to Rav Nosson Tzvi to get a *berachah* again. Upon meeting him again, the Rosh Yeshiva said to him "What took you so long to come back?" It was amazing that Rav Nosson Tzvi still remembered this *bachur*! The *bachur* is presently learning in a *kollel* in America as a result of his first encounter with Rav Nosson Tzvi.

During a fundraising trip in Argentina, Rav Nosson Tzvi was invited to attend a wedding. One of the *askanim* suggested that he take a side room in the hotel where the wedding was to take place, to accept people for individual audiences. Rav Nosson Tzvi declined the offer, even though the Yeshiva was very much in need of funds, because he felt that doing so would detract from the *simchah* of the wedding.

Rav Nosson Tzvi went to Brazil and stayed with a family whose young daughter had Down syndrome. She saw everyone getting a *berachah* from Rav Nosson Tzvi while she was standing at the side, overlooked. The Rosh Yeshiva noticed, and he called the little girl over to him. He smiled warmly to her, was exceptionally friendly to her and, of course, also gave her a *berachah*. This gesture of the Rosh Yeshiva gave *chizuk* to the entire *mishpachah*.

RABBI SHMUEL GOLDSTEIN, A *ROSH CHABURAH* IN YESHIVAS Mir, told me this story, which happened about 15 years ago:

**His Sensitivity to Others** "The Rosh Yeshiva *zt"l* asked everyone to write a *shtikel Torah* during *Elul zman*. I went to hand in my *shtikel Torah* on Erev Succos on the way to my parents' house in Neve Yaakov. My wife went straight from our house in Har Nof to Neve Yaakov, and I took my 1-year-old daughter and stopped off at the Rosh Yeshiva's apartment. I gave in my *shtikel Torah* and that huge smile broke out on his face. He said thank you and wished me a a good *Yom Tov*.

"I went to the bus stop but there was no bus, no cars, or anything; as I found out later, it was because of a bomb scare.

"Meanwhile, it was already almost candle-lighting time and my wife got worried. This was before cell phones — "the good old days." So she called the house of the Rosh Yeshiva *zt"l* and he asked for the phone and started telling my wife that I had been there with my daughter. He described exactly what my daughter was wearing (the Rosh Yeshiva *zt"l* noticed this because the children of his *talmidim* were like his own grandchildren to him). He calmed down my wife, assuring her that there was nothing to worry about. He continued talking for about 20 minutes, until I finally got back. Even minutes before *Yom Tov* the Rosh Yeshiva would not leave a wife to worry about her husband's welfare."

My son Rav Gedalya related to me: When his brother Rav Nosson Tzvi was a *yungerman* he raised money to pay *chavrusas* who were advanced in learning to learn with the weaker boys. He succeeded in arranging *chavrusas* for many boys in this way. He achieved two things at the same time: helping students with *parnasah* and at the same time giving confidence to the weaker boys who often were not aware of the financial arrangement.

A boy of 9 years was walking around the *beis midrash* during Rosh Hashanah. He was unable to find a place to sit. The Rosh Yeshiva called him over and asked him to sit next to him. Young or old, he always recognized their need.

A YOUNG WOMAN WHOSE HUSBAND IS AN *AVREICH* IN MIR came to me this morning and told me the following: "My husband grew

**Extending Himself**

up in similar environment as the Rosh Yeshiva *zt"l*. He felt that he also had potential, that the heights it was possible for him to reach were mirrored in the Rosh Yeshiva *zt"l* — what he could strive to become." She went on to tell me that her husband often attended a *shiur klali* of Rav Nosson Tzvi given in Yiddish. Even though he was not fluent in the language he kept coming week after week because he was so inspired by the Rosh Yeshiva *zt"l*. "He was so moved by the *mesirus nefesh* that the Rosh Yeshiva often displayed. There were times when the Rosh Yeshiva *zt"l* found it difficult to speak," she explained, "so he would pause for several minutes and the entire room was quiet — you could hear a pin drop, *mamash* — until he was able to start speaking again, until he resumed his *shiur* a few minutes later. To my husband," she went on, "it was a *shiur* in *mesirus nefesh*. He learned from the Rosh Yeshiva *zt"l* how it is important to persevere, to extend oneself." For this *yungerman* the Rosh Yeshiva's *shiur klali* was indeed a learning experience. He learned the important lesson of *mesirus nefesh* and what it entails, as well as how to achieve it. It was a lesson in striving, in working, a lesson not to give up when things become tough.

Rav Nosson Tzvi was customarily taken to the Yeshiva each morning by wheelchair to daven *Shacharis*, because it was difficult for him to walk. One day as someone was to take him with the wheelchair he said "This time I would like to try to walk to the Yeshiva in order to acquire *sechar halichah* for walking to the *beis knesses*."

A man who used to learn in the Yeshiva for some years was stricken with Parkinson's disease. He stopped learning because it was so difficult for him to concentrate, since the disease disturbed him constantly. Then he saw that his condition was of a considerably milder degree than that of Rav Nosson Tzvi's. When he learned of all that the Rosh Yeshiva was doing he was amazed; he had not dreamed it possible. This gave him a great deal of *chizuk*, an incentive to start learning again. And, indeed, he did.

I was told by the mother of Rav Nosson Tzvi's 8-year-old great-nephew that the young boy is trying very hard to follow his ways. This is what she told me: Her 8-year-old son came with her to the *levayah*. After he questioned her about his great-uncle's passing she explained to him that we cannot understand what Hashem is doing, and that we just need to think how to become better people. The little boy answered that he would try to take on himself to be *mevater*. He heard at the *levayah* how everyone was saying that Rav Nosson Tzvi *zt"l* cared so much about everyone, and he always was so kind to others, so the child decided that he would try to be nice to everyone. It's remarkable how Rav Nosson Tzvi's actions made such an impression even on a young boy.

The following story was told to me by my daughter-in-law, Rebbetzin Leah. She heard it directly from the person who gave the *hesped*. A prominent speaker from New York delivered a *hesped* in Lakewood, New Jersey to a large audience. After the event this speaker drove back to New York where he lived. As he was driving he became very sleepy and decided to pull over to the side of the road in order to rest a while. He fell asleep and dreamt that Rav Nosson Tzvi came to him asked him if he learned *mussar*. To which he answered, "Why do you ask?" Rav Nosson Tzvi answered, "Such a good *hesped* could only come from someone who learns *mussar*."

This story was told to me by my grandson, Rav Shmuel: An *avreich* came to Rav Nosson Tzvi, telling him that his wife was expecting and that the diagnosis was that the child would be crippled. Because of his sorrow and worry the *avreich* couldn't concentrate on his learning. He went to the Rosh Yeshiva to express his sadness. The Rosh Yeshiva listened sympathetically. He thought for a while and then asked the *avreich*, "Tell me, if I promise you that everything will be okay with your child, will be able to learn seriously?" The *avreich* answered positively, and the Rosh Yeshiva gave him the promise. Not long afterward the baby was born and the doctors informed the father that his child wouldn't survive more than a few weeks. The broken father ran to the Rosh Yeshiva and told him. The Rosh Yeshiva replied, "I gave you a promise and *b'ezras Hashem* he will be okay." Eventually the baby recovered and everything turned out well, just as the Rosh Yeshiva had guaranteed.

## Hakaras HaTov: A Man of Gratitude

RAV NOSSON TZVI ALWAYS FOUND A WAY OF SHOWING HIS appreciation for that which was done for him. After the wedding of his friend, Rav Nosson Tzvi recited the entire *Sefer Tehillim* on his behalf, davening that he should have a good life with his new bride. He did this as a gesture of *hakaras hatov*, because his friend had learned *Tehillim* with him many years earlier.

One of Rav Nosson Tzvi's *chavrusas*, Rav Meir Sirota, was very ill. On Purim, after the *tefillos* of *Shacharis*, Rav Nosson Zvi told Rav Sirota that he should call together fifty *avreichim* to make a *kollel*. Rav Nosson Tzvi would maintain it financially, and in that *zechus* Rav Sirota should have a full recovery. Rav Nosson Tzvi did this to show his *hakaras hatov* to Rav Sirota, because he had learned with him for a period of time.

# CHAPTER EIGHT

# MOURNING OUR LOSS

I
T IS THE FIRST EVE OF CHANUKAH, LESS THAN TWO
months after this tragic occurrence, the passing of my beloved
son. I thought the following ideas might be of help, a source of
consolation: the theme of victory, the theme of Chanukah; after all,
Chanukah is a time when *Am Yisrael* should rejoice. It seems I am con-

**The First Chanukah Without My Son, Rav Nosson Tzvi zt"l**

stantly trying to find consolation as I go
through my daily chores and activities.
But often it becomes quite a challenge. I
see his smiling face before me, I glance at
his picture on the covers of the periodicals on my dining-room table. But
do I need reminders? This is something a mother never forgets. It
remains etched in her heart. There are times when it is difficult to accept
the fact that it is a reality. Sometimes I just cannot believe it transpired.
As a matter of fact this was my initial reaction when I first heard the
tragic news. I said to Rav Tuvia Weiss, the *Av Beis Din* who is my down-
stairs neighbor, when he came up that morning to console me in the
presence of my son Gedalya, who rushed to my side; I said to this pres-
tigous Rav repeatedly, "I cannot believe it." I still wonder to myself, can
it really be true? I seem to look for him in every corner of my home. I look
at the door, waiting for it to open. Am I really waiting for him to come in,
I wonder ... Can it be a dream ... or is it a reality that I must face?

During Chanukah, a number of my grandchildren, Rav Nosson Tzvi's children and their youngsters, come to visit me after lighting the Chanukah menorah. It is an enjoyable time for all of us, and a tradition they maintain on the other holidays as well. Today is the third evening of the lighting, after which we are invited to attend the engagement party of a cousin. While sitting there exchanging conversation and mazal tovs with relatives and friends we get the wonderful news of a new baby boy born into the family — a son born to Rav Nosson Tzvi's youngest son, Rav Chaim, and

Rav Nosson Tzvi lighting Chanukah candles

his wife, which has great significance at this specific time. We learn from the *Shulchan Aruch* that when a baby boy is born in a family within the year of the *petirah*, it becomes a year of healing. The entire period of mourning for the immediate family is considered a time of judgment — we are being judged during this time of *aveilus* — and the birth of this son into the family during this time eases for us, the *aveilim*, this period of judgment. It is therefore an even greater *simchah* for the entire family that this baby boy was born at this time. In addition, the name Nosson Tzvi will continue to be perpetuated, for it will undoubtedly be given to him at the forthcoming *bris, im yirtzeh Hashem*. May this child continue to perpetuate our holy heritage and his namesake.

During the first week after Rav Nosson Tzvi *zt"l* was *niftar*, while we were sitting *shivah*, I heard of a good number of baby boys who were given the name Nosson Tzvi. I am constantly being told of more and more babies named for him. It seems that so many young people want to perpetuate Nosson Tzvi — his ways, his character traits, his *derech* — through his name.

During the *sheloshim*, I was at a *shiur* given weekly in my house when I received a call telling me that the United States Ambassador to

Israel was at my daughter-in-law Leah's house, and they were sending a car to pick me up so I could meet him. When I reached their apartment the first thing the Ambassador said to me, much to my surprise, was "Baruch Dayan Emes." He then asked me if when Rav Nosson Tzvi was young I thought he would achieve all that he had accomplished. I gave him a positive answer, while thinking — *what mother can ever really predict what will happen?*

## His Legacy Continues

MY DAUGHTER-IN-LAW REBBETZIN LEAH SHARED WITH ME some of what is going on with Mir today. She had just returned from New York where they attended the *Siyum HaShas,* where there was an overwhelming attendance of 2,500 people, the alumni from Mir. They divided the *Shas* among the alumni. Each one learned a few pages in order to finish the *Shas* before the *sheloshim.* My grandson, Rav Eliezer Yehudah, the new Rosh Yeshiva, inspired everyone with the depth of his knowledge, and the feeling that he has many of his father's personality traits.

When the new Rosh Yeshiva, my eldest grandson, took over, I reminded myself of what transpired when the previous Rosh Yeshiva, Reb Beinush, was *niftar* 22 years ago. Not long afterward I visited his widow, Rebbetzin Esther, my *mechutenesteh,* a truly great lady. I walked up the two flights of stairs at Rechov Slonim 11, just beyond Meah Shearim, to visit her. I told her that the new Rosh Yeshiva, my son and her son-in-law, Nosson Tzvi, appeared to be doing a great job. The enrollment was steadily increasing and the Yeshiva was moving ahead and making a lot of progress. To which she replied, "Sara, don't think it's because of that which is being done here. It's because of those who are already in the world of eternity, the *neshamos* on high that are bringing down the *siyata d'Shmaya,* that this is happening here in the Yeshiva." We are encouraged that we will merit that same *siyata d'Shmaya.* It is our hope that those who have already left this world and gone into the real world, the World of Truth, are making a favorable impact. The *neshamos* that have already reached those higher worlds are responsible for the success of the Yeshiva today.

Throughout all the years of Rav Nosson Tzvi's leadership of the Mir Yeshiva, he maintained a remarkable environment of harmony among the faculty as well as the students, that of unity and friendship, with each acknowledging the success of the other. This brotherly atmosphere was prevalent throughout the time he was Rosh Yeshiva. There is a genuine *kiddish Hashem* in this respect among the faculty as well as among the members of the family.

Our *tefillos* are that the new Rosh Yeshiva, Rav Eliezer Yehudah *shlita,* will continue his father's legacy and will maintain the same harmonious relationships. This is another of the admirable traits that the Mirrer Yeshiva has been known for — cooperation and harmony among the faculty and the students.

RAV MENACHEM ZARETSKY, ROSH YESHIVA OF YESHIVA Ketana of Mir in Ramat Shlomo in Yerushalayim, was a great help to

**Mourning ...
and Consolation**

Rav Nosson Tzvi in carrying out his sacred mission on behalf of the Mir Yeshiva. He came to his home every day to be of service to him. Rav Zaretsky accompanied the Rosh Yeshiva everywhere: to the various *simchas* he had to attend, when he was to be *sandek* at a *bris,* or *mesader kiddushin* at a wedding. He even accompanied him to Bnei Brak to consult with Rav Shteinman. Wherever the Rosh Yeshiva had to go, Rav Zaretsky went along with him, to help him, to be there with him.

Last week he picked me up to attend a wedding. As I walked down the steps from my apartment to the ground floor and approached the car, I glanced at Rebbetzin Leah in the back seat, where she always sat. Then my eyes took me to the front passenger seat where Rav Nosson Tzvi always sat when they picked me up the many times we went to *simchas.* But, alas, he was not there; he was not in the front seat of the car, he will not be there ever ... ever ... Instead, I saw my grandson, Rav Eliezer Yehudah, sitting there wearing his black frock as the new Rosh Yeshiva. I wondered to myself: *Could this be a source of consolation to me?* It's true, it is a real *nachas* for a grandmother to have a a grandson whom she loves dearly as a Rosh Yeshiva, a young Rosh Yeshiva of the largest Yeshiva in the world, Yeshivas Mir. But it is a big price for me to pay. A big price, indeed ... *Could it be a source of consolation,* I wondered. And then I thought to myself, *it will take time — it will take time ....*

*AS I DRAW THIS WRITING TO A CLOSE I WOULD LIKE TO SHARE with my readers a thought concerning that special place in my heart, the place where my precious son Rav Nosson Tzvi always was and will remain for ever and ever. He will be missed, I will deeply cherish his memory and I will never, ever forget him. Still I feel that he is truly a melitz yosher for me and my family. I see that he is continuing the kib-*

*bud eim that he so scrupulously observed throughout his lifetime. I can actually see his influence from above affecting us so favorably in many ways, that he is being an intermediary for me and for my family — for his family — for the success of his oldest son, Rav Eliezer Yehuda, the new Rosh Yeshiva — and of course for the continued success of the Yeshiva itself — for Yeshivas Mir, that he built into the largest yeshiva in the world today.*

# A MOTHER OFFERS IMPORTANT RULES OF CHILDREARING

# A MOTHER OFFERS IMPORTANT RULES OF CHILDREARING

By Rebbetzin Sara Finkel

IT IS VITAL THAT A CHILD FEELS AND KNOWS THAT HIS parents love him. It is of the utmost importance to tell a child every day **Love as a Tool** that you love him — and he should hear it from his father as well as from his mother. There should be a predominant atmosphere of love in the home. Love is not a luxury, it is a necessity.

IF A CHILD IS SECURE IN THE LOVE OF HIS PARENT, THEN DISCIplining will also be more effective. A child should not be made to feel **A child must** constantly on the defensive. He should not live **feel the love** with constant fear of punishment, for he will then try to find excuses for his misbehavior, and may even resort to lying. This is especially true if a child has a tendency to feel insecure.

A child should never be disciplined with anger or as a way of taking revenge from a child.

In families blessed with many children the parents should spend private as well as quality time with each child. Each child should feel that he is not just one of many children, but that he is special and unique.

IN OUR HOME, MY HUSBAND, THE CHILDREN'S FATHER, PUT A great deal of emphasis on discipline. Although my husband and I for-

**The Role of Discipline**

tunately agreed on most issues, he was the one who disciplined most and I served as more of a haven to them. With this "team effort" we avoided making things too tough for them. I was always there to caress them to make sure they did not feel rejected or forlorn. At the same time they had to know that there were certain rules to follow, certain behavior that was expected of them.

When there is a need to discipline it is important to still emphasize the positive side to the children, something good they did in connection with the problem.

When it is necessary to criticize, first mention something positive that the youngster did. For example, if you find his room to be a big mess, say to him, "You always keep your room so nice and neat, why is it messy today? Come, let's see it straightened up."

Never reprimand a child in anger or in the presence of others, especially his friends. A parent should always make sure to be calm and in control of herself when she disciplines a child. Simply take the child aside and explain to him in a quiet way what he did wrong and how he can correct it. This way the parent teaches the child what is expected of him and models good behavior as well.

RECENTLY I MET A WOMAN NOW IN HER 50'S WHO TOLD ME, "When I was about 6 years old, I was playing, and I gave a toy to

**Accentuate the Positive**

another child who wanted it. I was praised enthusiastically in front of all the people around me. I felt so proud and happy, I could hardly wait to do it again. I always remember that incident and it helped me to learn to become a sharing person." She remembered this for over 50 years! This illustrates how careful we must be in the way we speak to children, for these lessons carry over even in later years.

CHILDREN EMULATE THEIR PARENTS, THEREFORE IT IS IMPORtant for parents to set a good example for their children. If parents

**Be a Great Role Model**

constantly do things that are right, that are commendable, the children will follow suit. If a child sees that his parents are always truthful and honest, he will learn that from them; if he sees them involved in *chessed* he will copy that also. It is not difficult for children to pick up negative things as well, *chas v'shalom*, so parents must always be on the alert to set a good example in everything they say and do, which will then be carried out by the rest of the family, especially the youngsters.

**Be Happy!**

A HAPPY HOME IS THE KEY TO HAPPY CHILDREN. THIS includes *shalom bayis*, happiness between the parents, and open as well and frequent communication between parents and children. When children feel happy at home they do not need to search for happiness elsewhere.

Rav Avrohom Pam *zt"l* once told a *bachur* who was in *shidduchim* that there are three crucial points in a Yiddishe home. First is Torah, second is *kedushah,* and third is *simchah.*

**And Most Important ... Tefillah!**

MY SON RAV NOSSON TZVI PUT A GREAT DEAL OF EMPHASIS on *tefillah,* on davening, and on davening correctly. It is imperative that parents implement *tefillah* in order to have righteous children.

Rabbeinu Yonah, in his *sefer Iggeres HaTeshuvah*, points out that a mother should beg Hashem for help in raising her children. He also stresses that mothers should especially say a *tefillah* for their children when giving *tzedakah* and *bentching licht* on Erev Shabbos.

In Rav Wolbe's book on childrearing he points out that *tefillah* is the most important ingredient in raising children. He writes "If I have reached any level in Torah it is because of my mother's *tefillos*." He says that his mother davened for him several times a day.

In one of our early visits to the holy land in the 1960's, I visited Rebbetzin Batya Karelitz, who became the great-aunt of my son, Rav Nosson Tzvi, upon his marriage to Rebbetzin Leah. Rebbetzin Batya was the mother of the famed *posek*, Rav Nissim Karelitz, as well as the sister of the Chazon Ish. I traveled with my *mechutenesteh*, Rebbetzin Esther Finkel, her niece, to Bnei Brak, to meet her. I found her to be diminutive in physical stature, but a great lady spiritually. The perpetual smile on her face was captivating and her few words of wisdom made a marked impression on me.

Years later I read in a book about her life, called *Silence Is Thy Praise,* written by Esther Austern, the mother of Rebbetzin Batya's son-in-law, something that had a great impact on me. As is with many women, when I rose in the morning I felt eager to get into the day. I had laundry to put in the washing machine, telephone calls to return. Perhaps I wanted to get to the computer hurriedly to record a thought before it escaped my mind, or even to give a peek to see if I had received email from a friend abroad. Then I was reminded of what I read in this fascinating biography. It tells about Rebbetzin Batya consulting the Chazon Ish about a seemingly simple question. After rising one morning and going to the kitchen to daven, she noticed that the curtain hanging in the kitchen window was torn, and people passing by were able to look into the room, a fact that disturbed her. She called the Chazon Ish and asked him if she could mend the curtain before she davened. His answer, which made a marked impression on me to this very day, was that "before davening one must daven." From then on that was my first venture of the day — to daven — to seek contact with the One Above. It is, indeed, a spiritually uplifting way to begin the day.

The Gemara says that there are three partners in a child: the father, the mother, and, of course, Hashem. It is ultimately up to Hashem, our partner, to ensure that we have good, successful, righteous children. It's an important part of parenting. Remember that Hashem is your partner in your children. Daven to Him.

# BOOK 2:

# RAV NOSSON TZVI

## THROUGH THE EYES
## OF A TALMID

Rabbi Yehuda Heimowitz

# ᗐNTRODUCTION

ᗰANY PEOPLE STRUGGLED TO EXPRESS A FEELING that developed in the weeks and months after the sudden *petirah* of the beloved Mirrer Rosh Yeshiva, Rav Nosson Tzvi Finkel *zt"l*. In a *hesped*, Rav Yitzchok Berkowitz *shlita*, who was a close *talmid* of the Rosh Yeshiva nearly 40 years ago, helped crystallize the disquieting feeling many others shared.

At first, we were all too shocked at the passing of Rav Nosson Tzvi to process what he meant to the worldwide Torah community as a whole, and to each person as an individual. There is hardly a single *frum* family in the world that doesn't have a close relative — a son, a son-in-law, a brother, a grandson — who learned in the Mir. And out of those who learned in the world's largest yeshiva, how many *didn't* have at least a few personal moments or a special encounter with the Rosh Yeshiva that they cherish?

Yet how many times before Rav Nosson Tzvi's *petirah* had we given thought to what he meant to us? As Rabbi Berkowitz put it, "As the shock wears off, we realize that as the yeshiva grew, and the Rosh Yeshiva grew, we took it all for granted. And now we look back, and it's awesome."

Awesome indeed.

There is a feeling that I suspect has, at some point or other, paralyzed any author privileged to write a biography of a *gadol*. Commenting on the words *"ki ga'oh ga'ah"* that we say each day in *Az Yashir*, Rashi explains that no matter how much we praise Hashem, there is always more to praise. When writing a biography of a *gadol*, as you talk to those who knew him or reflect on your own memories of him, you constantly discover deeper levels of his greatness to probe. Far from making you grow weary of the subject, each new story adds to the overwhelming awe you develop for him — even if you knew him before! As you struggle to turn that awe into prose, you are keenly aware that no matter how much effort you put into writing about the *gadol*, it will always be *ki ga'oh ga'ah* – his greatness will exceed all the praise.

When the reality of Rav Nosson Tzvi's passing began to settle in, you didn't have to be his biographer to feel that overwhelming awe. Every *frum* Jew in the world came to feel, of his or her own accord, that the Mirrer Rosh Yeshiva was the ultimate *mechayev* (obligator). His illness provided the best possible excuse for him to live his life far from the public eye, perhaps emphasizing his personal advances in *ruchniyus*, or maybe even narrowing his focus to coping with his horrendous condition. Yet he went out and achieved more than dozens of others working together could have accomplished with healthy, well-functioning bodies.

For years, the phenomenon that was Rav Nosson Tzvi was just a fact of life. We took him — and all he represented — for granted. And when we woke up on that Tuesday morning and heard the news of his *petirah*, we were forced to face ourselves. We were forced to recognize that the excuses we make for ourselves just don't hold water when we have Rav Nosson Tzvi to compare to.

ALMOST PARADOXICALLY, HOWEVER, as this project became a reality, I began to wonder in what way Rav Nosson Tzvi truly obligates us. After all, the Gemara (*Yoma* 38b) teaches us that Hashem saw that there would be a minimal number of *tzaddikim* in the course of history, so He planted a few in each generation. Certainly, the *neshamos* of these *tzaddikim* are infused with *kochos hanefesh*, spiritual strengths that the rest of us just don't have. Furthermore, Rav Nosson Tzvi was molded by his great-uncle, Rav Leizer Yudel Finkel *zt"l*, who groomed him into the Rosh Yeshiva he would eventually become. Not many of us merit such close access to a *gadol* of Rav Leizer Yudel's stature.

So yes, we realize that he obligated us, but in what way? Does his existence in our generation require each of us to become a *gadol* in Torah, *middos*, or *chessed*?

There was one answer that was suggested independently by scores of family members and close *talmidim*: Rav Nosson Tzvi obligates each of us *not to accept limitations*.

His brother, Rav Gedalya Finkel *shlita*, may have put it best. In a *hesped*, he cited the Torah's narrative of the construction of the Mishkan, the final result of which would be to bring the Divine Presence down into this world. Hashem told Moshe to have the Jews donate gold, silver, and other items necessary for the construction. Moshe sent out the call, and before long, the amount of material was *"dayam ... vehoser —* enough for them ... and more"* (*Shemos* 36:7).

The Ohr HaChaim poses an obvious question: The donations received could either be enough, or more than enough. How could they be both?

The Ohr HaChaim suggests that since the Jewish people had the purest intentions in bringing these materials for the construction of the Mishkan, Hashem ordained that although there was indeed an excess, everything should miraculously fit so that no individual would be offended by having his offering turned away.

On one level, this interpretation represents Rav Nosson Tzvi. He was constantly building and bringing Hashem's Presence into the world, but never at the expense of the feelings of a single individual.

But this narrative represents Rav Nosson Tzvi on a much deeper level as well, noted Rav Gedalya.

Each person has what he considers his personal limitations. We have limitations on how much we think we can learn, how much *chessed* we can do, how much warmth and love we can spare for others.

Hashem knows, however, that when we reach the point of *dai* — we feel it's enough — there's always a point of *vehoser*: In reality, we can do a little more. In order to bring the *Shechinah* into this world, we have to break through that self-imposed glass ceiling, to reach above the point of *dai*, and enter the realm called *vehoser*.

That was the life of Rav Nosson Tzvi. No matter how much he did, he never considered it enough. He worked until he had no more energy — and then he worked some more.

The *vehoser* was present in everything he did.

It was there when he had no energy to move, but when it came time to say *shiur klali*, he said that he would just walk to the door of his house, because that much he could manage. And then he would reach the door, and he would say that he still had energy to walk outside. Then he would get outside, and push himself to walk to the yeshiva, and into the *beis midrash*, up to the podium ... and then he would somehow find the strength, fueled by his love of Torah, to deliver the entire *shiur klali*.

It was there every time he greeted somebody. He once revealed in a *vaad* the reason he smiled so much. When he was struck with his illness, he realized that children would be frightened by his appearance. He decided then that he would make a deliberate effort to smile as much as possible so that people would feel at ease around him. One can hardly fathom the level of *vehoser* that it took to force the muscles in his face to comply when he tried to smile.

And primarily, it was there in his thoughts. As his brother Rav Gedalya put it, "He always thought big." Whether it was the size of a building he wanted to build, in the financial incentives he would give to those who would excel in their learning or finish a *masechta*, or in any other area in life, he thought big.

The message of *dai vehoser* can change the lives of every one of us. We may not be able to spend 12 hours learning Torah each day for decades as Rav Nosson Tzvi did — although we might surprise ourselves if we tried, as many of his *talmidim* did. But even if we can't learn 12 hours each day, we can learn a little more than we've been doing; we can donate beyond what we consider our limit; or we can break through constraints that keep us from convincing others to become partners in building Torah.

If we can't succeed in those areas, perhaps we can look at the legendary *chassadim* of the Rosh Yeshiva and bring ourselves to do more *chessed* than we consider ourselves capable of doing.

And if we can't do more *chessed*, we can at least break the shackles of jealousy that don't allow us to be happy for another person when they accomplish something — to *fargin* others their success — as Rav Nosson Tzvi excelled in doing all his life.

The Rosh Yeshiva would often tell people, "There's no such thing as 'I can't.'" From anyone else, it may have been lip service. Coming from him, it was pure truth.

While we all realize that these brushstrokes of Rav Nosson Tzvi will fall short in painting the true picture of the *gadol* we lost, may they inspire us to reach beyond our limitations and achieve greatness — each in our own way.

# ABOUT THIS BOOK

I N THE AFTERMATH OF RAV NOSSON TZVI'S PASSING, stories about him made their way around the world at a rapid pace; some of them even grew "wings" in the process. Many stories turned out to either be false or severely embellished, and a great deal of work went into verifying each story before it was included in this book. For purposes of verification, I have attributed most of the stories to a specific source, unless it is obvious that the protagonist told the story. Even stories that are not sourced have been verified; the lack of attribution indicates that the source asked not to be quoted.

Most of the stories were written using only the first names of the people involved, for several reasons:

First, Rav Nosson Tzvi connected with hundreds of students each day, and often a story that happened with one *talmid* occurred with many others as well. To attribute it to one individual would be to limit the scope of the Rosh Yeshiva's influence.

Second, some stories contain personal details that the protagonist might prefer to keep private.

Third, some *talmidim* specifically requested that their full names not be used. Nevertheless, the first names in the stories are the actual names, unless the name appears in quotation marks the first time it is used.

Terms that have entered the vernacular of the yeshiva world – *shtikel Torah* and *chaburah*, for instance – have not been translated, though we do define each one the first time it is used. A glossary at the end of the book defines the Yiddish and Hebrew terms.

—YH

# SECTION ONE

# ROOTS OF A LEGACY

שְׁתוּלִים בְּבֵית ה' בְּחַצְרוֹת אֱלֹקֵינוּ יַפְרִיחוּ

*Planted in the house of Hashem, in the courtyards of our
G-d they will flourish* (Tehillim 92:14)

# CHAPTER NINE
# WHO WAS RAV NOSSON TZVI?

*In the months following Rav Nosson Tzvi's petirah, it seemed that everyone had a story to tell about him. Whether a Mir alumnus, a parent of a talmid, or even the few who didn't seem to have a direct connection to the yeshiva, the world buzzed for weeks, with new stories being told or emailed daily.*

*But who, exactly, was Rav Nosson Tzvi Finkel zt"l, the Mirrer Rosh Yeshiva? What defines his essence and explains why hundreds of thousands felt a personal bond with him and mourned his passing as a personal loss? If you were to poll a sample of the multitudes of mourners around the world, their answers to the question of "Who was Rav Nosson Tzvi?" would be surprisingly varied — even contradictory in some instances — and they might cite proofs from stories such as these:*

*D*OZENS OF PEOPLE WERE CRAMMED INTO THE LIV-
ing room at Rechov Ha'ameilim 33 in the Beis Yisrael
neighborhood for an extremely joyous occasion: the completion of a new Sefer Torah for the yeshiva.

The crowd grew silent as the Rosh Yeshiva prepared to address the

**Rav Nosson Tzvi, the Oheiv Torah**

gathering. But as happened on occasion in
the last few years of his life, as the Rosh
Yeshiva attempted to speak, the disease that
racked his body overwhelmed him. He tried to utter a word, but he
couldn't.

Some people shifted uncomfortably; others looked on in pity as Rav
Nosson Tzvi tried to speak a second time. No success.

He couldn't speak.

But he spoke nonetheless.

Reaching for the *mantel* (covering)
of the Sefer Torah, Rav Nosson Tzvi
laboriously pointed at each word
embroidered onto it: "*Mah ahavti
sorasecha, kol hayom hi sichasi* – O
how I love Your Torah! All day long
it is my conversation."

With that short "speech," Rav
Asher Arielli *shlita* recalled a day
after Rav Nosson Tzvi's *petirah*, the
Rosh Yeshiva had encapsulated his
life.

O, how he loved the Torah. All day
long it was his conversation.

Rav Nosson Tzvi writes the
final letter in a new Sefer Torah

SHAUL WAS A *BACHUR* IN MIR IN THE ERA BEFORE RAV NOSSON
Tzvi was Rosh Yeshiva. Once, he woke up in the middle of the night to

## Rav Nosson Tzvi, a Parent to Each Talmid

a sudden excruciating pain in his
mouth. Six thousand miles from
home and not familiar with the lan-
guage or the medical and dental system in Eretz Yisrael, he did what
any Mirrer *talmid* would do under the circumstances: he ran to Rav
Nosson Tzvi's house and knocked on his door.

Rav Nosson Tzvi came to the door, and when he heard the problem,
he determined that the only place where Shaul could get treatment at
that hour was in a hospital. He called a taxi and ushered Shaul into it,
sitting next to him and trying to calm him down.

The doctor on call examined Shaul and delivered the news that only
immediate oral surgery could alleviate the pain. They summoned a
surgeon, and Shaul, who was crying in pain at this point, settled into
the dental chair.

Rav Nosson Tzvi sat down alongside him, holding his hand as a
mother would do for her child. As the surgeon went to work, Shaul
squeezed Rav Nosson Tzvi's hand to release some pain. With his other
hand Rav Nosson Tzvi patted Shaul on the back, saying, "Shaul, it's
going to be okay, Shaul, everything's going to be fine," over and over
again, to soothe him.

Finally, when the direct cause of the pain was eliminated, the surgeon took a break. Shaul sat up in the chair and released Rav Nosson
Tzvi's hand. Noticing that his own hand was wet, he looked down and
was shocked to find blood on his fingers. He realized that he had been
cutting into Rav Nosson Tzvi's skin with his nails while squeezing his
hand. "Why didn't Rebbi tell me that I was hurting him?" he stammered.

Rav Nosson Tzvi just continued patting Shaul on the back, repeating
his soothing refrain: "Shaul, it's going to be okay, Shaul, everything's
going to be fine."

RAV YOSEF ELEFANT, ONE OF THE *MAGGIDEI SHIUR* IN THE MIR,
was once engaged in conversation with Rav Nosson Tzvi when an

## Rav Nosson Tzvi, the Torah Builder

alumnus came to visit, bringing his 6-year-
old son with him.
"What are you learning?" Rav Nosson
Tzvi asked the boy.

*"Parashas Lech Lecha,"* the boy replied.

"Let me ask you a question," the Rosh Yeshiva continued. "What if someone would tell you, 'Go'? He wouldn't tell you where to go, he would just say 'Go!' Would you do it?"

Somewhat bewildered by the question, the boy stood quietly, unsure of what to say.

Rav Nosson Tzvi then turned to Rabbi Elefant. "I have no idea where I'm going with all of this — the additional buildings, the learning incentives, bringing more and more groups into the yeshiva. But Hashem told me to go — so I'm going."


### Rav Nosson Tzvi, Everyone's Chavrusa

PINNY JOINED THE MIR IN 1995, WHEN THERE WERE APPROXImately 4,000 *talmidim* in the yeshiva. He arrived at the beginning of the winter *zman*, and was having some trouble acclimating. On the second Shabbos of the *zman*, Rav Nosson Tzvi approached him and asked, "How's it going?"

"Not that great," replied Pinny frankly. "My second-*seder chavrusa* didn't work out, and I haven't had a *chavrusa* in a week."

"Come to my house tomorrow at 3," the Rosh Yeshiva said simply.

On Sunday at 3, Pinny knocked on the Rosh Yeshiva's door. Rav Nosson Tzvi sat him down, gave him a drink, schmoozed with him a little, and then the two spent the next few hours learning. At 6 o'clock the Rosh Yeshiva said, "That was *gevaldik*."

"But I still don't have a *chavrusa*," Pinny pointed out.

"So come back tomorrow," the Rosh Yeshiva said.

So Pinny went back on Monday. And on Tuesday. And every day until Rosh Chodesh Nissan.

With both the spiritual and material needs of thousands of *talmidim* on his mind, Rav Nosson Tzvi could still find time for each individual *talmid*.


### Rav Nosson Tzvi, the Masmid

SHMUEL LEARNED WITH THE ROSH YESHIVA FOR MANY YEARS during *bein hazmanim*, sometimes joining him at a vacation home in Telz-Stone provided by a philanthropist who wanted to give the Rosh Yeshiva a much-needed opportunity to rest. Rav Nosson Tzvi would "disconnect" from the world in those weeks, without as much as a telephone to interrupt him, and he would prepare the *masechta* the yeshiva would be learning the next *zman*.

Once, the two were learning a difficult *Tosafos* together, and the Rosh Yeshiva was exhausted. He went to lie down on a couch that had no armrests or sides. As Shmuel suggested a possible explanation for the *Tosafos*, the Rosh Yeshiva was suddenly seized by a severe spasm that catapulted him off the couch and straight onto the floor, face down. The *bachur* froze in his seat. He wanted to run, call for help ... but in that moment, seeing the Rosh Yeshiva lying prone on the floor, he couldn't move. Before Shmuel could decide what to do, Rav Nosson Tzvi lifted his head slightly and said, "*Nuch a mohl. Vus iz der vort?* (Tell me again, what's your explanation?)"

Only after Shmuel repeated his entire approach to the *Tosafos* did the Rosh Yeshiva allow him to call the Rebbetzin to help him stand up.

### Rav Nosson Tzvi, the Tzaddik

SEVERAL YEARS AGO, RAV AVRAHAM CHESHIN, WHO HAD been one of Rav Nosson Tzvi's first *chavrusas* in the Mir, spotted the Rosh Yeshiva davening *Maariv* at a *chasunah*. He had an issue that he wanted to discuss with the Rosh Yeshiva, and he thought that this would be the perfect opportunity. The Rosh Yeshiva was in middle of davening *Shemoneh Esrei*, but since he had just bowed at the *berachah* of *Hatov Shimcha uLecha na'eh lehodos*, Rav Avraham figured that he would finish *Shemoneh Esrei* before long. But minute after minute ticked away, and Rav Nosson Tzvi still hadn't said *Oseh Shalom*. Finally, after a long while, he finished davening.

As a close friend, Rav Avraham felt comfortable enough to ask the Rosh Yeshiva what took so long to finish from *Hatov Shimcha* through the end.

"People bring me names of others who have fallen ill and need a *refuah sheleimah*," Rav Nosson Tzvi explained. "Before *Yihiyu Leratzon*, I mention each of those names. It takes me longer than my entire *Shemoneh Esrei*."

Amazingly, Rav Nosson Tzvi did not take a paper out of his pocket to read off the names. Though he didn't even know many of the people he was davening for, he cared so much for each individual in *Klal Yisrael* that he remembered their names.

IT WOULD BE FOOLHARDY TO TRY TO "ENCAPSULATE" RAV Nosson Tzvi's essence with any one description or any one story.

Was he a person who loved Torah, as the story of his *hachnasas Sefer Torah* illustrates, or was he the "*mammeh and the tatteh*" of the entire yeshiva, including that young man stricken with a toothache in the middle of the night?

Was he the visionary who filled his time planning the expansion of the yeshiva, or was he the Rosh Yeshiva who had time to learn with any person who requested an opportunity to learn with him?

Was he the quintessential *masmid* who wouldn't be deterred from understanding a *Tosafos* after landing face-down on the floor, or was he the *tzaddik* who would daven for anyone in *Klal Yisrael* who turned to him?

Rav Chaim Shmuelevitz, whom Rav Nosson Tzvi would often point to as an inspiration, provides an answer. "*Nisht der maaseh zugt oif der mench,*" he would say, "*nur der mench zugt oif der maaseh.*"[1] A story about a person does not define him; the person defines the stories told about him. Not every act of greatness is performed by a person who is truly great; every person is capable of performing great acts every now and then. Everyone can be a *masmid* or a *tzaddik* from time to time, and everyone can care for others every once in a while. A true *gadol* is someone whose every action is governed by his character perfection, and it is the overall picture that makes each individual story that much greater.

In a *hesped* delivered upon getting up from *shivah*, Rav Nosson Tzvi's son, Rav Shaya Finkel, related that during the *shivah* the family heard hundreds of stories — not huge stories, but small stories of events that occurred on a daily basis. As a close *talmid* who has been in the Mir for two decades delineated: "There were 50 or 100 stories occurring with the Rosh Yeshiva each day. Each time he would meet someone, that person would walk away feeling as though he had a story that no one else had."

The only conceivable answer to the question of "Who was Rav Nosson Tzvi?" is that he wasn't any one of the above. The entire Torah world mourned his loss, and many continue to grieve, for Rav Nosson Tzvi Finkel *zt"l* was all of the above — and much more.

---

1. See *Sichos Mussar*, 5733, *Mili D'Hespeida.*

CHAPTER ῘEN
# ῘHE ῤOOTS ῼPROUT IN ῌIR

*In explaining why the Torah records stories of
the lives of the Avos (Forefathers) in such detail, the
Ramban (Bereishis 12:6) explains that the concept
of "ma'aseh avos siman labanim[1] — the acts of the
Forefathers are a portent for the children" runs much
deeper than symbolism. When the Avos acted in a
certain way, they weren't merely serving as role
models for their descendants; they were "inventing"
the capacity for a Jew to act in that way and injecting
it into the spiritual genes of the Jewish nation.*

*We can illustrate Ramban's principle through
Akeidas Yitzchak. When Avraham Avinu passed the
test of the Akeidah by being ready to offer his son as
a korban, he was not merely the forerunner of the
countless fathers and mothers who would be willing to
sacrifice their children al Kiddush Hashem throughout
the generations. Rather, had Avraham not passed that
test, none of his offspring would have been able to
sacrifice their children either. His success spawned the
success of his descendants.*

*Although few laws of the Torah appear in Sefer
Bereishis, says the Ramban, it is a crucial component
of the Torah nonetheless, because it reveals the future*

---

1. *Midrash Tanchuma, Lech Lecha* 9.

*of the entire Jewish nation through the events in the lives of our Forefathers.*

*Similarly, it is impossible to write about — or learn from — the life of Rav Nosson Tzvi Finkel without understanding the spiritual roots of Yeshivas Mir. When we read about the history of the yeshiva, not only do we find striking parallels between the small yeshiva founded in a Polish hamlet and the flourishing institution it is today; we also find similarities, both in personality and in approach to leadership, between the founders of Yeshivas Mir, who were not ancestors of the Finkel family, and the roshei yeshiva who would lead it for the two centuries that followed — including, and perhaps especially, Rav Nosson Tzvi himself.*

*T*HE YEAR WAS 1815.[2] THE VENUE:[3] A SMALL, SLEEPY town in Poland, not far from Minsk, the capital of present-day Belarus, then known as White Russia. Even as late as 1935, Mir was still so minuscule that it could not be found on maps of the region. If not for the biannual fairs held in this village during the Middle Ages, few would ever have known it existed. No railway reached the town — the nearest train station was 10 miles away — nor were there any other organized modes of transportation to it.

In 5575/1815, what seemed to be a relatively minor event occurred in Mir, but it was an event that would change the face of Jewish history: A successful businessman, Rav Shmuel Tikutinsky, decided to open a yeshiva in his hometown. Little could anyone know that nearly two centuries later, Yeshivas Mir would not only continue to function as the longest-standing yeshiva in the world, but also as its largest, with an enrollment of nearly 7,000 students.

---

2. Unless otherwise indicated, the history of the Mir recorded in Chapters 10 and 11 is culled from two sources: (1) A historical account of the yeshiva from its inception through World War II written by Rav Yosef Dovid Epstein, the secretary of Rav Leizer Yudel Finkel in Europe and of Rav Chaim Shmuelevitz in Japan. Rav Epstein's account was printed in the book *Mosdos HaTorah b'Eiropa Bevinyanah Ubechurbanah*. (2) An essay by Rabbi Theodore (Tuvya) Lewis, who was in the Mir from 1935 to 1938, titled "Remembrances of the Mir," which he printed in the introduction to his book, "Bar Mitzvah Sermons at the Touro Synagogue."

3. In actuality, until World War I, the area that contained both Mir and Minsk — and many other towns that housed "Lithuanian" yeshivos — was in a country called Belarus, which was under Soviet control. (Belarus was part of the Pale of Settlement, an impoverished area of the Russian empire in which all Jews were required to live.) During World War I, the area fell under German control. After the war, on January 2, 1919, Belarus claimed its independence (although the government was Communist), but it was short-lived. By 1921, Russia and Poland had repartitioned the land. Mir was in Poland (which had also been under Russian control before World War I), and Minsk in Russia. For clarity, we use the classification that held true for the Golden Era of Yeshivas Mir (see p. 145), for which the historical records are more accurate.

THE HISTORY OF YESHIVAS MIR (ALTERNATIVELY KNOWN AS THE Mirrer Yeshiva, or simply as "the Mir") up to the point when it was reestablished in Eretz Yisrael can be divided into four eras.

**Four Eras**

The first era spanned from its founding in 1815 through 1899, during which the yeshiva was led by the Tikutinsky family.

The second and shortest era was from 1900 through 1909, when the yeshiva was led by Rabbi Elya Baruch Kammai, who then brought in his son-in-law, Rav Eliezer Yehuda Finkel, son of the Alter of Slabodka, Rav Nosson Tzvi Finkel, to be Rosh Yeshiva alongside him.

The third era was from 1909 through 1939, when the yeshiva thrived despite the difficulties of World War I.

The fourth and final era was when the yeshiva was on the run, evading the Nazi onslaught. Most of the yeshiva crossed the Soviet Union en route to Japan, eventually finding refuge in Shanghai, China. Once the yeshiva left for Japan, the Rosh Yeshiva, Rav Leizer Yudel Finkel *zt"l*, traveled to Eretz Yisrael, spending the war years toiling to reestablish the yeshiva in Yerushalayim and attempting to obtain immigration certificates for the entire yeshiva.

THE FOUNDER OF YESHIVAS MIR, RAV SHMUEL TIKUTINSKY, didn't only support — apparently singlehandedly — the nascent yeshi-

**The Tikutinsky Era (1815-1899)**

va; as a *talmid chacham* of note, he also delivered *shiurim* to the *bachurim* for the first eight years of the yeshiva's existence.

In 1823, Rav Shmuel had to travel on business, a trip that lasted for the last 12 years of his life. While he was on the road, his son Rav Avraham ran the yeshiva. A Torah giant and great *tzaddik*, Rav Avraham Tikutinsky left his business interests in the capable hands of his wife so he could devote himself to Torah. Under Rav Avraham's leadership, enrollment grew to approximately 120 *bachurim*, and he had to seek external sources of funding to sustain the yeshiva. At that point, yeshivos were generally supported by their host town, and when Rav Avraham embarked on a fundraising trip outside of Mir — an approach that was unheard of at the time — he met with resistance. His sterling reputation preceded him wherever he traveled, however, and eventually he was successful at raising the funds he needed.

Rav Avraham passed away when he was only 40, the same year in which his father passed away while still on the road. Rav Avraham's son, Rav Chaim Leib, was a very young man studying at a different yeshiva at the time.

The town of Mir, a sleepy hamlet that barely made it onto maps of prewar Europe

A map of the Mir area

The leadership gap in the yeshiva was filled by the Rav of the town of Mir, Rav Yosef Dovid Eisenstadt, who prevailed upon his son, Rav Moshe Avraham, to join him in running the yeshiva. When Rav Yosef Dovid Eisenstadt passed away in 5606/1846, Rav Moshe Avraham was appointed the Rav of Mir. Being the Rav of the city and running the yeshiva was too much of a burden for one person, and Rav Moshe Avraham realized that he needed someone to help him administer the yeshiva.

By that point, Rav Chaim Leib had become worthy of carrying on the Tikutinsky chain at the helm of the yeshiva, but there were some detractors who preferred another candidate. In the end, a panel of twenty rabbanim was appointed to determine which candidate should be appointed Rosh Yeshiva alongside Rav Moshe Avraham Eisenstadt.

An eyewitness account of the events[4] describes the fascinating selection process:

> The panel of twenty rabbanim, led by the Rav of Brisk, traveled to Mir to choose the Rosh Yeshiva. The first to appear before the panel was a Torah great named Rav Itzele [no other identifying characteristics were given for this candidate]. He prepared wonderful novella, displaying both sharp acuity and a broad range of knowledge. Upon concluding his shiur, he answered questions from the audience incisively. The yeshiva was filled with a sense of victory; many students felt that Rav Chaim Leib would be wasting his time trying to compete with this "lion."
>
> While almost everyone present celebrated with this gaon and showered him with blessings, two people remained silent: Rav Chaim Leib, and the elderly Rav of Brisk.
>
> On the next day, Rav Chaim Leib took his turn to deliver a shiur. As a young man,[5] this was his first appearance before such a distinguished audience. With his future at stake, he was stricken with eimsah detziburah (roughly: stage fright), and he spoke in such a soft voice that the Brisker Rav instructed him to speak louder.
>
> Some members of the yeshiva were surprised that this young man could mount a challenge after the astounding shiur they had heard a day before, and they were waiting to refute him at the first opportunity. But the "attack" never came, for there was nothing to attack.
>
> Rav Chaim Leib began to deliver his shiur. Twenty minutes passed, then half an hour, and no one could find any reason to interrupt with a question. He spoke without great oratorical garnishing, but his words ran pure as water, and all difficulties in the sugya (Talmudic topic) grew clear. All questions fell away before the young scholar's iron logic, presented with sweet simplicity.
>
> Sounds of blessings filled the room as the elderly Rav of Brisk, the first to reach the podium, declared joyously: "It was a pleasure to listen to you. Trust me, if not for the burden of my community, I would come to you and become your student."
>
> The second person to reach Rav Chaim Leib and bless him was none other than the competing candidate. Rav Chaim Leib himself was overwhelmed by the reaction. The crowd that had gathered placed him on

---

4. Cited in Rav Yosef Dovid Epstein's historical account.
5. Rav Chaim Leib was approximately 23 at the time.

*the seat [assigned to the Rosh Yeshiva], calling out, "Yechi Rabbeinu
– may our master live!"*

For all the fanfare associated with Rav Chaim Leib's appointment,
he was only the secondary Rosh Yeshiva, with Rav Moshe Avraham
Eisenstadt remaining the primary Rosh Yeshiva. When Rav Moshe
Avraham passed away in 5627/1867, his son-in-law, Rav Chaim Zalman
of Saltz, was appointed as Rav of Mir. Once again, there was a split
among the townspeople. Some felt that he should also inherit his father-
in-law's position in the yeshiva, while others felt that since the yeshiva
was a self-sufficient institution, which was not supported by the town,
the Rav's family no longer had a right to the position once Rav Chaim
Leib had restored the Tikutinsky chain to the yeshiva's helm.

The debate ultimately reached the desks of Rav Yitzchok Elchanan
Spector, the Kovno Rav, and Rav Dovberish Meislish of Warsaw. The
two ruled that Rav Chaim Leib should have control over the yeshiva,
and the Rav over the halachic issues of the town.

Rav Meislish wrote two strongly worded letters suggesting that if
the townspeople wouldn't agree to this arrangement, Rav Chaim Leib
should move the yeshiva elsewhere, especially since the funding wasn't
coming from the town.

Rav Yitzchok Elchanan toiled endlessly to foster peace between the
two sides, in order to save the yeshiva from the death knell of an all-out
*machlokes* (dispute).[6]


ONCE RAV CHAIM LEIB BECAME THE ESTABLISHED LEADER OF
the yeshiva, students starting streaming to Mir. Although his *derech
halimud* (style of learning) was simple, it impressed some of the greatest scholars of the generation, including Rav Chaim Soloveitchik of
Brisk. Rav Yisrael Salanter once remarked that anyone who wants
to understand a *daf* of Gemara properly must hear a *shiur* from Rav
Chaim Leib Tikutinsky.

Graced with a sweet disposition, Rav Chaim Leib would give
individual attention to each student and draw them close to him. A
*talmid* of his once related that although 40 years had passed since he

---

6. Years later, when the yeshiva was under intense financial stress in 5645/1885, Rav Yitzchok
Elchanan wrote letters to many of his supporters asking them to help prevent the closure of the
yeshiva.

The beloved Mirrer Rosh Yeshiva
for over 50 years,
Rav Chaim Leib Tikutinsky

Rav Yitzchok Elchanan Spector
supported Rav Chaim Leib
as sole Rosh Yeshiva.

left the yeshiva, he could not forget his rebbi's eyes. He remembered his first meeting with Rav Chaim Leib, stating that, "I was so taken by the sparkle in his eyes that I couldn't see the rest of him."

## Spiritual Genes

Although the Finkels were not descendants of the Tikutinsky family, it is impossible to miss the similarity between the descriptions of Rav Chaim Leib Tikutinsky and the accounts of thousands of *talmidim* who mourned the loss of Rav Nosson Tzvi Finkel. Apparently, love for each individual *talmid* was a fundamental element of the Mir that passed on through spiritual genetics.

Rav Chaim Leib stood at the helm of the yeshiva for over half a century. In the summer of 5658/1898, he delivered his last *shiur*, on the last section of the third chapter of *Eruvin*, ending with the word, "*Umashlimin* — we conclude."

In the winter of 5659/1899, at the age of 76, Rav Chaim Leib fell ill, never to recover. Several weeks before his passing, he traveled to Warsaw to visit greater doctors, but to no avail. On 19 Nissan 5659, Rav Chaim Leib was *niftar*. His funeral took place in Warsaw, but eulogies were held throughout the region, and even in Eretz Yisrael.

Well before his passing, in 5636/1876, Rav Chaim Leib had inducted his son, Rav Shmuel (named after the original founder of Mir), as a secondary Rosh Yeshiva, but Rav Shmuel was *niftar* at a young age in 5644/1884. Since the yeshiva had expanded to include several hundred students by that point, Rav Chaim Leib couldn't run it on his own. He appointed his younger son, Rav Avraham, as a Rosh Yeshiva, although he was a mere 17 years old. The two alternated between delivering *shiurim* and fundraising, with each doing a two-month stint at one job and then switching to the other.

After Rav Chaim Leib passed away, Rav Avraham took the entire financial responsibility of the yeshiva on his shoulders. An eyewitness describes him as having inherited his father's simple *derech halimud*. Unfortunately, Rav Avraham's tenure didn't last long. Shortly after Rav Chaim Leib's passing, Rav Avraham's vision deteriorated. He underwent surgery to repair his vision, but the operation was unsuccessful, and he remained blind for the rest of his life.

Although he was able to continue delivering *shiurim* from memory as if he were reading from a *sefer*, Rav Avraham realized that he had to bring in a rosh yeshiva to run the yeshiva alongside him. Among those considered were Rav Itzele of Ponovezh, who had served as a *maggid shiur* in the Slabodka Yeshiva, and Rav Zalman Sender, Rav and *maggid shiur* in Maltch. Ultimately, Rav Avraham and several other members of the yeshiva administration chose Rav Elya Baruch Kammai, who had been the Rav in Karelitz and Chechenovtzi, as the new Rosh Yeshiva, heralding the beginning of a new era for Mir.

RAV ELYA BARUCH KAMMAI'S ARRIVAL IN MIR IN 5660/1900 brought sweeping change to Mir. Several years after he became Rosh

**Rav Elya Baruch Kammai**

Yeshiva, the Rav of Mir, Rav Eliyahu David Rabinowitz-Teumim (known as the *Aderes*, his initials), left for Eretz Yisrael, and Rav Elya Baruch was appointed as Rav of Mir as well.

Rav Elya Baruch was known for his razor-sharp mind and his ability to develop novel interpretations of *sugyos* with ease. Having earned a sterling reputation among *gedolei Yisrael*, Rav Elya Baruch became a magnetic force, drawing some of the finest young scholars in Europe to Mir. The system in the yeshiva in those days was that the younger students would attend the *blatt shiur*, which was still delivered by Rav Avraham Tikutinsky despite his blindness, and the more seasoned

The Mirrer Rosh Yeshiva at the turn of the 20th century, Rav Avraham Tikutinsky, was able to deliver *shiurim*, quoting the Gemara and *Rashi* verbatim, after he went blind.

students would attend Rav Elya Baruch's complex *shiur*.

When Rav Elya Baruch would enter the *beis midrash* to deliver a *shiur*, a charged atmosphere could be felt in the room. On the way from the door to his seat, he would open *sefarim* en route and leaf through them, creating more *chiddushim* on this short walk. After the *shiur*, students would line up to discuss the *shiur* with him. He would read into their personalities and their level of learning based on these conversations, in which he would continue to develop more *chiddushim* as he delved deeper into the *sugya* with his students.

Rav Elya Baruch was able to relate to the *baalebatim* of Mir as well. His Shabbos HaGadol and Shabbos Shuvah *derashos*, masterful tapestries of *pilpul* and halachah, had his audience riveted for several hours.

Upon arriving in Mir, Rav Elya Baruch immediately instituted a new

Building of the Mirrer Yeshiva in Poland in the early 1900's

policy. Until then each student's stipend was based on the amount of money contributed to the yeshiva by that student's townspeople. Rav Elya Baruch began to distribute the money on a merit basis, giving more to accomplished students. His objective was to imbue his students with the realization that the entire world was being supported by their Torah study, and to make them appreciate the value of their spiritual ascent — a very important realization in the days when the *maskilim* ("enlightened ones") made every effort to heap scorn upon those who devoted their lives to Torah study.

Noticing the change in the world that required a new type of approach to *chinuch*, Rav Avraham Tikutinsky eventually stopped delivering *shiur* in the yeshiva, preferring to focus on a daily *shiur* for the *baalebatim* of Mir, in which he would recite the Gemara and Rashi, word-for-word, from memory. In recognition of the Tikutinsky family's seminal role in the yeshiva during its first 85 years of existence, the yeshiva continued to pay his salary of 25 rubles a month even after he moved from Mir to Minsk, until his passing sometime after World War I.

It would be just a few years before Rav Elya Baruch would be aided in the task of staving off the influence of the *Haskalah* by his son-in-law, Rav Leizer Yudel Finkel, the son of the man who is credited as one of the most masterful fighters against *Haskalah* — the Alter of Slabodka.

# CHAPTER ELEVEN
# THE FINKEL DYNASTY BEGINS

*After Rav Nosson Tzvi's petirah, Rav Yosef Elefant — a maggid shiur in Beis Yeshaya — reflected that although many Mirrer talmidim consider someone other than the Rosh Yeshiva their primary rebbi in Mir, it was actually Rav Nosson Tzvi who had the most profound influence on them.*

*"Rebbeim are able to build their talmidim slowly," explained Rabbi Elefant. "We can add layer upon layer of bricks to a bachur's development in Torah, and help him to gradually perfect his character. The Rosh Yeshiva was like a crane — he could lift a person up a few stories all at once and cause him to start viewing himself in a completely different light."*

*Many Mirrer alumni went on to become successful Kollel yungeleit, educators, and community leaders — in large part because Rav Nosson Tzvi had raised their own opinion of themselves by showing them that he respected them and expected great things from them.*

*Rav Nosson Tzvi's ability to elevate a person in his own estimation hails all the way back to the turn of the 20th century, to his great-grandfather, the first Rav Nosson Tzvi Finkel, the Alter of Slabodka.*

*T*HROUGHOUT THE 1800'S AND EARLY 1900'S STORMY winds of change swept through Europe, as the *Haskalah* led many of the continent's finest Jewish minds astray. Among Poland's Chassidim, the *Haskalah* was fought through Chassidus. In Hungary, the Chasam Sofer and his *talmidim* and descendants were the ones who took up the battle. In Lithuania, however, even some of those who were learning were falling prey to the *Haskalah*.

Tucked away in Kelm[1] was a young man by the name of Nosson Tzvi Finkel. After being orphaned from both of his parents at a young age, Nosson Tzvi had made such a name for himself by the age of 15 that Rav Simcha Zissel Ziv, the "Alter[2] of Kelm," had personally requested that he join his yeshiva.

After spending many years studying under the Alter of Kelm, Rav Nosson Tzvi realized that although the *batei midrash* in Lithuania were still filled with men studying Torah, young people were, by and large, studying without mentors who could guide them in learning and *avodas Hashem*. And since these young men were not being guided with the proper *hashkafah* (Torah outlook), they were very susceptible to being ensnared by the glamour of the *Haskalah*. He decided to open a yeshiva in the image of Volozhin,[3] but in which working on one's character traits through *mussar* would be a basic component of the daily schedule.

---

1. Kelm is generally regarded as the first *mussar* yeshiva. The "*Mussar* Movement," which was founded by Rav Yisrael Salanter, placed emphasis on perfecting one's traits by studying the words of our Sages relevant to character development. Not all Torah leaders of his day agreed that yeshiva men should be spending time learning *mussar*, and several yeshivos split up as the result of that dispute.

2. The title Alter, or Saba in modern Hebrew, literally means "the Elder." This appellation was reserved for the *menahel ruchani* (spiritual mentor) who led a *mussar* yeshiva. It had little to do with the age of the person to whom the title was applied; the Alter of Slabodka was known as such during his 30's.

3. The Volozhiner Yeshiva, founded by Rav Chaim of Volozhin in 5563/1803, was the first modern-day yeshiva.

Rav Simcha Zissel Ziv was born in 5584/1824 in Kelm. After his marriage, he moved to Kovno to study under Rav Yisrael Lipkin, better known as Rav Yisrael Salanter, the founder of the *Mussar* Movement.

In 1865, he opened the "Talmud Torah" in Kelm, a yeshiva in which he implemented the *mussar* teachings of Rav Yisrael Salanter. Kelm stressed strong self-discipline. Stories abound of people trying — unsuccessfully — to distract the students while they were learning.

Rav Simcha Zissel passed away on Erev Tishah B'Av of 5658/1898 while reciting *Ezras Avoseinu* during *Shacharis*.

Rav Nosson Tzvi, who would become known as the Alter of Slabodka in due time, is immortalized for his ability to build each student in his yeshiva into the greatest person he could be. While Kelm focused on self-control, the Alter of Slabodka forged his own approach based on the premise of *gadlus ha'adam*, the grandeur of man. The message of the *maskilim* that posed the greatest danger to yeshiva students was that they were wasting their time in yeshiva "splitting hairs" in their Talmudic studies, and that by joining the *Haskalah* they could become "productive members of society" and leave an imprint on the world. The Alter of Slabodka countered that message by imbuing his students with an appreciation for the inherent greatness of a Jewish soul, and by emphasizing that those studying Torah and working on themselves through *mussar* are the basis for Creation.

Alumni of the Slabodka approach would go on to build nearly every major Torah institution after the war. Rav Aron Kotler (Beth Medrash Govoha of Lakewood), Rav Yitzchok Hutner (Mesivta Rabbeinu Chaim Berlin), Rav Reuven Grozovsky (Torah Vodaath and Beth Medrash Elyon), Rav Yaakov Kamenetsky (Torah Vodaath), and Rav Yaakov Yitzchok Ruderman (Ner Israel, Baltimore) were among the future roshei yeshiva who were developed in Slabodka. That one rebbi could be the guiding force behind a group so varied in character and personality is the clearest testimonial to his ability to sense the depth of each person's nature and build each one accordingly.

Another innovation instituted by Rav Nosson Tzvi was the famed Slabodka Kollel, in which married students could study Torah and receive a stipend that would remove the burden of earning a livelihood.[4]

---

4. The terms for acceptance into the Slabodka Kollel were that after five years of study in the *kollel*,

The Alter of Slabodka,
known for his ability to help each
*talmid* grow according to his
strengths, spawned such Torah
giants as Rav Aron Kotler,
Rav Yitzchok Hutner,
Rav Yaakov Kamenetsky, and
Rav Yaakov Yitzchok Ruderman

Rav Aron Kotler

Rav Yitzchok Hutner

Rav Yaakov Kamenetsky

Rav Yaakov Yitzchok Ruderman

Chapter Eleven: The Finkel Dynasty Begins ☐ 137

**THE ALTER'S OWN SON, ELIEZER YEHUDA ("LEIZER YUDEL")**
Finkel, was one of the many to receive personal guidance.

**Rav Leizer Yudel Finkel Is Born**    Leizer Yudel was born in Elul of 5637/1877 in Kelm, while his father was still studying under Rav Simcha Zissel. His brilliance was notable from a very young age, as were many of the character traits that would define his life.

Taking note of his son's great genius and spiritual purity, the Alter sensed that Leizer Yudel would be a Torah leader of his generation, and invested great effort into developing his character.

During his developmental years, Leizer Yudel spent time studying in most major yeshivos in Europe under the Torah giants of the day. At first he was under his father's tutelage in Slabodka, but he then traveled to Telshe to learn under Rav Leizer Gordon, before moving on to Radin to learn under Rav Naftoli Tropp. In 5654/1894, the Alter sent him to Brisk, where Rav Chaim Brisker resided after the Russian authorities closed the Volozhin Yeshiva, delivering *shiurim* to a group of select *bachurim*.

After another brief stint back home in Slabodka, Rav Leizer Yudel was among fourteen *talmidim* sent by the Alter to Slutzk in 5657/1897 to establish a yeshiva there, upon request of the Ridvaz, the Rav of the city. The yeshiva was led by Rav Isser Zalman Meltzer, and the group of *bachurim* was of such quality that it was dubbed the *"Yad Hachazakah."*[5]

Unfortunately, an argument arose as to how much *mussar* would be studied in the yeshiva, and Leizer Yudel, who did not want to be involved in *machlokes*, left the yeshiva. At the time, Rav Baruch Ber Leibowitz began to deliver *shiurim* in the city of Holusk, and Leizer Yudel joined his yeshiva, meriting a *chavrusashaft* (study partnership) for a few hours each day with Rav Baruch Ber. He also tried to learn under the Chassidic master Rav Avraham of Sochotchov (the Avnei Nezer), but the cultural barrier proved to be too difficult to bridge. Before he returned home, the Avnei Nezer gave him a *berachah* for long life, and Rav Leizer Yudel would later attribute his longevity to that blessing.[6]

Rav Leizer Yudel's brilliant mind was able to synthesize the varying styles of learning of these yeshivos, although he was most influenced by

each person had to accept a rabbinic position.
5. The word *yad* has the numerical value of 14, which is why the Rambam named his halachic anthology, which is composed of fourteen sections, the *Yad HaChazakah*.
6. *Marbitz Torah HaGadol*, p. 82.

Rav Leizer Yudel Finkel studied under many Torah giants of prewar Europe, including Rav Leizer Gordon, Rav Naftoli Tropp, Rav Chaim Brisker, and Rav Isser Zalman Meltzer.

Rav Leizer Gordon

Rav Naftoli Tropp

Rav Chaim Brisker

Rav Isser Zalman Meltzer

the *derech halimud* of Rav Chaim Brisker. Decades later, he would still speak in amazement of his days in Brisk. He related that the *talmidim* would spend hours preparing the *sugya*, coming up with extremely difficult questions to pose during *shiur*, but then Rav Chaim would explain the *sugya* and all the questions would fall away.[7]

Rav Leizer Yudel once told his great-nephew Rav Nosson Tzvi that in Gan Eden, out of all of his *rebbeim* and the *geonim* of all the ages,

7. Ibid., p. 80.

Rav Leizer Yudel Finkel
as a young Rosh Yeshiva

he would choose to learn under Rav Chaim Brisker.[8]

Considered one of the top prospects of his time, Rav Leizer Yudel was chosen by Rav Elya Baruch Kammai, the Rav and Rosh Yeshiva of Mir, to marry his daughter Malka — setting the stage for the Finkel name to become synonymous with the Mirrer Yeshiva.

AFTER HIS MARRIAGE IN 5663/1903, Rav Leizer Yudel settled in Mir and

**Settling in Mir** began to learn in the yeshiva.

The Alter prevailed upon Rav Yaakov Yechiel Weinberg, one of his closest disciples and a great scholar, to study with his son. Rav Leizer Yudel devoted the early years of his marriage to growing in Torah and preparing *shiurim*. In 5667 (1907), Rav Elya Baruch Kammai appointed Rav Leizer Yudel as a rosh yeshiva in Mir, and the latter began to deliver *shiurim* to the *bachurim*. Having mastered the approaches of the various *Litvishe* strains of learning, Rav Leizer Yudel's range in Torah was phenomenal, and his *shiurim* grew very popular.

## Spiritual Genes

Perhaps because Rav Leizer Yudel mastered and amalgamated all of the Litvishe approaches to learning, to this very day, any valid approach to a *sugya* is appreciated and accepted in the Mir.

Although Rav Elya Baruch Kammai was not initially a proponent of the "*Mussar* Movement"[9] — he posited that the best *mussar* is to study Gemara — in the early years of his tenure, the yeshiva became a "*mussar* yeshiva."[10]

---

8. Rav Gedalya Finkel, who heard it from Rav Nosson Tzvi.

9. *Mussar* had not been a major component of the Mir during the Tikutinsky era.

10. It is unclear what caused Rav Elya Baruch Kammai to change his approach to *mussar*. Considering that the decision came not long after his son-in-law joined the yeshiva, the suggestion (in *Marbitzei Torah Umussar*, Vol. 3, p. 64) that Rav Leizer Yudel brought about the change seems plausible.

Upon recommendation from the Alter of Slabodka, Rav Zalman Dolinsky, who had studied in Kelm and Slabodka, was appointed the *menahel ruchani* (spiritual guide) of Mir. Like the Alter, Rav Zalman excelled in detecting a person's character and building him through those strengths.

A year later, the legendary Rav Yerucham Levovitz, another close disciple of the Alter of Kelm, joined the *hanhalah* of the yeshiva, after serving as a *mashgiach* in Radin. His magnetic personality and keen understanding of human nature drew all the *bachurim* to him, and his *shmuessen*, which have been immortalized in several sets of *sefarim*, are considered some of the basic texts of the modern era of *mussar*.

DURING WORLD WAR I, THE TOWN OF MIR WAS IN DANGER OF attack from both Russian and German forces, and the administration

**On the Move** decided to move the yeshiva. At first they settled in Stavitz,[11] a border town, then they moved to Minsk, and finally to Poltava, Ukraine, which was far from the battlefields. Rav Elya Baruch did not want to abandon his townspeople, so he sent Rav Leizer Yudel and Rav Yerucham to lead the yeshiva while he remained in Mir. He was hoping to see the yeshiva move back after the war — which it did — but unfortunately, Rav Elya Baruch would not be

---

## At a Glance — Rav Yerucham Levovitz

Rav Yerucham Levovitz was born in 5633/1873 in Lyuban, Belarus to R' Avraham and Chasha Levovitz. He studied in Kelm under Rav Simcha Zissel and in Slabodka under Rav Nosson Tzvi Finkel. He also learned in Radin, where he had a close relationship with the Chafetz Chaim.

He was *mashgiach* in Mir on two occasions, once before World War I and once after.

He was *niftar* on 18 Sivan, 5696/1936, but his legacy lives on through several sets of *sefarim*, most notably, *Daas Torah* on *Chumash*.

---

11. During their stay in Stavitz, Rav Leizer Yudel developed a close relationship with the Chazon Ish, who lived in the town.

able to enjoy the return of his beloved *talmidim*, for he passed away in Minsk in 1917 during a failed surgery.

An unfortunate — and fascinating — incident separated the *bachurim* from their beloved *mashgiach*, Rav Yerucham. While he traveled with the yeshiva through Stavitz and Minsk to Poltava, Rav Yerucham had left his wife and children behind in Lithuania. Missing his family, he wanted to illegally cross the border back into Lithuania, which was then controlled by the Germans, to visit them, and then return to rejoin the yeshiva in Poland. His first plan was to sneak into Lithuania by traversing the German-Russian border near the city of Lunchin. When he was suddenly filled with apprehension about that plan, he decided to do a *Goral HaGra*.[12] The verse that emerged was, "*Lo sa'avor bi, pen bacherev eitzei likrasecha* — Do not pass through [my territory], lest I come toward you with a sword" (*Bamidbar* 20:18).

The message was clear, and Rav Yerucham moved on to another border crossing near Danzig. This time, a *Goral HaGra* turned up the verse, "*Bechol hamakom asher azkir es shmi, avo eilecha uveirachticha* — In each place that you will mention My Name, I will come to you and bless you" (*Shemos* 20:21). He interpreted this verse as a sign that he could cross safely, and indeed, he was able to rejoin his family. But the joy of the reunion was short-lived. Immediately after he managed to get into Lithuania the border was hermetically sealed by the Russians, and he could not return to Poland. In a poignant letter to the *talmidim*, he wrote, "I am wandering on the road, and you are able to sit in the holy house of Hashem. Fortunate are you ... Had I known in Poltava that crossing the border would become impossible, I would never have made this trip, but now I cannot return."[13]

## The War Ends

THE YESHIVA WENT THROUGH DESPERATE FINANCIAL STRAITS during the war years, and only the self-sacrifice of Rav Leizer Yudel saved the students from utter starvation. He would travel frequently to solicit funds, despite the danger of being on the road in wartime. He found himself under threat of death several times. Once, on a train ride to Charkov, he had to hide

---

12. This is a special "lottery" in which a *pasuk* in the Torah is selected through a method known to certain *talmidei chachamim*, and the message in the *pasuk* is interpreted as a sign from Heaven on how to proceed in a matter in life.

13. *Marbitzei Torah Umussar*, Vol. 3, p. 66.

under a pile of luggage when a group of Ukrainian thugs boarded the train searching for Jews to kill.

After the war, there were still skirmishes between Poland and Lithuania, and the yeshiva had to remain in Vilna for the summer of 5680/1920. Interestingly, being in safe territory and being able to learn under ordinary conditions for the first time in many years led to a substantial decrease in the number of students in the yeshiva. While stranded in Lithuania without the yeshiva, Rav Yerucham had joined the Slabodka Yeshiva in 5678/1918. When the *talmidim* of Mir heard that he was there, many top students made their way to Slabodka, and the yeshiva was left with only a few dozen young students.

At the same time, however, many yeshiva students began to arrive in Vilna, helping to rebuild the yeshiva. By 5681/1921, when the yeshiva was finally able to return to Mir, enrollment reached 130.

Although Rav Yisrael Shlomowitz was retained as a *mashpia ruchani*, Rav Leizer Yudel tried to convince Rav Yerucham to rejoin the yeshiva. By that point, however, Rav Yerucham had plans to become a "traveling *mashgiach*" for several yeshivos throughout Lithuania, and he did not want to commit to settling in Mir again. He recommended that they appoint his student from his days in Radin, Rav Yechezkel Levenstein, as *masghiach*, and his recommendation was accepted.

## At a Glance — Rav Yechezkel Levenstein

Rav Yechezkel Levenstein, known as "Reb Chatzkel," was born in 5655/1895 in Warsaw. After studying in Radin, where he became a disciple of Rav Yerucham Levovitz, Rav Chatzkel became the *mashgiach* in Mir after World War I, and again after Rav Yerucham's passing in 5696/1936. He traveled with the yeshiva when it fled Mir, all the way through Japan and China, where it spent the war years. After the war, he moved to America with the yeshiva, but he then immigrated to Eretz Yisrael to reassume his position in Mir. After a number of years, he became *mashgiach* in Ponovezh, where he remained until he passed away on 18 Adar, 5734/1974.

UPON THE YESHIVA'S RETURN TO MIR, RAV AVRAHAM TZVI Kammai, who had succeeded his father as Rav of the town, was

**Back to Mir** appointed as a Rosh Yeshiva as well. Although his *derech halimud* differed from the approaches that had become popular in most *Litvishe* yeshivos in those days, Rav Avraham Tzvi astounded the students at his weekly *shiur* with a breadth of knowledge that literally spanned all of *Shas*. A charming, humble man, Rav Avraham Tzvi did not take an active role in running the yeshiva, limiting his influence to his weekly *shiur*.

At Pesach time of 5684/1924, Rav Yerucham Levovitz rejoined the Mir, bringing along a group of close disciples who had been with him at Ponovezh, where he had been serving as *menahel ruchani* after his stint in Slabodka. Before making the decision to return, however, Rav Yerucham had visited Kelm, and many *bnei Torah* from the surrounding towns requested that he stay there and become their spiritual guide.

Rav Yerucham was torn, and only years later, in a letter to Rav Shimon Shkop written in 5689/1929, did he reveal the reason for his decision to return to Mir: He had once again turned to a *Goral*

Rav Avraham Tzvi Kammai, Rav of the town of Mir, became Rosh Yeshiva alongside Rav Leizer Yudel when the yeshiva returned to Mir after World War I.

*HaGra*, and the verse that emerged was, *"Betab'os ha'aron yihiyu habadim, lo yasuru mimenu* — In the rings of the Ark shall the poles remain; they should not be removed from it"* (*Shemos* 25:15). Rav Yerucham interpreted this verse to mean that he should attach himself to the yeshiva with which he had bonded in the past.[14]

The timing of his return couldn't have been better. The yeshiva was undergoing a financial crisis at the time, and if not for the spiritual energy Rav Yerucham breathed into the Mir, many *bachurim* might have caved under the pressure and left the yeshiva.

Rav Leizer Yudel realized that the

---

14 Although we have recorded three instances in which Rav Yerucham turned to a *Goral HaGra*, it was not a system that he overused; he did a *Goral HaGra* only when he needed to make a decision on a significant matter. In his humility, he wrote to Rav Shimon Shkop that it was not in his own merit that he received a sign from Heaven through this *Goral*, but in the merit of the *rabbim* (public) that would be affected by this decision (*Marbitzei Torah Umussar*, Vol. 3, pp. 66-67).

yeshiva wouldn't survive unless he made a trip to America to solicit funds. He was accompanied by the Rav of Rakov, Rav Avraham Kalmanowitz, who, after establishing a support base in the United States during this year-long trip together with Rav Leizer Yudel, continued to travel to the States biannually on behalf of the Mir.

Rav Yechezkel Levenstein, who had served as *mashgiach* alongside Rav Yerucham during the summer of 5684/1924, moved on to Kletzk at the advice of Rav Isser Zalman Meltzer. When Rav Leizer Yudel was in America, Rav Yerucham had to shoulder both the spiritual and administrative duties of the yeshiva. He was aided by the secretary of the yeshiva, Rav Shmuel Greineman (a brother-in-law of the Chazon Ish).[15]

Rav Yerucham Levovitz's dynamic personality revitalized the spirit of Mir even as starvation was a constant threat.

## The Golden Era

THE YEARS BETWEEN 1926 AND 1938 are often described as "The Golden Era" of prewar Mir.

Despite the yeshiva's financial difficulties during those years, the *talmidim* continued learning with legendary *hasmadah* (diligence), and students from many other yeshivos across Europe began to stream into Mir.

The first contingent to join was the "Grodno group," students of the elderly

Rav Shimon Shkop, whose *talmidim* constituted the first group to join the Mir as a unit

Rav Shimon Shkop, who arrived during the winter of 5686/1926. Some of them arrived while Rav Leizer Yudel was still in America, and some came after his return. Among them was Rav Chaim Shmuelevitz, who

---

15. Rav Shmuel Greineman would eventually become the father-in-law of Rav Beinush Finkel, Rav Leizer Yudel's son and successor as Rosh Yeshiva of Mir. (See p. 218.)

was then known as Chaim Stutchiner (from the city of Stutchin). He quickly caught the eye of Rav Leizer Yudel, who selected him as a son-in-law. The *chasunah* was held on the last day of Chanukah, 5690/1930.[16]

Several years after the wedding, in the winter of 5684/1934, Rav Leizer Yudel appointed Rav Chaim Shmuelevitz as a *maggid shiur*.

Next to join were students of Rav Naftoli Tropp, the Rosh Yeshiva of Radin. Though this group was smaller than the Grodna contingent, they brought their own novelty: notebooks containing Rav Naftoli's Torah. A new trend quickly took root, in which *talmidim* of the Mir would copy (by hand) the notes of Rav Naftoli's *shiurim*.

In 5688/1928, the Kamenitz contingent arrived. These were actually Mirrer *talmidim* whom Rav Lazer Yudel had sent to shore up the Kamenitz Yeshiva, Knesses Beis Yitzchak, which was under the leadership of Rav Baruch Ber Leibowitz, when it returned to its home in Kamenitz after spending the war in Kremenchug. The nine students that Rav Leizer Yudel had sent to Kamenitz returned after a period ranging between half a year and a year, having absorbed the Torah

## At a Glance — Rav Chaim Shmuelevitz

Rav Chaim Leib Shmuelevitz was born on the second day of Rosh Hashanah 5663/1902 in Kovno, Lithuania, to Rabbi Refoel Alter Shmuelevitz and Ettel, a daughter of Rabbi Yosef Yoizel Horowitz, the Alter of Novardhok.

In Chaim Leib's youth, his family moved to Stutchin. In 1919, he was orphaned of both his father and mother.

Rav Chaim's father had been Rosh Yeshiva of Shaarei Yosher, a position that was filled, upon his *petirah*, by Rav Shimon Shkop. Rav Chaim developed a close bond with Rav Shimon, and when he turned 18 Rav Shimon asked him to begin delivering *shiur* for younger *talmidim*. He would continue to teach Torah for close to 60 years, until his *petirah* on 3 Teves 5739/1979.

---

16. Since Rav Chaim Shmuelevitz was a grandson of Rav Yosef Yoizel Horowitz, the Alter of Novardhok, this union between the granddaughter of the Alter of Slabodka and the grandson of the Alter of Novaradok "fused" the major schools of *mussar* at the time.

of Rav Baruch Ber. They also brought along several other *talmidim* who had been learning under Rav Baruch Ber for several years.

The final influence on the Mir's *derech halimud* was the return of students who had spent some time learning under the Brisker Rav, Rav Velvel (Yitzchak Zev) Soloveitchik. Although he did not have a formal yeshiva, he maintained his father's practice of disseminating Torah to a select group of students while he carried out his duties as the Rav of Brisk. Rav Isser Zalman Meltzer, who was a Mir native, stopped off in his hometown while en route to Kletzk to establish his own yeshiva there. He urged Rav Leizer Yudel to send a group of *talmidim* to Brisk to study under the Brisker Rav. Rav Leizer Yudel was so enamored with this idea that he sent his own son, Rav Avrohom Meir *Hy"d* (who was killed during World War II), as part of the group. Not only did he send a group of four students each year, he also sent them the monthly stipend that they would have received had they remained in Mir!

Rav Baruch Ber returned Rav Leizer Yudel's *talmidim* to him ... with interest.

This was apparently the first of many instances in which roshei yeshiva from the Finkel dynasty would demonstrate their utter love of Torah by aiding the growth of Torah in other yeshivos, not only in the Mir.

Rav Leizer Yudel continued to pay monthly stipends to the *talmidim* he sent to learn under the Brisker Rav, Rav Yitzchok Zev Soloveitchik.

## The Bekiyus "Drive"

WITH ALL OF THESE STRAINS OF *LOMdus*, complex analyses of *sugyos*, taking root in Mir, Rav Leizer Yudel began to worry that *bekiyus*, broad knowledge of *masechtos* in *Shas*, would be lost. In the winter of 5689/1929 he announced a special "drive" (as it was called) in the yeshiva: Anyone who would learn *Bava Kamma, Bava Metzia, Bava Basra,* and *Kesubos* (over 500 *blatt* in all) in one year and master the Gemara with *Tosafos* would receive $50, a princely sum in those days. Twenty

A famous historic poster of the entire Mirrer Yeshiva during its Golden Era

people took up the challenge, but only nine managed to complete the rigorous course of study. Their *hasmadah* during that year served as a catalyst for all of the students of the Mir to become more diligent. On Simchas Torah of 5690, a special *Mi Shebeirach* was made for "those who accepted upon themselves to learn with *hasmadah*."

The nine who completed the "drive" were tested by a triumvirate of Rav Avraham Tzvi Kammai, Rav Leizer Yudel, and Rav Yerucham, although the latter famously declared, "I don't have to test them. I can tell on their faces that they know." All three were duly impressed by the group's mastery of the four major tractates.

DURING THE LATER YEARS OF THIS GOLDEN ERA, MIR BEGAN to draw students from other parts of the globe, primarily from America[17]

## The "Auslander"

and Germany, but also from England, Belgium, Switzerland, Sweden, and other European countries, and even one from South Africa. Known as the "Auslander," many of these students weren't on the same level as those from Poland,

---

17. A detailed account of how an American adjusted to life in Mir is recorded in *All for the Boss* by Ruchama Shain, who settled in Mir with her husband after their marriage.

Lithuania, and Russia. Rav Yerucham had the difficult task of training them — and especially the free-spirited Americans, who were unaccustomed to the reserved way of life in Mir — to become true *bnei Torah*. To their credit, these *talmidim* exercised great *mesiras nefesh* in making the decision to join the Mir. Many already had professional degrees and could have remained in the comfort of their respective hometowns to earn a decent living. Instead, they traveled to Mir, a town described by Rabbi Theodore (Tuvya) Lewis[18] as being relatively primitive:

> *As there was no indoor plumbing in the homes, water was unavailable from the faucet. Instead, water had to be transported, physically, in buckets from a well in the center of the town. Some poor Jews eked out a meager livelihood by filling two buckets of water at the well and carrying them yoke-wise and selling the water to the house owners.*

Along with the antiquated way of life, however, the Auslander found a highly uplifted spiritual existence, as Rabbi Lewis recounts in the tale of his initiation into the Mir:

A group of *talmidim* in the *beis midrash* in Mir, circa 1933

18. Rabbi Theodore Lewis was born in Dublin, Ireland in 1915. After graduating from Dublin University, he studied Torah in London and then in Mir. He eventually became the rabbi of the largest synagogue in Ireland, the Adelaide Road Synagogue in Dublin. He then immigrated to America, where he became the rabbi of the Touro Synagogue in Newport, Rhode Island, the oldest synagogue in North America, established in 1763. Rabbi Lewis held that position for 36 years, retiring in 1985 to live in Israel and then in Brooklyn, New York, where he davened at the Mirrer Minyan in Boro Park. He passed away in Brooklyn on 27 Tishrei, 5771 (October 5, 2010) at the age of 95. See Chapter 10, footnote 2.

*My first impression of the Yeshiva was a soul-stirring one. It was at night, when all the students were engaged in the study of Mussar – personal ethics and piety. As I traversed the grounds of the Yeshiva, I heard a voice of yearning, a yearning toward spiritual uplifting, a voice sublime, which made all things material recede in the distance. I can still hear that sound, its deep emotion ringing in my ears. It is one of the few experiences I will never forget. As I entered the glass doors, a most impressive scene met my eyes. Over four hundred young men were poring over books of Mussar, in which they were intensely engrossed. The sincerity of the sight, which I witnessed, moved me profoundly ...*

*Hours of study were rather long. Officially, nine hours of study a day were required, but few were content with such "limited" hours. The majority of the students studied until the early hours in the morning, and on Thursday nights, some students studied until 5 o'clock in the morning. Electric light was switched off in the whole town at 1 a.m. From that hour, study was only possible by the flickering light of huge oil lamps, which were suspended from the ceiling. This, however, did not deter the students. No difficulty which was connected with study was deemed insuperable. At the end of the term when books were put in order, and the library was temporarily closed, most students felt life difficult. It seemed that some vital component had been removed from their lives. Everybody studied with boundless zeal and enthusiasm. All had but one thought in mind — to waste as little time, and to gain as much knowledge, as possible ....*

*One of the most important periods during the year was the month preceding Rosh Hashanah. Former students of the yeshiva, Rabbis holding responsible positions, came from the most distant parts of Poland. As many as six hundred students crowded the yeshiva at these times. All came to be inspired by the brilliant ethical discourses of the Mashgiach, who delivered as many as three or four lectures each day. This was spiritual preparation for Rosh Hashanah.*

The Auslander gained immeasurably from the Mir, but they also contributed greatly to the advance of the local *talmidim*, helping them attain perfection by learning to understand and tolerate Jews from different cultures. In addition, many local *talmidim* were hired as *"rebbeim"* to study with the less-learned students.[19]

---

19. Interestingly, this practice continues to this very day in Mir in Yerushalayim; many *yungeleit*, both Israeli and American, are hired to learn with *bachurim* whose parents would like them to advance in learning.

During 1933, with the Nazi rise to power in Germany, there was an influx of refugees who fled the danger back home by joining the yeshiva. Not only couldn't the new German students pay their own way, but even the German students who had been in the yeshiva until that point and had brought funding to the yeshiva — covering not only the salaries of their own *rebbeim*, but other parts of the budget as well — could no longer do so once the Nazis *ym"sh* froze their parents' assets and began restricting Jewish commerce. This placed a further financial burden on the yeshiva, even as funding from America was drying up due to the Great Depression. In June 1933, Rav Leizer Yudel wrote a letter to Yosef Heiman, the secretary of the Joint Distribution Committee,[20] asking him to cover the costs of 20 German students, 15 of whom were already in Mir and another five who were en route from Hamburg. Eventually, the number of German students grew to 45. Over the course of the years from 1933 through 1939, the Joint and several other relief organizations were able to help the yeshiva in some measure, but by 1939, contact with the outside world was lost as Europe was thrown into the turmoil of World War II.

In 5696/1936, the yeshiva suffered a great tragedy. Rav Yerucham Levovitz, the revered *mashgiach*, fell extremely ill. Doctors were brought from Vilna and R' Carlebach[21] sent Dr. Adler, a respected doctor from Leipzig, to try to find a cure, but to no avail. On 18 Sivan, 5696, one of the greatest *baalei mussar* of the last two centuries passed away. To quote Rabbi Lewis, who was in Mir for the six months prior to Rav Yerucham's *petirah* and remained there for another two-and-a-half years afterward:

> *His death was very keenly felt by the thousands of students who received spiritual guidance from him. To many, it was as if they had been bereaved of a parent. How deeply he affected his disciples may be understood from the fact that when one of his elder pupils, a Rabbi, delivered a hesped at his graveside, he disclosed that scarcely a day went by without a vision of the mashgiach appearing before him.*

---

20. The Joint Distribution Committee, also referred to simply as "The Joint" or the JDC, was a relief organization founded in 1914 to alleviate the suffering of the Jews in war-torn Europe. It was called the Joint because it distributed funds collected by three bodies: (1) The Central Relief Committee, which was run by Orthodox leaders; (2) The American Jewish Relief Committee, led by secular Jews. (3) These two groups were later joined by the People's Relief Committee, which represented labor organizations.

21. R' Moshe Carlebach was the father of Rav Naftoli Carlebach, who would eventually learn in Mir in Europe, and who eventually became *mechutanim* with both the Israeli and the Chicago Finkels (see pp. 60 and 181).

Rav Yerucham Levovitz escorted by his beloved *talmidim* through the streets of Mir.

ON TZOM GEDALIAH 5700 (SEPTEMBER 16, 1939), SEVERAL WEEKS after the outbreak of World War II, the Luftwaffe, the German air force,

**Escape to Vilna** began to bomb Poland. Although the Germans didn't reach Mir, which was close to the Russian border, the sounds of the bombardment of Baranovitz, which was 50 kilometers away, could be heard in Mir. The first group of Polish war refugees, including Rav Elchonon Wasserman *Hy"d*, arrived in Mir during *Aseres Yemei Teshuvah*. The combination of the *Yamim Noraim* atmosphere and the looming Nazi onslaught sowed fear in the hearts of all those in Mir.

Then *talmidim* spotted what they thought were German airplanes in the skies above Mir, and panic gripped many of the residents and the students. Before long, however, someone brought news that these were actually Russian aircraft on surveillance missions, to the collective relief of the entire town. A short time later, Russian tanks were seen arriving from the East, driving all the way into Mir. While there was a measure of celebration in the streets because the Nazi invasion seemed to have been forestalled, a sense of foreboding still prevailed. The future seemed bleak — at best.

As local homeowners began to stock up on food products, leaving empty shelves at the local stores, the *bachurim* were the first to suffer. Many of the townspeople who had been feeding the students, for pay, over the years, preferred to hold onto supplies. Some *bachurim* began to work for local farmers, pulling potatoes out of the ground, so they could purchase their own food.

As the Soviet government set up shop in Mir, everyone began to worry about the future of the yeshiva. Although the Soviets treated the yeshiva very well at first, the assumption was that it wouldn't be long before anti-Semites and Torah-haters would begin to dismantle it.

Rather than being frozen in fear, however, the *talmidim* began to learn and daven with extra vigor. Those present on that last Simchas Torah in the village of Mir never forgot how the students danced almost endlessly as they sang, "*Utzu eitzah v'sufar, dabru davar velo yakum, ki imanu Keil* — Plan a conspiracy and it will be annulled; speak your piece and it shall not stand, for G-d is with us" (*Yeshayah* 8:10).

Right after Simchas Torah, news came that Vilna was being annexed by Lithuania. No one knew exactly what to make of this development, but everyone felt that it would be a good idea to head to Vilna. The thinking went that perhaps Lithuania would remain neutral throughout the war, and the Jews would be spared the oppression of both Nazi Germany and Communist Russia.

On the second day of Cheshvan, the students began to leave Mir. It was a dark day for the town. Even townspeople who weren't particularly fond of the yeshiva felt that "*panah zivah, panah hadarah*" — the beauty and glory of their town was departing.[22] Following his father's lead, Rav Avraham Tzvi Kammai decided to remain behind with the members of his flock rather than travel with the yeshiva. It was particularly painful for him to be left bereft of his beloved *talmidim*.

The road to Vilna was paved with obstacles. Though thoroughly defeated by the Nazis, the Polish soldiers returning from the warfront made sure to display their own brand of anti-Semitism. Movement toward Vilna was interrupted frequently by overpopulated trains, and students were often forced to sleep on the floor of train stations along the way while waiting for another train to arrive.

By mid-October, the entire yeshiva had reached Vilna. The city itself was in transition, with the Soviet government in the midst of pulling out and the Lithuanian government taking hold of the reins. Having trouble regrouping during this chaotic period, the yeshiva split up between several shuls and *batei midrash* throughout the city. Some students found a relative or family friend to board with. The most

---

22. See *Rashi* to *Bereishis* 28:10.

concentrated group of students settled in the building of the Rameilles Yeshiva, sleeping on their luggage.

With little food available in the city, the *talmidim* were starving, and some of the younger students took to roaming the streets. Eventually, the administration was able to receive assistance from the Vaad HaYeshivos.

Weighing the limited prospects for the future of the yeshiva, Rav Leizer Yudel felt that moving the entire yeshiva to Eretz Yisrael was the best option, and he began a tireless battle to obtain immigration certificates[23] for all the students.

## To Keidan ... and Onward

TWO MONTHS AFTER ARRIVING IN VILNA, A LEGAL PROBLEM arose, and the yeshiva had to move away from the center of the country. A secretary of the Kovna community, Mr. Itzkowitz, was able to obtain a special permit to move the yeshiva to Keidan.

Life in Keidan was much more conducive to learning than the chaotic circumstances in Vilna had been. The slower pace of a small village allowed the *talmidim* to begin learning with intensity once again. On the very first day in Keidan, Rav Leizer Yudel ascended to the *bimah* and announced, "Our yeshiva, which was founded 120 years ago, will continue to survive. All *sedarim* (learning sessions) will continue through this exile as well, and we will strive to be worthy to hand over the keys of the yeshiva to the Melech HaMashiach."

Nevertheless, everyone realized that the situation was untenable. Surrounded by bellicose nations such as Nazi Germany and Communist

Yeshiva students leaving Mir at the onset of World War II

---

23. Eretz Yisrael, or Palestine as it was called then, was under British rule, and the British were limiting immigration. Each *bachur* who wanted to emigrate needed a certificate, which was hard to obtain.

Russia, how long could the Lithuanian government remain autonomous? Rav Leizer Yudel, who had managed to receive immigration certificates for himself and his Rebbetzin, felt that he could be more successful in his quest to secure visas for all of the *talmidim* if he would be in Eretz Yisrael. He left for Riga, hoping to catch a plane to Eretz Yisrael, but a plane crash prevented him from making the trip, and he returned to Keidan.

That relative tranquility of Keidan didn't hold for long. In Tammuz of 5700/1940, approximately nine months after the yeshiva had left Mir and seven months after they had arrived in Keidan, a political war erupted between the Lithuanian and Russian governments. Communist troops entered Keidan for a short time, but were driven back quickly by Lithuanian forces. The yeshiva once again felt the threat of war, and bad news was not long in coming. On the first of Av, the Lithuanian government decided that this was no time to have a large, organized yeshiva in its midst, and issued a decree, effective immediately, to disband the yeshiva.

The yeshiva split into four groups, each of which settled in a small town. One group, led by Rav Chaim Shmuelevitz and Rav Chatzkel Levenstein, settled in Karkinova; the other three settled in Remigola, Shat, and Krok.

The *bnei hayeshiva* received a warm welcome in these small towns. The simple, idealistic Jews in these villages considered themselves lucky to host a yeshiva for the first time ever, and they were willing to share their fare with the *bachurim*. Rav Chatzkel Levenstein would make the rounds between the four towns every few weeks, providing much-needed *chizuk* to all the groups.

Rav Leizer Yudel settled in a fifth hamlet called Grinkishok and embarked on yet another campaign to organize a mass *aliyah*. He was under extreme danger, because the Communists, who did not take kindly to emigration, were scrutinizing every movement of the yeshiva leaders. The only chances for success would be to keep the operation under wraps, and tiny Grinkishok was the most appropriate setting for secrecy. The townspeople did not know the identity of the elderly gentleman who had settled at the far end of a block that housed the local Communist club, or what he was doing in their midst. He lived there with his wife and his devoted secretary, Yosef Dovid Epstein. If any members of the *hanhalah* had to visit him, they would come after the villagers had gone to sleep and would leave before morning light.

Unfortunately, Rav Leizer Yudel's plans fell short, and he could not

A famous picture of the Mirrer Yeshiva in the Beis Aharon shul in Shanghai, China.
At the bottom left is Rav Chatzkel Levenstein.

obtain the immigration certificates. Instead, in the winter of 1941 a now-famous plan materialized: the yeshiva would escape, in its entirety, to Curacao, a Dutch island in the Caribbean, by traveling through Japan via Russia. Many members of the *hanhalah* were initially skeptical of the safety of traveling directly through the Communist stronghold. Rav Leizer Yudel himself was still set on trying to move the yeshiva to Eretz Yisrael, and his doctors forbade him from traveling to Japan due to health concerns.[24] But with few other choices available, the yeshiva, led by Rav Chaim Shmuelevitz and Rav Chatzkel Levenstein, took the initiative and fled in one of the most miraculous stories of escape from World War II Europe.[25] They ended up spending six years in the Far East, first in Kobe, Japan and then in Shanghai, China. The miracle of the survival of Mir is, in a way, a miracle that belongs to all of *Klal*

24. Printed in *Hazricha B'paasei Kedem*, Vol. 3, p. 1024.
25. The story of the miraculous salvation of the Mirrer Yeshiva is the subject of many full-length books, such as Yechezkel Leitner's *Operation Torah Rescue* (Feldheim, 1987), the three-volume Hebrew work *Hazricha B'paasei Kedem*, and another Hebrew volume titled *Nes Hahatzalah*.

*Yisrael,* for many of the *talmidim* who were saved through this journey to Japan became roshei yeshiva after the war.[26]

After seeing the yeshiva off, Rav Leizer Yudel fled to Eretz Yisrael via Turkey on the same boat that carried the Brisker Rav, Rav Yitzchak Zev Soloveitchik. Rav Leizer Yudel's son, Rav Beinush, who would eventually become the Rosh Yeshiva in Mir, followed him a short while later.

The two personalities who would reestablish the Mir in Yerushalayim arrived in Eretz Yisrael in the winter of 1941.

IN *PARASHAS VAYEIRA,* DIRECTLY AFTER THE *AKEIDAH,* WE read about the descendants of Avraham's brother Nachor. *Rashi* explains that the *Akeidah* caused Avraham to contemplate that had Yitzchak been offered as an actual sacrifice, Avraham would not have left any descendants through him. Hashem therefore now informed Avraham of the birth of Rivkah, who would be the conduit for the continuity of Avraham's lineage.

Although of course Rav Leizer Yudel could not know it at the time, as he began toiling to reestablish his yeshiva in Yerushalayim, in another part of the world a child was born to his nephew and niece. Named Nosson Tzvi after the Alter of Slabodka, this Nosson Tzvi would ultimately be groomed by Rav Leizer Yudel to carry on the Finkel chain and expand the yeshiva to proportions that Rav Leizer Yudel could hardly have envisioned during that difficult chapter in the history of the Mir.

---

26. Rav Shmuel Berenbaum, Rav Elyah Chazzan, Rav Zelik Epstein, Rav Dovid Kviat, and Rav Nachum Partzovitz (who would become Rav Chaim Shmuelevitz's son-in-law), among many others.

# CHAPTER TWELVE
# YOUTH IN CHICAGO

*If there is one dictum from Chazal that can summarize the trajectory Rav Nosson Tzvi Finkel took through life, from his youth on the north side of Chicago to Rosh Yeshiva of the largest yeshiva in the world, that dictum would be, "Derech eretz kadmah laTorah."[1]*

*The exemplary character traits that would become famous when he was Rosh Yeshiva — his easy manner with people, his unflappable nature, his love for all those around him, his endless patience for others — already graced his personality from his youngest years. And although Jewish life in Chicago in the 40's and 50's bore little resemblance to the way frum kids grow up today, Rav Nosson Tzvi would state openly — both in public and in private conversations — that he excelled in his role as Rosh Yeshiva of the Mir because of his childhood, not despite it.*

---

1. *Vayikra Rabbah* 9:3.

*L*IKE THE FINKEL FAMILY IN ERETZ YISRAEL INTO WHICH Rav Nosson Tzvi would eventually marry, the Chicago Finkels were direct descendants of the first Rav Nosson Tzvi Finkel, the Alter of Slabodka, after whom Rav Nosson Tzvi was named.[2] The Alter's son, Rav Avraham Shmuel Finkel, had been a Rav in Europe before moving to Eretz Yisrael and becoming a

**Roots in Slabodka**

*mashpia ruchani* in the Chevron Yeshiva.[3]

Rav Avraham Shmuel was remembered as a devout *baal mussar*. When the family reprinted his work, *Nesivos HaMussar*, in 5766/2005, Rav Michel Yehuda Lefkowitz *zt"l*, Rosh Yeshiva of Ponevezh Latze'irim, wrote a letter in which he described Rav Avraham Shmuel as follows:

> *Seventy years ago, I merited to hear mussar talks from the gaon and tzaddik Rav Avraham Shmuel zt"l, when he influenced the bachurim in fear [of Hashem] and mussar through his discourses in Yeshiva Knesses Yisrael/Chevron … Aside from the discourses delivered to the talmidim, we were influenced greatly by his noble character — he was a purely spiritual person, completely removed from Olam Hazeh … Just seeing his nobility and the way he conducted himself certainly had a profound effect on us talmidim.*

Although Rav Michel Yehuda Lefkowitz also describes Rav Avraham Shmuel as a *"shaskan"* — a person who spoke very little — the few stories that are told about him point to a person who was very sensitive to the feelings and needs of others.

---

2. See family tree, p. 471
3. Chevron was the relocated Slabodka Yeshiva founded by the Alter of Slabodka, and was in fact led by the Alter after he moved with the yeshiva to Eretz Yisrael in 5685/1925, until his passing on 29 Shevat, 5687, two years before the bloody massacre in Chevron would force the yeshiva to move to Yerushalayim.

LOOKING BACK AT RAV NOSSON TZVI'S GRANDFATHER AND father, it is apparent that many good *middos* were in the Finkel genes.

**Tracing the Character Traits**
Rav Avraham Shmuel Finkel[4] got married shortly before World War I. He received a sizable dowry, and he traveled to Warsaw to invest his money in some sort of safe investment. After consulting with friends in Warsaw, he decided to invest in several food commodities. He bought flour and other basic staples in large quantity at wholesale prices, which he planned to resell to grocery stores.

But then the world went black. With the outbreak of World War I Poland came under attack, and food staples began to disappear off the shelves of the local stores. This turn of events could have signaled the beginning of a bright financial future for the 30-year-old Rav Avraham Shmuel. He could have sold his merchandise at a significant markup and lived off the profits for many years to come. But his own finances were the furthest thing from his mind. Not only didn't he raise the prices, he didn't sell his merchandise at all. Rather, he distributed it free of charge to *rabbanim* and other *talmidei chachamim* who were suffering from the severe food shortage.

Rav Michel Yehuda Lefkowitz arriving in Rav Nosson Tzvi's home for a meeting of the Moetzes Gedolei HaTorah.
Seated at the table is Rav Yissachar Meir *zt"l*, Rosh Yeshiva of Yeshivas HaNegev.

---

4. The information on Rav Avraham Shmuel Finkel was culled primarily from a biographical sketch printed in the newly formatted *Nesivos HaMussar*.

His friends thought he was being irresponsible, but Rav Avraham Shmuel said, "In such times, when supplies are limited, everyone worries only about their own money and their own families. The *rabbanim* and *talmidei chachamim* are in grave danger of starvation, because no one is taking care of them. Anyone who can help them is obligated to do so."

Not only did Rav Avraham Shmuel distribute all of his merchandise to the *talmidei chachamim*, he also disbursed the remaining funds from his dowry to widows, orphans, and others who were in dire straits; he even gave away his own *Yom Tov* clothing.

## Empathy for a Talmid

WHEN RAV MOSHE MORDECHAI EPSTEIN, THE ROSH YESHIVA of Chevron, was *niftar* on 20 Kislev, 5694/1934, the entire Chevron Yeshiva was thrown into mourning. Rav Moshe Mordechai had led the yeshiva from Slabodka in Europe to Chevron, where it remained until the massacre in 1929.[5] Aside from the great *geonus* with which he led one of the top yeshivos in the world for over 40 years, he was extremely devoted to his *talmidim*. After the attack in 1929, in which twenty-four *talmidim* were killed and many more were injured by the marauding Arabs (as the British officials looked on), the yeshiva moved to Geulah in Yerushalayim. The day after the massacre, the British agreed to evacuate the remainder of the Chevron community and the yeshiva, but they decided to move a few people at a time for fear that the bloodthirsty mobs would attack again. When community leaders urged Rav Moshe Mordechai to leave first, he staunchly refused, insisting that he would remain until every other member of the yeshiva and the community had left.

Having lost such a dedicated Rosh Yeshiva, the *talmidim* were overcome with grief.

As the *levayah* (funeral) procession reached Har Hazeisim and the *niftar* was being buried, one of the *talmidim* was grieving for another reason: His *chasunah* was to take place that very night. With the yeshiva in mourning, would anyone attend his wedding, or would he be celebrating his *simchah* in an empty hall?

One other person was envisioning that empty hall and empathizing with this *bachur*. As he stood to deliver his eulogy at the open grave, Rav Avraham Shmuel Finkel declared, "*Rabbeinu HaKadosh*! You have risen above, to the *Yeshiva shel Maalah*, but here, in the *Yeshiva shel Matah*,

---

5. See p. 34, where Rebbetzin Finkel tells the miraculous story of her husband's survival of the massacre.

Rav Moshe Mordechai Epstein,
Rosh Yeshiva of Chevron
for over 40 years

in Chevron Yeshiva in Yerushalayim, one of the *bnei chaburah* is scheduled to walk to his *chuppah* tonight. We may not allow the mourning to diminish his honor or cast a pall over his *simchah*. We are all required to participate in his day of joy, with love and friendship. This is the highest level of *gemillus chassadim,* for *gemillus chassadim* with a live person is greater [than with a deceased person] …"

As a writer who was present at that burial recalled, those present felt as though the *niftar* himself, from the depth of his open grave, was nodding his head in agreement, declaring, "Rejoice, my children …"

RAV AVRAHAM SHMUEL WAS SO SENSITIVE TO OTHERS' FEEL-ings that he could quickly size up a situation in which someone would

## The Sandak That Wasn't

be embarrassed and act immediately to forestall that person from being shamed.

When his nephew Rav Chaim Zev (a son of his older brother Rav Leizer Yudel) made a *bris,* he wanted Rav Avraham Shmuel to serve as *sandak.* R' Avraham Shmuel donned his *tefillin,* as is customary, and the *mohel* announced that another relative, who had arrived from Germany, would act as "*kvatter.*" That relative rose, but instead of walking to the *ezras nashim* to receive the baby from his wife and bring him into the hall, he walked to the seat set aside for the *sandak* and settled himself comfortably in it, waiting for the baby to be brought to him. Dozens of sets of eyes followed this guest's movements, wondering why he had chosen to sit in the *sandak's* seat. It suddenly dawned on a few participants that in Germany, the *sandak* is referred to as *kvatter,* but they were unsure of what to do.

Rav Avraham Shmuel also realized what had happened, and he quickly motioned that no one should say anything to the guest. The baby was brought to the guest's lap by another attendee, and the *bris* commenced as Rav Avraham Shmuel slipped away to take off his *tefillin.*

AT THE *SHIVAH* FOR RAV NOSSON TZVI, SOMEONE REVEALED to the family that their grandfather, Rav Avraham Shmuel, had been

**A Gadol Will Come From Him**

offered a very respectable position when he was still in Europe. He was interested in the position, which would have provided for his family and given him the opportunity to remain ensconced in Torah study. He heard, however, that there was a *machlokes* (dispute) brewing over who would be appointed to the post, and he immediately removed himself from the running. When Rav Yerucham Levovitz heard this story, he remarked, "I am sure that a *gadol b'Yisrael* will come out of him."

It took two generations for his prediction to materialize.[6]

The exemplary character traits displayed by Rav Avraham Shmuel in these incidents — generosity, empathy for a *talmid*, humility, and avoiding *machlokes* — would become some of the hallmarks of his grandson, Rav Nosson Tzvi Finkel.

HAVING GROWN UP IN THE HOME OF SUCH A NOBLE *TZADDIK*, R' Eliyahu Meir Finkel, Rav Nosson Tzvi's father, arrived in Chicago

**R' Eliyahu Meir Finkel**

equipped to build a solid Jewish home. Although he was by nature a quiet person — to the extent that members of the community who lived there for over 50 years hardly realized the extent of his *klal* work there — in actuality he worked behind the scenes to build Chicago's Jewish community. He was active, for instance, in bringing the Telshe Yeshiva to Chicago, and in establishing an Agudah there, though few people knew that he was behind those initiatives.

In a *hesped* delivered on his father's *sheloshim*,[7] Rav Nosson Tzvi noted that it was hard to know much about his father, because he hid most of his greatness. He would hide behind the mask of a businessman, while building Torah in the United States and beyond.

In highlighting one of his father's *middos* in that *hesped*, Rav Nosson Tzvi could easily have been describing himself: "Perhaps my father's most unique quality," he said, "was that he respected each person and held everyone in high esteem. He never saw people's flaws."

---

6. Rav Gedalya Finkel.
7. This *hesped* is printed, along with that of Rav Aryeh Finkel (quoted below, that was delivered on the same occasion), in the back of *Imrei Gedaliah*, one of Rav Gedalya Finkel's eight *sefarim* on *Shas*, in the volume on *Pesachim* and *Gittin*.

Upon settling in Chicago, R' Eliyahu Meir (commonly known as E. Meir or just Meir in those days) began to teach in a local school. At some point, he and R' Yaakov Brodie, a brother of Rav Simcha Zissel Brodie, one of the roshei yeshiva of Chevron, opened a catering business together — the first major kosher catering business in Chicago. The business was very successful, to the extent that the partners were able to sell it in the 1970's and move to Eretz Yisrael.

R' Meir was a quiet *baal chessed*, helping family members and others who were unable to make ends meet. Rav Gedalya Finkel recalls overhearing a conversation in which a distinguished member of the community asked his father for a $5,000 loan — a handsome sum in those days. The very fact that someone so prestigious could feel comfortable asking for a large loan indicates that it was commonplace to receive such loans from R' Meir.

R' Meir shared a close relationship with his uncle, Rav Leizer Yudel, the Mirrer Rosh Yeshiva. At a *hesped* delivered upon R' Meir's *sheloshim*, Rav Aryeh Finkel[8] said that Rav Leizer Yudel displayed a level of affection for R' Meir that he hardly displayed for his own progeny. In the course of the years, Rav Leizer Yudel wrote many letters to the Chicago Finkels. One of those letters, penned several months before Rav Leizer Yudel passed away, demonstrates the trust and respect Rav Leizer Yudel had for his nephew:

> As I have reached old age, and I feel that I no longer have the energy of my early years, the burden of the yeshiva has become too difficult for me to shoulder myself. Out of concern for the future of the yeshiva that has been my life's work,[9] I feel obligated to bring new, fresh energy into the directorate of the yeshiva, in order to breathe life into the institution and to support it.
>
> Therefore, I call upon the two Rabbanim, Hageonim Moreinu Harav R' Meir Finkel shlita of Chicago and Moreinu Harav R' Shamshon Raphael Weiss shlita of Brooklyn, to join the presidium of the yeshiva, and appoint them as members of the executive board of the yeshiva.[10]

---

8. A son of Rav Chaim Zev, currently Rosh Yeshiva of Mir Brachfeld.
9. At the point when he was writing this letter, Rav Leizer Yudel had been the Rosh Yeshiva for over 60 years, and had navigated it through two world wars and a rebuilding process in Eretz Yisrael.
10. This is a free-flowing translation of the first section of the letter on p. 167, dated 5 Adar, 5725 (1965).

Letter from Rav Leizer Yudel adding R' Eliyahu Meir Finkel to the presidium of the Mir

Perhaps the most remarkable aspect of the relationship between Rav Leizer Yudel and R' Meir was the absolute *hisbatlus* (abnegation) the latter had for his uncle, as Rav Nosson Tzvi himself related at his father's *hesped*.

By all accounts, Rav Nosson Tzvi's path to greatness was through his own *hisbatlus* to Rav Leizer Yudel[11] — and his father clearly served as a role model in this *middah*.

RAV NOSSON TZVI'S CHILDHOOD FRIENDS FONDLY RECALL
the warmth of the Finkel home, which they attribute to the Rosh

**Rebbetzin Sara Finkel**
Yeshiva's mother, Rebbetzin Sara Finkel. The stories that abound of the *middos* for which Rav Nosson Tzvi is remembered mirror the descriptions of his mother from 50 years ago. "It was always a wonderful house to visit," recalls Mr. Shael Bellows, a schoolmate during the 1950's. "Their house was always open to visitors. Rebbetzin Finkel brought an entirely different definition of the word *chessed* into the community. At a time when

11. See pp. 187-194

women in the community would commonly open their homes to benefit educational causes near and dear to their heart, she became a role model on how to host an event — not by design, but by the way she carried herself. When she opened her home, it was an experience, because she would take pride in making people feel welcome."

"Rebbetzin Finkel always had a smile on her face," recalls Rabbi Harvey Well, Rav Nosson Tzvi's closest friend from their junior year in high school through their first post high-school year in Eretz Yisrael. "She always had a kind word to say to everybody. You felt good being in their house, because she always saw the positive in everyone and everything."

Another trait that Rav Nosson Tzvi inherited was his mother's humility. "She could easily have shown off," says Rabbi Well. "They had a very nice home, and she could have afforded expensive jewelry, but that wasn't her. She was a non-materialistic, sweet woman."

Some five decades later, anyone who meets Rebbetzin Finkel would describe her exactly the same way.

## A Jewish School West of the Hudson

AFTER GRADUATING FROM THE ARIE CROWN DAY SCHOOL (which was then known as Central Park Hebrew Day School), the choices for young Nosson Tzvi were limited. *Frum* Jews in Chicago were actually the fortunate ones, because Chicago was home to two out of three[12] post-elementary Jewish schools west of the Hudson River: a high school, which was called the Chicago Jewish Academy, or Ida Crown; and a yeshiva, called the Hebrew Theological College/Beis Midrash L'Torah.

For the first few years of high school, students would attend the Academy full time, studying *limudei kodesh* (Jewish studies) in the morning and *limudei chol* (secular studies) in the afternoon. When a boy would reach the point where he could advance beyond the level of the *limudei kodesh shiurim* at the Academy, he would travel to the yeshiva in the morning to study *limudei kodesh* there, and he would return to the Academy for secular studies in the afternoon.

In his first two years in the Academy, Rav Nosson Tzvi's *rebbeim* were Rabbi Saks, who had studied in Telshe in Europe, and Rabbi Silver, both of whom Rabbi Well remembers as being wonderful *rebbeim*. During

---

12. The Telshe Yeshiva in Cleveland was the other institution.

his senior year in high school, Rav Nosson Tzvi traveled to the yeshiva in the morning, where his rebbi was Rav Herzl Kaplan, a brother of the legendary Rav Mendel Kaplan, who at that time gave the higher *shiur* in the yeshiva.[13] It was common, however, for *talmidim* to go to Eretz Yisrael for the second year of *beis midrash*, skipping Rav Mendel Kaplan's *shiur*, and then to return to Chicago and enter a *semichah* program led by Rabbi Rogoff and Rav Chaim Zimmerman.

Although he took his studies seriously, Nosson Tzvi didn't show a unique level of interest or aptitude in learning in his early years in high school. At 14, he traveled to Eretz Yisrael, and, at the request of Rav Leizer Yudel, he remained in Mir for several months.[14] Rav Leizer Yudel set him up with a *chavrusa*, Rav Yosef Stern, currently the *mashgiach* in Torah Ore, who learned *Perek Merubah* in *Bava Kamma* with him.

Rav Daniel Lehrfeld *shlita*, now Rosh Yeshiva of Yeshiva Beis Yisrael in Neve Yaakov, was several years older than Rav Nosson Tzvi. As one of the best yeshiva students in Chicago, he came to Eretz Yisrael to learn in the late 1950's, one year after Nosson Tzvi's return to Chicago. When Rav Daniel went to talk in learning with Rav Leizer Yudel, the latter expressed pride in what his great-nephew had accomplished during that visit. "*Ehr hut gehuruvet, uhn ehr hut gut gekent Merubah,*" he said. "He toiled, and he knew *Merubah* well." Rav Nosson Tzvi later revealed that he learned *Merubah* eight times during that trip.[15]

Rav Leizer Yudel was so taken by his great-nephew that he asked no less a personage than Rav Chaim Shmuelevitz and Rav Chaim's son Refoel (then a teenager) to escort Nosson Tzvi to the airport, in the hope that he would be left with warm memories of the Mir and choose to return as soon as he finished high school.

Despite his obvious success in Eretz Yisrael, Nosson Tzvi's friends don't remember a marked difference in his learning upon his return to the States.

Although nothing about Rav Nosson Tzvi's early years indicated that he would eventually become a great Rosh Yeshiva, one aspect of his eventual success as an educator did shine through even in those early years. Rav Nosson Tzvi's younger brother, Rav Gedalya, recalls that when he attended shul as a youngster, Rav Nosson Tzvi would

---

13. Rav Mendel later became a Rosh Yeshiva in Philadelphia. He had an unusual ability to understand and inspire American boys, and his influence lasted a lifetime for many of his students.

14 See p. 46

15. Heard from the Rosh Yeshiva by Rabbi Paysach J. Krohn.

dramatize the *Krias HaTorah* with hand motions to make the proceedings interesting for him.

Years later, Rav Nosson Tzvi would excel in making Torah study interesting to everybody, even *talmidim* who had not enjoyed learning until they arrived in Mir.

R' MEIR FINKEL WAS EXTREMELY DEVOTED TO THE TORAH upbringing of Nosson Tzvi and Gedalya. Although there were some

**"Rebbi, Rebbi, All That I Have Is Yours!"** excellent *rebbeim* at the Arie Crown Day School and the Chicago Jewish Academy high school — the most famous of whom was Rav Yaakov Nayman, a *talmid* of the Brisker Rav who would go on to become the Rav of the Kehillas Adas Yisrael — R' Meir wanted his sons to be more successful in their learning, so he engaged Rav Yehoshua Levinson to learn privately with them after school.

A native Chicagoan,[16] Rav Levinson had been living in Monsey, New York, for several years while studying in Beis Midrash Elyon. He returned to Chicago to tend to his father, who had fallen ill, and he subsequently began learning with the young Nosson Tzvi Finkel. In hindsight, it seems that Heaven orchestrated his return to Chicago so that he could influence the life of the future Rosh Yeshiva of Mir.

During the *shivah* for R' Meir Finkel, Rav Aryeh Fredman, a son-in-law of Rav Levinson, came to be *menachem avel* Rav Nosson Tzvi. The Rosh Yeshiva said, "I consider it a *shevach* (praise) of my father that he chose such a big *tzaddik* and *lamdan* — your father-in-law — as a private rebbi for me." He also said that if there are thirty-six *tzaddikim* in our generation, Rav Levinson was undoubtedly one of them.

Rav Gershon Meltzer,[17] another son-in-law of Rav Levinson, related that both his father-in-law and Rav Nosson Tzvi independently told him that Rav Levinson would constantly cajole his young *talmid* to strive for more. "You are a Finkel, an *einikel* of the Alter of Slabodka," he would remind him. "You are capable of more."

Rav Levinson learned with Rav Nosson Tzvi for about three years, beginning when Rav Nosson Tzvi returned from his first trip to

---

16. The information about Rav Levinson was culled from interviews with Rebbetzin Levinson and her son-in-law, Rav Aryeh Fredman, and from a *hesped* by Rav Levinson's son-in-law, Rav Gershon Meltzer.

17. Rav Meltzer is famous in the Mir for giving daily halachah *shiurim* in English and in Hebrew. Although the *shiur* is given during *bein hasedarim* (the lunch break), dozens of *talmidim* give up their only free time of the day to attend his *shiur*.

Eretz Yisrael. Later, he was one of the people responsible for convincing the Finkels to send Rav Nosson Tzvi back to Eretz Yisrael at the age of 17.

Rav Nosson Tzvi considered himself forever indebted to Rav Levinson. Whenever he heard that Rav Levinson was in Yerushalayim, Rav Nosson Tzvi would drop everything and run to see him. He considered his rebbi so meritorious that in his later years, when his Parkinson's disease kept growing worse, he would ask Rav Levinson for a *berachah* that he should get better. For his part, Rav Levinson cried the first time

Rav Nosson Tzvi greets Rav Yaakov Nayman, his eighth-grade rebbi, at a Mir event in America.

he saw Rav Nosson Tzvi suffering from his disease. "He's my *talmid*; he's younger than me. How can he be so sick?" he said with anguish. He would daven constantly for Rav Nosson Tzvi's recovery.

Rav Levinson related that when he would visit Rav Nosson Tzvi and would see him in a weakened state, he would ask him about the *"meluchah"* (kingdom) he was building. "Suddenly," Rav Levinson would say, "it would be like I was looking at a different person. He would jump up and run to get papers to show me just what he was building."

A particularly poignant moment of Rav Nosson Tzvi's life took place at Rav Levinson's *levayah*. He was *niftar* on Erev Shabbos Chol HaMoed Pesach 5770, a year and a half before Rav Nosson Tzvi. By that point, the Rosh Yeshiva was very weak most of the time. The *levayah* was to take place close to Shabbos, and Rav Meltzer called the Rosh Yeshiva's house out of courtesy, assuming that he wouldn't make it to the *levayah*. To everyone's surprise, not only did Rav Nosson Tzvi join the *levayah*, but he ran after the *mittah* and tried to grab onto it, crying bitterly, "Rebbi, rebbi, all that I have is yours!"

At the *shivah* for Rav Nosson Tzvi, when Rebbetzin Levinson came to be *menachem avel*, everyone stood up for her when she entered the

Rav Nosson Tzvi dancing with his rebbi, Rav Yehoshua Levinson,
at the wedding of Rav Levinson's grandchild, with Rav Gershon Meltzer looking on

room. Rav Nosson Tzvi's daughter turned to her and said, "We can never forget the influence your husband had on our father, because he wouldn't stop talking about it."

IN *EMUNAH UBITACHON* (1:11) THE *CHAZON ISH* DETAILS A PERsonality profile in which he could have been describing Rav Nosson Tzvi, even in his teenage years:

## A Good Friend to All

*There is a person who desires to do good for others. Meeting a friend fills his heart with joy, and he greets him with a cheerful face. He worries that perhaps he didn't hit the mark in [gladdening] his friend's spirit, and whether he might say something that is not to his friend's liking, for nothing brings him sadness as much as hurting his friend's feelings or not granting his friend kindness.*

*[This person] will never be hurt by what his friend does, because his heart, which is full of love, will hide all iniquities [of his friend]. He is willing to lovingly accept all wounds and insults that his friend will deliver, because he realizes that not everyone has noble character traits. [He thinks,] "What can you expect of him?" Yet he respects and honors him, for he does not harbor in his heart any ill thoughts that amount to lack of respect for other humans.*

*[Furthermore,] this soul can indulge itself by grasping onto contradictory sides of the very same issue in order to attain the greater*

*good. He will therefore blame himself for even the slightest deviance from character perfection, yet he will see his friend's actions as being perfectly meritorious even when that friend has sinned grievously.*

*This precious soul does not need to exercise great self-control in order to avoid the natural feelings of anger [toward others] or to avoid embarrassing another person, because his soul is already polished and shined and it cannot become sullied. He is filled with happiness and retains his sweet disposition constantly.*

Friends from Chicago recall that the young Nosson Tzvi was very popular, thanks in large part to his easygoing, friendly personality. Rabbi Well relates — from the vantage point of a close friend who spent much of each day with him in his youth — that he doesn't remember a single instance in which Nosson Tzvi grew impatient or angry with anyone, nor does he recall him ever saying *lashon hara* or something hurtful to anyone. Another schoolmate related that although Nosson Tzvi was exquisitely sensitive to other people's feelings and would go out of his way not to hurt anyone, he was not nearly as sensitive to his own feelings and would shrug off any hurtful words or actions aimed at him. Even when a friend snubbed him, his attitude and respect for that person did not change.

Nosson Tzvi already exhibited leadership qualities in high school. He was vice president of the student council in his senior year (Harvey Well was the president), and he was a tireless leader of a drive to raise funds for the needy in Eretz Yisrael. Even back then, he had perfected some aspects of the style of leadership he would use when he would

Rav Nosson Tzvi visits Chicago some 40 years after he left as a typical American teenager in 1960, flanked by his brother-in-law and a Rosh Yeshiva in Mir, Rav Nachman Levovitz, and his trusted helper and fellow Chicagoan, R' Yehuda Neuhaus.

Chapter Twelve: Youth in Chicago □ 173

become Rosh Yeshiva some 30 years later — the smile never left his face and no one felt that he was overbearing or demanding.

## Graduating From the Academy

UPON GRADUATING FROM THE CHICAGO JEWISH ACADEMY IN 1960, Nosson Tzvi joined a *"chaburah"* of approximately 10 boys who went to Eretz Yisrael, although the yeshivos they attended were quite varied. One boy, who was a grandson of the great *mashgiach* Rav Elyah Lopian, enrolled in Kfar Chassidim to be near his grandfather. Another boy attended Ponovezh. One went to Kerem B'Yavneh. And Nosson Tzvi Finkel enrolled in Mir, rejoining his great-uncle Rav Leizer Yudel, who eagerly awaited his return.

# SECTION TWO

# A LEGACY IN BLOOM

וְהָיָה כְּעֵץ שָׁתוּל עַל פַּלְגֵי מָיִם אֲשֶׁר פִּרְיוֹ יִתֵּן בְּעִתּוֹ
וְעָלֵהוּ לֹא יִבּוֹל וְכֹל אֲשֶׁר יַעֲשֶׂה יַצְלִיחַ

*He shall be like a tree deeply rooted alongside brooks of water, that yields its fruit in its season, and whose leaf never withers; and everything that he does will succeed*

(Tehillim 1:3)

# CHAPTER THIRTEEN
# MIR YERUSHALAYIM

*Construction of the main building of Mir Yerushalayim began in 1949. At the time, many people in Yerushalayim were starving due to extreme food shortages, and physical labor was sought by many who needed income to feed their families. The Mir building was built by several Yerushalmi yungeleit, one of whom would go on to become a mashgiach in a yeshiva. While they worked, they discussed Torah topics, infusing the mortar and bricks that have now housed the Mirrer Yeshiva for over six decades with the holiness of the Torah.*

*Years later, when Rav Nosson Tzvi began to construct additional buildings, he would insist on being present to press the button on the cement mixer to pour the foundation for each of the buildings — reenacting history, in a sense, and infusing each new Mir building with the same holiness as the main building.*

HE MIR YESHIVA IN YERUSHALAYIM TO WHICH THE 17-year-old Nosson Tzvi Finkel would return in 1960 had already experienced considerable growing pains.

Rav Leizer Yudel Finkel arrived in Eretz Yisrael in the winter of 5701/1941. He initially moved into the home of his eldest son, Rav Chaim Zev, who was a Rosh Yeshiva in Heichal HaTorah in Tel Aviv at the time. Several months after Rav Leizer Yudel's arrival, he moved to Yerushalayim, where he began to work to reestablish the Yeshiva.[1]

Although he was nearing 70, Rav Leizer Yudel began from scratch, even as he retained the hope that his students who were marooned in the Far East would eventually make their way to Eretz Yisrael. From his humble home in the Yegias Kapayim neighborhood of Yerushalayim, he sent dozens of letters each day to patrons and alumni of the Mir who were living in America, beseeching them to come to his aid in rebuilding the yeshiva.

It took several years to raise the necessary funds, especially

Starting from scratch at 70, Rav Leizer Yudel embarked on a campaign to reestablish the Mir in Yerushalayim.

---

1. Unless otherwise indicated, the story of the reestablishment of the Mir is based on an interview with Rav Nachman Levovitz *shlita*, a grandchild of Rav Yerucham Levovitz, who married the daughter of Rav Beinush Finkel, thus uniting the Levovitz and Finkel families, and on information culled from *Marbitzei Torah Umussar*, Vol. 3.

"The Torah returns to its host": Rav Isser Zalman Meltzer in his later years, when he returned Rav Leizer Yudel's favor by sending him *talmidim* with whom to reestablish the Mir

because he was still sending food packages and other forms of aid to his students in Shanghai, while working to reopen the yeshiva in Yerushalayim.

In 5704/1944, Rav Leizer Yudel was finally ready to establish the new Mir Yerushalayim. In a turn of events that exemplifies the principle of *"Torah machzeres el ha'achsanyah shelah* — the Torah returns to its host" (*Bava Metzia* 85a), the very same Rav Isser Zalman Meltzer who had asked Rav Leizer Yudel to send his *talmidim* to shore up various yeshivos in Europe (see Chapter 3) was now the Rosh Yeshiva of Eitz Chaim, and he returned the favor by sending a group of his top *talmidim* to help Rav Leizer Yudel rebuild the Mirrer Yeshiva.

At first, this group began to learn in the Beis Baruch shul in Meah Shearim.[2] They then moved to the Vizhnitz *shtiebel* in the Beis Yisrael neighborhood.[3] During the Israeli War of Independence in 1948, Beis Yisrael — which was situated at the Jordanian border — came under incessant shelling, and the yeshiva moved into the Achvah shul in Geulah.

IN 1947, AS THE WORLD WAS JUST BEGINNING TO RECOVER from the devastation of World War II, the Mir students and faculty who had spent the war years in the Far East immigrated to America, though some of them went via Canada. In the years that followed, a group of these *talmidim* began to make their way to Eretz Yisrael. Rav Chaim Shmuelevitz was one of the first to move, leaving America after only six months, bringing along some of the "Shanghai" *talmidim*, and the yeshiva began to grow.[4]

**A Time to Build**

---

2. *Oros MiMir*, p. 62.
3. In yet another case of the aforementioned principle that the Torah returns to its host, the Vizhnitz shul — which is a short walk from the main building of the Mir — has hosted Mirrer *talmidim* many times over the years, serving *bachurim* and *yungeleit* who cannot find seats in one of the Mir's buildings.
4. Heard from Rav Aharon Chodosh.

In 5709/1949, Rav Leizer Yudel decided that it was time to construct a building. In order to finance it, he traveled to America during the winter of that year. His *mechutan*, Rav Shmuel Greineman, arranged for him to stay at the Broadway Central Hotel in New York City.

On Rav Leizer Yudel's first day in America, Rav Shamshon Raphael Weiss, who had studied in Mir in Europe before the war, came to visit his rebbi, and found him eating store-bought herring on a paper bag. He rushed to call Rav Shmuel Greineman and tell him that Rav Leizer Yudel didn't feel comfortable with his accommodations.

Rav Shamshon Raphael Weiss, flanked by his son, Rav Yisroel Meir Weiss, now Rosh Yeshiva of Nachlas Halevi'im in Haifa, and Rav Dovid Greineman, a son of Rav Shmuel Greineman

"What can I do?" asked Rav Shmuel. "I don't have a better option."

Rav Weiss said, "Let me take him to my home."

Rav Greineman agreed, as did Rav Leizer Yudel, who ended up staying in the Weiss home for six months, except when he traveled out of the city. The Weiss children recall that in those six months he became a surrogate grandfather to them.

Rav Leizer Yudel had a relative in Detroit who had left Europe long before the war, and the family had lost contact with him. The Rosh Yeshiva wanted to locate him and bring him back into the fold, so he spent Pesach of that year in Detroit in the home of Rav Naftoli Carlebach.[5] Rav Leizer Yudel offered to bring his relative back to Eretz Yisrael, but the latter unfortunately refused.

As *hashgachah* would have it, both of Rav Leizer Yudel's hosts in the United States would later become his children's *mechutanim*: Rav Weiss' son Rav Yisroel Meir (currently Rosh Yeshiva of Yeshivas Nachlas Halevi'im in Haifa) married Rav Chaim Shmuelevitz's daughter, and Rav Binyamin Carlebach married Rav Beinush Finkel's fourth daughter.

Although the main purpose of Rav Leizer Yudel's visit to America was to fundraise for the yeshiva, he also used his visit as an opportunity to help

---

5. His two hosts were siblings: Mrs. Weiss was Rav Naftoli Carlebach's sister.

his *talmidim* who had settled in the United States establish their homes.

In a telling episode, as he was leaving the home of a *talmid* he had visited, the woman of the house asked him to bless her children that they should grow up to be *yirei Shamayim*. "I remember thinking that after hosting such a *tzaddik* and *gadol baTorah* and receiving a *berachah* from him, I would be on easy street with my children's *chinuch*," she relates.

But she would soon be disappointed. "I'll give you a *berachah*," Rav Leizer Yudel replied, "but *mein tei'ereh Yiddeneh* (my dear Jewish woman), you don't succeed in *chinuch* through *berachos*. You need *zechusim* (merits) — your *tefillos*, and your effort."

"When the door closed behind him," the woman recalls, "I burst into tears, realizing that I would still have to work very hard to raise my children."

Her sons are now great *talmidei chachamim*, and her daughter is married to one of the finest *maggidei shiur* in the world, but when complimented that her efforts obviously bore fruit, she demurs. "It was Rav Leizer Yudel's *berachah*," she insists.

## Foreseeing the Growth

BY THE TIME RAV LEIZER YUDEL returned to Eretz Yisrael, he had amassed enough funds to begin building the large, multistory building he envisioned. But when he revealed his plans to others, they laughed. The yeshiva numbered only a few dozen *talmidim* at the time. "Why build such a large edifice for such a small number of students?" they wondered.[6]

Rav Leizer Yudel shaking *arba minim* in the new Mir building. With enrollment at fifty when he started building, his vision for the yeshiva's growth was met with doubt.

---

6. Heard from Rav Binyamin Finkel, in an impromptu *hesped* delivered as part of his regular Tuesday-night *shmuess* given several hours after Rav Nosson Tzvi's *levayah*.

The Ponovezher Rav faced similar opposition when he set out to build the Ponovezh Yeshiva building in Bnei Brak, which was large enough to contain over 2,000 *talmidim*. The Torah world had been decimated during World War II, and few believed that it would thrive yet again. The architects of the Torah regeneration through the world — the Ponovezher Rav and Rav Leizer Yudel Finkel in Eretz Yisrael, and Rav Aron Kotler in America — were certain that Hashem's promise that the Torah would never be lost to the Jewish people would be fulfilled, and they conducted their building campaigns according to this belief. And how wonderfully has history borne out their visions!

The original
Mir Yerushalayim
building under
construction

Their argument wasn't unfounded. During the first years in the new building, Rav Chaim Shmuelevitz insisted that all *talmidim* had to learn in the main *beis midrash* so that the benches wouldn't be too sparsely populated. A *bachur* who came to Eretz Yisrael during the 1950's chose to attend Yeshivas Chevron over the Mir because "there weren't many people learning in the Mir at the time."[7]

The growth Rav Leizer Yudel envisioned for the Mir would take decades. During the 1960's, when someone came to complain that there was no space left in the *beis midrash*, Rav Chaim ran upstairs to see this sight for himself. Later, in the 1970's, when attendance at his *shmuessin* reached standing-room-only proportions, he cried tears of joy, saying, "*Aza hatzlachah* – such success!"[8]

Despite the naysayers, Rav Leizer Yudel wouldn't be deterred, and he built the three-story building he had planned. His vision was prophetic. Even during his son Rav Beinush's years as Rosh Yeshiva, the yeshiva was already bursting at the seams, and he had to add a floor to accommodate more *talmidim*.

EVEN BEFORE HE BEGAN TO REESTABLISH THE YESHIVA, RAV Leizer Yudel was already building Torah scholarship in Eretz Yisrael in

**The Yeshiva Without a Door** his trademark fashion: distributing funds to anyone who would come tell him a *shtikel Torah* (novel interpretation of a Torah topic) — even to those who were not enrolled in the yeshiva.[9] In the 1940's and

---

7. *A Treasure of Letters*, by Rabbi Elozor Reich.
8. Rav Yitzchok Berkowitz.
9. Rav Leizer Yudel actually took up this "hobby" as a young *bachur* in Telz. His father, the Alter

Rav Chaim Shmuelevitz walking out of the "building without a door"

1950's, it became known among Yerushalayim's Jews that if you didn't have money for Shabbos, you could go to Rav Leizer Yudel and tell him a *chiddush*, and he would invariably give you enough to buy food for Shabbos. Many a Yerushalmi family would not have had basic staples if not for this "deal."[10]

In planning the building, Rav Leizer Yudel left out a basic component of every building in the world: a door. This oddity was a symbol of the policy that has existed in Mir Yerushalayim from the day it was established: the Mir is open to anyone who would like to enroll, regardless of his background or his level of scholarship — as long as he is sincerely interested in studying Torah.[11]

Once, a *bachur* came to Rav Leizer Yudel to take a *farher* (entrance exam). Rav Leizer Yudel asked him where he had learned previously, and the boy named one of the prominent yeshivos in Eretz Yisrael. But when Rav Leizer Yudel asked him to say a *shtikel Torah*, the boy replied that he didn't have anything to say. He explained that he had not seen *hatzlachah* in his learning in his previous yeshiva — nor had he succeeded in any other institution.

"On what basis should I accept you?" asked Rav Leizer Yudel.

---

of Slabodka, would send him money for food, but Rav Leizer Yudel wanted to pay his own way. He would use that money to pay for *shtiklach Torah,* and he would pay for his meager subsistence by tutoring younger *talmidim.*

10. Rav Tzvi Cheshin and Rav Binyamin Finkel.

11. The building remained door-less for several decades, until the danger of Arabs infiltrating from nearby East Jerusalem posed a threat to the safety of the *talmidim.* But the "open-door policy" of the Mir has remained in effect until this very day.

"I want to start learning now," replied the boy. "Are you closing the door on someone who wants to have a new start?"

Rav Leizer Yudel accepted the boy — who has now served as a Rosh Kollel of one of the most prestigious *kollelim* in Eretz Yisrael for several decades.

Not only would Rav Leizer Yudel accept every *bachur*, he was extremely hesitant to expel anyone. In one incident, two *bachurim* acted so egregiously that other boys in yeshiva insisted that they be thrown out. Rav Leizer Yudel was loath to expel them, but the sever-

Rav Leizer Yudel's son, Rav Chaim Zev Finkel, the *mashgiach* of Mir Yerushalayim

ity of their actions left him no choice. For months after expelling the boys, however, he would remind the *bachurim* who had insisted that he throw them out that it was their fault that these boys were no longer in the yeshiva.[12]

When the yeshiva was already established, Rav Leizer Yudel asked his son, Rav Chaim Zev, to serve as the *mashgiach*, a position he held until an illness made it impossible for him to continue delivering *shmuessen*. His son in-law and successor as *mashghiach*, *yblcht"a*, Rav Aharon Chodosh, recalls that in Rav Leizer Yudel's days, the *hanhalah* generally would not expel a *bachur*; rather, they would tell him to go learn elsewhere for a year and then come back.

PERHAPS THE MOST ASTOUNDING STATISTIC REGARDING MIR Yerushalayim is its growth from the time Rav Nosson Tzvi enrolled as

**A Mini Mir** a 17-year-old in 5720/1960 until his *petirah* 52 years later. When Rav Nosson Tzvi arrived, there were fewer than 200 *talmidim* in the yeshiva; about 75 percent of them were married and only 25 percent were *bachurim*. The yeshiva Rav Nosson Tzvi left after his *petirah* numbered approximately 7,000 *talmidim* — some 35 times the size of the yeshiva he entered! And although the

---

12. Rav Moshe Meir Heizler.

seeds for that growth were planted by Rav Leizer Yudel and watered by Rav Chaim Shmuelevitz, Rav Chaim Zev Finkel, Rav Beinush Finkel, and Rav Nochum Partzovitz, the main growth of the yeshiva occurred under the leadership of a young man, who, unbeknownst to anyone, had already made a decision to rejoin the Mir — a decision that would change the face of the Torah world forevermore.

# CHAPTER FOURTEEN

# RAV NOSSON TZVI'S RETURN TO MIR

*"Everyone talks about how much Rav Leizer Yudel invested in Rav Nosson Tzvi, and how he guided him into becoming a rosh yeshiva. That's all true, as I can bear witness. But no one focuses on the flip side. Rav Leizer Yudel demanded a lot from everyone. He had ideas about how fast people should learn, when they should learn, how much they should review, and so on. Not everyone could handle his demands. Rav Nosson Tzvi was unique in his absolute hisbatlus (self-abnegation) to Rav Leizer Yudel. The Rosh Yeshiva instructed him **what** to learn, **how** to learn, **with whom** to learn, and **when** to learn — and Rav Nosson Tzvi followed every single directive faithfully."*

*— Rav Avraham Shmuelevitz, at Rav Nosson Tzvi's kever at the end of shivah*

**T**HE 17-YEAR-OLD NOSSON TZVI FINKEL RETURNED TO Mir, excited to engross himself in full-time learning. His entire extended family, especially Rav Leizer Yudel, was thrilled to have him back, and he often ate meals with his relatives.

Both *hanhalah* members and former *talmidim* who learned in Mir in those days remember Rav Leizer Yudel expressing and demonstrating tremendous belief in Nosson Tzvi, and demanding a lot from him because he was certain that Nosson Tzvi would become great.[1] Rav Leizer Yudel arranged for some of the foremost *talmidei chachamim* in the yeshiva to learn with Nosson Tzvi.

His morning *chavrusa* was Rav Yosef Stern,[2] who had learned with him when he came to Mir as a 14-year-old. Because Rav Yosef was one of the only English speakers in the Mir at the time, Rav Leizer Yudel asked him not only to learn with Nosson Tzvi, but also to oversee all areas of his spiritual growth. Rav Nosson Tzvi considered Rav Yosef a mentor for many years; even after he married he would still visit Rav Yosef on occasion to consult with him on various matters. Their *chavrusashaft* lasted for about four years.

In the afternoon Nosson

The young Nosson Tzvi Finkel returns to Mir.

---

1. Heard from Rav Aharon Chodosh and Rav Moshe Meir Heizler.
2. Currently *mashgiach* of Torah Ore, Rav Yosef Stern was one of Rav Leizer Yudel's closest and most trusted *talmidim*.

Rav Yosef Stern

Tzvi learned with Rav Yehoshua Korlansky, and at night he learned with Rav Chaim Kamiel, whom he would consider his *rebbi muvhak* (primary rebbi) until Rav Chaim passed away in 5765/2005. After Rav Chaim moved to Ofakim, in the south of Israel, he would return to Yerushalayim every so often, and during those visits he would learn with a group that included Rav Nosson Tzvi, Rav Aryeh Finkel, and Rav Elya Baruch Finkel. And even after he became Rosh Yeshiva, Rav Nosson Tzvi would travel to Ofakim to learn with Rav Chaim on many occasions – especially during *bein hazmanim*, but also on Thursday nights every so often.

Many of Rav Nosson Tzvi's practices, which he followed the rest of his life, were acquired from Rav Kamiel. For instance, Rav Chaim insisted that in order to grow in Torah, one must learn diligently even during *bein hazmanim*. Once, when Rav Nosson Tzvi was already ill, he came to learn with Rav Chaim during *bein hazmanim*, but he was too weak to get out of the car. His driver informed Rav Chaim that Rav Nosson Tzvi

Rav Nosson Tzvi with his *rebbi muvhak* and mentor, Rav Chaim Kamiel *zt"l*

was there. The driver found Rav Chaim in the *beis midrash*, in middle of a *bein hazmanim* learning program. With characteristic warmth, Rav Chaim took Rav Nosson Tzvi's driver by the hand and walked with him through the *beis midrash* until he found the person in charge of the learning program, and he apologized to him that he had to leave the *beis midrash* because Rav Nosson Tzvi was waiting for him. Although no one would have suspected that Rav Chaim Kamiel was "slacking off," he didn't want to diminish the seriousness of the program.

Following his rebbi's example, Rav Nosson Tzvi's *hasmadah* during *bein hazmanim* was not only as rigorous as during the rest of the year — he actually learned even *more* diligently then because there weren't as many interruptions. In fact, he spent many a *bein hazmanim* in Telz-Stone, disconnected entirely from the world, without as much as a telephone to disrupt his learning.

Rav Chaim Kamiel was also Rav Nosson Tzvi's primary mentor in life, and he treated Rav Nosson Tzvi like a son. Whenever Rav Chaim would visit the Rosh Yeshiva, he would first ask about Rav Nosson Tzvi's health, how the yeshiva was doing financially, whether Rav Nosson Tzvi was able to handle the burden of the yeshiva, and other questions that only a loving father would ask.

Another key figure in Rav Nosson Tzvi's life was Rav Chaim Brim *zt"l*, a great *tzaddik* and *gaon* who was known for his magnetic person-

Rav Nosson Tzvi greets Rav Chaim Brim at the wedding of one of his children

ality and love for every Yid. Rav Brim attracted many *talmidim* to the various *chaburos* and *vaadim* that he delivered for Mirrer *talmidim* in his home for many decades. But he always reserved an extra measure of love and respect for Rav Nosson Tzvi.[3]

## Chiddushim From Day One

IT IS UNCLEAR EXACTLY WHEN NOSSON TZVI BEGAN TO LEARN with the extraordinary *hasmadah* that would eventually transform him into Rav Nosson Tzvi, the Rosh Yeshiva of Mir. It is clear that like any profound and lasting change, the transformation occurred gradually, in stages, over time. Rabbi Harvey Well, his childhood friend from Chicago, recalls spending a lot of time with Nosson Tzvi during their first year in Eretz Yisrael. Although Nosson Tzvi was a serious student, arriving on time to every *seder*[4] and not leaving the *beis midrash* until *seder* was over, he would take some time during *bein hasedarim* (breaks between learning sessions) to take walks and schmooze with his friends. One Motza'ei Shabbos, for instance, Nosson Tzvi suggested to Harvey Well that they visit the Gerrer Rebbe, Rav Yisrael Alter (the "Beis Yisrael"). After receiving *berachos* from the Beis Yisrael, they visited the Sarna family of the Chevron Yeshiva; they were related to the Finkels through the Alter of Slabodka.

While the intense *hasmadah* and focus that characterized Rav Nosson Tzvi later did take time to develop, Rav Leizer Yudel did not allow him any leeway in creating *chiddushei Torah* (novellae). Rav Nosson Tzvi used to eat all three Shabbos meals together with Rav Refoel Shmuelevitz *shlita* (a grandson of Rav Leizer Yudel), who was then a *bachur*. The two would eat the Friday-night *seudah* and *seudah shlishis* at the home of Rav Leizer Yudel and the Shabbos-day *seudah* at the Shmuelevitz home. Rav Refoel was expected to say a *shtikel Torah* at the Friday-night *seudah*, and Rav Nosson Tzvi was expected to say a *shtikel Torah* at *seudah shlishis* — even after he first rejoined the Mir at the age of 17.

Some people doubted Rav Leizer Yudel's approach, thinking that it

---

3. See p. 306
4. A yeshiva day is generally divided into three learning sessions, or *sedarim* (plural of *seder*) – a morning *seder*, afternoon *seder*, and night *seder* (they are also referred to by number: first *seder*, second *seder*, third *seder* – although the latter is almost always referred to as night *seder*). The breaks between *sedarim* are called *bein hasedarim*. A typical day in Mir ran for a minimum of 10 hours – a 4-hour first *seder*, a 3½-hour second *seder* followed by half an hour of *mussar*, and a night *seder* that started at approximately 8:30 and would last as long as each individual *bachur* could muster.

Rav Nochum Partzovitz *zt"l* (L) and *yblcht"a* Rav Refoel Shmuelevitz (R) in a Torah discussion, as Rav Chaim Shmuelevitz (second from left) listens in. Second from right is Rav Gutfarb, an administrator in the yeshiva.

would be better to wait for Rav Nosson Tzvi to develop more *yedios* (breadth of Torah knowledge) before asking him to say *chiddushim*, but Rav Leizer Yudel apparently felt that requiring him to say *chiddushim* even at his stage of learning would teach him to develop the intellectual skills necessary to create more complex ones when he would gain more *yedios*.

Later, when Rav Refoel Shmuelevitz married, Rav Avraham, his younger brother, took his place at the Shabbos *seudos*, and Rav Nosson Tzvi then began to say his *shtikel Torah* on Friday night.

In the later years of his life, Rav Leizer Yudel suffered a heart attack. After being hospitalized for some time, he returned home. Despite his weak condition, he nevertheless sat at the *seudah* that night and asked to hear a *shtikel Torah* from Rav Nosson Tzvi. Rav Nosson Tzvi had prepared a particularly complex *chiddush*, in which he posed 36 questions on a *sugya* and suggested a single principle that could resolve all his questions. Rav Leizer Yudel managed to listen for some time, although he was too weak to listen to the entire *chiddush*.

Rav Chaim Shmuelevitz generally did not ask Rav Nosson Tzvi to repeat his *chiddushim* at the day meal, but that week he told Rav Nosson Tzvi that he wanted to hear the *shtikel Torah* that Rav Leizer Yudel had sat and listened to even though he had barely recovered from his heart attack. Rav Nosson Tzvi repeated it to Rav Chaim, who listened intently. Rav Nosson Tzvi would describe the ensuing interaction on many occasions in the years that followed:[5]

---

5. Rav Chaim Shmuelevitz's *yahrtzeit* during 5771 (Rav Nosson Tzvi's last full year) fell on a Friday, and Rav Nosson Tzvi's Friday *vaad* was a eulogy for Rav Chaim, whom he considered one

"When Rav Chaim would think in learning," Rav Nosson Tzvi recounted, "he would occasionally issue a deep, guttural sound from his throat. During that particular *seudah*, which lasted about half an hour, he did not say a word, but made that guttural noise three times. And then he *shlugged up* (refuted) my entire *shtikel Torah*!"

**The Transformation**

WHILE IT TOOK SOME TIME FOR RAV NOSSON TZVI TO DEVELOP his exceptional *hasmadah* and level of scholarship, other areas of his spiritual greatness were discernible even from his first days back in the Mir. Friends from those early days recall that his *tefillos* were extraordinary. He would sit and say each word of davening slowly and carefully, and he would never remove his *tefillin* until after *Aleinu*.[6]

By 5722/1962, two years after his return to Eretz Yisrael, a transformation had clearly taken place in him. Rav Moshe Meir Heizler, who went on to author several classic *sefarim* on the mitzvos of Eretz Yisrael, developed a close relationship with Rav Nosson Tzvi during the summer *zman* of that year. He remembers Rav Nosson Tzvi as being "a Rav Chaim Volozhiner *masmid*": Rav Chaim Volozhiner used to say that a *masmid* is someone who eats at the correct time, sleeps at the correct time, and learns at all other times.

Rav Heizler attended Rav Nochum Partzovitz's *shiur* in the Mir, and he was part of a *chaburah*[7] led by Rav Yosef Chaim Blau.[8] Rav Yosef Chaim would give *chaburah* each week, and his words would be followed by another *chaburah* delivered by one of the *bachurim* in the group on a rotating basis. Rav Leizer Yudel pressed Rav Nosson Tzvi to join that group, and he gave *chaburah* twice that *zman*. The yeshiva was learning *Bava Kamma* then, and Rav Leizer Yudel would proudly tell people, "*Nosson Tzvi hut azoi geshteigen, ehr hut gezugt chaburah oif Pi Parah* – Nosson Tzvi has advanced so much in his learning that he even said a *chaburah* on *Pi Parah* (a topic on *daf* 23a that few others discuss)."

---

of his role models. This story – which was clarified in an interview with R' Refoel Katz – was part of that *vaad*.

6. Rav Moshe Meir Heizler.

7. *Chaburah* literally means "a group." In yeshiva parlance, it is generally used to describe a group that gathers to deliver *chiddushei Torah* to one another. That group is called a *chaburah*, and the members are called the "*bnei hachaburah*." But a *chiddush* delivered at such a session is also called "a *chaburah*," presumably because it is delivered to the group, which can lead to some confusion when considering that one can "say a *chaburah* (i.e., a *chiddush*) to his *chaburah* (group)."

8. Currently Rav of Ashkelon.

Rav Leizer Yudel also encouraged him to become an active participant in other people's *chaburos*, asking him from time to time what the other members of the *chaburah* had said and asking him to analyze their *shtiklach Torah*.

Just as Rav Nosson Tzvi's high-school friends recall his gracious way of interacting with others, Rav Heizler remembers clearly how *eidel* (refined) Rav Nosson Tzvi was during those early years. The nature of *chaburos* is that there is a great deal of give and take. When a person delivers what he considers a proper *chiddush*, others will often argue – sometimes quite vehemently – that his approach is wrong. Not Rav Nosson Tzvi. Even if he disagreed with a person's thesis, Rav Nosson Tzvi would approach him only after the *chaburah,* so as not to embarrass him in front of the others. He would ask softly, "Can you please explain this section to me? I didn't understand it."

Only then would the person sense that Rav Nosson Tzvi had been harboring a question that refuted his entire *chaburah*.

MANY *GEDOLEI YISRAEL* ARE REPUTED TO HAVE BEEN BORN geniuses, and the heights they reached in Torah study are credited to

**Unabashed in Learning**
their unusual intellectual prowess. This was not the case with Rav Nosson Tzvi. Later in life, he did astound people with his incredible range of Torah knowledge[9] – but that knowledge came from hard work rather than genius. Those who knew him in his youth say that he was of above-average intelligence, but his success came primarily from his incredible *hasmadah* and drive to grow in learning.[10] This makes his success in Torah learning all the more inspiring, because if he could reach the level he did, then so can many, many others – if they would devote themselves to growth in Torah as he did. "Rav Nosson Tzvi was a big *maamin*," recalls Rav Heizler. "He believed strongly that learning was paramount, and that gave him the will to learn with incredible *hasmadah*."

But belief alone wouldn't have propelled Rav Nosson Tzvi to the level he managed to attain in those first few years at the Mir. The Mishnah states, "*Lo habayshan lameid* – one who is easily shamed cannot learn," Rav Nosson Tzvi proved that a person who is unabashed in his struggle to advance in learning can eventually become a superior

9. See pp. 241-244
10. His first rebbi, Rav Yosef Stern, whose words were echoed by several family members in *hespedim*.

*talmid chacham*. In his deep humility, for instance, he would approach Rav Heizler, whose brilliant *kitzur sefarim* (compendia of halachos) would later attest to his ability to organize Torah thoughts, and ask him to listen to his *shtiklach Torah* and help him organize them properly – never considering it beneath him to ask for help from others in learning.

Another factor in Rav Nosson Tzvi's growth is what seems to have been an inborn love for *chazarah* (review). During one of his first *zmanim* in the Mir, he learned the first half of *Bava Kamma* 13 times – twice with each of his three *chavrusas*, and another seven times himself! As we will see, the importance of *chazarah* would become not only his own trademark, but also a key message that he would impart to *talmidim* and other *bachurim* any time he discussed *gadlus* in Torah.

## First Rays of the Legendary Hasmadah

AS RAV NOSSON TZVI ADVANCED IN HIS LEARNING, RAV Leizer Yudel would take much pride in each of his accomplishments, and he would spare no praise when discussing him. "*Ich hub aza Nosson!*" he would tell people with excitement.[11]

During the summer *zman* of 5722/1962, the yeshiva learned *Bava Metzia*. Rav Chaim Shmuelevitz took ill during that *zman*, and there was concern that he had contracted a life-threatening disease. The *bachurim* decided to make a "*mishmar*" – to learn an entire Thursday night, except for a brief break to recite *Tehillim*, as a merit for Rav Chaim's recovery. [This was no easy task, because Rav Chaim lived in the yeshiva building, and the *bachurim* had to close the windows – during the summer, without air-conditioning – to ensure that he wouldn't hear them reciting *Tehillim* for him.] Moshe Meir Heizler and Nosson Tzvi Finkel learned together that night in what they thought would be a one-time *chavrusashaft*, but they ended up maintaining a marathon *seder* each Thursday night for close to a year: They would start learning at 9 p.m. and continue straight through the night until the *vasikin minyan*. They would then break for approximately two hours to daven and eat breakfast, and then resume learning until about noon on Friday – learning 13 out of 15 hours! They set a goal of learning between two-and-a-half and three *blatt* a week *b'iyun*, and they did not stop until they reached that goal.

---

11. Rav Avraham Shmuelevitz.

DURING THOSE LONG THURSDAY NIGHTS, ANOTHER ASPECT of Rav Nosson Tzvi's personality manifested itself in Mir.[12] There was

**A Generous Soul** one *bachur* who would have liked to be part of the group that studied through the night on Thursday nights, but he just wasn't capable of sitting for so long. Rav Nosson Tzvi would give him money each week and ask him to go to Brizel's Bakery on Rechov Meah Shearim – which was open all night on Thursdays to bake *challos* for Shabbos – and purchase the best pastries for the *bachurim* who were learning.

Another *chavrusa* from Rav Nosson Tzvi's first days in yeshiva, Rav Avraham,[13] began to study *Sefer Tehillim* with Rav Nosson Tzvi when the latter first arrived in yeshiva, at Rav Leizer Yudel's request. When they finished the *sefer*, Rav Nosson Tzvi asked if they could review the entire thing. They also learned *Reishis Chochmah*, an advanced *mussar sefer*. This *chavrusashaft* developed into a friendship that would last a lifetime.

Rav Avraham's family are Breslover Chassidim, and Rav Avraham would daven in the Breslover *beis midrash* on Rechov Meah Shearim during *Yamim Noraim*. Poverty was rampant in those days in Yerushalayim, and rarely could a family afford to buy new clothing for *Yom Tov*. One year, however, when Rav Avraham was close to *shidduch* age, his parents put together enough money to order a new *chalat* (long coat) for their son. Much to Rav Avraham's chagrin, while he was walking in the Breslover *beis midrash* on Rosh Hashanah, he suddenly heard the sound of cloth being torn. He looked down and saw that his new *chalat* had become caught on an iron stud protruding from a table, and there was now a large, L-shaped gash running through the front of it. Embarrassed to go home that way, he went to his married sister's home near the *beis midrash* and asked her to go to their parents' home and bring him his old *chalat*, which he wore for the rest of Rosh Hashanah.

On Tzom Gedaliah, he dejectedly told Rav Nosson Tzvi what had happened. "Your parents don't know about it yet?" Rav Nosson Tzvi asked.

"No," Rav Avraham replied.

"Come," Rav Nosson Tzvi beckoned. "We're going to the tailor who made your *chalat*."

When they reached the store, Rav Nosson Tzvi asked the tailor how

---

12. High-school friends recall incidents in which his generosity was apparent even earlier.
13. Family name withheld upon request.

soon he could make another *chalat* out of the same material. "Depends how much you are willing to pay!" he replied. He explained that he could finish it in one day – but the work would cost double the price of a regular *chalat*. Rav Nosson Tzvi instructed the tailor to make it on that same day, and Rav Avraham was able to wear it the next time he returned home – his mother none the wiser.

It took half a year before Rav Avraham worked up the nerve to tell his mother what had transpired. When she heard the story, she insisted that Rav Avraham bring Rav Nosson Tzvi home so she could thank him personally.

AN INCIDENT THAT TOOK PLACE A DECADE AFTER RAV NOSSON Tzvi arrived in Eretz Yisrael captures his mindset during his early days in the Mir.

**You Can!**

Rav Chaim Shmuelevitz began to deliver *mussar shmuessin* late in his life, during the years 5731-5733 (1971-1973). Each year after Shabbos *Parashas Vayeitzei*, he would give a *shmuess* in which he would quote the Midrash that deduces from the *pasuk* of *"Vayishkav bamakom hahu* – [Yaakov] slept in *that place"* (*Bereishis* 28:11) that it was only in *that place* that Yaakov slept, but he hadn't slept during the 14 preceding years in which he learned at the yeshiva of Shem and Ever. Rav Chaim would point out that Yaakov's first night of sleep was on a stone, which means that during his 14 years at Yeshivas Shem V'Ever, he hadn't slept even on a stone.

We assume that this must have been a miraculous phenomenon, Rav Chaim would say. After all, the Gemara (*Nedarim* 15a et al.) states that if someone swears that he won't sleep for three days, we give him *malkos* (lashes) immediately, because it's impossible to remain awake for so long.

Rav Chaim would then bang on the *shtender* and say, *"M'ken, m'ken* – you can, you can!" He would explain that just as a person experiences an adrenaline rush to save his or her child from a burning building, a person would be able to do things that are physically impossible if he would really push himself to the limit.

"Everyone would sit and listen to the *shmuess*," recalls Rav Yitzchak Berkowitz, "and we all understood that this was Rav Chaim Shmuelevitz speaking – and Rav Chaim could say such a thing because of who he was. And while we all knew that what he was saying was true, only one person took it to heart. I sat behind Rav Nosson Tzvi and watched him soak up every word.

*"M'ken."*

AS RAV NOSSON TZVI CONTINUED TO GROW IN HIS LEARNING, eventually developing a remarkable ability to be *mechadesh* (create

**Rav Leizer Yudel's Nachas**

novel expositions on *sugyos*), Rav Leizer Yudel's pride in him grew by leaps and bounds. He would express this pride to many people, but especially to R' Meir and Rebbetzin Sara Finkel, Nosson Tzvi's parents.

In a letter dated 21 Iyar, 5722, 2½ years after Rav Nosson Tzvi returned to Mir, Rav Leizer Yudel writes:

> *I see your son at his current level — a beloved, sweet bachur who, with siyata d'Shmaya, has attached himself to Torah study and is succeeding to the maximum capacity in the short time that he has been learning. He has already reached a wonderful level of understanding in his learning, and he is able to develop chiddushim with the proper reasoning … I see him "living his learning" and feeling the sweetness of Torah, which is causing him to become very diligent. His future, if he continues on this path, cannot be described in words. He will have a future that will be l'sheim ul'siferes — it will bring glory to himself and to you as well …*
>
> *To be honest, I myself would never have imagined when he first began to learn here that he would reach the level he has merited to attain. I never imagined any of it — not that he would learn with such hasmadah, not that he would enjoy his learning to this extent, and not that he would reach the heights he has attained in his learning at this point.*

A year and a half later, in Elul of 5723/1963, Rav Leizer Yudel wrote R' Meir and his wife a Rosh Hashanah greeting in which he describes Rav Nosson Tzvi's growth yet again:

> *You would have taken immeasurable pleasure had you heard the chiddushim that your son, my dear Nosson, said on a certain sugya. He sat in my house for a full hour and spoke about the sugya, delivering deep and wonderful chiddushim that gave me much pleasure …*

But perhaps most astounding is a letter dated a few months before this one. On 4 Nissan, 5723, Rav Leizer Yudel sent the Finkels a letter with Rav Nosson Tzvi when he returned home for Pesach. The brief note included a startling prediction:

*First of all, I bless you together with your precious son, my dear Nosson, upon his return to spend the Festival of Freedom with you. I feel that as I get to know your son, I am certain that the house fills with light on his arrival – the light of his refinement, the light of his Torah, of which he has been able to absorb, at his young age, far more than we could have imagined.*

*I tell visitors from chutz la'aretz that he is already a gadol baTorah, developing his own chiddushim – precious pearls – **and that he will end up serving as a Rosh Yeshiva** ...*

*I thank Hashem for His great chessed that He allowed me to bring [Nosson Tzvi] to this great level in Torah and in the Yirah, fear of Heaven, which precedes his wisdom. Between the two, he will keep rising from one level to the next, **and his place will be among the Gedolei Yisrael**, which will be your greatest glory ...*

Considering that less than three years after Rav Nosson Tzvi's arrival in Eretz Yisrael, his great-uncle Rav Leizer Yudel – who, aside from his own reputation as one of the Torah giants of his day, had studied under the greatest roshei yeshiva of prewar Europe – was already describing Rav Nosson Tzvi as a "*gadol baTorah*" and predicting that he would eventually be a Rosh Yeshiva, one can only imagine the amazing strides he had made in those three short years.

SOME PEOPLE WHO UNDERGO A TRANSFORMATION AND CLIMB to a loftier spiritual level lose their ability to interact patiently and kindly with others who are not so fortunate.

**Still the Same Person**

During the years of transformation specifically, a *bachur* might feel a need to distance himself from those who are weaker – perhaps out of fear that they might drag him down, or out of a need to prove that he is now "one of the better boys."

*Talmidim* of Mir in those years recall that Rav Nosson Tzvi didn't change in his stellar *bein adam la'chaveiro* in the least. When a *bachur* who wasn't so motivated to learn would come over to talk to him during lunch, he didn't try to brush the boy off. He would schmooze with the *bachur* and make him feel comfortable, despite his reputation as the *masmid* of Mir.[14]

Decades later, when Rav Nosson Tzvi would become a *maggid shiur*

---

14. Rav Moshe Meir Heizler.

ב"ה, ד' ניסן תשכ"ג, ירושלם ת"ו

כבוד
ידי"נ היקר הרב הג' , ב"א
מוהר"ר מאיר פינקל הי"ו
ורעיתך הכבודה והמהוללת עדינת הנפש
מרת שרה תחי'
שיקאגו

אחדש"ס ורב ברכה.

ראשית דברי הריני לברך אתכם יחד עם בנכם היקר
חביבי הרב נתן הי"ו בברוך הבא שבא להיות יחד אתכם בימי חג החרות
הכעל"מס, כפי הרגשתי ומה שאני מכיר ויודע את בנכם הלוא בבוא
הביתה נתמלא הבית אורה – באור אצילותו ובאור תורתו שהספיק כבר
עוד בהיותו צעיר לימים ושנים לספוג בו הרבה הרבה יותר ממה שיכולנו
לתאר לעצמנו מקודם, כזאת אני מפרסם ואומר לכל המבקרים אותי מחו"ל
וכזאת אני אומר לכם, כי הנה כבר גדול בתורה מחדש חדושים בעצמו
בפנינים יקרים ומיועד הוא להיות ולשמש כראש ישיבה בעזי"ה, ××××××××
××××××××××××××××××××××××××××××××××××××××××××××××××××××××××××××××
×××××××× אודה לד' על חסדו הגדול שהסיב ואת בידי להעמידו על
עליונותו התורנית ויראתו הקודמת למחכמתו ובשניהם יעלה מעלה מעלה
אשר מקומו תהא בין גדולי ישראל וזאת תהא לאשריכם הגדול והמפואר,
יהא רעוה שתזכו לראות ממנו ומבנכם אחיו הקטן שיחי' רב נחת וכל
הטוב בגו"ר בעשמיות וברוחניות אכי"ר, תבלו יחד מתוך חדוה ושמחה
את חג החרות בבריות גופא ורב נחת, והשמיענו על הטוב אשר אתכם
תמיד. כי יש לכם במה לשמוח ולהתענג את נפשיכם בהרגשת אשריכם הגדול.

אגב בזה אשתף גם אתכם בשמחתנו שרכשנו שני בנינים
להרחבת הישיבה, בנין אחד קנינו לפני כמה שבועות ובנין השני קנינו
בזו השבוע, שעלה לנו יותר ממאתים אלף לירות, ע"ז הזמין לנו ד'
נדיב לב שנותן תרמה בסך של כ–50 אלפים לירות ועל היתר לע"ע אין
תחת ידינו מאומה אבל נקוה כי 8 יזמן ד' לנו ע"י פעילותם ××××××××
והתעינותם של נאמני הישיבה אשר כ"א יצליח בדבר מה החשוב למטרה זו.

אסיים בברכתי הלבבית לקראת חג הפסח הבעל"מ לכם
ולבנכם היקר חביבי הרב נתן הי"ו ויקירכם אהובי מר גדליה שיחי'
תתברכו מגג כשר ושמח ויראו עיניכם בנפלאות ד' שידאנו כימי הוציאנו
ממצרים בישועתנו הנצחית בלאכול מן הזבחים ומן הפסחים בב"א.

בכל הכבוד הראוי ונבדכת התורה

ראש הישיבה

Rav Leizer Yudel's letter predicting that
Rav Nosson Tzvi would yet serve as a Rosh Yeshiva

Rav Nosson Tzvi as a beloved *bachur* in Mir, surrounded by Yerushalmi friends

and then a rosh yeshiva, people were drawn to him because they felt that he was totally "normal" – he had no airs about him, and everyone felt good around him. That wasn't anything new about Rav Nosson Tzvi. The soft-spoken, friendly Chicagoan never let his meteoric growth – going from a 17-year-old newcomer to one of the top prospects in Mir in a short few years – go to his head. No matter how distinguished he became, he never considered others unworthy of his respect and attention.

# CHAPTER FIFTEEN
# THE FINKEL HOME

*Many a child has marveled at Daf 77a in Bava Kamma, which contains just nine words of Gemara, a few Rashis, and a humongous Tosafos. One Shavuos night, Rav Leizer Yudel zt"l told Rav Nosson Tzvi to learn that Tosafos and come up with a chiddush by morning light. Rav Nosson Tzvi would later bemoan the fact that he never managed to commit that chiddush to paper — but the chiddush had made its mark. When he finished telling it to Rav Leizer Yudel, the latter said, "You are ready for a shidduch."*

**q**N THE SUMMER OF 1964, RAV NOSSON TZVI MARRIED Rebbetzin Leah, the daughter of Rav Beinush Finkel and granddaughter of Rav Leizer Yudel – who had hand-picked Rav Nosson Tzvi for his own granddaughter.[1]

After their wedding, Rav Nosson Tzvi and his wife moved into an apartment on the border of the Bucharim and Geulah neighborhoods. To this day, any *talmid* who learned in Mir during that era (from 1964 through 1997, when he moved into his home near the yeshiva) can immediately recall Rav Nosson Tzvi's address, Yisa Brachah 10. From that humble dwelling, the couple began their life of devotion to the three

Rav Nosson Tzvi at his vort, flanked by his father (R) and Rav Chaim Shmuelevitz (L)

1. See p. 58.

pillars that hold up the world: *Torah, Avodah,* and *Gemillus Chassadim* (*Avos* 1:2).

AFTER HIS TRANSITION FROM *BACHUR* TO *YUNGERMAN,* RAV Nosson Tzvi maintained the intense *hasmadah* he was known for before

**Torah in the Finkel Home**

his marriage.

Much later, as a Rosh Yeshiva, Rav Nosson Tzvi joined the first Friday-night *seudah* held for *bachurim* studying in the Beis Yeshayah building. On that occasion, he recounted that at the beginning of his marriage, his apartment wasn't connected to a generator for Shabbos, and he and the Rebbetzin didn't use the regu-

Rav Nosson Tzvi as a *yungerman*

lar electricity in their apartment.[2] Instead, he would learn by the light of a lamp called a *Lux,* which burned kerosene. The halachah is that one may not learn by such a lamp on Shabbos without a *shomer* (guard) ensuring that he doesn't try to increase the light by tilting the lamp so that more oil reaches the wick. Rav Nosson Tzvi told the *bachurim* that the Rebbetzin would stay up into the wee hours of the morning, acting as a *shomer* so that he could learn with the *Lux.*[3]

The Finkel children relate[4] that as they were growing up, days were divided into two parts – the part

---

2. There is a dispute among halachic authorities whether one may use electricity in Eretz Yisrael on Shabbos, because there is a chance that the electric company's Jewish employees are desecrating Shabbos in order to generate the electricity. The Chazon Ish, among other *gedolim,* ruled very stringently on this issue. To this day, the Mir runs on electricity from its own generators, which had to be upgraded every few years in order to handle the ever-increasing heating and air-conditioning needs of the various buildings and growing enrollment. The current generator, which is on the roof of the main building, powers all of the buildings on campus.

Since they followed the Chazon Ish's ruling, and at the time they did not have a generator in their neighborhood with which to power their electricity, Rav Nosson Tzvi and his wife wouldn't use electricity at all on Shabbos.

3. Rav Yosef Elefant.

4. Much of the family-related information in this chapter is based on interviews with Rav Nosson Tzvi's sons Rav Shaya and Rav Yosef Shmaryahu Finkel, and on *hespedim* delivered by several other sons and sons-in-law.

when Rav Nosson Tzvi was learning in yeshiva, and the part when he was learning at home. He wasn't an absentee father – the children recall his involvement in their upbringing, and especially the interest that he took in their learning – but his primary role in the house was as a role model of *hasmadah*.

Rav Nosson Tzvi would often say in his Friday *vaadim* that he never changed a diaper, and that he went to the *makolet* – which was located directly across the street from his original apartment on Rechov Yisa Brachah – only three times in the 30 years he lived there, one of which was to weigh the matzos to know how much would constitute a *kezayis*. The Rebbetzin took the entire burden of running the home upon herself so that he would be free to learn.

[In private conversation with *chassanim*, however, Rav Nosson Tzvi would point out that most women are not able to carry the burden of the home independently, and he would urge those close to him to help their wives as much as necessary. He nevertheless recounted his own experience in public, apparently to teach *talmidim* that when their wives *would* be able to free them to learn, they should take advantage of that time and use it for Torah study.]

Even with his *hasmadah*, Rav Nosson Tzvi's daughters related[5] that he was always a presence in the home, and from a mere facial expression of his they were able to tell when he was pleased with something and when he wasn't. And though he never made demands or delineated his expectations of his children, several of them relate that seeing him constantly sitting and learning at the table accomplished more than all the *shmuessin* about *hasmadah* could have achieved.

Torah would continue to be a constant in the home of Rav Nosson Tzvi and the Rebbetzin throughout their marriage. As one *chavrusa* put it, Rav Nosson Tzvi's home was an extension of the *beis midrash*, with the addition of a family in the background. Even during the Yisa Brachah years, when he had many boisterous young children running around his apartment, Rav Nosson Tzvi would learn with *chavrusas* in his home during the evening hours, keeping focused on his learning no matter what else was going on in the room.

When he moved to Rechov Ha'ameilim, across the street from the yeshiva, in 1997, he began to learn with his *chavrusas* and hold *vaadim* and *chaburos* in his home during all hours of the day and night. One *bachur* who was part of a *vaad* that studied *Ohr Yisrael* (the writings

---

5. As told to the wife of one of the Rosh Yeshiva's *chavrusas*.

of Rav Yisrael Salanter) with the Rosh Yeshiva in 2006 recalls that the wedding of one of Rav Nosson Tzvi's daughters coincided with a busy time for the yeshiva, which was preparing for the *chanukas habayis* of the Beis Yeshayah building. Their weekly *vaad* happened to be on the morning of the wedding, and they showed up at the Rosh Yeshiva's house fully expecting to hear that he was too preoccupied to have the *vaad* that day.

To their surprise, not only did the Rosh Yeshiva learn with them, but it seemed to them that he deliberately kept the *vaad* going for longer than it usually did, perhaps to show them that a person should not allow life circumstances to distract him from his learning.

IN YESHIVA, TOO, RAV NOSSON TZVI CONTINUED TO SERVE AS a model of *hasmadah*. Rav Binyamin Carlebach arrived in Eretz Yisrael as a *bachur* in 5725/1965, less than a year after Rav Nosson Tzvi's wedding. Though he wasn't learning in the Mir at the time, he would visit often because of the close connection his family had with the yeshiva and the Finkels, dating back to Europe. He remembers that there was one constant in the Mir: Rav Nosson Tzvi was always to be found in the *beis midrash*. Rav Chaim Mendel Brodsky,[6] who arrived during the 1970's, recalls that the sight of Rav Nosson Tzvi sitting and learning with *chavrusas* all day with phenomenal *hasmadah* was a lesson for everybody.

"He was always in the *beis midrash*." Rav Chaim Mendel Brodsky, Rosh Yeshiva of Yeshiva Gedolah Zichron Shmayahu, visits Rav Nosson Tzvi during a trip to Toronto.

6. From a *hesped* delivered in Toronto during the *shivah* for Rav Nosson Tzvi. Rabbi Brodsky is the Rosh Yeshiva of Yeshiva Gedolah Zichron Shmayahu in Toronto, Canada. A son-in-law of Rav Nochum Partzovitz, he gave *chaburah* in the Mir for several years in the 1980's before moving to Canada.

And one more thing was a constant with Rav Nosson Tzvi: his smile, and his love for every Jew. Rabbi Brodsky adds that even back then, Rav Nosson Tzvi was not a man of many words, but the words that he did say exuded warmth and love, and every word he uttered was meaningful, because it came from deep within his heart.

Rav Yitzchak Berkowitz[7] remembers Rav Nosson Tzvi's sweet disposition and the soft-spoken manner in which he greeted everyone. "There was no *shtick*. He was so *temimusdik* (wholesome). Everything was straightforward with him. If you had a question, he had a logical answer. And he wouldn't scream and yell to get his point across. He would tell it to you softly and calmly."

Rav Nosson Tzvi would also apportion hours of the day to help others advance in their learning.

Rav Tzvi Partzovitz[8] remembers how Rav Nosson Tzvi, who was already an accomplished *talmid chacham* and could easily have filled his day with top *chavrusas*, would regularly learn with newcomers to in-depth Torah study. He would split his time between these beginners, giving each one 45 minutes or an hour. He would call these *bachurim* his "*chavrusas*," when in reality he was teaching them how to learn.

Rav Asher Arielli[9] revealed that Rav Nosson Tzvi would also raise funds quietly and use the money to hire *yungeleit* to learn with specific *bachurim* who needed extra encouragement. These *bachurim* had no idea that their *chavrusas* were being paid; they thought that the *yungerman* Rav Nosson Tzvi paired them with had *chosen* to learn with them, and that gave them the confidence to advance in their learning.

But Rav Nosson Tzvi didn't limit himself to helping the *bachurim*

---

7. Rav Yitzchak Berkowitz is the Rav of Minyan Avreichim in Sanhedria Hamurchevet and Rosh Kollel of the Jerusalem Kollel, formerly Rosh Yeshiva of Aish HaTorah. Rav Berkowitz was a member of Rav Nosson Tzvi's first *chaburah* in the Mir, which began during the 1970's, and he maintained a relationship with him in the four decades that followed.

8. Rav Tzvi is a son of Rav Nochum *zt"l*. In the years following his father's *petirah*, he gave *shiur* in the Mir. He later became a *maggid shiur* in Ohr Yisrael in Petach Tikva, but when Rav Nosson Tzvi opened the yeshiva in Brachfeld, he tapped Rav Tzvi to become one of the roshei yeshiva there.

9. Rav Asher Arielli, who is also a son-in-law of Rav Nochum Partzovitz, delivers the largest daily *shiur* in the world, disseminating Torah to over 500 *talmidim* varying from *yungeleit* who have been in his *shiur* for over a decade to a large contingent of *chassidishe bachurim* who flock to Mir, a *Litvishe* yeshiva, in order to hear *shiur* from him. Known for his *hasmadah* and his deep humility, Rav Asher is one of the most respected and beloved figures in the yeshiva.

Recordings of Rav Asher's *shiurim* are available throughout the world, and many people from all walks of life who never sat in his *shiur* consider themselves *talmidim* of his because they have gained so much from listening to these recordings. He has also been the catalyst for many other *shiurim* in Mir – most of the *maggidei shiur* in Beis Yeshayah are *talmidim* of Rav Asher, as are several *roshei chaburah* in other *chaburos* in the yeshiva.

who needed assistance in their learning. As early as the 1970's, he would arrange *chavrusas* for many others. There were only about 300 *talmidim* in the yeshiva in those days, but Rav Nosson Tzvi made sure to get to know each one personally, so that he could pinpoint his strengths and find him the most appropriate *chavrusa*.[10]

ALREADY FROM HIS FIRST DAYS AS A *BACHUR* IN MIR, RAV Nosson Tzvi's *tefillos* stood out.[11] After his marriage and through the rest

**Avodah**
of his life, he continued to daven in Mir whenever he possibly could; perhaps the sole protracted period in which he did not daven in the yeshiva was when his *chavrusashaft* with his father-in-law, Rav Beinush, precluded it.

His devotion to *tefillah* went far beyond joining the yeshiva for davening. Watching him daven was the most profound *mussar shmuess* on how to stand before Hashem. His *tefillos* were *behishtapchus hanefesh*, pouring his soul out to his Creator.[12]

Even later in life, when Parkinson's disease made it more and more difficult for him to stand during *Shemoneh Esrei*, he would still force

At the *bris* of Rav Nosson Tzvi's son and successor, Rav Eleizer Yehuda *shlita*. (R-L) Rav Beinush, Rav Nosson Tzvi, a young Rav Avraham Shmuelevitz, and R' Eliyahu Meir Finkel

10. Rav Yitzchak Berkowitz at a *hesped*.
11. See p. 194.
12. Rav Ephraim Wachsman, at a *hesped* in Chicago.

himself to stand as much as he could. Somehow, as Rav Nosson Tzvi went, so went many others in yeshiva. Both *hanhalah* members and *talmidim* related that when they would see Rav Nosson Tzvi walking into yeshiva on his own, the *tefillos* in yeshiva would invariably be more intense, and when he was wheeled in devoid of energy, the rest of the yeshiva would be affected by it.[13]

But no matter how weak Rav Nosson Tzvi was, he always fell *kor'im* (prostrating himself) during the *chazzan's* repetition of *Mussaf* on Rosh Hashanah and Yom Kippur.[14]

Rav Nosson Tzvi loved analyzing the words of the *tefillos*. In the last year of his life, when a *talmid* asked him a question about the order of two *berachos* in *Shemoneh Esrei*, the Rosh Yeshiva became so excited that his face lit up, and he called over other people to repeat the question to them.[15]

## Gemillus Chassadim

THE COUNTLESS STORIES OF *CHESSED* THAT OCCURRED IN the Finkel home – first at Yisa Brachah 10 and then at Rechov Ha'ameilim 33 – would fill a book of their own. After Rav Nosson Tzvi's *petirah*, people from around the world revealed their personal stories of how they were helped by Rav Nosson Tzvi and his Rebbetzin.[16]

From the time of Rav Nosson Tzvi's marriage in 1964 through the ensuing decades, as he went from *Rosh Chaburah* in the 70's to *maggid shiur* in the 80's and then to Rosh Yeshiva from 1990 through 2012, one thing every *talmid* in Mir knew is that if you were in need of help, you went to Rav Nosson Tzvi Finkel. And if you didn't go to him, he would seek you out and take care of you anyway.

Legendary *hasmadah* notwithstanding, Rav Nosson Tzvi would drop everything and run if he knew that a *talmid* needed assistance.

In the late 1970's, one of the *bachurim* in Rav Nosson Tzvi's newly formed *iyun shiur* fainted suddenly with no apparent cause. Rav Nosson Tzvi insisted that the boy move into his home to recuperate until the doctors would determine what had caused him to faint.

---

13. Rav Yitzchak Ezrachi, at his *hesped* at the end of *shivah*, among others.

14. Rav Refoel Katz, who sat across from the Rosh Yeshiva in the *beis midrash* during *Yamim Noraim* and merited to help him throughout the davening, especially during *kor'im*. He recalls that Rav Nosson Tzvi would crane his neck while bent to the ground to watch Rav Aryeh Finkel fall *kor'im* and recite the words of the *Avodah*.

15. Heard from Eli Fogel, the *talmid* who asked the question.

16. Details of the stories in this section have been changed to protect the privacy of the protagonists.

Rav Nosson Tzvi, with his trademark smile, always ready to help a *talmid*

More than three decades later, this *bachur* – now a popular *mesivta maggid shiur* in America – still remembers how Rav Nosson Tzvi cared for him. "He accompanied me to one doctor, and later, when I went to another doctor alone and suddenly realized that I didn't have the money to pay for a test that the doctor wanted to administer, I called Rav Nosson Tzvi's house. He told me to wait at the doctor's office, and before long, he was there with the money."

The doctors never did determine why the boy had fainted, but Rav Nosson Tzvi kept the boy in his home for over a week until he felt certain that the *bachur* had recovered fully.

A while later, the boy's mother sent the Finkels a tablecloth as a token of her appreciation for their devotion to her son. The Rebbetzin insisted that the person who delivered the tablecloth take it back, refusing to accept a gift in exchange for the mitzvah.

And the open door remained open throughout the years. Less than a year before Rav Nosson Tzvi's passing, an American *bachur* underwent a surgery that he didn't want his parents to know about, out of fear that they would get nervous and insist that he come home in the middle of a *zman*. To be certain that his parents would not find out, the *bachur* didn't tell anyone in yeshiva that he was having the surgery.

One day, the *bachur* received a phone call from the Rebbetzin, who had somehow found out about the surgery, and wished to invite him to recover in her home. When he refused, she insisted that he let her know if there was anything she could do for him.

"SHIMSHON," ONE OF THE MEMBERS OF RAV NOSSON TZVI'S first *chaburah*, had a daughter who attended seminary in Eretz Yisrael in the 1990's, two decades after her father had learned in Mir. One day, around Chanukah time, Shimshon was on the phone with his daughter, and he suddenly realized that the other girls were having a negative influence on his daughter. The seminary was brand new, and apparently the staff had not been selective enough in their vetting process. Shimshon was concerned that a full year in bad company would have a lasting effect on his daughter, and having no relatives in Eretz Yisrael to turn to, he did what he would have done 20 years earlier as a *talmid* of the yeshiva: he called Rav Nosson Tzvi to ask him what to do.

"Get her out of the seminary, *now*," Rav Nosson Tzvi replied with uncharacteristic firmness.

"But Rebbi," Shimshon replied, "it's afternoon in Eretz Yisrael now. What am I going to do with her? Where am I going to send her tonight?"

"Send her here," Rav Nosson Tzvi replied. "She can stay here as long as she needs to."

Sure enough, the girl packed her bags and left the seminary that very day, moving in with the Finkels. The Rebbetzin tried valiantly to place her elsewhere, but all the seminaries that were appropriate for a girl of her academic level were already full. Ultimately, the girl went back to America in the middle of the year, and Rav Nosson Tzvi instructed her father to observe her carefully to ensure that there was no long-term damage from the girls she had been in seminary with. But for several weeks before she departed for America, she lived with the Finkels and was made to feel like part of the family.

ALREADY IN HIS FIRST YEARS AS A *ROSH CHABURAH,* RAV NOSSON Tzvi would invite *bachurim* to eat Shabbos meals with his family, at Yisa Brachah 10. His *talmidim* from those days recall how comfortable they always felt around his table.

**"Don't Bother Me Less"**

When the family moved to Rechov Ha'ameilim, it became rarer for *bachurim* to eat with them, because the Finkels felt that the deluge of guests at each *seudah* would be too much for their children to handle. Nevertheless, Rav Nosson Tzvi called together a group of *bachurim* and asked them to deliver a message to the rest of the yeshiva: "You are probably thinking," he said, "that I moved closer to yeshiva because I don't have energy anymore, and that you should now leave me alone. That's not true. I moved here so that you can feel free to come by even more than you used to."[17]

In his later years, he would often tell *talmidim* after they took their entrance exam, "Come by if you need something – and even when you

---

17. Rav Yosef Jacobs, in a *hesped*.

don't need anything!"

And with the warm atmosphere that pervaded the Finkel home built on these three great pillars of *Torah*, *Avodah*, and *Gemillus Chassadim*, many *talmidim* took his offer quite literally, making their way to his house whenever they found an opportunity to visit.

## CHAPTER SIXTEEN
# THE RAV BEINUSH YEARS

One of Rav Nosson Tzvi's legacies is the Daily
Daf program, in which yungeleit study a daf each day
with all of the Rishonim. Most people don't realize,
however, that Rav Nosson Tzvi wasn't the originator
of this approach; he carried on the program instituted
by his father-in-law, Rav Beinush Finkel. Even less
known is that until receiving the mandate from Rav
Beinush to lead the Daf chaburah, Rav Nosson Tzvi
did not enjoy learning fast; he preferred to learn with
more depth. Yet, just as he had done in the days of Rav
Leizer Yudel, Rav Nosson Tzvi completely abnegated
his own will and followed Rav Beinush's guidance — to
the extent that five years into the Daf program, he was
able to deliver daily shiurim on two blatt in different
masechtos aside from his regular iyun shiur!

Eventually, Rav Nosson Tzvi would become a great
proponent of the daily daf, and until his last day, he
urged as many yungeleit as he could to undertake the
rigorous study schedule established by Rav Beinush.

O NE OF THE MOST ENIGMATIC AND UNDERAPPRECI-
ated figures in the history of the yeshiva world was Rav
Nosson Tzvi's father-in-law, Rav Binyamin Beinush Finkel,
who succeeded Rav Leizer Yudel as Rosh Yeshiva of Mir. As Rav
Nosson Tzvi himself put it: "Everyone looked at him, yet no one saw
him; everyone knew him, yet no one understood him."[1]

Although Rav Nosson Tzvi's style of leadership mirrored his father-
in-law's in some ways, it was impossible to emulate many aspects of Rav
Beinush's conduct.

Born on Erev Yom Kippur 5672 (1911) in Mir, Rav Beinush (as he
would come to be known) spent his childhood years studying under

"Everyone looked
at him, yet no one
saw him; everyone
knew him, yet no one
understood him."
– Rav Nosson Tzvi (L)
encapsulates the life
of his father-in-law,
Rav Beinush Finkel. (C)

---

1. Unless otherwise indicated, these remembrances of Rav Beinush are culled from interviews
with his sons-in-law, Rav Binyamin Carlebach and Rav Aaron Lopiansky, and from a tribute to Rav
Beinush entitled "*A Gem Called Yashpeh*" (printed first in *The Jewish Observer* and then in *Torah
Luminaries* [ArtScroll Judaiscope Series]) written by Rav Lopiansky.

The Chazon Ish

his father, Rav Leizer Yudel. When he was approximately 20 years old, Rav Beinush went to study under the Chofetz Chaim in Radin, and he later studied under the Brisker Rav, Rav Yitzchak Zev Soloveitchik.

In 1941, shortly after Rav Leizer Yudel escaped Europe through the port of Odessa, Rav Beinush followed the same route to safety, arriving in Eretz Yisrael at around Purim of that year.

## The Chazon Ish's Choice

RAV BEINUSH MARRIED ESTHER, the daughter of Rav Shmuel Greineman, who, after serving as the secretary of the Mir in Europe, had moved to Eretz Yisrael with his family. Before World War II, Rav Shmuel traveled from Eretz Yisrael to the United States, and he was stranded there when the war broke out. He was hired as the *menahel ruchani* of Mesivta Tiferes Yerushalayim (MTJ), on the Lower East Side of Manhattan.

Since Esther Greineman's father was not in Eretz Yisrael, the task of filtering her *shidduchim* prospects fell into the capable hands of her uncle, the Chazon Ish.

When the Mirrer Yeshiva fled Europe and arrived in Kobe, Japan, a difficult halachic issue arose regarding the international dateline. This halachic battle had many ramifications, such as on which day to keep Shabbos. The most critical question, however, was when Yom Kippur should be observed. The Chazon Ish had ruled that it should be observed the day *after* it was kept in Eretz Yisrael, while most other authorities ruled that it should be observed the same day as in Eretz Yisrael. Since the largest group to be affected by this ruling was the Mirrer Yeshiva,[2] Rav Leizer Yudel was very active in trying to resolve the issue. At one point during the debate, Rav Beinush, who was still single, traveled to Bnei Brak to discuss the matter with the Chazon Ish.[3] The Chazon Ish

---

2. There were several other yeshivos that traveled along with them, including a remnant of Yeshivas Chachmei Lublin.
3. It is astounding that as such a young man, Rav Beinush could discuss so difficult a topic with the Chazon Ish, the undisputed Torah giant of his time:
   The dateline problem centered around the simple fact that daybreak does not occur simultane-

was so impressed with this young man that when Rav Beinush left, the Chazon Ish informed his niece that he had found the right boy for her.

EVEN IN HIS YOUTH, RAV BEINUSH WAS KNOWN TO BE EXTREMELY sharp-witted.

**The Brisker Rav's Smile**

During the *shivah* for Rav Beinush, Rav Dovid Soloveitchik related that when the Brisker Rav began delivering *shiur* in Eretz Yisrael, he stipulated that the *shiur* was only for his own sons and their *chavrusas*. On the first day of *shiur*, he locked the door to the room in which he was delivering *shiur*. The next day, he walked into the room and wanted to lock the door, but the key was not in the door. A minute later, Rav Beinush walked into the room holding a chair, which he placed next to the door. After sitting down, he pulled the key out of his pocket and locked the door. The Brisker Rav looked up and smiled, which was extremely out of character.

Rav Dovid also related that Rav Beinush once came to visit the Brisker Rav, and as soon as he arrived, the Rav handed him a packet of

---

ously at all points on the globe. Rather, day begins and ends later in the Western Hemisphere than in the Eastern Hemisphere, because the sun rises in the east before it does elsewhere. This means that when it is day in one place, it is night elsewhere, and when it is Sunday morning in points in the east, it is still Shabbos in points to the west.

Because the world is round, there is no one place that can be isolated as the first place where the sun rises. As far to the east as one can go, he will eventually be able to go farther, into territory that we consider the west. In order to make the calendar run smoothly, scientists created an imaginary line called the International Dateline, where the date officially changes. To avoid confusion, this line was placed in the middle of the Pacific Ocean, far from any land mass or civilization. This way, someone traveling over this point in the Pacific Ocean would have to change his calendar a full day ahead if he is traveling eastward, or a full day behind if he is traveling westward, but at least no two adjacent points inland are separated by a full day.

When the yeshiva students headed for Japan, a question arose: Where is the halachic dateline? From a geographic standpoint, Kobe is situated 100 degrees east of Jerusalem. Does Shabbos in Kobe therefore begin approximately six hours *before* it begins in Eretz Yisrael, or do we ignore the scientific dateline and have Shabbos begin approximately 18 hours *after* it begins in Eretz Yisrael? Or, in a practical sense, should the yeshiva students keep Shabbos on Japan's Saturday or on its Sunday?

The yeshiva ultimately ended up refraining from *melachah* on both days as a stringency, but following the opinion of the Chazon Ish, they davened the Shabbos *tefillos* on the day the Japanese considered Sunday.

*Hashgachah* arranged that for the most part, Yom Kippur did not end up being an issue, because the yeshiva was exiled from Kobe, Japan to Shanghai, China, before Yom Kippur of 1941. Shanghai does not have a dateline issue; all agree that Shabbos is observed on the local Saturday. There were a few students who were still in Kobe, however. Some followed the Chazon Ish's ruling and fasted only on Thursday, but others were stringent and fasted both days.

(For a full treatment and fascinating documentation of this debate, see *Hazricha B'Paasei Kedem*, *vol*. 2, Ch. 21.)

his notes, asking him to review them by 1:30 that day. They met at 1:30 and sat together for hours, as the Brisker Rav listened to Rav Beinush's critique of his *chiddushei Torah*.

True to form with Rav Beinush, although everyone knew that he was close to the Brisker Rav, no one knew until after Rav Beinush was *niftar* that the Rav respected him enough to ask him to critique his *chiddushim*.

RAV BEINUSH'S MOST MEMORABLE CHARACTERISTIC WAS HIS desire to hide his greatness from others. The Chazon Ish once remarked

### Hiding at the Mizrach Vant

that Rav Beinush was a *tzaddik nistar*,[4] and Rav Shlomo Wolbe said that Rav Beinush "managed to hide on the *mizrach vant* (the Eastern wall)."[5]

Rav Beinush would go to great lengths to prevent anyone from seeing him learning. Rav Nosson Tzvi, his first son-in-law, once awoke at 2:30 a.m. when he was staying at Rav Beinush's house. Noticing the light on in the dining room, he figured he would "catch" Rav Beinush learning. By the time he entered the dining room, however, Rav Beinush was in the kitchen, having left the *Hamodia* newspaper spread over the dining-room table. Upon further investigation, Rav Nosson Tzvi noticed that the newspaper wasn't lying evenly on the table. He lifted it up and saw that Rav Beinush had quickly pulled the newspaper over his Gemara before going into the kitchen so that he would not be apprehended.

One might think that Rav Beinush would have taken a different approach toward *talmidim*, from whom he would want to command respect, but he didn't.

My oldest brother, R' Moishe, who arrived in Mir in 1988, recalled his initial meeting with Rav Beinush, in which the latter's colorful persona was immediately revealed.

Rav Beinush lived on a tiny street, Rechov Slonim, that was extremely difficult to find – especially in the dark. My brother went with a group of friends to take a *farher* (exam) so that he could be admitted into the yeshiva. When they finally found Rav Beinush's home, they noticed that he had just received a delivery of groceries. The door was still slightly ajar from after the delivery, and the boys could see Rav Beinush sitting in his shirtsleeves learning out of a Gemara. When he heard them knock on the

---

4. Heard from Rav Nosson Tzvi's rebbi, Rav Yosef Stern *shlita*, at a *hesped*.
5. The *mizrach vant* is customarily designated for the leaders of a shul or yeshiva. Rav Wolbe meant that people saw Rav Beinush at the Eastern wall, but because he hid his greatness everyone thought he didn't belong there – and Rav Beinush considered that his ultimate success!

door, he quickly snapped the Gemara shut and pulled a *Hamodia* open in front of him – apparently unaware that he had been "caught" learning.

Rav Beinish used his wit to hide his greatness.

He called out for the boys to enter, figuring that their first impression would be of him reading a newspaper. "*Ah, ihr vilt arainkumen in yeshiva?*" he asked. "You want to enroll in yeshiva?"

When they answered in the affirmative, he rose to his feet, and with a twinkle in his eye he said, "*Koidem lu'mich veren a Rosh Yeshiva* – first allow me to become a Rosh Yeshiva."

He donned his frock ceremoniously, and then said, "*Ah, yetzt bin ich a Rosh Yeshiva* – now I'm a Rosh Yeshiva," and then proceeded to listen to their *shtiklach Torah*.

## Avoiding Honor

RAV BEINUSH'S WIT WAS LEGENDARY, ALTHOUGH HE USED IT primarily to conceal his greatness and to find ways to shy away from kavod (displays of honor). If a *talmid* would approach him the day after the *shiur* with a question, he would say, "You think I remember what I said yesterday?" If someone rushed up to him after the *shiur* to ask a question, Rav Beinush would quickly assess why the person was asking the question. If he determined that the person was seeking his own honor – i.e., he wanted to be seen talking to Rav Beinush in learning or be able to brag afterward that he had spoken to the Rosh Yeshiva – he would find a way to put an immediate end to the conversation. "And no one could fool him," recalls Rav Binyamin Carlebach. "He was too sharp."

Some of the approximately 1,200 *talmidim* who were enrolled in Mir at the time of Rav Beinush's *petirah* didn't even know who he was – even though he was their Rosh Yeshiva! Because of the cryptic style of his *shiur*, many of the students would leave the *beis midrash* before he arrived. Legend has it that once, when he was on his way up the steps to the *beis midrash* to deliver a *shiur klali*, he passed a group of *talmidim* running down. "*Loift shnell*," he urged them, "*Rav Beinush kumt!*" (Run away fast, Rav Beinush is coming!).

In general, he took great glee in avoiding any display of honor aimed at him.

Once, Rav Beinush showed up very late to a family *sheva berachos* held in the Shmuelevitz apartment in the Mir building. Everyone was already seated, and Rav Beinush's sister, Rebbetzin Shmuelevitz, was distraught because she didn't have a spot for him at the head table – or at any table. A family member quickly brought in a little table and set it up perpendicular to the main table, but because it jutted into a doorway, Rav Beinush was sitting halfway into the adjacent room and was barely visible. The *sheva berachos* continued, and when it came time for *Bircas HaMazon*, the hosts wanted to honor Rav Beinush to lead the *zimun*. "But I'm not ready to *bentch*," he protested.

"So we'll wait for you," his sister replied.

"But I haven't even washed yet!" he said with a smile.

Only later did it dawn on those present that Rav Beinush had deliberately come late and waited to wash so that they wouldn't be able to seat him at the head table or accord him any honor.


RAV BEINUSH USED TO DAVEN ON FRIDAY NIGHT IN THE MEAH Shearim *shtieblach*.[6] The *gabbai* would announce that they wouldn't begin davening until the Mirrer Rosh Yeshiva would enter, but Rav Beinush refused to enter until they would recite *Borchu*, when everyone was already standing, because he didn't everyone to rise in his honor.

Stories also abound of how Rav Beinush would prevent people from opening doors for him. If he saw someone running to grab the door, he would rush to get there first. If the other person managed to open it, he would close it and reopen it.

Once, a *talmid* thought he might get the better of Rav Beinush, telling him that he wanted to open the car door for him to fulfill the mitzvah of *shimush talmidei chachamim*. "It's a mitzvah?" Rav Beinush wondered aloud.

"Sure," the *talmid* replied.

"In that case," Rav Beinush retorted while opening the car door, "I want the mitzvah too."

No one in his family was allowed to do anything for him, either. Once, after he had undergone an emergency surgery, his sons-in-law

---

6. Though no one knew it at the time, the reason Rav Beinush avoided davening in the yeshiva on Friday night was because the yeshiva's electricity was not yet on a generator, and he didn't want to derive benefit from the electric company's power (see p. 206, fn. 2).

wanted to help him get off of his hospital bed. *"Maybe* I'll allow you to hold the bed so it shouldn't roll," he said with a smile.

Rav Binyamin Carlebach remembers only one instance in which Rav Beinush departed from his usual approach of not allowing anyone to do anything for him. Once, when they were in America together, Rav Beinush allowed Rav Binyamin to do something for him that he normally only allowed the Rebbetzin to do. "I was trying to figure out afterward why he allowed me to help him," explains Rav Carlebach, "and I realized that that was his way of showing his appreciation for something I had done for the yeshiva."

IF RAV BEINUSH WAS PARTICULAR ABOUT NOT RECEIVING honor, he was even more insistent about not accepting money, favors,

**Never Taking From Anyone**
or gifts from anyone – including his own parents. Family members relate that he calculated how much Rav Leizer Yudel had spent on his *chasunah*, and repaid him in full.

After his wedding, Rav Beinush settled in Bnei Brak. Both his parents and his in-laws wanted to support him, but Rav Beinush told each one that the other was supporting him. Someone once asked the Chazon Ish, with whom Rav Beinush maintained an extremely close relationship until the former's *petirah* in Cheshvan of 5714/1953, how Rav Beinush survived. "Each time I ask him," the Chazon Ish lamented, "he just cracks a joke to change the subject."

It seems that Rav Beinush actually supported himself by renting out his own apartment and moving into a shack on the premises of an ice factory. The owners of the factory provided this shack to him free of charge because it obviated the need for a night watchman, and he used the rent he received from his tenants to pay for all of his living expenses.

Shortly after his *chasunah*, Rav Beinush began to travel in from Bnei Brak to deliver *shiurim* in Yeshiva Beis Baruch in Yerushalayim.[7] When Rav Leizer Yudel reestablished the Mir Yeshiva in 5704/1944, he prevailed upon Rav Beinush to begin delivering *shiur klali* in Mir every week. He insisted that Rav Beinush accept a salary for delivering these *shiurim*, but he later told a family member that each month, when he would review the yeshiva's budget, he would find that the money paid to Rav Beinush had somehow made it back into the yeshiva's account.

---

7. *Oros Mi'Mir.*

This continued for over 20 years, until Rav Leizer Yudel was *niftar*.

During those years, Rav Beinush traveled to America several times on behalf of the yeshiva. Rav Leizer Yudel would pay for his tickets from yeshiva funds, but he would ultimately find that the exact ticket price had mysteriously been "refunded" to the yeshiva.

Upon returning from his third trip to America, Rav Beinush sighed with relief when relating to his wife that he had managed to cover his own travel expenses yet again – not taking a dime from the yeshiva for any of the three trips. He was crafty in his efforts to repay the funds to the yeshiva, but wasn't always successful in getting it by Rav Leizer Yudel. Once, upon returning to Eretz Yisrael, he handed Rav Leizer Yudel $1,000, explaining that someone had donated it to the yeshiva. Rav Leizer Yudel realized that his son was returning the amount he had been given for the expenses of the trip. Rav Leizer Yudel said, "*Ich veis shoin dein shtick* (I know your tricks)."

Even when Rav Leizer Yudel was *niftar* and Rav Beinush became Rosh Yeshiva of Mir, he refused to take a salary from the yeshiva. He managed to support himself in other ways, though no one knew what sort of business interests he had. Before he passed away, he left his wife instructions regarding bank accounts that no one knew existed, accounts that held the remaining profits of his secret business ventures.

In Rav Beinush's dealings with his *mechutanim* when his daughters got engaged, he evaded the subject of how much money each side would give. Each time they would raise the issue, he would change the topic immediately. At the end of one such conversation, he dismissed the question the other side had tried to raise tactfully several times by saying, "*Zorgt zach nit, eiyer zun vet zein tzufriden* – Don't worry, your son will be happy."

ALTHOUGH IT WAS IMPOSSIBLE TO RUN THE YESHIVA WITH-out fundraising, in a certain way, Rav Beinush's refusal to take from

**"Give Him the Money"** others extended even to financing the yeshiva.

One year, when a few philanthropists came to Eretz Yisrael for Succos, Rav Beinush begged Rav Binyamin Carlebach not to bring them to him. And when one of the philanthropists did come to his *succah* and withdrew a wad of bills from his pocket, Rav Beinush pointed to Rav Carlebach and said, "*Git es tzu em; s'hut nisht tzu tun mit mir* – Give it to him; it has nothing to do with me."

Rav Carlebach explains that Rav Beinush wanted philanthropists to realize that they weren't doing *him* a favor. If they wanted to take part in supporting Torah, they would receive eternal merit – but it was for their sake, not for his.

Rav Beinush on Succos:
"Don't bring the philanthropists to me."

Fundraising together with Rav Beinush was difficult, to say the least. The *hanhalah* chose the guest of honor for the Mir's first dinner without asking him beforehand how much he would donate to the yeshiva. After the dinner, a son of the guest of honor mentioned to Rav Binyamin Carlebach that a personal visit from Rav Beinush would mean a lot to his father, and he would be likely to give a larger donation.

When Rav Beinush heard that they wanted him to visit the guest of honor, he was aghast. *"Vi azoi ken ich gein? Ehr vet meinen az ich mein gelt* – how can I go? He'll think I'm visiting him only to get his money!"

Two days after that dinner, there was a parlor meeting in Chicago for the Mir. Rav Beinush agreed to come along, but only on one condition: that as soon as the subject turned to money, he would leave the room. And that's exactly what he did. When he sensed that people were about to discuss contributing to the yeshiva, he went upstairs to sleep.

In typical Rav Beinush style, he kept the particulars of the yeshiva's finances to himself. No one could know whether he would be able to pay the *kollel* salaries at the end of the month effortlessly, or whether he had a serious shortfall. Somehow, though, he always paid on time.

The other Roshei Yeshiva – Rav Chaim Shmuelevitz and Rav Nochum Partzovitz – were extremely grateful to Rav Beinush for taking sole responsibility for the yeshiva's budget, freeing them to focus on their learning. For his part, however, Rav Beinush would fade into the shadows when it came to learning, insisting that people approach Rav Chaim and Rav Nochum with matters related to learning. After delivering a *shiur klali* in yeshiva, for instance, he would quickly move away from the podium, and would rarely answer questions that people posed on his *shiur klali*, instructing them to pose their difficulties on a *sugya* to Rav Chaim or Rav Nochum

And yet Rav Nochum – who was considered one of the greatest *lamdanim* in the world at the time – truly valued Rav Beinush's Torah. He would make sure to be at his *shiur klali*, where he would sit and listen with his full attention, as a *talmid* before his rebbi.

Rav Nosson Tzvi's respect for Rav Beinush's Torah went far beyond the usual rebbi-*talmid* relationship. Rav Binyamin Carlebach relates that at one point, Rav Beinush agreed to learn with his four oldest sons-in-law (Rav Aaron Lopiansky had not yet married into the family) each morning. Rav Nosson Tzvi, Rav Binyamin Carlebach, Rav Nachman Levovitz, and Rav Yisroel Glustein would all daven *Shacharis* at *neitz* (sunrise) each day, and they would begin to learn at 7 a.m. Rebbetzin Esther would bring coffee, tea, and cookies, and the men would gather around the dining-room table to learn.

Rav Binyamin recalls that he would arrive at first *seder* at 9 o'clock each morning completely exhausted, because he would often challenge Rav Beinush's approach to a *sugya*, and he would then have to argue it out with Rav Nosson Tzvi, who invariably defended Rav Beinush's approach.

### Rav Nosson Tzvi's Inheritance

THE MOST DIRECT INHERITANCE FROM RAV BEINUSH TO RAV Nosson Tzvi was the Daily Daf program.

For many years after Rav Beinush accepted the mantle of leadership upon his father's passing, he bemoaned the fact that people were learning too slowly in yeshiva, and that they couldn't grow into true *talmidei chachamim* by learning at such a pace. In the winter of 5742/1982, when the yeshiva was learning *Bava Basra*, he decided to take action. A few days into the *zman*, he announced that he was starting a new learning program: a daily *daf* with all of the *Rishonim*. After 30 years of fading into the woodwork and delivering only his *shiur klali*, he suddenly began to deliver a *blatt shiur* each day from 2:00 to 3:15.

When people complained that there was no *meshichah* (draw) toward learning a *daf* each day, Rav Beinush said, "Well, if I can't be *koneh* (acquire) them with *meshichah*, I'll be *koneh* them with *kesef* (money),"[8] and he began to offer an additional stipend each month to

---

8. This is a play on words based on the ways a person can acquire an object, as per the Mishnayos

those who would learn the *daf*.

Shortly after Purim of that *zman*, he made a *siyum* on *Maseches Bava Basra*, having read every single Gemara with *Rashbam* and having said a *shtikel Torah* at each *shiur*![9]

The next *zman*, in which the yeshiva learned *Gittin*, Rav Beinush handed the *blatt shiur* over to Rav Nosson Tzvi, who continued to lead the *Daf shiur* until Rav Beinush passed away and he became Rosh Yeshiva. Five years after they started this learning program, the *Daf chaburah* finished the yeshiva's cycle.[10] The naysayers were quelled: a group of *yungeleit*, led by the indefatigable Rav Nosson Tzvi, had now mastered eleven *masechtos* from cover to cover.

The core group that had participated in this program wanted to learn other *masechtos* that were not in the yeshiva cycle, and Rav Nosson Tzvi agreed to give *shiur* on an additional *masechta*. The group chose to learn *Beitzah* first. At the same time, Rav Nosson Tzvi continued to lead those who had joined in the middle of the previous cycle and had some yeshiva *masechtos* to complete. And he had already started to deliver a regular *iyun* (in-depth) *shiur* to *bachurim* learning the yeshiva *masechta* at a much slower pace.

Consequently, Rav Nosson Tzvi would deliver three *shiurim* each day: an *iyun shiur* in *Gittin*, the daily *daf* in *Gittin*, and a daily *daf* in *Beitzah*!

While others would spend a full day sweating over a single *sugya* in order to come up with a daily *shiur*, Rav Nosson Tzvi would sit and listen to his *chavrusas* read all of the *Rishonim* on three different *sugyos*, and then come up with an approach to each of the three.

After two *zmanim* of delivering three daily *shiurim*, he asked his brother-in-law Rav Binyamin Carlebach to deliver the *shiur* on the additional *masechta*, while he carried on with his regular *iyun shiur* and the daily *daf* in the yeshiva *masechta* until the *petirah* of Rav Beinush.

---

in the first *perek* of *Kiddushin*. Large items are acquired with *meshichah*, by pulling them, and other items are acquired as soon as the money (*kesef*) paid for them changes hands.

9. One would have imagined that it would be difficult enough to just explain the basic concepts of each *blatt* in such a limited time frame, but Rav Beinush wouldn't suffice with that; he would deliver a complex, novel approach to at least one portion of the *daf*.

10. Most yeshivos in the world have a specific cycle in which they study *masechtos*. In the Mir, the winter *masechtos* are *Bava Kamma*, *Bava Metzia*, *Bava Basra*, *Yevamos*, and *Kesubos*. The summer *masechtos* are *Kiddushin*, *Gittin*, *Pesachim*, *Succah* (until Tishah B'Av), and *Makkos* (in Elul), and *Nedarim*. When a person finishes the cycle, he has the option of reviewing it or moving on to additional *masechtos* or sections of Torah, such as halachah, that he has yet to study.

ANOTHER ASPECT OF RAV BEINUSH'S PERSONALITY THAT HAS filtered down to his descendants is his love for the regular Yid on the street, and especially for the downtrodden.

**Pity for the Downtrodden**

When Rav Beinush passed away, many beggars and simple laborers showed up at the *shivah*. Several of them asked to see a picture of Rav Beinush, because they had heard that the gentleman who would always share a joke or a kind word with them was the same man they read about on the placards announcing the *petirah* of the Mirrer Rosh Yeshiva, but they couldn't believe that it was true!

Rav Beinush would daven at the *neitz minyan* at the Kosel each morning.[11] One woman who sat and collected charity every morning was particularly distraught when she showed up toward the end of the *shivah*, explaining that she hadn't known that her daily benefactor – both in terms of the money he gave her and the kind words that carried her through the day – was the Mirrer Rosh Yeshiva. Only after he hadn't

Many of those Rav Beinush gladdened each day en route to the *neitz minyan* at the Kosel didn't know that he was the Mirrer Rosh Yeshiva.

appeared for a few days did she ask someone what had happened to him. When she was told that the tall man with the white beard was none other than Rav Beinush, she ran to the Finkel home to tearfully share her story.

Rav Beinush's Rebbetzin, Rebbetzin Esther Finkel, was a *chessed* powerhouse as well, serving as the first medical referral specialist in Israel. She knew every top doctor in the country, and could arrange appointments with even the busiest practitioners at the drop of a hat. Rav Beinush encouraged her in her efforts, insisting that she answer phones on Shabbos

11. For many years, Rav Beinush walked to the Kosel, but in his later years, R' Meyer Birnbaum ("Lieutenant Birnbaum") would pick him up and drive him there.

because it would usually be someone with a *pikuach nefesh* (life-threatening) issue, for which we are obligated to desecrate Shabbos.

RAV BEINUSH FELL ILL IN THE BEGINNING OF THE WINTER OF 5750/1990. He refused to have a surgery that might have saved his life,

**Passing the Torch**

out of fear that some people would think that he used yeshiva funds to pay for it. Though his illness caused him terrible pain, he showed no sign of the agony he was in until his last days, when he lost consciousness. Only when he slipped into a state of delirium would his face distort in pain.

Several days before Rav Beinush's *petirah*, he summoned the family and requested that they change the yeshiva's legal documents, signing control over to Rav Nosson Tzvi. Rav Nosson Tzvi understood that this was, in essence, an implicit sign that Rav Beinush was appointing him the next Rosh Yeshiva, and in his deep humility, he asked that he not be the only one in control. Rav Beinush refused to hear of adding anyone else to the documents, however.

On 18 Shevat, 5750/1990, a nurse sensed a change in Rav Beinush's breathing. A *minyan* was summoned, and as they recited *Krias Shema*, they saw Rav Beinush's lips moving. The *minyan* moved onto *Kabbalas Malchus Shamayim*,[12] and as they recited the seventh *Hashem Hu HaElokim*, Rav Beinush took his last breath and closed his eyes.

---

12. The "acceptance of the yoke of Heaven," which we recite at the conclusion of *Ne'ilah* on Yom Kippur.

Rav Shach delivers a hesped at Rav Beinush's levayah, as Rav Nosson Tzvi is at right

Rav Nosson Tzvi at the grave of Rav Beinush *zt"l*

Little could anyone know then that Rav Nosson Tzvi, who was already afflicted with Parkinson's disease and did not seem, at first, to possess the leadership skills necessary to maintain the yeshiva, would spend the next two decades nurturing tens of thousands of Mirrer *talmidim* and transforming the Mir into the largest Torah institution since the times of the Talmud.

# SECTION THREE
# ENDURING LEGACY

אִמְרוּ צַדִּיק כִּי טוֹב כִּי פְרִי מַעַלְלֵיהֶם יֹאכֵלוּ

*Tell the righteous man that [he has done] good; for they
shall eat the fruit of their deeds* (Yeshaya 3:10)

# CHAPTER SEVENTEEN
## FOR LOVE OF TORAH

---

*Rav Nosson Tzvi was often visited by 13-year-old boys who came to receive a berachah upon the occasion of their becoming bar mitzvah. These boys expected the Rosh Yeshiva to wish them "mazal tov" and perhaps bless them that they should grow up to become a talmid chacham and a yerei Shamayim.*

*But along with these wishes, Rav Nosson Tzvi had an additional message to impart to bar mitzvah boys — a message that emanated from his own love of Torah. He would take the boy's hand in his, and looking into the boy's eyes, he would ask tenderly, "Do you know that the Torah is zees (sweet)?"*

---

AV ASHER ARIELLI'S *HESPED* ON RAV NOSSON Tzvi, delivered a day after the *levayah*, focused on the Rosh Yeshiva's favorite *pasuk*: "*Ma ahavti sorasecha, kol hayom hi sichasi* – How I love Your Torah! All day long it is my conversation" (*Tehillim* 119:91).[1]

This *pasuk*, explained Rav Asher, describes a cycle that was embodied in Rav Nosson Tzvi: If someone loves the Torah, he makes it his conversation all day. And the more one makes the Torah his conversation, the more love he develops for it.

Rav Nosson Tzvi's love of Torah also had another direct outcome: Because he loved to learn Torah so much, he wanted to build Torah, and to enable others to learn. His singular ability to fuse personal *hasmadah* with building Torah was one of the most remarkable aspects of his greatness. In the history of the yeshiva world, how many *masmidim* of Rav

The *Aron Kodesh* in Beis Shalom carries the Rosh Yeshiva's favorite *pasuk:* "If I could, I would emblazon '*Mah ahavti* …' on every *Aron Kodesh* in Mir."

---

1. These words were so beloved to Rav Nosson Tzvi that he once remarked that he would love to emblazon this *pasuk* on every *Aron Kodesh* in the Mir Yeshiva.

Nosson Tzvi's caliber have devoted themselves to enabling thousands of others to learn while still maintaining their own rigorous daily learning schedules? And among those who crisscross the world to garner support for Torah, how many are capable of learning Torah for 12 hours a day or more in all situations?

In Rav Nosson Tzvi's case, one wasn't a contradiction to the other. When the reins of Mir Yerushalayim were thrust into his hands after the *petirah* of Rav Beinush, he accepted the immense fundraising burden of the yeshiva upon his already fragile shoulders – but he remained a *masmid* for the rest of his life, even as he built a Torah empire.


AT SOME POINT AFTER RAV NOSSON TZVI'S WEDDING, RAV Leizer Yudel told him that in order to continue his trajectory toward

**Twelve Hours** becoming a great *gadol baTorah*, he should join a small *chaburah* of *yungeleit* in the Mir who were learning 12 hours every day. As with every other directive he received from Rav Leizer Yudel, Rav Nosson Tzvi followed this prescription faithfully.

Later in life he would recount that in order to complete his 12-hour quota each day, he needed a *chavrusa* to accompany him on his walk to and from yeshiva and review material with him by heart.

It's unclear for how long a period Rav Leizer Yudel wanted Rav Nosson Tzvi to keep to this grueling schedule. It is clear, however, that Rav Nosson Tzvi kept to it for many, many years, and that in essence, he never made a conscious decision that he was no longer aiming to learn 12 hours a day.

My rebbi, Rav Chaim Kitevits of Yeshiva U'Mesivta Rabbeinu Chaim Berlin, related that approximately 5 years before Rav Nosson Tzvi passed away, he told Rav Chaim about Rav Leizer Yudel's 12-hour program. When Rav Chaim asked him whether he still kept to it, Rav Nosson Tzvi replied, "I try."

While family members have a hard time determining how this was possible, considering the hours he set aside for his thousands of *talmidim* and for handling the financial burden of the yeshiva, one thing everyone who entered his house did know: Every moment Rav Nosson Tzvi could possibly learn, he did.

Rav Menachem Zaretsky, Rav Nosson Tzvi's close confidant, related that when he would escort him back home after a *shiur klali* and remove the Rosh Yeshiva's frock, it would be so drenched with perspiration from the exertion of delivering the *shiur* that Rav Menachem would have to hang it up to dry. Drained as he was, however, the Rosh Yeshiva never went to rest. As soon as he had a bite for lunch, he would head straight back to his table to learn.

Rav Menachem would remain in Rav Nosson Tzvi's home until he retired for the night. He doesn't recall a single time when he went to sleep before he reached the point of utter exhaustion and simply couldn't learn any longer.

At times when the Rosh Yeshiva's schedule was less demanding – such as during *bein hazmanim* – and he was able to

Using every available moment to learn – even while waiting for a *seudah* to begin

free himself from his public duties to some extent, he would spend all of his time learning. At those times, he may even have exceeded Rav Leizer Yudel's 12-hour-a-day learning quota.

RAV ASHER ARIELLI, A LEGENDARY *MASMID* IN HIS OWN RIGHT, recalled that Rav Nosson Tzvi learned at times that "no one else consid-

## When No One Else Had Time

ered a time to learn." Rav Zundel Stern, a neighbor from Rechov Yisa Brachah, related that on Erev Pesach, when everyone else was busy burning their *chametz*, Rav Nosson Tzvi was already walking to yeshiva, Gemara in hand.

Throughout his life, Rav Nosson Tzvi stressed the importance of learning not only during the "full days" in yeshiva, but also on Friday and Shabbos.[2] His son and successor, Rav Eliezer Yehuda *shlita*, recounted[3] that Rav Nosson Tzvi would learn 17 hours over Friday and Shabbos! *Bein Hazmanim*, too, was devoted to uninterrupted learning

---

2. See p. 260.
3. At a *hesped* delivered at the end of *shivah*.

"I remember how Abba would learn 17 hours between Friday and Shabbos."
Rav Nosson Tzvi with his son and successor,
Rav Eliezer Yehuda *shlita*, writing letters in a new Sefer Torah.

– that was the Rosh Yeshiva's idea of vacationing.[4] And a son-in-law,
R' Aharon Kessler, recalled that at times when no one else had energy
to learn – such as on Motza'ei Yom Kippur or Tishah B'Av – the Rosh
Yeshiva would return immediately to his Gemara.

IN CODIFYING THE OBLIGATION TO STUDY TORAH, THE
Rambam (*Hilchos Talmud Torah* 3:4) famously writes, "If one has two
obligations before him – doing a mitzvah, and

**"… And Then
Return to His
Learning"**
studying Torah – if the mitzvah can be done by
others, he should not stop learning [to do it]. If it
can't be done by others, he should do the mitzvah
*and then return to his learning."*

Rav Nosson Tzvi adhered to this Rambam faithfully every second
of his adult life. Even before he became Rosh Yeshiva, he often paused
from his learning to take care of a *talmid* in need.[5] After he became Rosh
Yeshiva, many other obligations fell on him, such as fundraising for the
yeshiva and caring for his thousands of *talmidim*.

4. See pp. 190-191.
5. See pp. 211-214.

Many others who are capable of learning with his level of *hasmadah* might have viewed these obligations as annoyances, and would have either delegated them to others or done them halfheartedly and hurriedly so that they could get back to their learning. But Rav Nosson Tzvi never considered his obligations to be a nuisance or a distraction; they were merely an extension of his service of Hashem. He gave each item on his schedule the time and attention it needed, but when he was finished, he returned to his learning immediately, as per the Rambam.

Incredibly, despite his packed schedule, he never rushed people, nor did he make others feel as though they were taking him away from his learning. When he attended *simchos* of relatives, and even *mechutanim*, he would stay for a long time, never glancing at his watch or making the *baalei simchah* feel as though he wanted to leave. And he would often attend four or five weddings a night! Even when he was so weak that he couldn't get out of his car, and the *baal simchah* had to be summoned outside so the Rosh Yeshiva could say mazal tov, he continued giving freely of his time to gladden other people's lives.

But when he was finished, he would get right back to his learning.

In fact, Rav Menachem Zaretsky relates that Rav Nosson Tzvi would work his *chasunah* schedule around his planned learning sessions. Even when he had to be at a wedding for the *chuppah* and the dancing, if there was a *chaburah* with a group of *talmidim* scheduled for that night, he would return home after the *chuppah*, participate in the *chaburah*, and then return to the wedding for the dancing.

Trips to and from events or visits were spent learning. R' Aharon Yosef, a close *talmid*, once informed the Rosh Yeshiva on Erev Rosh Hashanah that a boy who was learning in a different yeshiva, but was planning to enroll in Mir for the winter *zman*, had lost his father and was sitting *shivah* that day only. Rav Nosson Tzvi was learning with a *chavrusa* when he heard the news. He immediately told his *chavrusa* to come along for the car ride, and he went to be *menachem avel*.

En route to the house where the boy was sitting *shivah*, Rav Nosson Tzvi continued to review the *shakla vetarya* (roughly: dialogue) of the Gemara with his *chavrusa*. When they reached the house of mourning, Rav Nosson Tzvi asked his *chavrusa* to wait in the car. R' Aharon Yosef escorted the Rosh Yeshiva inside, and Rav Nosson Tzvi spent a considerable amount of time with the boy. "As soon as he settled back into the car," says R' Aharon Yosef, "he picked up with the exact words of the Gemara at which he had left off!"

Most astounding, however, is the testimony of Rav Binyamin Carlebach, who accompanied Rav Nosson Tzvi on most of his trips to the United States. "We would get back to Eretz Yisrael," says Rav Carlebach, "and the Rosh Yeshiva could go directly from the car into the *beis midrash* and deliver a *shiur klali*. It took the rest of his retinue a few days to recover from the jet lag, but it was as if the Rosh Yeshiva had never left the country altogether!"

WITH RAV NOSSON TZVI, THERE WAS NO SUCH THING AS wasting time. If he wasn't involved in either tending to the administrative needs of the yeshiva or caring for a *talmid*, he was learning.

## No Minutes Wasted

R' Ari, who sat right next to the Rosh Yeshiva during davening, recalls that in the years before the yeshiva added a ramp enabling the Rosh Yeshiva to go straight to his seat – bypassing the steps and the main entrance to the *beis midrash* – he would often arrive for *Maariv* thoroughly winded, having walked from his home and dragged himself up the steps. Yet if he would get to his seat even just a minute or two before *Maariv*, he would open a Gemara and use those minutes to learn.

Rav Nosson Tzvi would also take advantage of every possible moment en route to and from the United States to learn. R' Yehuda Neuhaus relates that the Rosh Yeshiva would learn *Chumash* and *Rashi* with him on flights.

Even when he wasn't able to look into a *sefer*, he was still learning. When he was too weak to hold a *sefer*, or even sit at a table, he had *chavrusas* read the words of the Gemara aloud to him. And when he walked outside, he spoke to his companions in learning.

R' Mendy Horowitz, who was a member of Rav Nosson Tzvi's first *chaburah* and eventually served as the Rosh Yeshiva's primary host in the New York area, relates that during the 1970's, when he would accompany Rav Nosson Tzvi for the 15-20-minute walk to his home on Yisa Brachah, Rav Nosson Tzvi would invariably have a question on a Gemara or an approach to a *sugya* to discuss.

When Mendy learned at night with Rav Nosson Tzvi, their learning session would sometimes continue as late as 1 o'clock. As Mendy would leave, Rav Nosson Tzvi would sometimes lament, "Mendy, I don't have anything to say in *shiur* tomorrow!"

Somehow, though, by the next morning he would have a *shiur* prepared – apparently having stayed up and learned for an additional few hours after Mendy left. (Rav Nosson Tzvi's brother, Rav Gedalya, relates that he would often arrive at a spontaneous *chiddush* during a *shiur* as well.)

RAV NOSSON TZVI WOULD NEVER INTENTIONALLY SHOWCASE his breadth of Torah knowledge, but short snippets culled from dozens

## Amazing Breadth of Knowledge

of his *talmidim* and *chavrusas* point to an encyclopedic recall of numerous *masechtos* in *Shas* and many other sections of the Torah.

Some of his *shiurim* were based on more than a dozen quotes from the *Rambam*. Although he occasionally prepared a list of points that he wanted to discuss at the *shiur*, he would leave the list at home; he knew the *Rambams* so well, he didn't need any notes.

Even in a *shiur* comparing the various approaches of many *Rishonim*, he never lost his train of thought or confused one *Rishon*'s approach with another's. He could go from one *Rishon* to the next effortlessly, as if he had each one open in front of him.

A sign announcing a *shiur klali* in which the Rosh Yeshiva would develop an approach based on fifteen halachos in the *Rambam*

ישיבת מיר ירושלים

*MIRRER YESHIVAH JERUSALEM*

Founded in Mir 1817. In Jerusalem 1944    בס"ד   נוסדה במיר בשנת תקע"ז. בירושלים בשנת תש"ד

**RABBI N.Z. FINKEL**    **הרב נ.צ. פינקל**
DEAN    ראש הישיבה

בס"ד, יום ראשון י"ג כסלו, תשס"א

## הודעה

ביום שני, י"ד כסלו, בשעה 6:30 בערב,
יתקיים אי"ה שיעור כללי בהיכל הישיבה הק'
ע"י ראש הישיבה הרב הגאון רבי נתן צבי פינקל שליט"א
בענין: שי' הרמב"ם בחיוב שבועה.
[הל' טוען ונטען: פ"א ה"ב, פ"א ה"ג, פ"א ה"ד, פ"ב ה"ה, פ"ג ה"ז,
פ"ד ה"ד, פ"יד ה"ו, פ"ה ה"ה, פ"ה ה"ט, פ"יט ה"ח, פ"ט הי"ב, פ"יר ה"ו
פכ"ב מהל' עדות ה"ב, פט"ז מהל' אישות ה"ד ופ"יד מהל' גזילה הט"ז]

A paper Rav Nosson Tzvi prepared before the first *shiur klali* that he delivered at the beginning of the winter *zman* of 5772, just a week before he passed away. His original list contained 22 points to discuss, and he then restructured the order of the first 11 points (see two sets of numbers at the right margin). At the bottom of the paper, he restructured it once again. With all the restructuring, he never took the paper with him; he had total recall on what he wanted to discuss.

RAV TZVI KAPLAN, THE ROSH YESHIVA OF YESHIVAS KODSHIM, a large yeshiva in Yerushalayim, related that he was once sitting next to Rav Nosson Tzvi at a *simchah*, and he asked whether the Rosh Yeshiva had any proof from *Maseches Pesachim* to support the Vilna Gaon's principle that one fulfills a mitzvah with each *kezayis* (olive-size piece) of matzah he eats on Pesach. "Rav Nosson Tzvi started to go through the *masechta* by heart, page by page, suggesting proofs from Gemara, *Rashi*, and *Tosafos*," Rav Tzvi remembered.[6]

WHEN RAV NOSSON TZVI WAS A GUEST AT THE HOME OF R' Tzali Edelstein in Flatbush for a Shabbos, the home was open to the community for *seudah shlishis*. After *Havdalah*, a group of 13-to 15-year-old *bachurim* began an impromptu question-and-answer session, peppering Rav Nosson Tzvi with questions from all over *Shas*, Mishnayos, and *Tanach*. They asked every question they could think of, and Rav Nosson Tzvi answered each one without hesitation. After approximately 45 minutes of nonstop bombardment on a diverse array of Torah subjects, R' Tzali said, "Okay, boys. I think the Rosh Yeshiva passed the test."

When the *bachurim* left, R' Yehuda Neuhaus asked the Rosh Yeshiva when he had last learned *Masechtos Taanis* and *Sotah* (which are not in the yeshiva cycle) and several books of *Tanach* on which the *bachurim* had asked him questions. Rav Nosson Tzvi admitted that it had been many years. "But when I learned them," he explained, "I reviewed them many times, so I remember them."

RAV NOSSON TZVI WAS ONCE SITTING WITH A GROUP OF *bachurim* at the end of a *zman*, and he mentioned that if one learned the *masechta* in yeshiva well, he should know the number of *Tosafos* on each page of the Gemara. The *bachurim* looked at him incredulously. "Does the Rosh Yeshiva know how many *Tosafos* there are on each page?" a boy ventured to ask.

"Let's see," Rav Nosson Tzvi replied.

That *zman*, the yeshiva had learned *Yevamos*, which is known as one of the hardest *masechtos* in all of Shas.

A boy fetched a Gemara so they could test the Rosh Yeshiva, and the boys took turns asking the Rosh Yeshiva for the number of *Tosafos* on

---

6. Heard from R' Mordechai Linzer.

each *daf*. Page by page, Rav Nosson Tzvi listed the number of *Tosafos*, much to the amazement of the *bachurim*. Finally, when the Rosh Yeshiva said that a certain *daf* had nine *Tosafos*, the boys said, "It has ten!"

"The first one starts on the previous *amud*," the Rosh Yeshiva replied – correctly – without hesitation.

ONE OF RAV NOSSON TZVI'S *CHAVRUSOS* RELATED THAT HE was once learning with the Rosh Yeshiva on *Yom Tov* when a Yerushalmi fellow came with his teenage son to wish him *Gut Yom Tov*. "What are you learning?" Rav Nosson Tzvi asked the son.

"*Bava Kamma*," he replied.

"Do you know what *mav'eh* is?" the Rosh Yeshiva asked.[7]

"No," the boy answered. "I only learned the Mishnah so far."

"And what does *Rashi* say?" the Rosh Yeshiva pressed.

"*B'Gemara mefaresh* (the Gemara will explain)," the boy replied.

"Actually," corrected the Rosh Yeshiva, "*Rashi* says '*mefaresh b'Gemara*.' There's a difference between the two."

R' YEHUDA NEUHAUS, THE ROSH YESHIVA'S TRUSTED HELPER in his last decade, had several learning sessions with Rav Nosson Tzvi over the course of the years. Sometimes, when the Rosh Yeshiva was particularly drained and couldn't sit at the table, he would lie on the couch and ask R' Yehuda to keep reading. At times, it appeared that he had fallen asleep, but he would suddenly open his eyes and say, "You skipped a word."

THE ROSH YESHIVA'S SCOPE OF TORAH KNOWLEDGE WASN'T limited to Gemara and *Rishonim*. R' Leib (Greg) Fragin[8] related that on a visit to Eretz Yisrael, he asked Rav Nosson Tzvi a question on a Gemara he had learned in *Daf Yomi* – which was not the *masechta* the yeshiva was studying at that point. Rav Nosson Tzvi asked for a Gemara, and without a moment's hesitation he leafed to the back and pointed to a *Maharatz Chayes* that asked R' Leib's question and answered it.

---

7. The term *mav'eh*, which appears in the very first Mishnah in *Bava Kamma*, is a type of damage one can inflict on another person or his property. The Gemara (4b) cites a dispute whether *mav'eh* refers to an animal that ate someone else's produce or crop, or to a person who has inflicted damage on another person or his property.

8. See p. 331.

RABBI AKIVA EIGER WAS ONCE TRAVELING, THE STORY IS TOLD, and he spent the night in an inn. When he asked the innkeeper if he had

**Chazarah, Chazarah, Chazarah** any *sefarim*, the innkeeper brought him a volume of *Teshuvos HaRashba*. During the night, Rabbi Akiva Eiger noticed that a page was missing from the volume – so he took a paper and wrote out the missing words from memory!

A *maggid shiur* in Mir once pointed out that on a basic level, one can be impressed with the fact that Rabbi Akiva Eiger knew *Teshuvos HaRashba* by heart and was able to fill in the missing words. But there is a much deeper level to this story: Despite the fact that Rabbi Akiva Eiger knew the *sefer* by heart, he stayed up late into the night studying it!

In a similar vein, one of the most incredible aspects of the Rosh Yeshiva's learning was that despite his encyclopedic Torah knowledge, he thirsted for Torah so much that he could review the very same material over and over, never tiring of it. Rav Zaretsky, who spent hours in the Rosh Yeshiva's house each day, relates that Rav Nosson Tzvi would prepare the *sugyos* for his *shiur klali* with tens of *chavrusas*, and each time he would start the Gemara with the same *geshmak* (zest). Even after he had already learned a *sugya* ten times in one week, if one of

Three ingredients to success in learning: *chazarah, chazarah,* and *chazarah*

a group of four *chavrusas* came late, he would start the Gemara again from the beginning — with enthusiasm — as though he had never seen it in his life.

The best summation of Rav Nosson Tzvi's devotion to Torah may have come from his own address to a group of young teenagers in Monsey, New York, who were just starting to learn seriously: "If you want to succeed in learning," he told them, "there are three things you need to do: *chazarah, chazarah,* and *chazarah* (review, review, and review)."[9]

---

9. R' Yehuda Neuhaus.

# CHAPTER EIGHTEEN
# AT THE HELM OF MIR

*When a Jew davens Shemoneh Esrei, no matter where in the world he is, he faces Eretz Yisrael. In Eretz Yisrael, he faces Yerushalayim, and in Yerushalayim, he faces the Makom HaMikdash, the spot on the Temple Mount where the Beis HaMikdash once stood.*

*It is also proper to face the Aron Kodesh when davening Shemoneh Esrei. In general, therefore, an Aron Kodesh in a shul or beis midrash is placed in the direction of Har HaBayis, so that when one faces it, he automatically faces the correct direction.*

*In the Mir, however, this halachah could not be fulfilled due to a technical issue: The Aron Kodesh, which stood at the center of the beis midrash, did not face the direction of the Makom HaMikdash. People who stood to the right of the Aron Kodesh had two choices: they could face either Har HaBayis or the Aron Kodesh — but not both.*

*When the Fragin wing of the beis midrash was being added in 1994, Mr. Fragin offered to have the architects place the Aron Kodesh in the corner of the room so that everyone could face both the Aron Kodesh and Har HaBayis during davening.*

*But Rav Nosson Tzvi didn't want to move the Aron Kodesh. "If this is where Rav Leizer Yudel placed it," he explained, "then this is our mesorah (tradition), and we are going to stick to it."*

WHEN RAV NOSSON TZVI RECEIVED THE MANtle of leadership after Rav Beinush, he resolved that *mesorah*, the traditions that Rav Leizer Yudel and Rav Beinush had set in place, would be his guiding light.

Even seemingly simple matters, such as where to place an *Aron Kodesh*, were weighed through the lens of Mirrer tradition, and that was the basis for many a decision by the Rosh Yeshiva.

Surprisingly, even Rav Nosson Tzvi's prodigious effort to expand the Mir – which at first glance seems to have been a break with tradition – was actually a continuation of a *mesorah*. Rav Binyamin Carlebach relates that in a letter to Rav Shamshon Raphael Weiss, Rav Leizer Yudel

Rav Nosson Tzvi (L) clung to the *mesorah* from Rav Leizer Yudel and his father-in-law, Rav Beinush (C)

describes his dream of the yeshiva's unencumbered growth – a dream that was fulfilled by Rav Nosson Tzvi.

*Talmidim* of the Mir cannot help but absorb the *hanhalah*'s veneration of the Torah of the yeshiva's past leaders – Rav Leizer Yudel, Rav Chaim Shmuelevitz, Rav Beinush, and Rav Nochum Partzovitz. What they may not realize, however, is that so many of the administrative policies and operating procedures implemented by Rav Nosson Tzvi were based on the *mesorah* established by these giants as well.

## Derech HaLimud

BACHURIM WHO ARRIVE IN THE MIR FROM *CHUTZ LA'ARETZ* (outside Eretz Yisrael) are often shocked by the speed at which one is expected to learn in the Mir. Once a *bachur* joins Mir, gone are his days of learning one *blatt* a month and spending hours, if not days, dissecting the approach of a single *Acharon* (recent commentary) to a *sugya*. In Mir, the emphasis is on developing one's *own* understanding of *sugyos* by analyzing the different approaches of the *Rishonim* – and then moving on, with the goal of mastering large amounts of material.

At the beginning of each *zman*, signs composed by Rav Nosson Tzvi were posted detailing how people could finish the entire *masechta* being studied that *zman* if they use their time properly.

The importance of finishing the *masechta* was handed down in a *mesorah* from Rav Leizer Yudel[1] to Rav Beinush. Even in Rav Beinush's waning moments, when he was overcome by delirium due to his illness, he would talk to Rav Nosson Tzvi about the *kedushah* of learning a full *masechta*.

Aside from the obvious benefits of knowing an entire *masechta*, the feeling of joy and accomplishment that fills a *talmid* who learns over 100 *blatt* in a winter *zman* – and in the case of *Bava Basra*, 176 *blatt* – is indescribable. Many *talmidim* who felt that they couldn't handle intense learning, and came to the Mir as their last stop before leaving full-time learning, went on to become outstanding *talmidei chachamim* because of the satisfaction they experienced upon completing *masechta* after *masechta*. Those who took the *bechinos* (written exams)[2] felt an even greater sense of accomplishment, because they had proven to themselves that not only could they learn a full *masechta*, they could also retain the material.

---

1. See p. 462.
2. See p. 255.

Founded in Mir 1817. In Jerusalem 1944
RABBI N.Z. FINKEL
DEAN

ישיבת מיר ירושלים
**YESHIVAS MIR YERUSHALAYIM**

בס"ד נוסדה במיר בשנת תקע"ז. בירושלים בשנת תש"ד

עי"ר 580037638

הרב נ.צ. פינקל
ראש הישיבה

# מסכת כתובות

## ההספק וההבחינות לזמן חורף תשס"ט

|   |   |   |
|---|---|---|
| 1. (חדש חשון) יום ראשון ג' כסלו: | תחילת המסכת | עד דף כ: מתני' זה אומר |
| 2. (חדש כסלו) יום ראשון ב' טבת: | מדף כא. | עד דף לח. מתני' נערה |
| 3. (חדש טבת) יום ראשון כ"ט טבת: | מדף לח. | עד סוף פרק נערה שנתפתתה |
| 4. (חדש שבט) יום ראשון כ"ח שבט: | מתחילת פ' אע"פ | עד דף עב: מתני' המקדש |
| 5. (חדש אדר) יום שני כ"ט אדר: | מדף עב: | עד סוף פרק הכותב דף צ. |

חדש ניסן -   מתחילת פרק מי שהיה עד סוף המסכת

## ביום שלישי כ"ט ניסן תשס"ט  תתקיים אי"ה בחינה על כל מסכת כתובות

## לבחורי הישיבה - לומדי עמוד ליום

|   |   |   |   |
|---|---|---|---|
| א. יום ראשוןג' כסלו: | תחילת אלו נערות | מדף כט. | עד דף לט. מתני' |
| ב. יום ראשון ב' טבת: | מדף לט. | עד דף מח. מתני' |
| ג. יום ראשון כ"ט טבת: | מדף מח. | עד דף נז. מתני' |
| ד. יום ראשון כ"ח שבט: | מדף נז. | עד דף סו. מתני' |
| ה. יום שני כ"ט אדר: | מדף סו. | עד דף עה: מתני' |

## בימי שישי ושב"ק אחה"צ:

מדף עח: תחילת פרק האשה שנפלו   עד דף קא: ס"פ אלמנה

## בימי בין הזמנים ניסן:

מדף קא: תחילת פרק הנושא   עד סוף המסכת
ומדף עה: מתני'   עד דף עח. ס"פ המדיר

## ביום חמישי כ"ט ניסן תתקיים אי"ה בחינה על כל מסכת כתובות

## ההספק הלימוד בעיון

|   |   |   |
|---|---|---|
| א. ר"ח חשון - ט"ו חשון: | ב' א' | - ג' ב' כדתניא |
| ב. י"ח חשון - ז' כסלו: | ג' ב' | - ח סוף ע"ב [ג' שבועות] |
| ג. י' כסלו - כ"א כסלו: | ט' א' | - ט' ב' |
| ד. כ"ד כסלו - ה' טבת: | י' א' | - י"ב ב' מתני' |
| ה. ח' טבת – י"ט טבת: | י"ב ב' | - י"ג ג' ארוס וארוסתו |
| ו. כ"ב טבת - ד' שבט: | י"ד א' | - ט"ו ו ב' סוף הפרק |
| ז. ז' שבט – י"ח שבט: | ט"ז א' | - י"ח ב' אנוסין היינו |
| ח. כ"א שבט - ב' אדר: | י"ח ב' | - כ' אין מזימין |
| ט. ה' אדר - ט"ז אדר: | כ' א' | - כ"ב ב' מתני' |
| י. י"ט אדר – כ"ט אדר: | כ"ב א' | - כ"ג ב' מתני' |

3 Beth Israel St. P.O.B. 5022 Jerusalem 91050 Tel. 02-5410999 Fax. 02-5323446 ● עי"ר 580037638 ● 02-5323446 פקס. 02-5410999 טל. ירושלים 91050 ת.ד. 5022 רח. בית ישראל 3

The schedule detailing how one could complete
the 111 *blatt* in *Maseches Kesubos* in one winter *zman*

Under Rav Nosson Tzvi, in order to be accepted into the *kollel,* a *yungerman* had to follow the Daily *Daf* program instituted by his father-in-law, Rav Beinush, for at least a year and a half.[3]

Approximately 14 years before he passed away, Rav Nosson Tzvi instituted an additional program for *bachurim,* after a fateful encounter with Rabbi Dr. Yaakov Mordechai Greenwald, then of Monsey, New York.

During one of the Rosh Yeshiva's trips to America, Rabbi Greenwald came to visit him. Characteristically, Rav Nosson Tzvi asked him what he was learning. Rabbi Greenwald answered that he had just finished *Shas* for the second time in a *chaburah* in Beis Midrash Elyon that learned an *amud* a day.

The Rosh Yeshiva lapsed into silence. Rav Binyamin Carlebach, who was sitting next to Rabbi Greenwald and across from the Rosh Yeshiva, whispered, "You know what the Rosh Yeshiva is thinking about? He's thinking of a way to bring this idea into Yeshivas Mir."[4]

Sure enough, a short while later, the Rosh Yeshiva instituted a learning program – one of the most popular programs in the yeshiva – in which hundreds of *bachurim* study a full *amud* of Gemara, *Rashi,* and *Tosafos* each day during second *seder.* Many *talmidim* also take monthly *bechinos* on this material.

Today, the Mir has two general tracks for finishing the yeshiva *masechta*: the daily *daf* for *yungeleit,* and the daily *amud*[5] for *bachurim.*[6]

It was extremely important to Rav Nosson Tzvi that his *talmidim* maintain a certain pace while learning the *masechta.* When the Shalmei Simchah *beis midrash* was inaugurated, it was assigned to *chaburos* that learned at a pace that was relatively slow, at least for the Mir. One day, Rav Nosson Tzvi came in and began walking around the *beis midrash,* asking each *chavrusashaft* where they were up to in the *masechta.* In his humility, he approached the *talmidim* himself, even though he could easily have appointed someone to perform this "fact-finding mission" for him.

---

3. See pp. 226-228. Although this was a general rule, the Rosh Yeshiva made exceptions for individuals whom he felt could grow more by pursuing a different course of study.

Rav Binyamin Carlebach would explain the general policy with the parable of a mother trying to convince a child to eat a new dish. When the child resists, the mother says, "You don't have to eat all of it, but at least try it. Maybe you'll like it." Often, after a *yungerman* joined the *Daf* program for this trial period, he took a liking to it and followed through to the rest of the *masechtos.*

4. Heard from Abbish Rand, who heard it from Dr. Greenwald.

5. A *daf* is two sides of a folio of the Talmud, and an *amud* is one side.

6. See schedule (p. 251). The *daf* schedule is on the upper third of the page, and the *amud* schedule (which includes a quota for learning first *seder* at a slower pace) is beneath it.

When he saw that the *talmidim* were learning at what he felt was too slow a pace, he indicated that he wanted to deliver an impromptu address. A microphone was set up, and he began to cry, shedding tears at the thought of his *talmidim* knowing only a few *sugyos* in depth, but not mastering the *masechta* they were learning.

"Don't be *talmidei chachamim ameratzim* (Torah scholars who are ignoramuses)!" he begged.

He didn't berate anyone in particular, but the sight of the beloved Rosh Yeshiva crying at what he perceived as a weakness in learning was the most powerful *mussar shmuess* of all.

## It's All in the Words

ANOTHER UNIQUE FEATURE OF THE MIR *DERECH HALIMUD* IS the system of *diyukim*, in which a word or even an extra letter in a *Rishon* is noted, analyzed, and explained. Often, when several such *diyukim* are added together, they lead to a novel way of understanding the *Rishon's* approach to the *sugya*.

*Diyukim* were a key element in Rav Nochum Partzovitz's Torah – in fact, Rav Nosson Tzvi remarked that one can learn from Rav Nochum how to read a *Rishon* – and the Rosh Yeshiva amplified that *mesorah* by making *diyukim* a focal point of many of his own *shiur klalis*.

"One can learn from Rav Nochum how to read a *Rishon*."
Rav Nochum Partzovitz delivering *shiur klali*, as Rav Leizer Yudel (L) and
Rav Chaim Shmuelevitz (R) listen in

But what was most famous about the Rosh Yeshiva's Torah were his "*leshitaso*" analyses. The Rosh Yeshiva would frequently compare a statement made by a *Rishon* in one place with another statement made by that same *Rishon* elsewhere in the *masechta,* or even in a different *masechta.* He would then either resolve the contradictory positions held by the *Rishon* or prove that the *Rishon's* words were *leshitaso* – in line with the positions he expressed elsewhere.

The most famous example of the Rosh Yeshiva's *leshitaso* approach was in *Maseches Nedarim,* in which he pointed to over 100 disputes between the *Ran* and the *Rosh* that could all be explained by their different understandings of the way a *neder* (vow) affects an object.

When the Rosh Yeshiva reached a point in a *shiur klali* or *chaburah* that he could explain with a *leshitaso,* he would often grin widely, radiating his deep joy at having demonstrated that the *Rishon's* opinion was consistent with his opinions elsewhere.

Interestingly, this approach to Torah study was not acquired from any of his *rebbeim*; it was simply an outgrowth of his absolute mastery of the yeshiva *masechtos* with *Rishonim.* Because he had a great command of the entire *masechta,* he saw the *leshitaso*s so clearly that they became a central focus of his approach.[7]

RAV NOSSON TZVI'S CLARITY ON EACH *DAF* OF THE YESHIVA *masechta* also enabled him to deliver an in-depth analysis of any *sugya*

**Always Ready** on demand, even when he had absolutely no preparation time.

One of his *chaburos* in the 1990's comprised a select group of *yungeleit* whose learning was at an extremely advanced level. Rav Nosson Tzvi would walk into the dining room, where the *chaburah* was held, and ask, "Where is the *olam* (public) holding?" Someone would say, "*Nas'cha d'Rabi Abba*" (a *sugya* in *Bava Basra*). Without hesitating for a moment, the Rosh Yeshiva delivered a *chaburah* on *Nas'cha d'Rabi Abba.*

Sometimes, five minutes into a *chaburah,* someone would call out, "Rosh Yeshiva, most of us are not holding there yet; we would like to hear a *chaburah* on the previous *sugya.*"

A different *chaburah*? No problem. The Rosh Yeshiva would stop in his tracks, and without even pausing to gather his thoughts, he would start to deliver a *chaburah* on the previous *sugya.* And this was to a

---

7. Rav Menachem Zaretsky.

*Chaburos* on demand. Rav Nosson Tzvi with a group of *Chassidishe talmidim.*
His son and successor, Rav Eliezer Yehuda *shlita*, is seated to his left.

group of accomplished *talmidei chachamim*, not mere beginners!

Even in recent years, with the ever-growing burden of the yeshiva weighing constantly on his mind, he was still able to give a *chaburah* on the spot. He would travel to the Mir Yeshiva in Brachfeld, enter a room where some of Brachfeld's finest *kollel yungeleit* had gathered, and ask them on which topic they wanted to hear a *chaburah* – and he would begin talking as soon as he got the answer.

AS THE YESHIVA GREW, AND MORE AND MORE *YUNGELEIT* finished learning all of the yeshiva *masechtos*, new *chaburos* were

**Quotas and Tests**

formed to study areas of Torah other than the *masechtos* in the yeshiva cycle. Rav Nosson Tzvi encouraged *yungeleit* who were capable of establishing such *chaburos* to do so. But whatever subject matter a *chaburah* was learning, Rav Nosson Tzvi would demand two things: "*hespek*" – a certain quota of how much material the group would cover each month,[8] and that the group take *bechinos*, written examinations on the material.

*Bechinos* in Mir, which were often composed or at least reviewed by the Rosh Yeshiva himself, were extremely comprehensive. A typical question, taken from a *bechinah* on *Bava Basra*, was, "List 12 reasons

---

8. Heard from his son, Rav Yosef Shmaryahu.

found in this *perek* explaining why we would not rely on *migui*." And *yungeleit* were expected to be able to answer such questions on 20 *blatt* each month!

A monthly testing station in the Mir could have *yungeleit* sitting at a table in the dining room taking *bechinos* on an astonishing range of Torah subjects. *Bechinos* were given on many *masechtos* in *Shas*, as well as on intricate halachic topics such as *Hilchos Shabbos* and *Issur V'heter*. There were even *bechinos* on obscure subjects such as the difficult Mishnayos of *Seder Taharos*, which *yungeleit* studied on buses to and from yeshiva. As Rav Binyamin Finkel once summed it up, the Mir as a whole is learning all sections of the Torah at once.

ASIDE FROM ENCOURAGING *BACHURIM* AND *YUNGELEIT* TO deliver *chaburos* to their peers – often at his home, but even just among

**The Written Word**

themselves – Rav Nosson Tzvi also urged all Mir *talmidim* to write *chiddushei Torah*.

Long before he was Rosh Yeshiva, Rav Nosson Tzvi founded an initiative called *Yad Eliezer*. Named after Rav Leizer Yudel *zt"l*, *Yad Eliezer* was a series of compilations of *chiddushim* written by both *hanhalah* members and *talmidim*. There are now 22 volumes of the *Yad Eliezer* series. Rav Tzvi Partzovitz recounts that in those early years, Rav Nosson Tzvi would read each *shtikel Torah* himself. Often, instead of rejecting a piece, he would approach the writer and help him improve it to make it worthy of inclusion in *Yad Eliezer*.

Later, as Rosh Yeshiva, Rav Nosson Tzvi would pay *bachurim* and *yungeleit* for writing *shtiklach Torah*. Closer to his *petirah*, he urged *talmidim* to write "*ma'arachos*," deep analyses of an entire *sugya*.

THE ROSH YESHIVA ALSO ENCOURAGED *TALMIDIM* TO WRITE and publish *sefarim* containing their Torah *chiddushim* and insights. He

**Becoming a Partner**

took great pleasure in giving *haskamos* to *sefarim* written by *talmidim* of the yeshiva, and he happily gave *haskamos* to hundreds such *sefarim*.

Rav Hillel Cooperman – a longtime Mirrer *talmid* who is best known for running the largest Gemach (free-loan fund) in Eretz Yisrael, along with Rav Mordechai Yoffe – wrote a set of *sefarim* that indexes the entire *Shas*. Before publishing his work, he received a *haskamah* from the Rosh Yeshiva, and when the *sefarim* were printed, he presented the Rosh Yeshiva with a set as a gift.

ישיבת מיר ירושלים

**YESHIVAS MIR YERUSHALAYIM**

Founded in Mir 1817. In Jerusalem 1944

RABBI N.Z. FINKEL
DEAN

עיר 580037638

בס"ד נוסדה במיר בשנת תקע"ז. בירושלים בשנת תש"ד

הרב נ.צ. פינקל
ראש הישיבה

כ"ג אייר תשס"ט

יתיב הוינא ואתה לקדמנא הרב הנעלה והמצוין ר' יהודה היימוביץ שליט"א ועמו

צרור כתבים בענינים העומדים ברומו של עולם ובחובתו של כל אחד ואחד, שש

מצוות התמידיות המוזכרים בדברי רבנו בעל החינוך זת"ע. הנה המחבר היקר

למד בישיבתנו הק' לפני נישואיו ומאז לא מש מתוך האהל ועלה שם במעלות

התורה. יראת שמים היא אוצרו הטוב ואהוב על חבריו ורבותיו במדות טובות שמנו

חכמים. עתה כאשר נתן עינו ולבו לעיין בענין הנ"ל ולהעלות מסקנתיו על הגליון

ולהפיץ מעיינותיו לתועלת הרבים, אמרתי לברכו שחפץ ה' יצליח בידו ויתגלגל

זכות על ידי זכאי כמוהו לעורר את הרבים ולחזקם לקיום הדברים כראוי. יהי רצון

שיזכה לשבת על התורה ועל העבודה ללמוד וללמד לשמר ולעשות ולקיים את כל

דברי התוה"ק ולהאיר עיני הרבים במאור התורה.

הכו"ח בכבוד ויקר

*[signature]*

הרב נתן צבי פינקל
ראש הישיבה

Rav Nosson Tzvi's *haskamah* to my book, "The Six Constant Mitzvos"

Chapter Eighteen: At the Helm of Mir ☐ 257

To Rav Hillel's surprise, the Rosh Yeshiva immediately pulled out 2,000 *shekel* from his pocket and handed it to him.

"What's this?" asked Rav Hillel in confusion.

"You accomplished something very important," the Rosh Yeshiva replied. "This work will be very helpful to people, and I want to have a *chelek* in it."

Rav Hillel did not want to take the money, but the Rosh Yeshiva insisted.

## "Don't Take Away My Baby"

EPHRAIM, A CLOSE *TALMID* AND *CHAVRUSA* OF RAV NOSSON Tzvi, had a friend who had learned in Mir and then moved back to America. The friend authored a *sefer* and had received a *haskamah* from Rav Nosson Tzvi, and he asked Ephraim to present a copy to the Rosh Yeshiva.

Ephraim approached the Rosh Yeshiva one day after a *shiur klali* in the Shalmei Simchah *beis midrash* and handed him the *sefer*. The Rosh Yeshiva had not yet moved away from his spot at the podium, and *Minchah* was about to begin. Ephraim realized that it would be hard for the Rosh Yeshiva to descend from the podium while holding the *sefer*. He tried to remove the *sefer* from the Rosh Yeshiva's hand, but as he tugged at it, he realized that Rav Nosson Tzvi was exerting more strength to hold onto the *sefer*. When the Rosh Yeshiva realized what Ephraim was trying to do, he grinned broadly and said, "That's like pulling a brand new baby out of a mother's grasp!"

He continued to clutch the *sefer* tightly until he began *Shemoneh Esrei*.

## Incentives

ANOTHER *MESORAH* FROM RAV LEIZER YUDEL WAS OFFERING monetary incentives for Torah study.[9]

Rav Nosson Tzvi was so single minded in his desire to encourage Torah study that he once remarked that when the Parkinson's sapped his energy to the point that he could no longer even think in learning, he would lie in bed and daydream of ways to get people to learn more.

Over the years, Rav Nosson Tzvi instituted a number of standard

---

9. Rav Leizer Yudel began to pay others for their *chiddushei Torah* when he was a *bachur* in Telz. When he reestablished Mir in Yerushalayim, he underwrote the Shabbos expenses for many a Yerushalmi home by paying the father of the family for a Torah *chiddush* – even if the person wasn't enrolled in Mir (see p. 183).

financial incentives: for passing the monthly written exams, for writing *chiddushei Torah*, for being punctual and learning full *sedarim*, and even for learning *mussar* in yeshiva each day.

But there were also *"mivtza'im"* – one-time initiatives – in which Rav Nosson Tzvi would offer a considerable sum to those who would accomplish something extremely significant in learning.

Perhaps the most common *mivtza* was the "Twelve Hour" program. Every so often, toward the end of a *zman*, Rav Nosson Tzvi would sense that the spirit of *hasmadah* in the Mir was slipping, and he would call a meeting of the *bachurim* and *yungeleit* or use his Friday *vaad* to announce a 12-hour learning campaign. He would describe how Rav Leizer Yudel had instructed him to learn 12 hours each day, and he would offer a monetary prize to anyone who would manage to stick to the program through the end of the *zman*. But beyond the monetary prize offered, Rav Nosson Tzvi would guarantee that the lives of those who would manage to learn 12 hours a day for those weeks would never be the same.

Aside from announcing the *mivtza* to the whole yeshiva, Rav Nosson Tzvi would sometimes summon specific individuals – many of whom did not consider themselves capable of learning with such diligence – and demand that they add their names to the list of those joining the drive.

One such *bachur* recalls that when the Rosh Yeshiva first told him to learn 12 hours, he adamantly refused. But the Rosh Yeshiva wouldn't take no for an answer, and he added the *bachur's* name to the list in his own handwriting.

The boy, whose learning during that *zman* had been limited to the one *seder* in which he had a *chavrusashaft* with Rav Nosson Tzvi, had no choice but to learn three solid *sedarim* a day from then until the end of the *zman*.

At the end of the third day of this program, he went back to his apartment totally exhausted, but he realized that he had 15 minutes left to fill his 12-hour quota. He lay down in bed, took a *Kitzur Shulchan Aruch* and started to learn. A few hours later, he awoke with a start, finding the *Kitzur* on his face – and his mind on the words of the *Kitzur Shulchan Aruch*!

The *bachur* ran to the Rosh Yeshiva's apartment, which was then on Rechov Yisa Brachah, and knocked on the door. Rav Nosson Tzvi came to the door, somewhat surprised to see a *bachur* there in the wee hours of the morning, and asked the boy what had happened. "Rebbi," the boy exclaimed, "this is the first time in my life that I woke up and the first thing I thought about was Torah."

Rav Nosson Tzvi pulled him inside and made a *l'chaim* to mark the milestone.

**Friday and Shabbos**

WHEN RAV NOSSON TZVI FIRST BECAME ROSH YESHIVA, MANY *bachurim* would take a break from learning on Friday and Shabbos, apparently feeling spent from a week of intense learning. Rav Nosson Tzvi always insisted that learning on Friday and Shabbos was critical to the growth of a *ben Torah*, and he decided to change the perception that those days were "off days." He announced a *mivtza* in which anyone who learned 12 hours from Friday morning until Motza'ei Shabbos for an entire *zman* would receive 1,000 *shekel* – a hefty sum – at the end of the *zman*.

Not all of those who joined this campaign managed to follow through until the end of the *zman*, but even those who didn't earn the 1,000 *shekel* proved to themselves that Friday and Shabbos could be used for further growth in Torah.

**Until the Very End**

ANOTHER LONGSTANDING PHENOMENON THAT RAV NOSSON Tzvi successfully combated was that of *bachurim* from abroad leaving before the end of the *zman*. This phenomenon was especially prevalent during winter *zman*, when *bachurim* were often aching to see their families after being in Eretz Yisrael for a long period, and could not resist the temptation to leave shortly after Purim, when the *zman* was winding down.

It was so common for *bachurim* to leave early, in fact, that Rav Chaim Shmuelevitz famously stated: "Those who leave before Purim leave without permission and without a *berachah*. Those who leave after Purim leave with permission but without a *berachah*. And those who leave on Rosh Chodesh Nissan *tantzt men zei arois fun beis midrash* – we dance them out of the *beis midrash*!"

Rav Nosson Tzvi would urge *bachurim* to stay until Rosh Chodesh Nissan, and his efforts were remarkably successful. Sometimes he achieved success by offering one of his 12-hour-a-day financial incentives, but there were *zmanim* when he simply issued a personal request that *bachurim* remain until the end of the *zman* – and many *bachurim* obliged, out of love for him.

ONE STORY THAT SPREAD RAPIDLY THROUGH THE YESHIVA highlighted Rav Nosson Tzvi's devotion to each *seder* at the end of the *zman*. Ephraim, who was extremely close to the Rosh Yeshiva, was booked on a flight that required him to leave for the airport midday on the last day of the

**$400 for One Seder**

*zman*. Since he was in Rav Asher Arielli's *shiur*, this meant missing second *seder* and one *shiur* – but no more than that.

Rav Asher specifically asked his *talmidim* to stay until the end of the *zman*, which left Ephraim in a quandary: Should he pay the $400 to have his ticket changed, or should he miss that one *seder* and *shiur*?

Ephraim discussed it with his father, who advised him to ask the Rosh Yeshiva what to do. "If the Rosh Yeshiva tells you to stay," his father said, "I'll pay the change fee on the ticket."

When Ephraim went to Rav Nosson Tzvi to discuss the matter, the Rosh Yeshiva thought about it for a few minutes and then said, "I think you should stay."

Ephraim accepted the Rosh Yeshiva's answer and turned to leave. As he was walking out the door, however, Rav Nosson Tzvi called him back. "I know that $400 is quite a sum," he said. "Since I'm the one who wants you to stay, it's my business, not yours." The Rosh Yeshiva then reached into his pocket, counted out $400, and handed the money to Ephraim.

No price was too steep for a few more hours of *hasmadah*.

"I can't take this money," Ephraim stammered, trying to return it to the Rosh Yeshiva. The Rosh Yeshiva would not hear of taking back the money, however. He wanted to make a point about the importance of every minute of learning and the value of a single *shiur* – but not at someone else's expense.

RAV HILLEL COOPERMAN SERVES AS THE *MASHGIACH* OF A yeshiva, in addition to learning in Mir each morning and running his

**Today's Battlefield**

Gemach. After noticing how effective the Rosh Yeshiva's financial incentives were in encouraging Mirrer *talmidim* to excel in their learning, he wanted to implement similar incentives in his yeshiva. When he discussed this move with the administration of his yeshiva, however, he met with staunch disapproval. "What's next?" a member of the administration asked cynically. "We'll offer the *bachurim* money to recite *berachos*?"

Rav Hillel relayed this question to Rav Nosson Tzvi, who admitted that he, too, had detractors who frowned upon his approach of offering financial incentives for learning. He explained that his decision to continue offering new incentives was based on a story told of the Chazon Ish:

*In the early 1900's, a pitched battle was fought between the chareidi leaders of the old Yishuv of Yerushalayim and the secular-Zionist settlers of what was then British Palestine over whether to establish Ivrit (Modern Hebrew) as the official language of Palestine's Jewish residents. The leaders of the Yishuv – most notably, Rav Yosef Chaim Sonnenfeld zt"l – were adamantly opposed to the efforts of Eliezer ben Yehuda, the "father" of Modern Ivrit, and his cohorts to make Ivrit the country's spoken language. The gedolim felt that modern Ivrit was a defilement of Lashon Hakodesh, and that the language was being used as a tool in developing a culture antithetical to Torah and mitzvos.*

*Several decades later, in the early 1950's, a group of ziknei Yerushalayim (the elders of Yerushalayim) traveled to Bnei Brak to ask the Chazon Ish to sign a letter against a school whose language of instruction was Ivrit. The Chazon Ish was known for taking a stance against the secular government on many issues, and the group assumed that he would certainly sign this letter.*

*The Chazon Ish refused to sign, however. Seeing their shock, he explained with a parable. "There was once a decorated general who won many important battles for his country. Even after he retired, his*

*successor would often consult with him in the preparation of military strategies. Once, the country was attacked by a neighboring country, and the younger general rushed to his predecessor for guidance.*

*"The older general surveyed the maps of the area, and then issued instructions: 'Send this number of troops to this area with the following weaponry, and send an additional battalion to another front ...'*

*"When he was finished, the younger general thanked him, but explained that he didn't think that the strategy would work.*

*"'Why not?'*

*"'Your strategy would have worked wonderfully for the battles you used to fight, with the weapons that were in use at that time,' explained the younger general. 'But today's weapons are vastly different, and I have to develop a strategy based on current realities.'*

*"I'm not defending the use of Ivrit in schools," the Chazon Ish explained, "but that is no longer the battlefield today. We need to fight our battles elsewhere."*

"The same principle applies to offering incentives for learning," Rav Nosson Tzvi explained to Rav Hillel Cooperman. "It is true that in a perfect world, everyone would learn Torah *lishmah*, only for its own sake. But nowadays, when there are so many distractions, Torah *lishmah* is no longer the battlefield. Just getting people to learn and master the material they are learning is enough of a battle."

The Rosh Yeshiva paused, and then reflected, "This *zman*, I offered 500 *shekel* to anyone who would do well on a test on all of *Maseches Nedarim* at the end of the *zman*. I added that I would give another 2,000 *shekel* to anyone who would write a *ma'arachah* on each *perek* of the *masechta*.

"It cost me a lot of money," the Rosh Yeshiva concluded, "but I know that 500 *yungeleit* in Yeshivas Mir learned *Maseches Nedarim* from cover to cover this *zman* and know it well."

AT THE END OF EACH *ZMAN*, THE YESHIVA WOULD HOLD A FES-
tive *siyum* upon finishing the *masechta* of that *zman*. The Rosh Yeshiva

**Celebrating Torah** would often announce a new *mivtza* at a *siyum*, encouraging the *bachurim* and *yungeleit* to use their *bein hazmanim* well. In his last years, when money became extremely tight, members of the *hanhalah* would beg him not to announce a new financial incentive, which would be a further strain on the yeshiva's budget – and the Rosh Yeshiva would give them a verbal agreement. Sometimes, however, during the *siyum* he would be overcome with love for Torah and the thought of accruing more hours of learning, and he would announce a new incentive while smiling apologetically toward the other *hanhalah* members to acknowledge that he just couldn't resist, despite his prior agreement.

The Rosh Yeshiva also loved to celebrate *siyumim* of his *talmidim*, and he would invite them to make their *siyumim* in his home. He was especially enthusiastic about hosting *siyumim* for *talmidim* who had studied the daily *daf* according to Rav Beinush's system. The menu at a *siyum* would either be rugelach and cake or a full meat meal, depending on the magnitude of the accomplishment, all funded by the Rosh Yeshiva and prepared by the Rebbetzin.

When a *yungerman* would make a *siyum* on the entire *Shas*, Rav Nosson Tzvi would make every effort to attend the *siyum*, wherever it was. On such occasions, he would make a point of asking the *yungerman* to call over his wife, and he would wish her a separate mazal tov before he left.

Once, one of the yeshiva's donors wanted to do something for the Rosh Yeshiva personally, and he commissioned an artist to produce

Rav Nosson Tzvi was always happy to host a *siyum*.

a large, illuminated *Al Hamichyah* to hang on the wall of the Rosh Yeshiva's home. Upon seeing this big *Al Hamichyah* sign, some *talmidim* joked – or simply assumed – that it was there so that they could recite *Al Hamichyah* after each of the myriad *siyumin* hosted by the Rosh Yeshiva.

Celebrating Torah wasn't limited to *siyumim*. About 12 years before Rav Nosson Tzvi's *petirah*, a *talmid* began to provide a service that enabled Mirrer *talmidim* to get a tape of the *shiurim* given by their *rebbeim* without having to record it themselves.[10] This undertaking required the *talmid* to purchase specialized equipment and set up a complex system for recording and distributing the various *shiurim*. When the system was up and running, this *talmid* met the Rosh Yeshiva in the street and told him that he had succeeded in his efforts to make it easier for the *talmidim* to review their *rebbeim's shiurim*. Upon hearing this, the Rosh Yeshiva began to dance with him in the street.

## Combating Bitul Torah

ALTHOUGH THE ROSH YESHIVA WAS COMMITTED TO FAITHfully upholding the Mirrer *mesorah*, he was not afraid to innovate and chart new courses for the yeshiva when necessary. Some of his innovations arose in response to the rapidly changing times, while others were a reflection of his personal yearnings.

Approximately six years before his *petirah*, after meeting with *gedolei Yisrael* to discuss the severe *bitul Torah* in yeshivos caused by cell phones, Rav Nosson Tzvi made waves throughout the yeshiva world when he became the first Rosh Yeshiva to call a general meeting of his *talmidim* and ban cell phones from the *batei midrash*. Though most *talmidim* were careful not to disturb others by answering phones in the *beis midrash* even before the ban, some people did disturb the learning by carrying on phone conversations.

---

10. Before this service began, a *talmid* who sat next to the *maggid shiur* would be charged with the task of "flipping the tapes." Half an hour or three-quarters of an hour into the *shiur* (depending on the length of the tapes), this *bachur* or *yungerman* would flip dozens of tapes as quickly as he could so that the owners of the recorders wouldn't have to run to the front of the room to turn their tapes over. In recent years, this service has morphed into several other initiatives, including one on the part of Kol Halashon to provide free MP3 recordings of all *shiurim* in Mir – and hundreds of others from *maggidei shiur* throughout the world. Set up by R' Zevy Chodosh, a son of the *Mashgiach* Rav Aharon Chodosh, the Kol Halashon downloading center is located in a basement near the Mir. At the time of the Rosh Yeshiva's passing, over 160,000 hours of *shiurim* were being downloaded in that room each month! In addition, R' Zevy set up 14 computers in that room running the latest *sefarim* databases, enabling *talmidim* to search for obscure sources that relate to the material they are learning.

Shortly after this meeting, R' Beinish Mandel, a *talmid* from the 1970's, visited him and found piles of cell phones on the table. The Rosh Yeshiva explained that he had not actually asked the *talmidim* to hand in their phones, but many had done so voluntarily to show that they were complying with the ruling.[11]

Rav Nosson Tzvi was, in a sense, responsible for cell phones becoming off-limits in *batei midrash* around the world, because only after seeing his success did other roshei yeshiva enact similar rulings in their own institutions.

## The Call

A SHORT WHILE AFTER RAV NOSSON TZVI ISSUED HIS BAN ON cell phones, a *yungerman* in yeshiva who was a grandson of Rav Zeidel Epstein *zt"l*, *mashgiach* of Yeshiva Torah Ore, had a serious dilemma: Rav Zeidel was well into his 90's at the time and was very frail. Since none of his children lived in Eretz Yisrael, this grandson was charged with the task of making medical decisions for his grandfather. The grandson originally complied with the cellphone ban, but after Rav Zeidel was hospitalized a few times, his grandson felt that he should be accessible at all times in case an urgent decision had to be made.

The young man asked Rav Nosson Tzvi what to do. He told him that he should go outside and make a phone call every 15 minutes if necessary, but not to bring his phone into the *beis midrash*.

One day, this grandson happened to pass a friend who was a Hatzalah member, and he asked his friend, half-jokingly, "Why didn't you alert me when my grandfather was hospitalized a few weeks ago?"

Ten minutes later, this friend came running over to the grandson. "What did you ask me before?"

"I asked why you didn't alert me when my grandfather was hospitalized a few weeks ago."

The Hatzalah member withdrew his beeper, and showed Rav Zeidel's grandson that a call had just been placed regarding a medical emergency at Rav Zeidel's address. The grandson ran out of the *beis midrash* and called his grandfather's apartment. The relative who answered the phone asked incredulously, "How did you know to call? *Zeideh* just fell ill a minute or two ago!"

---

11. In order to help people manage without cell phones, the yeshiva set up a phone system with reasonable calling rates and free voicemail for use by all *talmidim*.

"I think," the grandson says in hindsight, "that the *zechus* of the Rosh Yeshiva set off the chain of events that enabled me to know immediately when my grandfather needed me."

IN HIS QUEST TO BOLSTER THE LEVEL OF *HASMADAH* IN yeshiva, the Rosh Yeshiva enacted several other *takanos* in his two

## No Hafganos

decades as Rosh Yeshiva. One of these *takanos* was a "No *Hafganah*" policy.

*Hafganos*, demonstrations, are very common in Eretz Yisrael, and especially in the Meah Shearim neighborhood, which is just a 2-minute walk from the Mir. While the issues at the heart of the demonstrations are often very serious, the demonstrations themselves can become rowdy, and even dangerous. In addition to his concern for the physical safety of the *bachurim*, Rav Nosson Tzvi considered it pure *bitul Torah* for the *bachurim* to participate in these demonstrations, and he would put up a sign each time there was a *hafganah* warning the *bachurim* to stay far away from the demonstrations.

There was only one time when he actively instructed his *talmidim* to attend a demonstration, and that was when a peaceful *atzeres tefillah* (prayer gathering) was held at the entrance to Yerushalayim, drawing a crowd of half a million. The *atzeres tefillah* was called by the *gedolim* of Eretz Yisrael to protest the Israeli Supreme Court's repeated efforts to dismantle the religious structure of the State. Even then, Mirrer *talmidim* knew that after participating in the demonstration, they were expected to immediately return to the yeshiva and resume learning.

ALTHOUGH RAV NOSSON TZVI WAS NOT AFRAID TO TAKE A strong stance against anything that could jeopardize his *bachurim's*

## The Kitchen Is Always Open

well-being, bans and prohibitions were hardly his preferred method of guiding *talmidim*.

Aside from the monetary incentives he offered to promote Torah study, he also made sure that the yeshiva provided its *talmidim* with good food and even leisure activities *bein hazmanim*. During *bein hazmanim*, he would invest heavily to ensure that the *talmidim* of the yeshiva – and even those of other yeshivos – would be able to learn. Rav Asher Arielli recalled that the Rosh Yeshiva let it be known that the kitchen would be providing delicious meals during *bein hazmanim*. With permission from the *mashgiach*, Rav Aharon Chodosh,

"Camp Mir" on a mountain-biking excursion

*bachurim* from all yeshivos were allowed to eat in the Mir, as long as they learned in the *beis midrash* for at least one *seder*.

A few years after he became Rosh Yeshiva, Rav Nosson Tzvi instituted another innovation: he would subsidize trips for *bachurim* who learned first *seder* in the yeshiva during *bein hazmanim*. His intent was not only to increase attendance in the *beis midrash* during *bein hazmanim*, but also to prevent *bachurim* from organizing their own trips to places that were either dangerous or inappropriate for *bnei Torah*.

Some days, "Camp Mir" – as the *talmidim* affectionately dubbed it – would go to a beach with separate swimming; other days they would go bike-riding; and at the end of each *bein hazmanim* there would be a trip to *kivrei tzaddikim*.

Rav Nosson Tzvi also wrote a letter – which the yeshiva would post in each building before *bein hazmanim* – begging *bachurim* not to rent cars and not to visit attractions that posed a physical or spiritual hazard.

AS WE WILL SEE IN SUBSEQUENT CHAPTERS, THE ROSH YESHIVA wanted to have a deep, lasting *kesher* with each of his thousands of

**Shabbos Getaways**

*talmidim*, and he constantly sought ways to develop those bonds. Aside from the *chavrusashafts* that he had with hundreds of *talmidim* over the years, he would also go to lengths to make sure that *bachurim* felt free to come to his

Rav Nosson Tzvi derives pleasure from watching the *bachurim* playing chess and basketball during a weekend getaway during his last summer *bein hazmanim*, three months before he passed away.

home. After accepting a *bachur* into yeshiva, he would often say, "Please come to me if you need anything. And even if you don't need anything, come anyway!"

These weren't empty words; he sincerely wanted his home to be open to the *bachurim* and *yungeleit*. People sensed the sincerity of his invitation, and they accepted it – by the thousands.

In another effort to develop a lasting *kesher,* during the last six or seven summers of his life, the Rosh Yeshiva came up with yet another innovation: he asked some of the Mir's dedicated staff members to organize a weekend getaway during *bein hazmanim* for the *bachurim.* The Rosh Yeshiva himself joined the *bachurim* for Shabbos – sometimes arriving early on Friday to spend more time with them.

*Talmidim* who were fortunate enough to participate in the getaways recall that those were some of the most uplifting moments of their lives.

On Friday, the Rosh Yeshiva would make his way from one playing field to the next, watching *bachurim* playing ball or competing in a game of chess. He had pleasure from watching other people enjoy themselves, even if they weren't in the *beis midrash* learning.

The Rosh Yeshiva wouldn't miss a Shabbos getaway for anything. On the Friday of the very first getaway, in which the yeshiva traveled to Har Tavor, the Rosh Yeshiva felt extremely weak, and his family sent a message to the organizers that it didn't seem as though he would be able to make it for Shabbos. When the organizers explained that the *bachurim* greatly desired to have him there – even without energy – the Rosh Yeshiva decided that he would go. Not only did he participate wholeheartedly in the Shabbos meals, but he even arrived a little early to be part of the Friday activities.

Zevy, one of the organizers of that Shabbos, remembers how he was sitting and schmoozing at a picnic table, having finished a learning *seder* with a *chavrusa,* when the Rosh Yeshiva arrived, led by Rav Menachem Zaretsky. "At first," he recalls, "we weren't sure what to do with ourselves. We felt uncomfortable having been 'caught' with our Gemaras closed.

"To our surprise, the Rosh Yeshiva didn't just nod and walk past us. Rav Zaretsky brought a chair, and the Rosh Yeshiva sat down at the head of the picnic table and joined our conversation."

After that, a crowd gathered where the Rosh Yeshiva was sitting, and someone brought the booklets that the yeshiva had prepared for the getaway. One booklet contained general-knowledge questions on

Sitting among the *talmidim* at a Shabbos getaway: "I don't have a home big enough to fit you all, so I rent out a home that can accommodate you!"

Torah topics, and another contained questions about the yeshiva's history. There were also photos of random spots or signs in the yeshiva, and the objective was to guess where that spot was. The Rosh Yeshiva went through the booklets with the *bachurim*, enjoying the challenge of answering the questions with them.

His participation on that first Friday set the tone for the entire Shabbos, and for all those to follow in subsequent summers.

During the meals, Rav Nosson Tzvi wouldn't sit at a "head table." Rather, he would spend a few minutes at each table, sitting among the *bachurim* and schmoozing with them. "I would love to have all of you over for a Shabbos *seudah*," he once explained. "But I don't have an American home big enough to fit you all. So I rent out a home that *can* accommodate you!"

The obvious love that flowed between the Rosh Yeshiva and the *talmidim* on those Shabbosos remains indelibly imprinted on the memories of the *bachurim*. But there were also moments during the getaways when the Rosh Yeshiva imparted subtle *mussar*. At one *seudah*, he spoke about the concept of always remembering that we are *banim laShem*, children of Hashem. It was clear to all in the room that

The *mashgiach*, Rav Aharon Chodosh (R), explained Rav Nosson Tzvi's subtle message after the Rosh Yeshiva left the room.

something was bothering him, but in his characteristic manner of issuing rebuke,[12] he didn't explain exactly what he meant.

Later, when the Rosh Yeshiva was no longer in the room, the *mashgiach*, Rav Aharon Chodosh, explained that the Rosh Yeshiva had observed a game of basketball earlier that day, and had seen some *bachurim* whose yarmulkes had fallen off their heads. Rather than retrieve their yarmulkes immediately, these *bachurim* finished the play and only then went back for their yarmulkes. The Rosh Yeshiva wanted everyone to know that no matter where a Jew finds himself – in the *beis midrash*, on a basketball court, or in any other place a person might find himself – he must be constantly aware that he is a child of Hashem, and behave accordingly.

For ultimately, whether Rav Nosson Tzvi was following a *mesorah* or adapting a tradition to the needs of the generation, whether he was implementing a ban or innovating a new way of encouraging *bachurim* and *yungeleit*, the Rosh Yeshiva sought to guide his *talmidim* to be *banim laShem*.

---

12. See pp. 460-462.

Rav Nosson Tzvi with his beloved *talmidim:* "Remember that you are all children of Hashem."

# CHAPTER NINETEEN
# EVERYONE'S CHAVRUSA

In 1975, "Yaakov," an 18-year-old boy, traveled from America to to join the Mir. He arrived before Succos, and spent Yom Tov in the yeshiva dormitory, where he promptly contracted the flu. After Succos he took his farher (entrance exam), which turned into somewhat of a disaster. The member of the hanhalah who administered the bechinah was unimpressed, and although he didn't tell Yaakov that he couldn't join the yeshiva, he definitely did not seem interested in having him. Yaakov left the office in tears. He would have seriously considered returning to the United States and perhaps go to work, but he had a problem: his plane ticket had been subsidized by a loan from the Jewish Agency that would be waived if he remained in Eretz Yisrael for a year, and he couldn't afford to repay that loan.

Suddenly, he remembered that before he had left for Eretz Yisrael, a yungerman learning in the yeshiva he had studied at in New York had given him a letter. "As soon as you get to the Mir," he had said, "please find Nosson Tzvi Finkel – everyone over there knows him – and give him this letter.

"It's very important," the yungerman emphasized, "so try to make it a priority."

Yaakov walked into the beis midrash and asked someone to point out Nosson Tzvi Finkel. He *approached Rav Nosson Tzvi, who greeted him with a friendly smile and shook his hand warmly. "I was asked to deliver a letter to you," Yaakov said.*

*Rav Nosson Tzvi opened the letter, continuing to hold Yaakov's hand in his while he read it. "Thank you so much for bringing this," Rav Nosson Tzvi said when he finished reading the letter. "It's very important. What did you say your name was?" Yaakov said his name, and Rav Nosson Tzvi asked, "Are you new?"*

*"Yes."*

*"Do you have where to sleep?"*

*"Well, I have a dorm room I'm using for now ..."*

*"Do you have chavrusas?"*

*"No."*

*"Well," Rav Nosson Tzvi said, "I don't have a first seder chavrusa. Would you like to learn with me?"*

*"I guess so," Yaakov replied, not realizing that he was talking to one of the finest talmidei chachamim in Mir and the son-in-law of Rav Beinush Finkel, the Rosh Yeshiva. "I don't have anyone else ..."*

*Thus began one of the hundreds of chavrusashafts Rav Nosson Tzvi would have in his life — not necessarily with the cream of the Mir crop, but with anyone who wanted to learn with him.*

**Y**ESHIVOS ALL AROUND THE WORLD – AND LARGE yeshivos especially – undergo a unique process called *"chavrusa tumul"* at the beginning of each *zman*. The name says it all: it's a tumult. For the first few days of the *zman*, *talmidim* who have not yet secured a *chavrusa* scramble about the *beis midrash* trying to find an appropriate study partner.

## Everyone's Chavrusa

Generally, a serious *lamdan* and *masmid* will seek a *chavrusa* whose level of scholarship is on par with his, so that he can advance in his learning and be challenged by his *chavrusa*. Rarely will one of the top *lomdim* in a yeshiva deliberately choose a *chavrusa* whose level of scholarship is far lower than his own.

Rav Nosson Tzvi was different. He was willing to learn with *anyone*. No matter who asked – an advanced *bachur* or a beginner; a great *lamdan* or someone of relatively weak intelligence – Rav Nosson Tzvi

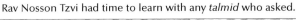
Rav Nosson Tzvi had time to learn with any *talmid* who asked.

would immediately agree to learn with him.

This practice of learning with anyone who approached him would have been difficult enough to adhere to when he was a newly married *yungerman* or a young *maggid shiur*. But Rav Nosson Tzvi kept up the practice until the last day of his life!

He would learn with some *chavrusas* for a few hours each week; with others for only half an hour. With some he would learn Gemara and prepare for his *shiur klali*; with others he would learn *mussar* or halachah. But no matter how much time a *chavrusa* had with Rav Nosson Tzvi and no matter what they learned, the *chavrusa* couldn't help but walk away from that encounter with an enhanced love for Torah that would remain with him for years to come.

ONE OF RAV NOSSON TZVI'S *CHAVRUSAS* IN HIS DAYS AS A *ROSH chaburah* was a *bachur* named Mendy, who arrived in the Mir in 1975,

**"More for Me Than for Him"**
when Rav Nochum Partzovitz was one of the primary attractions in the Mir. The rule was, however, that you couldn't go straight into Rav Nochum's *shiur*: you had to first hear *shiur* from either Rav Aryeh Finkel, Rav Yitzchak Ezrachi, or Rav Nosson Tzvi for a *zman*.

Mendy arrived late for the *zman* and he couldn't find a *chavrusa*.

He went to Rav Nosson Tzvi, who would help many *bachurim* find *chavrusas* during those years, and told him that he was having a hard time finding a *chavrusa*. "I'll work on it for you," Rav Nosson Tzvi assured Mendy. "If I don't find a *chavrusa* for you, you'll learn with me."

Rav Nosson Tzvi didn't manage to find one, so Mendy became his *chavrusa* – joining the *chavrusa* who was already learning with him.

"That's how it started," Mendy recalls, "and from there it grew and grew and grew. We learned morning *seder* together and sometimes night *seder* as well. We would learn on Shabbos morning before davening – Rav Nosson Tzvi would come to the dorm at 5:30 on Shabbos morning to wake me up."

Later, after the Shabbos davening, one of Rav Nosson Tzvi's sons would tell Mendy, "You're eating at our house, right?" Mendy became a *ben bayis* (family member) of sorts in the Finkel home, and he continued learning with Rav Nosson Tzvi for three years.

"He even took me along with him to Kiryat Sanz in Netanya for *bein hazmanim*," Mendy recalls, "on condition that I would learn with him first *seder*. 'After that you can do what you want,' he told me.

"He said he needed a *chavrusa* in Netanya, but it was more for me than for him," Mendy acknowledged wryly.

## A Ten-Year Chavrusashaft

ABOUT 10 YEARS BEFORE THE ROSH YESHIVA WAS *NIFTAR*, A *bachur* by the name of Yitzchak found out that his parents were planning to spend Pesach in Eretz Yisrael, which meant that he would not have to return to the States for *bein hazmanim*. Yitzchak had been hoping to ask the Rosh Yeshiva for a *chavrusashaft* ever since he had entered the yeshiva nearly a year earlier, but he hadn't found the opportunity. When he heard that he was going to be in Eretz Yisrael for Pesach, Yitzchak asked the Rosh Yeshiva if he could learn with him during *bein hazmanim*. The Rosh Yeshiva agreed, and told him to come to his home at 9 o'clock on Rosh Chodesh Nissan.

When Yitzchak arrived, he found that three other *bachurim* were there to learn with the Rosh Yeshiva as well. The Rosh Yeshiva was very weak, and he had to lie on the couch during this learning session. All four *bachurim* lined their chairs up next to the couch and the Rosh Yeshiva motioned to one of them to begin reading the first Gemara in *Maseches Gittin*. (The Rosh Yeshiva would use *bein hazmanim* to prepare his *shiur klalis* for the next *zman*.) The *bachur* read the Mishnah at the beginning of the *masechta* and explained it. Before he could go further, Rav Nosson Tzvi began to recite the *Rashi* – from memory.

"I followed along with my finger on the place," recalls R' Yitzchak, "and I saw that the Rosh Yeshiva didn't miss a single word! I remember thinking, *This is like reading a biography of a gadol from a previous generation!* I decided then and there that I would never give up the opportunity to learn with him."

Indeed, for a decade or so after that first learning session with Rav Nosson Tzvi, R' Yitzchak clung tenaciously to his *sedarim* with the Rosh Yeshiva. They would learn together during *bein hazmanim* for the next 10 years, but he also added another two regular *sedarim*: R' Yitzchak would repeat Rav Asher Arielli's *shiur* to Rav Nosson Tzvi on Friday night,[1] and he began to prepare *shiur klali* with the Rosh Yeshiva every Shabbos during the *zman* as well.

R' Yitzchak recalls that the Rosh Yeshiva was able to learn in the most

---

1. Rav Nosson Tzvi had been listening to *bachurim* tell over Rav Asher's *shiurim* for over a decade by that time. Two of Rav Asher's top *talmidim* would repeat Rav Asher's *shiurim* to him on *Leil Shabbos*, and when one of them got married, R' Yitzchak took over his slot.

noisy, frenetic conditions. His young grandchildren would be running around the room, and people would be coming in and out, but the Rosh Yeshiva would remain focused on his learning. R' Yitzchak relates that Rav Nosson Tzvi seemed to *enjoy* being in the family setting while he learned.

Although the Rosh Yeshiva wouldn't waste time with idle chatter during their scheduled learning times, after they finished learning the Rosh Yeshiva would discuss various *hashkafah* topics. In R' Yitzchak's words, "He watered me – he was constantly concerned with my growth."

Along with the clarity in Torah that could be gained by learning with Rav Nosson Tzvi, says R' Yitzchak, his appreciation and love of Torah were infectious.

Once, when they finished learning a particularly satisfying *shtikel* from Rav Chaim Shmuelevitz that resolved a contradiction between two *Rashis*, Rav Nosson Tzvi was grinning broadly. "*Ah, the Sar HaTorah,*" he exclaimed, using the words he had written for a plaque commemorating Rav Chaim *zt"l* in the main *beis midrash* of Mir.

R' Yitzchak seized the opportunity to ask, "How do you reach Rav Chaim's level of depth and understanding?"

"*Only* through *horavanyeh* (delving intensely into learning)," Rav Nosson Tzvi replied. "You have to learn, and learn, and learn in order to get there!"

THE ROSH YESHIVA'S MULTITUDES OF *CHAVRUSAS* RECALL that when they would check with the Rosh Yeshiva to ensure that their

**Never Saying No** learning session was on, he was always extremely careful not to say no. Even if he couldn't make it to a learning session one week, he would never say, "No, we can't learn." Rather, he would say, "I'm sorry, but we'll learn next week" or "I don't think it's going to be possible today." His love of Torah was so great that he couldn't bear to say no to a *chavrusa*.

When he *would* be able to learn, he would say, "I'm looking forward to learning with you," thereby giving his *chavrusas* a great feeling about their learning session.

ONCE, WHEN R' BEINISH MANDEL, A *TALMID* FROM RAV NOSSON Tzvi's early days as a *rosh chaburah,* was visiting Eretz Yisrael, he visited

**"They Asked!"** the Rosh Yeshiva's home on a Friday afternoon and saw him sitting with two young men wearing jeans and T-shirts, with *Chumashim* open in front of each of them.

When they left, R' Beinish asked the Rosh Yeshiva, "You were learning *Chumash* and *Rashi* with them?"

"Yes," the Rosh Yeshiva replied.

These boys were obviously not in the Mir, and R' Beinish couldn't help but ask, "Why?"

"Because they asked," the Rosh Yeshiva said with a shrug.

EVEN IN THE ROSH YESHIVA'S LAST YEARS, WHEN MOUNTING budget deficits forced him to travel to the United States more often, he still

**One of the Last** managed to find a time slot for anyone who asked to learn with him. During the *shivah*, it became apparent that he had been learning with some 80 people every week!

As the accounts of *chavrusashafts* poured in from alumni around the world, even people who were well aware of the Rosh Yeshiva's policy were shocked by the sheer number of people who had learned with him over the years.

Rav Yosef Elefant, a *maggid shiur* in the Mir, related that he was astounded at how many of his *talmidim* called him crying during the days after the *petirah*. "You were so close to the Rosh Yeshiva?" he asked in surprise.

The rejoinder was the same with nearly every such *talmid*: "What do you mean? I had a *chavrusashaft* with him!"

A letter received by the Mir office in America from a *talmid* named Akiva, who learned in the Mir in the late 1990's, effectively captures the concept that even *chavrusas* who had a sporadic connection with Rav Nosson Tzvi gained immensely from those sessions:

> As a young bachur learning in Mir Yerushalayim, it can be extremely
> disconcerting to find one's place in a yeshiva of over 3000 talmidim. I
> had come from a small yeshiva and was not used to the hustle and bustle
> of a large institution. As I started to get settled into my new yeshiva,
> I was told that as large as the yeshiva was, the Rosh Yeshiva zt"l, in
> his tzidkus, was willing to learn with any bachur who asked to learn
> with him. To say that I was a bit skeptical would be an understatement.
> How could it be that Harav Nosson Tzvi Finkel, a man who ran the
> largest yeshiva in the world at the time and lived with Parkinson's dis-
> ease, could possibly find time to learn with anyone who simply asked?
> Nevertheless, I approached the Rosh Yeshiva one evening, introduced
> myself, and asked him if he had any time to learn with me. To my

amazement, the Rosh Yeshiva thought for a moment, and asked me to come to his house on the following Tuesday evening.

Needless to say, as I approached the house I was a bit nervous. I knocked on the door and was greeted by a member of the family. I proudly said that I had an appointment to learn with the Rosh Yeshiva and asked if he was available. To my chagrin I was told that the Rosh Yeshiva was at the chasunah of a talmid and would not be able to meet me tonight. I was very disappointed but I understood that the Rosh Yeshiva was an extremely busy man. I was sure that there was not a night that went by without a myriad of obligations that the Rosh Yeshiva had to take care of. I was not yet ready to give up, though, and decided to try again the following week.

The next week I once again knocked on the Rosh Yeshiva's door only to be told that the Rosh Yeshiva was home but was too tired to meet with anyone. All of the talmidim knew about the superhuman strength the Rosh Yeshiva needed just to get up in the morning, and I just couldn't bring myself to try and talk my way in. But I was extremely disappointed, and I pretty much gave up at that point.

I did not realize it at the time, but the next encounter I would have with the Rosh Yeshiva would change my life forever. The Tuesday after I was turned away from the door of the Rosh Yeshiva for the second time, I was walking out of the Mir after lunch when I was approached by none other than the Rosh Yeshiva himself. In his incredibly quiet manner, he apologized for not being able to meet with me the previous two weeks and guaranteed me that if I would stop by that night, he would make sure he was available. I could not believe that the Rosh Yeshiva actually remembered me enough to recognize me and approach me.

I showed up that night and once again knocked on the door. This time I was ushered right in. The Rosh Yeshiva was lying on the couch resting from a long day. It was obvious to me that he was absolutely spent. He did not have one ounce of strength left. In utter exhaustion, he got up from his couch and slowly walked with me over to the table. We sat down together and I waited for the Rosh Yeshiva to speak. Instead, he just looked at me, waiting for me to speak. "Uh, what does the Rosh HaYeshiva want to learn?" I asked, like a schoolboy in the principal's office.

He smiled at me and said, "You're the boss, what do you think?" I told him that I wanted to learn mussar, perhaps something about laziness. At this point I assumed the Rosh Yeshiva would give me a shmuess *about the importance of making every moment count, or perhaps tell me over some divrei Torah focusing on the middah of zerizus. Instead, the Rosh Yeshiva did something that I will never forget for the rest of my life. Without a second thought – and as tired and weak as he was – he literally jumped out of his chair, hurried to the bookshelf and pulled out a mussar sefer. It was as if a sudden burst of energy suddenly filled his body. I watched in utter shock as a man who had been completely exhausted just moments ago came back to life right before my eyes. We learned together for half an hour – a half-hour that was me'ein Olam Haba, a touch of the World to Come.*

*To tell you the truth, I don't even remember what the sefer was and I don't remember a word of what we learned. But I will never forget the incredible energy the Rosh Yeshiva suddenly exhibited. It was a lesson not of words, but of action – and I have put that lesson to use many times in the 15 years that have passed since this incident. Whenever I feel tired after a long day at work and am not in the mood to do something, I remember the incredible actions of the Rosh Yeshiva.*

*Unfortunately, I learned with the Rosh Yeshiva only one more time, but the lessons I learned have lasted a lifetime. The Rosh Yeshiva zt"l will be sorely missed by everyone – especially by this talmid, who was just one of 3,000.*

## The Youngest Chavrusa

ONE NIGHT DURING THE LAST SUMMER OF THE ROSH YESHIVA'S life, a *yungerman* in Mir named R' Yosef was reading a book called *The Gedolei Yisrael Album*[2] to his children at bedtime. The book contains pictures and vignettes of many *gedolei Yisrael*, including Rav Nosson Tzvi, and the vignette about Rav Nosson Tzvi tells how he not only took time out of his busy schedule to learn with a *talmid*, he even asked the *talmid* what time was good for *him*. Hearing this, R' Yosef's 7-year-old son Eliyahu looked up at his father and announced, "I want to learn with the Rosh Yeshiva too."

Eliyahu had actually met the Rosh Yeshiva a year before this incident. Eliyahu's family was visiting their grandparents in Baltimore for the summer, and Eliyahu joined his grandfather's first-grade class in Torah Institute, a local *cheder*. During that summer, Rav Nosson Tzvi visited Baltimore, and one of his stops was at the Torah Institute. Now that

---

2. By Mattis Goldberg, Feldheim Publishers, Jerusalem, 2010.

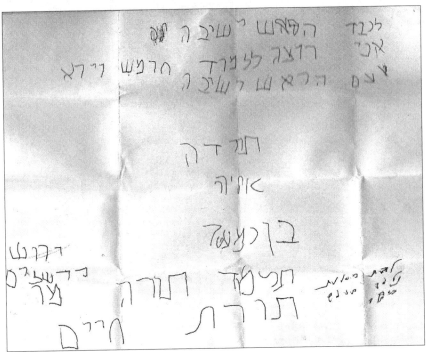

The note little Eliyahu sent Rav Nosson Tzvi. In the lower right-hand corner is
Rav Nosson Tzvi's response.

Eliyahu had heard about the Rosh Yeshiva's willingness to learn with
*talmidim*, he wanted a *chavrusashaft* with him as well.

R' Yosef felt that it wasn't proper to ask the Rosh Yeshiva to learn with
a 7-year-old, but the little boy was insistent. Finally, R' Yosef told his son
that if he would write a letter to the Rosh Yeshiva requesting the learning session, R' Yosef would deliver it to Rav Nosson Tzvi.

The next morning, Eliyahu awoke early and scrawled a letter to
Rav Nosson Tzvi before going to *cheder*. "Lichvod HaRosh Yeshiva –
Dear Rosh Yeshiva," he wrote. "*Ani rotzeh lilmod Chumash Vayeira
im HaRosh Yeshiva* – I want to learn *Chumash Vayeira* with the Rosh
Yeshiva." He signed it with his name, his age (*"ben kimat 7* – almost 7"),
the name of his *cheder*, and his location, Yerushalayim.

R' Yosef brought the letter to the Rosh Yeshiva, who wrote back on
the letter, "*Lehitra'ot, nilmad Chumash beyachad* – I'll see you, and we'll
learn *Chumash* together."

The first time they learned together was on Shabbos Shuvah. Little
Eliyahu came with his father to the Rosh Yeshiva's house toting his
papers from *cheder*, and the Rosh Yeshiva sat next to him at the table

and listened to him review the *pesukim* and *teitch* (interpretations) he had learned that week.

The next time they learned was Shabbos Chol HaMoed Succos. When R' Yosef arrived at the Rosh Yeshiva's house with Eliyahu, the Rosh Yeshiva was learning with his regular Shabbos *chavrusa*, R' Yitzchak, and by the time the two finished it was almost time for *Minchah*. Rav Nosson Tzvi began learning with Eliyahu, even though only a few minutes remained before he had to leave to *Minchah*.

When it was time to stop, he motioned to R' Yosef to tell his son that the Rosh Yeshiva had to go. Characteristically, Rav Nosson Tzvi did not want to be the one to tell his young *chavrusa* that it was time to stop learning.

R' Yosef indicated to his son that it was time to leave. Several minutes later, as they were walking together outside, they passed the wheelchair-bound Rav Nosson Tzvi on his way to *Minchah*, and he waved to Eliyahu.

"The Rosh Yeshiva loves me," Eliyahu confided to his father. "The Rosh Yeshiva is my friend."

Unfortunately, that Shabbos was the last time they learned together. During the three Shabbosos that followed, either the Rosh Yeshiva or Eliyahu's family was away, and the Rosh Yeshiva passed away the week of *Parashas Vayeira* – the *parashah* he had been learning with Eliyahu.

Little Eliyahu will forever remember his special, if short-lived, *chavrusashaft* with Rav Nosson Tzvi, the Rosh Yeshiva of the largest yeshiva in the world who made time to learn with anyone – even a *talmid*'s 7-year-old son.

# CHAPTER TWENTY
# ACHDUS IN THE MIR

*Every Rosh Hashanah, the Rosh Yeshiva would speak in each of the three batei midrash where the Mir held minyanim, addressing thousands of participants between the three.*

*On the last Rosh Hashanah of his life, Rav Nosson Tzvi rose to the podium in each beis midrash and said, "People want to know what kavanos they should have during tekiyas shofar. You want to know what you should think about during tekiyos? Think about someone else."*

ANY A *BACHUR* ARRIVING AT RAV NOSSON Tzvi's Mir – home to thousands upon thousands of *talmidim* – was astounded by the warm reception extended to him by the *hanhalah* and nearly everyone else he would meet in yeshiva. This atmosphere was fostered by Rav Nosson Tzvi himself. When he would speak at the first *seudah shlishis* at the beginning of a *zman*, he would quote Rav Chaim Shmuelevitz's teaching that *"Ve'ahavtem es hager* – you shall love the convert" refers not only to newcomers to Judaism, but to newcomers to a yeshiva as well.

"You want to know what to think about during *tekiyos*? Think about someone else."

In Mir, it made no difference where you came from, what kind of yeshivos you had attended, or who your father was. The *mashgiach*, Rav Aharon Chodosh *shlita*, explains that the sole criterion for accepting a *bachur* into yeshiva was if he was truly interested in learning. If the answer was yes, then he was welcome in Mir.[1]

And Mir wasn't reserved only for Mirrers. *Bachurim*

---

1. Although this policy began when Rav Leizer Yudel established the yeshiva in Yerushalayim, it was more of a challenge to maintain over the years as the Torah world grew and an open-door policy meant accepting hundreds of new *bachurim* each *zman* and supplying them with seats, *rebbeim*, and three meals a day.

*Chassidish* and *Litvish*,
young and old,
join together to learn
in the Mir.

learning in other yeshivos were invited to eat in the dining room or use
an empty bed in the dormitory on Shabbos or during *bein hazmanim*,
as long as they would spend some time learning in the Mir.

One might expect that *bachurim* coming from such a panoply
of backgrounds – Israeli, American, and European; *Chassidish* and
*Litvish*; Sephardic and Ashkenazic – would not have been able to meld
into a cohesive unit, but they did. And the reason they were able to do
so is because they were following the example of the *hanhalah*.

RAV BINYAMIN FINKEL, SON OF RAV ARYEH FINKEL,[2] IS A beloved figure in the yeshiva. With his heartwarming smile and humor-

**A "Personal Request" at the Chanukah Mesibah**

ous, light way of delivering *mussar* and *chizuk*, his *Shmuessen* and *vaadim* have always attracted a large crowd of *bachurim* from *Chutz La'aretz*.

"R' Binyamin HaTzaddik," as he is affectionately known, pointed out[3] that Rav Nosson Tzvi's Mir was built in the image of the Jewish people traveling through the *Yam Suf*. *Chazal* tell us that during *Kriyas Yam Suf* (the Splitting of the Reed Sea), there were 12 paths running through the Sea, one path for each *shevet* (tribe). Hashem made the walls of water between the paths transparent so that the members of the different *shevatim* could see each other and feel part of the overall nation.

So, too, explained Rav Binyamin Finkel, Rav Nosson Tzvi wanted each group of *bachurim* and *yungeleit* to feel that they had their own home in the Mir. As an example, he arranged for the *chassidishe* contingent in Mir to have a separate *minyan* so that they could daven in their familiar *Nusach Sefard,* and he would join that *minyan* several times a year. But when it came to learning, he wanted everyone to be *b'achdus*, to feel part of the greater whole. And indeed, one of the most heartening sights in the Mir is to see *talmidim* from five continents, representing the gamut of Jewish communities and backgrounds, mingling together

The *achdus* in yeshiva mirrors that of the *hanhalah*. (R-L) Rav Nosson Tzvi, Rav Binyamin Finkel, Rav Refoel Shmuelevitz, and Rav Binyamin Carlebach at a Purim gathering in the Mir

---

2. Rav Aryeh has been delivering *Shmuessen* in the Mir since his father, Rav Chaim Zev, passed away. In addition, he has served as Rosh Yeshiva of Mir Brachfeld since shortly after its inception.
3. At an impromptu *hesped* delivered at his regularly scheduled Tuesday-night *shmuess*, the night after the *levayah*.

"Turn to the person on your right and your left and say hello."
The *hanhalah* dances at a Chanukah gathering in the 1990's. (R-L): Rav Aharon Lopiansky,
Rav Refoel Shmuelevitz, Rav Yitzchak Ezrachi, Rav Nosson Tzvi, Rav Aryeh Finkel,
Rav Nachman Levovitz, and Rav Binyamin Carlebach

in the *batei midrash*, each contributing to the overwhelming roar of Torah being studied in several languages and dialects.

During the Chanukah *mesibos* of his last years, Rav Nosson Tzvi would interrupt his speech to issue what he called "a personal request": he wanted each *talmid* to turn to the person to his right and to his left, say *Shalom Aleichem*, and ask him his name.

To ensure that the *talmidim* wouldn't feel sheepish about fulfilling his request, the entire *hanhalah* seated at the head table heeded the Rosh Yeshiva's request, turning to one another and shaking hands!

THE THEME OF *ACHDUS* WAS ALWAYS ON RAV NOSSON TZVI'S lips. He would often repeat a saying from Rav Chaim Zev Finkel, **"How Could You Not?"** brother of his father-in-law, Rav Beinush, who was the *mashgiach* when Rav Nosson Tzvi arrived. Rav Chaim Zev would say, "I don't know how someone can walk up or down a flight of steps in yeshiva and not say 'Good morning' to each person he passes."

My own initiation to the respect and love the *hanhalah* had for each *talmid* actually happened in an encounter with a son of Rav Chaim Zev.

Although the Mir already owned a few buildings when I enrolled there in Elul 5768 (August 1998), everyone would daven *Shacharis* and *Maariv* in the main *beis midrash* in the original Mir building. Understandably, seats were at a premium. I noticed that one bench could easily be pulled into the aisle just a bit, and then I could place a *shtender* in front of it and "create" a new seat.

I davened in that seat one day. The next morning, as I arrived at "my spot," an elderly, distinguished-looking person immediately jumped to his feet, helped me pull the bench out and pushed a *shtender* in my direction. This continued for a while, until one day someone informed me, almost parenthetically, that this person was Rav Aryeh Finkel, who had been a *maggid shiur* in yeshiva for decades and began to deliver *shmuessen* in Mir after his father Rav Chaim Zev's passing.[4] In the days that followed, I tried to arrange my own "accommodations" without allowing Rav Aryeh to help me, but to no avail. He insisted on helping me, day after day. Eventually, feeling uncomfortable with accepting this daily *chessed*, I found myself an empty seat in a different part of the *beis midrash*.

IF THE ROSH YESHIVA WANTED EVERYONE TO FEEL FOR ONE another under ordinary circumstances, during trying times he would

**A Prerequisite to Greatness**

demand an even greater level of *achdus*.

Once, a *bachur* in the yeshiva collapsed in the *miklat*[5] during lunchtime. Someone rushed to call an ambulance, and someone else ran to inform the Rosh Yeshiva. Bystanders recall seeing Rav Nosson Tzvi race down the two flights of steep steps to the *miklat*. When he got there, he heard from the medics that the *bachur* was in critical condition. He begged the medics not to give up the fight for the boy's life. The medics heeded his pleas, and after working on him for a long time, they finally got a pulse and transported him to the hospital. If not for the Rosh Yeshiva rushing to his side and exhorting the medics not to give up, the boy – whose vital signs had been undetectable for a while – might have died.

That night, the Rosh Yeshiva addressed the *bachurim* to be *mechazek* (strengthen) them through this crisis – and also to ensure that they were feeling the pain of a fellow *talmid*. He quoted the Gemara in *Berachos* that states that one who is in a position to beg for Divine mercy on behalf of a friend and doesn't do so is considered a sinner. If that friend is a *talmid chacham*, the Gemara adds, one must beg with great intensity until he himself feels ill.

---

4. When the Mir in Brachfeld opened, Rav Aryeh became Rosh Yeshiva there, while continuing to deliver *shmuessen* in Mir Yerushalayim.

5. A *miklat* is a fortified basement that serves as a bomb shelter in many Israeli buildings. As is the case with every space in the Mir, the *miklat* is pressed into use as a *beis midrash*. For many years, it was also used as a *shiur* room by both Rav Elya Baruch Finkel *zt"l* and *yblcht"a* Rav Asher Arielli.

"Our friend is a *talmid chacham!*" declared the Rosh Yeshiva. He then recited five *kapitlach* of *Tehillim*, and the *talmidim* repeated after him, verse by verse.

At *seudah shlishis* that Shabbos, which was *Parashas Shemos*, the Rosh Yeshiva spoke again. This time, he quoted the verse that states that Moshe Rabbeinu "saw the pain of his brethren" (*Shemos* 2:11). The Midrash teaches that it was this empathy that earned Moshe Rabbeinu his position as leader of *Klal Yisrael*.

"We must feel the pain of a friend in need," the Rosh Yeshiva implored. "It is a prerequisite for greatness."[6]

## Echad Mibnei HaChaburah

BEFORE RAV NOSSON TZVI WAS ROSH YESHIVA, HE HARDLY ever addressed large audiences in the yeshiva. There was one instance, however, in which he did make a rare public speech.

During the winter *zman* of 1990, a few months before Rav Beinush passed away and Rav Nosson Tzvi became Rosh Yeshiva, a British *bachur* in yeshiva went missing during *seder* one day. He had told his *chavrusa* that he had to use the restroom, and he had never returned. The next morning, he was found in a restroom stall, apparently having died shortly after leaving his *chavrusa*.

A few days after the boy was found, when many in yeshiva were still reeling from the shocking news, Rav Nosson Tzvi addressed a large group of *talmidim*. The words he spoke then reverberate to this day in the minds of those who were present:

"The Gemara says, '*Echad min ha'achin shemeis, yid'agu kol ha'achin kulan; echad mibnei hachaburah shemeis, tid'ag kol hachaburah kulah –* If one of the brothers dies, all of the brothers should worry; if a member of the group dies, every member of the group should worry' (*Shabbos* 106a).

"A member of our *chaburah* was *niftar*, and we all have to fear for our own lives."

Rav Nosson Tzvi paused for a moment, and then said with uncharacteristic forcefulness: "So you might think to yourself, *This was a British bachur who just came to yeshiva. What does it have to do with me? I didn't even know him!* The answer to that is that if a *bachur* could be in yeshiva for two and a half months and you don't know him – *oy yid'agu* – how much more must the entire *chaburah* worry!"

---

6. Rav Yechezkel Leiman.

"How can it be that there is a *bachur* in Mir whom you don't consider *echad mibnei hachaburah*? *Oy yid'agu!*"[7]

PERHAPS BECAUSE OF HIS DESIRE FOR *ACHDUS* IN THE YESHIVA, Rav Nosson Tzvi would encourage the development of friendships among the *talmidim*.

## Friendships

For instance, one of my roommates in the Mir dormitory was scheduled to get married in America during the last week of Adar. Now, everyone knew that the Rosh Yeshiva tried valiantly to combat the phenomenon of *bachurim* leaving yeshiva before the *zman* officially ended on Rosh Chodesh Nissan.[8] When my roommate expressed his dismay that none of his friends would be at his *chasunah*, I went to Rav Nosson Tzvi to discuss with him whether I should leave early to be able to attend the wedding, fully expecting him to say that it was more important to stay in yeshiva until the end of the *zman*. To my surprise, he told me to go to America and attend the *chasunah*.

To Rav Nosson Tzvi, friendship overrode the importance of being in yeshiva until the last day of the *zman*.

RAV NOSSON TZVI HAD A KNACK FOR KEEPING TRACK OF WHO was a friend of whom.

Yaakov and Yitzchak were two *bachurim* who had the privilege of conveying to Rav Nosson Tzvi each Friday night the Torah that Rav Asher Arielli *shlita* had said during the week. The two met and married their respective wives at around the same time, and then continued to go to Rav Nosson Tzvi's house as *yungeleit* for their special Friday-night *chavrusashaft*. The parallelism in their lives continued when their respective first children were born a few weeks apart. At that point, although Yitzchak continued the *chavrusashaft* with Rav Nosson Tzvi, Yaakov could no longer attend.

Shortly before Yitzchak's second child was born, Rav Nosson Tzvi approached him one morning after *Shacharis* and wished him mazal tov.

"But Rebbi," Yitzchak said in confusion, "the baby wasn't born yet!"

"What do you mean?" Rav Nosson Tzvi replied. "Your friend Yaakov had a baby yesterday, so I'm wishing you mazal tov!"

---

7. Heard from Rav Simcha Ellis, *mashgiach* in the branch of the Lakewood Yeshiva in Eretz Yisrael, who was present at this gathering.
8. See pp. 260-261.

AND FRIENDSHIPS MEANT SO MUCH TO HIM THAT HE WOULD remember them for decades. R' Beinish Mandel, who was part of Rav Nosson Tzvi's first *chaburah* in the mid-70's and remained close to him for the next 35 years, recalls that even in recent years, the Rosh Yeshiva would ask him, "How's Mendy?" or "How's Uri?"

When Beinish would explain that he had lost contact with those friends from his old *chaburah*, Rav Nosson Tzvi would be aghast. "How could you not keep up with a friend?" he would wonder aloud.

## Mirroring the Hanhalah

THE UNDERLYING PRINCIPLE OF THE *ACHDUS* AMONG THE *talmidim* was a direct outgrowth of the respect that each member of the *hanhalah* had for every single *talmid*. *Shmuessen* in the Mir, especially during *Sefirah*, would focus on the story of Rabbi Akiva's *talmidim*, who all died during *Sefirah* "*mipnei shelo nahagu kavod zeh lazeh* – because they didn't treat one another with respect" (*Yevamos* 62b).

Respect for each individual is one of the very foundations of the Mir.[9] Rav Binyamin Carlebach, who was one of the Rosh Yeshiva's closest partners in expanding and fundraising for the yeshiva, could often be spotted waiting outside Rav Nosson Tzvi's room while a *bachur* was inside discussing something with the Rosh Yeshiva. Although Rav Binyamin was coming to discuss yeshiva matters, he wouldn't interrupt a *bachur's* audience with the Rosh Yeshiva.

And the respect the *hanhalah* members displayed toward the *talmidim* mirrored the respect they had for one another.

At yeshiva functions, the Roshei Yeshiva would often be seen "arguing" with each other as to who should enter the room first. For instance, when Rav Aryeh Finkel and Rav Yitzchak Ezrachi once reached the dining room for a Chanukah *Mesibah* at the same time, the deliberations over who should enter first lasted for quite a few minutes. Rav Yitzchak insisted that Rav Aryeh enter first, and vice versa. Rav Aryeh pointed out that Rav Yitzchak was carrying *sefarim*, so he should certainly have the right-of-way. Rav Yitzchak couldn't bring himself to enter before Rav Aryeh, however, so he asked Rav Aryeh to take the *sefarim* from him and enter first.

Rav Nosson Tzvi himself would rise each time Rav Aryeh, Rav

---

9. Rav Aryeh Finkel noted at Rav Nosson Tzvi's *levayah* that *achdus* is so central to Mir, that in a certain sense the message of unity was Rav Nosson Tzvi's *tzava'ah* (will) to the yeshiva. (See p. 350 for the story.)

Honoring each other at every Mir event. (R-L) Rav Yitzchok Ezrachi (singing at microphone), Rav Nosson Tzvi, and Rav Aryeh Finkel

Aharon, or anyone else on the *hanhalah* would enter the room, no matter how severe his Parkinson's symptoms were at the time.

And the rest of the *hanhalah* reciprocated, even those who were older than Rav Nosson Tzvi and could theoretically have been named Rosh Yeshiva after Rav Beinush's passing. One Simchas Torah, as the *bachurim* were dancing in lively circles around Rav Nosson Tzvi, Rav Refoel Shmuelevitz took Rav Binyamin Carlebach aside and said, "Do you know why he gets this honor? Because he proved that he's worthy of it!"

THE RESPECT THE *HANHALAH* MEMBERS HAD FOR ONE ANOTHER was even more apparent in the lengths they would go to avoid hurting

**Avoiding Hurting Another's Feelings**
another's feelings. Children and close *talmidim* relate that Rav Nosson Tzvi would often be *mevater* on (forgo) an initiative he wanted to institute because he felt that someone on the *hanhalah* who was opposed to the initiative might be insulted that the Rosh Yeshiva hadn't followed his advice.

There was one person who would visit Rav Nosson Tzvi frequently to share his own vision for the yeshiva and criticize the way the Rosh Yeshiva was running it. One of Rav Nosson Tzvi's children once heard him admit, uncharacteristically, that it was difficult for him when this person would visit. *"Ich bin nisht bei zich* – I'm not myself [when he comes]," the Rosh Yeshiva sighed.

Yet in the decades of their relationship, this person never once sensed that the Rosh Yeshiva didn't appreciate his visits, or that he found the criticism disconcerting – as evidenced by the fact that he kept coming back, certain that the Rosh Yeshiva was interested in his advice.

THE ROSH YESHIVA'S RESPECT AND LOVE FOR EVERY PERSON rubbed off on the *talmidim*, but those closest to him were the most deeply affected.

### "What Would the Rosh Yeshiva Do?"

"R' Yechezkel," a *talmid* who was particularly close to the Rosh Yeshiva for many years and was eventually appointed to the *hanhalah* of the Mir Yeshiva Ketanah,[10] related that he was walking alongside a respected *talmid chacham* at the *levayah*. The *talmid chacham* wanted to hear about R' Yechezkel's relationship with the Rosh Yeshiva. Shocked as everyone else was by the sudden loss, R' Yechezkel drew comfort in reminiscing about the Rosh Yeshiva.

While he was talking, a *yungerman* walked over to R' Yechezkel and began to share his own memories of the Rosh Yeshiva. R' Yechezkel wanted to tell this interloper that he was in the middle of a conversation – but then he caught himself.

*What would the Rosh Yeshiva do in this situation?* he thought to himself. *He would put his own need for consolation aside and listen to this yungerman.*

With that in mind, he apologized quietly to the *talmid chacham* and turned his full attention to the *yungerman*.

IN *PARASHAS MIKEITZ, RASHI* REVEALS THAT WHEN YOSEF HaTzaddik was on the verge of sinning grievously, the image of his father Yaakov implanted itself in his mind, inspiring him to control his urge.

### "But the Rosh Yeshiva Respects Me!"

Because of the respect Rav Nosson

---

10. A *yeshiva ketanah* in Eretz Yisrael is equivalent to an American *mesivta* high school.

Tzvi had for each *talmid*, he had the very same effect on *talmidim* for years – and even decades – after they left the yeshiva.

A *talmid* who had been in Rav Nosson Tzvi's first *chaburah* and maintained ties with him for nearly 40 years relates that not once did he hear a single word of *tochachah* (rebuke) from the Rosh Yeshiva. Yet there were countless times when he was tempted to enter into a business deal that wasn't perfectly honest, and he refrained from doing so because he was suddenly struck by the thought, *How can I do this? Rav Nosson Tzvi respects me!*

## Torah of Unity

THE *ACHDUS* RAV NOSSON TZVI DEVELOPED IN THE YESHIVA wasn't only an exercise in *bein adam la'chaveiro* (obligations between man and his fellow) – it also fostered an atmosphere of camaraderie in which Torah could flourish.

Any Mir venue – from the dining rooms to the *otzar hasefarim* (library), from the buses that bring thousands of *yungeleit* to yeshiva each morning to the lines of people waiting to receive their monthly stipends – turns into a *"beis midrash"* of sorts.

The breakfast table is filled with *divrei Torah*, as one *talmid* poses a question on the weekly *parashah* and the others respond with their own insights. On the bus to yeshiva, many a *yungerman* is animatedly delivering a deep analysis of a *sugya* to another. Even people who never met, and who might hail from opposite ends of the planet, enthusiastically share *chiddushim* with each other.

For after all, in Mir we had one father – Rav Nosson Tzvi – and that made us all brothers!

Turning every venue into a *beis midrash*. Two *yungeleit* make the most of the ride home.

# CHAPTER TWENTY-ONE
# A TATTEH AND A MAMMEH

*The Rosh Yeshiva was a tatteh and a mammeh. He took care of every one of us — in ruchniyus, like a tatteh, and in gashmiyus, like a mammeh.*
*— Rav Eliezer Yehuda Finkel shlita, Rav Nosson Tzvi's son and successor, describing his father in his hesped at the levayah*

**W**HEN ONE HEARS OF A ROSH YESHIVA WITH thousands of *talmidim* – and especially one who is a big *masmid* – one naturally assumes that he oversees the yeshiva in a general way, and has no time to be very involved with the day-to-day operations. Mirrer *talmidim* knew that with their Rosh Yeshiva, the opposite was true.

No matter how much the yeshiva grew, Rav Nosson Tzvi had time for every *talmid* who turned to him. He was there to guide and help in any way possible, and perhaps most of all – to listen.

His son Rav Shaya related that until Rav Nosson Tzvi was *niftar*, everyone felt as though he were a *ben yachid*, an only child to the Rosh Yeshiva. At the *shivah*, each of these "only children" suddenly experienced a revelation: thousands of others felt exactly the same way.

"And the truth," concluded Rav Shaya, "is that each one was right. Because each person truly was a *ben yachid* to him."

AS EARLY AS THE LATE 1960'S, SHORTLY AFTER HIS WEDDING and long before he held a position in the Mir, Rav Nosson Tzvi showed

**A Tatteh in Ruchniyus**

his concern for each *talmid*. Not only did he fundraise quietly to pay *chavrusas* to learn with weaker *bachurim*, he also gave freely of his own time to help them advance in their learning.[1]

He never changed. Even when he was a Rosh Yeshiva with thousands of *talmidim*, he would graciously put aside dozens of pressing matters to tend to the spiritual growth of even one *bachur*.

I experienced this myself as a young *bachur*. About a year after I joined the Mir, I was considering switching to a different *shiur*, but I wasn't sure whether to make the move. One of the easiest times to have

---

1. See p. 209.

an audience with the Rosh Yeshiva was after *Shacharis*, when he would sit and make himself available for *talmidim*. Not wanting to burden him during the hours he set aside each day for receiving the public (both Mirrer *talmidim* and outsiders), I waited on line after *Shacharis* and told the Rosh Yeshiva that I wanted to discuss switching *shiurim*. "Come to my house at 11 o'clock tonight," he replied.

I knocked at the door at 11, and the Rosh Yeshiva himself opened the door and greeted me with a broad smile. I didn't want to waste his time, so as I sat down in his living room and explained my dilemma as briefly as possible. He wasn't satisfied with this concise explanation. He asked me many questions about myself: which yeshivos I had learned in before Mir, who my *chavrusas* were, and so on. It took me 15 minutes to answer all of his questions. Finally, he advised me to switch *shiurim*.

The Rosh Yeshiva could easily have answered my question in that 30-second meeting after *Shacharis*. But the *ruchniyus* of one of his 4,000 *talmidim* was so important to him that he wanted to hear all the details surrounding the question before responding.

DESPITE ALL OF HIS OBLIGATIONS, THE ROSH YESHIVA DIDN'T mind when people came to him to discuss even the most insignificant

**A Spiritual Guide**

matters. In fact, a *maggid shiur* in yeshiva estimated that at least 70 percent of the people Rav Nosson Tzvi dealt with each day were nudniks, people who came to pester him about trivialities.

When I quoted this to Rav Nosson Tzvi's son, Rav Shaya, he corrected the statement. "Abba didn't consider anyone a nudnik. Often there were extremely weighty issues on his table – a *talmid's* medical crisis, a deep budgetary shortfall, or an issue affecting all of *Klal Yisrael*. Yet when a *yungerman* came to ask for a raise so he could afford some leben and cottage cheese, the Rosh Yeshiva didn't think, *How can you bother me about your leben when I'm dealing with such important issues?* He was able to put himself into the shoes of the person he was talking to. Since the issue was important to that person, it was important to him."

His ability to put himself into the shoes of others was even more noticeable when the issue was of spiritual significance. In the course of a day, he could guide scores of *talmidim* and offer many simple nuggets of advice, such as the following:[2]

---

2. This list is a small sampling of the tens of pieces of advice recorded in detail by R' Moshe Dov Fox, a *talmid* who had a long-term *chavrusashaft* with Rav Nosson Tzvi and recorded each piece

- How should one review his learning in a way that will maximize the amount he will remember?
  **Say the words aloud, and write summaries of what you learned.**

- I finished learning *Chovos HaLevavos*. Should I review it, or start a new *mussar* work?
  **Start a new work, because it's good to expose yourself to different ways of thinking.**

- If someone reviews his learning frequently, so that he finishes a *masechta* frequently, should he make a *siyum* each time?
  **When I was learning many *blatt* each day with Rav Zundel Kroizer,[3] he would make a *l'chaim* each time we finished a *masechta*.**

R' Moshe Dov Fox relates, however, that the Rosh Yeshiva often asked him what *he* thought was correct. "He wanted to train me to think."

When R' Moshe Dov would give his opinion and the Rosh Yeshiva disagreed, he would not say "You're wrong." He would always stress the positive – "The other option would have been better."

Even when answering a yes-or-no question, the Rosh Yeshiva would look for a way to express himself in a positive way. When asked, for instance, whether one should call his friends by their last names, Rav Nosson Tzvi replied, "It's nicer to call people by their first names."

"He wanted to train me to think." Rav Nosson Tzvi learning with Moshe Dov Fox in his days as a *bachur* in Mir

---

of advice he received from the Rosh Yeshiva in the Rosh Yeshiva's exact words. The Rosh Yeshiva's responses, which are paraphrased here for the sake of clarity (he often mixed Yiddish words into his answers), are in bold.

3. The Rosh Yeshiva had a learning session with one of the greatest *talmidei chachamim* in Yerushalayim, *yblcht"a* Rav Zundel Kroizer, in which they would learn approximately five *blatt* a day!

THE MISHNAH (*AVOS* 5:9) TEACHES THAT ONE OF THE QUALITIES
of a wise person is that he doesn't rush to answer questions. When Rav

**The Gedolim's Trust**     Nosson Tzvi was asked for advice on an
                            issue upon which he didn't feel capable
of rendering a decision, he would say simply, "I don't know."

Nevertheless, other *gedolim* expressed their wholehearted confidence
in his ability to decide on important matters.

Rav Simcha Ellis, formerly *mashgiach* of the Israel branch of Beth
Medrash Govoha, relates that he once had a dilemma regarding whom
to honor at the *bris* of his son. He was close to Rav Chaim Brim, and
went to discuss the issue with him. When Rav Chaim heard the question, he said, "This question has to be posed to Rav Nosson Tzvi."

Rav Simcha stared at him incredulously. Rav Chaim Brim was not
only a few decades older than Rav Nosson Tzvi, but everyone knew that
the Rosh Yeshiva considered Rav Chaim one of *his* mentors!

"You need *siyata d'Shmaya* (Divine assistance) to answer such a
question," explained Rav Chaim. "With the force of the [then] 4,000
people learning in yeshiva behind him, Rav Nosson Tzvi has a lot of
*siyata d'Shmaya*."

IN ISRAEL, ALL 18-YEAR-OLDS ARE SUBJECT TO ARMY DRAFT,
unless they can claim an exemption (*petur*) on various grounds. One type

**"I Have to Learn**     of exemption, which was entered into law by
**the Sugya"**           Israel's first prime minister, David Ben Gurion,
                         is a *petur* for yeshiva students who learn all
day. The process of receiving such an exemption is not simple. Each
yeshiva student must obtain a paper from the yeshiva declaring that this
*talmid* is "*Toraso umnaso*" – his occupation is Torah – and then submit
the *petur* to the local army enrollment center. Sometimes, the army will
try to fight the exemption in one way or another.

Several months before becoming Rosh Yeshiva, Rav Beinush handed
over the task of determining eligibility and signing documents for these
exemptions to Rav Nosson Tzvi. That same day, a *talmid* approached
him to discuss his deferment. Characteristically, Rav Nosson Tzvi didn't
answer off-the-cuff. "It's a '*sugya*,'" he said, "and I have to learn it.
Come back to me tomorrow."

In later years, he would champion the cause of those who were having trouble getting deferments.

There was an Israeli *yungerman* who came from a more modern background, and his parents wanted him to go to the army. The army, too, refused him a deferment. The *yungerman* came to the Rosh Yeshiva and told him that the army was trying to draft him.

"Should I leave the country so that I can continue learning?" he asked.

"You'll stay here," the Rosh Yeshiva said resolutely, "and you'll continue learning."

Rav Nosson Tzvi spent hours contacting Knesset members and other activists for help. When the Rosh Yeshiva was *niftar*, nine years later, the *yungerman* was still learning.

## "His" Shidduch

ONCE, A *BACHUR* CAME TO THE ROSH YESHIVA TO DISCUSS A *shidduch* that had been suggested for him. He felt that he was too young to go back to America and start *shidduchim*, but his parents wanted him to look into the *shidduch*. The Rosh Yeshiva told him to come back in a few hours. When he returned, the Rosh Yeshiva told him to proceed with the *shidduch*.

It seems that in those few hours, the Rosh Yeshiva had made the necessary inquiries, and had learned that this was indeed an appropriate match.

The boy went back to America to meet this girl, and eventually they married. A few months later, the couple returned to settle in Eretz Yisrael. Without reminding the Rosh Yeshiva about the conversation they had had a few months before, the *yungerman* asked him if he could join the Mir *kollel*. "Of course," the Rosh Yeshiva said with a smile. "Your *shidduch* happened because of me; how can I *not* take you into the *kollel*?"[4]

## "He Needs a Push"

AS AN OUTGROWTH OF THEIR JOINT CONCERN FOR EACH *talmid*, the Rosh Yeshiva and the Rebbetzin devoted themselves to helping the *bachurim* find *shidduchim* – especially those *bachurim* who were getting on in years and had not found their mate.

Abbish, who had attended the Rosh Yeshiva's daily *iyun shiur*, had gone back to America to find a *shidduch*, but several years had passed and he was still not married. Once, when he was visiting the Rosh Yeshiva, the Rebbetzin asked, "*Nu*, what's taking you so long?"

---

4. There were times when Rav Nosson Tzvi couldn't afford to pay all the *yungeleit* who wanted to join the *kollel*, but they were still welcome to learn in the yeshiva and eat meals there, without a monthly stipend.

"He needs a good push," the Rosh Yeshiva said with a smile. With that, he reached up and gave the *bachur* a playful slap on his cheek to reinforce his point that this *bachur* was being too particular.

Daniel, an older single who had trained as a lawyer and had then taken a year off to learn in Eretz Yisrael, was having a very hard time with *shidduchim*. One day the *mashgiach*, Rav Aharon Chodosh, told him that the Rosh Yeshiva wanted to speak to him. Daniel hurried to the Rosh Yeshiva, who told him that he had a *shidduch* for him. The parents of the girl were in Eretz Yisrael and wanted to meet him. They set up a meeting, and the parents were favorably impressed – so much so, that they were willing to pay for his airfare and accommodations so he could fly in to America to meet their daughter. Daniel returned to the Rosh Yeshiva and asked him what to do. He had taken this break from his career plans in order to learn, and this trip would cause a major interruption of his learning. "I want to discuss it with the Rebbetzin," the Rosh Yeshiva replied. "Come back to me tomorrow."

When Daniel returned, the Rosh Yeshiva told him not to make the trip.

A short time later, the Rosh Yeshiva summoned him once again and suggested a different *shidduch*. This time, Daniel met the girl twice and then told the Rosh Yeshiva that he didn't really think it was for him for a certain reason, which the Rosh Yeshiva didn't accept. "You don't have to be so picky," the Rosh Yeshiva chided. Although he generally didn't rebuke people so openly, he apparently felt that it was important for Daniel to hear that he was limiting his chances at a *shidduch* by waiting for the "perfect" mate to come along.

The Rosh Yeshiva didn't limit his role in *shidduchim* to older *talmidim*; at times, he would get involved in *shidduchim* for those who were "fresh off the boat" as well.

Shortly after Ari, a very close *talmid*, went back home for *shidduchim*, the Rosh Yeshiva made a short visit to America, his first visit ever during the month of Elul. Knowing that Rav Nosson Tzvi was visiting for only a few days, Ari rushed over to the home of the Rosh Yeshiva's host to greet him. As soon as he entered the room, Rav Nosson Tzvi asked, "How's it going with *shidduchim*?"

Ari reported that there were several offers on the table. "Can I suggest someone?" asked the Rosh Yeshiva.

"Sure," a surprised Ari replied, "but my mother handles my *shidduchim*."

The Rosh Yeshiva asked for her telephone number, and Ari gave it to him. The conversation continued for a few more minutes after that, and then Ari left.

Later that day, Ari's mother told him that she had received an unusual phone call.

"Mrs. So-and-so?" a quavering voice intoned.

"Yes," she replied.

"Hello, this is Nosson Tzvi Finkel." (Ari's mother related that she nearly dropped the phone when she heard the Rosh Yeshiva identify himself.) "Can I suggest a *shidduch* for Ari?"

"Certainly," Ari's mother stammered, getting out her *shidduchim* notebook.

The Rosh Yeshiva told her the girl's name, and then explained that his brother-in-law Rav Binyamin Carlebach knew more details. He then asked if he could hand the telephone to Rav Binyamin.

Ari, who has since returned to Eretz Yisrael to rejoin the yeshiva, still can't get over the story. The Rosh Yeshiva was on an urgent visit to the States that would last for only a few days, yet he took the time to help a young *bachur* with *shidduchim*!

CHAIM'KE, AN ISRAELI *YUNGERMAN*, WAS PART OF AN ELITE, hardworking *chaburah* that learned a full *daf* every day and reviewed

**Chiddushei Torah From Overseas**

each *daf* many times, according to a system designed to help people retain their learning. Aside from this intensive learning schedule, Chaim'ke would also tell his *chiddushei Torah* to the Rosh Yeshiva every two weeks.

After a few years of marriage, Chaim'ke's wife was diagnosed with a severe form of lymphoma, and the couple had no choice but to leave their children and travel to the United States so she could be treated in Memorial Sloan-Kettering Hospital in New York.

Before they left, Rav Nosson Tzvi told Chaim'ke that he expected him to continue delivering *chiddushei Torah* to him by writing them and faxing them. He also asked Chaim'ke to call every week with an update on his wife's condition.

Several months later, the phone rang in Chaim'ke's parents' house. It was one of the Rosh Yeshiva's attendants, asking for Chaim'ke's number in the States. "He hasn't called in a few weeks," the attendant explained, "and the Rosh Yeshiva wants to call him to find out what's doing."

Sure enough, the Rosh Yeshiva called Chaim'ke in New York. But that wasn't the only time the Rosh Yeshiva called him.

The next time the Rosh Yeshiva traveled to the States, he called Chaim'ke again. "How's your wife?" he asked.

"She's doing well, *baruch Hashem*," Chaim'ke answered.

"I want to see for myself," the Rosh Yeshiva said. "Come with your wife to the house where I'm staying."

The couple came and had breakfast with the Rosh Yeshiva and the Rebbetzin. As busy as he was on his trips to America, he *had* to check on Chaim'ke and his wife.

## "I Am Their Father"

ONE *CHABURAH* IN THE MIR WAS COMPOSED OF LONGTIME Mirrer *talmidim* who had proven themselves in learning over the course of many years. Each candidate for this advanced *chaburah* had to be approved by Rav Nosson Tzvi himself. These *yungeleit* were assigned seats in one of the yeshiva's *batei midrash*, but – as often happens in the Mir – there weren't enough seats for all of them.

The seats adjacent to this *chaburah* belonged to a group that one might consider the polar opposite of these *yungeleit*. Out of his deep love of every Jew and his desire to give every *bachur* a chance to learn, Rav Nosson Tzvi had established a *chaburah* for boys who had not done well in any other yeshiva. Some of them were on the verge of leaving Yiddishkeit when they joined the Mir, and this *chaburah* was their last-ditch effort to rejuvenate themselves. But as a result of their lackadaisical attitude toward Yiddishkeit, these boys would consistently come late.

Some of the seat-less *yungeleit* in the advanced *chaburah* wanted to use the seats designated for the other group – at least until they arrived – but the *mashgiach* would not hear of it. "If you're sitting in their seats when they walk in," he explained, "they'll leave without learning at all that day."

"Boruch," the person in charge of the advanced *chaburah,* was close to Rav Nosson Tzvi, and some of the *yungeleit* urged him repeatedly to discuss the situation with the Rosh Yeshiva. After several weeks, Boruch worked up the courage to approach the Rosh Yeshiva. He explained, "We have *yungeleit* stationed in hallways and near the restrooms, while some seats in the *beis midrash* are vacant most of the morning" – hoping that the Rosh Yeshiva would allow the *yungeleit* to use those seats at least until the *bachurim* showed up.

Rav Nosson Tzvi heard Boruch's request, and responded with a question of his own. "What will I do when a father of one of these boys comes to me and cries, 'My son was finally beginning to learn after failing everywhere else, and now he comes into yeshiva and sees someone sitting in his seat, so he doesn't learn that day!' What will I answer him?"

Rav Nosson Tzvi always had time for each individual *talmid*.

"If that's the problem," Boruch replied, "then we can formulate a diplomatic answer for those fathers."

Rav Nosson Tzvi fixed his gaze on Boruch. Pointing to himself he said, "*I* am their father."

## ... And a Mammeh

RAV NOSSON TZVI'S CONCERN FOR EACH *TALMID* EXTENDED far beyond caring for their spiritual well-being; he was equally concerned with each person's physical and emotional well-being.

Many of the thousands of stories that surfaced in the months after the Rosh Yeshiva's *petirah* were stories of how he would take the well-being of every single *talmid* to heart – even though he almost always ignored his own physical disability.

One summer, he met one of the younger *maggidei shiur* in the Mir and asked whether he was going away on vacation during *bein hazmanim*. The *maggid shiur* replied that he could not afford it. Rav Nosson Tzvi reached into his pocket and withdrew a sizable sum of money. "It's important for you to get away with your family," he explained, pressing the money into the *maggid shiur's* hand.

## Arranging the Vacation

ALTHOUGH RAV NOSSON TZVI ALWAYS SPOKE ABOUT THE need for *retzifus*, uninterrupted study that spanned from the beginning of each *zman* through the end of the *zman*, he also knew when someone needed a break.

During Rav Nosson Tzvi's last year, a *yungerman* who has been learning in Rav Asher Arielli's *shiur* for close to a decade was going through a particularly hectic and stressful period. Rav Nosson Tzvi instructed him to get away with his wife for the Shabbos after Shavuos, in order to recoup their energy. The Rosh Yeshiva even helped him plan the trip so that he wouldn't miss any *shiur*.

THE WIFE OF ONE OF RAV NOSSON TZVI'S *CHAVRUSAS* WAS going through a difficult labor, and her husband called the Rosh

## "We Were Up, So We Called"

Yeshiva's house at 10 p.m. to ask the Rosh Yeshiva to daven that the birth should go easily. The Rebbetzin asked for his wife's name, and said that she would pass on the message. At 1 a.m., the woman delivered a healthy baby girl.

The next morning, the *yungerman* came to inform Rav Nosson Tzvi about his mazal tov. When he entered the house shortly after *Shacharis*, Rav Nosson Tzvi and the Rebbetzin were eating breakfast, and they immediately wished him mazal tov on the birth of a girl.

"How did you know that it was a girl?" the *yungerman* asked incredulously.

"We were up at 3 a.m.," they explained, "and we were worried about you. We called the maternity ward to find out what happened, and they told us that your wife delivered a girl and mother and child were doing well."

RAV NOSSON TZVI WAS BLESSED WITH A SIXTH SENSE THAT picked up people's inner feelings. This sense was so acute that he could

## A Quick Lift

discern when a *talmid* felt down just from passing him on the street. Once, when walking home from yeshiva, he passed "R' Chaim," a *yungerman* with whom he was close. Without uttering a word, he walked over to R' Chaim and gave him a kiss on his forehead.

"That was the first and last time the Rosh Yeshiva did something like that to me," R' Chaim later confided to a friend. "The timing couldn't have been better. I had been going through a difficult period, and nothing seemed to be working out for me. My learning wasn't going well, and there was trouble in my family, among other issues. I had fallen into despair, and that affected my learning even more. That kiss was a watershed moment. It reminded me that the Rosh Yeshiva loved me, and that gave me the strength to deal with my problems."

No matter how large the yeshiva grew, Rav Nosson Tzvi loved each *talmid* as an individual.

ONE OF THE EARLIEST – AND MOST ASTOUNDING – TESTIMONIALS to Rav Nosson Tzvi's concern for each *talmid* goes back to the 1970's,

## "Rebbi, You're the Greatest"

when he had his first *chaburah*. A member of the *chaburah* contracted measles, which, if not treated properly, can affect the nervous system. This *bachur* went crazy – quite literally. Among other dangerous behaviors, he tried jumping off the roof.

Thankfully, Rav Beinush's wife, Rebbetzin Esther, was able to arrange for a top doctor[5] to examine the *bachur* early in the morning, before the neurology ward in Hadassah Hospital opened. The *bachur*'s roommates brought him to the hospital – and then who should show up but Rav Nosson Tzvi!

Rav Nosson Tzvi wouldn't leave this *bachur* alone in the hospital. He cared for him day after day, making sure that no one besides his roommates, who already knew what had happened, would know of the disturbing symptoms of his illness, so as not to ruin his prospects for a *shidduch* once he recovered.[6] Rav Nosson Tzvi stayed with him until his parents came to take him back to America.

---

5. See p. 228.
6. Rav Beinush knew that a *bachur* had contracted a mental illness, and he asked for the *bachur*'s first name and his mother's name, but he also asked that he not be told the family name. "I want to daven for him," he explained, "but I don't want to know his family name, in case people ask me about him for a *shidduch*."

This *bachur* was so disturbed that he wrote a "last will and testament," which included barbs for every single person he knew. His *chavrusas*, his roommates – no one he knew was spared from his sharp criticism.

But then there was the last line in his "will," which he wrote for Rav Nosson Tzvi.

"Rebbi," he wrote, "you are the greatest."


JUST AS THE LOVE FLOWED FROM THE ROSH YESHIVA TO EVERY single *talmid*, so did the love flow back to him.

## An Ocean of Love

During the 1990's, the Rosh Yeshiva made a *chasunah* in Bnei Brak. A large group of Mirrer *bachurim* traveled to Bnei Brak – not out of a feeling of obligation, but because they truly wanted to take part in the Rosh Yeshiva's *simchah*, just as they would for a member of their own family. In attendance at the *chasunah* were many *gedolei Yisrael*, political figures, and philanthropists who had donated large sums to the yeshiva. But the Rosh Yeshiva focused most of his time and energy on the *bachurim*, who danced indefatigably around him.

That Friday, as Rav Nosson Tzvi's living room filled up for his weekly *vaad*, he sat there silently with a big smile on his lips, his gaze moving from face to face around the room. Finally, he spoke. "Gentlemen," he said, "I want to share something with you.

"My *mechutan* has been a *mechanech* for decades. After the *chasunah*, he told me that in all his years in *chinuch*, he has never seen an outpouring of love the likes of which he saw between us at the *chasunah*. He said it was an '*Okiyanus shel ahavah* – an ocean of love.'"

The Rosh Yeshiva paused for a second, his smile growing larger. "I just wanted to say thank you."

# CHAPTER TWENTY-TWO
# CARING: BEYOND THE WALLS OF MIR

*Rav Nosson Tzvi would often recount, in vivid detail, a story that occurred when he slept in the room of Rav Leizer Yudel's house where the sefarim were kept. One morning, Rav Leizer Yudel came into that room very early, thinking that young Nosson Tzvi was sleeping. He was actually awake, but he pretended to be asleep so he could watch how Rav Leizer Yudel began his day.*

*What he saw remained with him for the rest of his life: Rav Leizer Yudel stretched out his hands and embraced the entire Shas, and then went from one volume to the next kissing each one individually. Rav Nosson Tzvi would say that he learned how to love the Torah from this incident.*

*After Rav Nosson Tzvi's petirah, Rav Tzvi Cheshin, whose family was close to him from his first years in the Mir, remarked, "Everyone knows that the Rosh Yeshiva used to say that he developed his own love of Torah from seeing Rav Leizer Yudel kiss every volume of Shas. But what did Rav Nosson Tzvi's own children see?*

*"They saw how a living Shas kisses every Jew."*

**W**HEN MOSHE RABBEINU STOOD AT THE *SNEH* (burning bush) and received the instruction to lead the Jewish people from Egypt, he began a week-long dialogue with Hashem.[1] At the end, when Moshe still declined the mission, Hashem grew angry and commanded him to go. Apparently, though, what Moshe had discussed with Hashem until his final refusal had been acceptable.

The Torah doesn't record the entire conversation between Hashem and Moshe, but a Midrash (*Shemos Rabbah* 3:4) fills in the details. The Midrash states that Moshe asked, "How can You send me to take all the Jewish people into a wilderness? There are many new mothers, expectant women, and children among them. Do we have enough food for the new mothers? Will we have soft foods to give the expectant women? And will we have sweets to give the children?"

We see, noted Rav Moshe Chait, the Rosh Yeshiva of Yeshiva Chofetz Chaim in Yerushalayim, that a true leader thinks of everyone – from the adults to the smallest children. And we see that as long as Moshe's focus was on the people, Hashem continued the discussion. Only when Moshe turned the conversation toward his own discomfort did Hashem put an end to the dialogue by instructing him to go.

It is astounding enough that Rav Nosson Tzvi was able to train his focus on each of the thousands of individuals in his yeshiva, caring for each one as an only child. It is almost unfathomable that he had the same concern for every member of *Klal Yisrael* – man, woman, or child.

Rav Binyamin Carlebach relates that just as Rav Nosson Tzvi asked his *talmid* Chaim'ke to call him every two weeks with an update on his wife's condition (see p. 310), he made the same request of many people

---

1. See *Rashi* to *Shemos* 4:10.

who came to him to pour out their woes – whether or not they were connected to the Mir. And he truly wanted them to call – he remembered them, and waited to hear their updates. How he found the time to fit these phone calls into his grueling schedule, no one knows.

ONCE, A WOMAN FROM CANADA CAME WITH HER DAUGHTER to Rav Nosson Tzvi and told him of their terrible personal plight. Rav

**Tehillim and Tears**

Nosson Tzvi said, "I wish I could help you, but the only thing I can do is daven. Come, let's say some *Tehillim* together." Rav Nosson Tzvi opened his *Tehillim* – to the very chapter that this woman used to say whenever she was overwhelmed by her tragic circumstances.

Later, she related that of all the many *tzaddikim* she had visited in Eretz Yisrael, the one who had given her the most comfort was Rav Nosson Tzvi.

Even when he was too weak to recite *Tehillim*, Rav Nosson Tzvi still had the capacity to offer solace. In his last year, someone came to unburden himself. A difficult health issue was affecting someone in his family, and it was becoming too much for him to bear. Rav Nosson Tzvi was lying on the couch, thoroughly drained. After hearing the story, he said, "I don't have *koach* (energy) to do anything – not even to daven. All I can do now is cry."

Rav Nosson Tzvi then instructed the person to bring a *Tehillim*. The person sat down next to Rav Nosson Tzvi and started to say *Tehillim*, while Rav Nosson Tzvi lay there and cried.

MANY PEOPLE – ESPECIALLY AMERICANS, BUT ALSO EUROPEANS and Israelis – had the feeling that Rav Nosson Tzvi was "our *gadol*."

**An American Gadol in Eretz Yisrael**

Rav Yitzchak Berkowitz expressed this feeling in a *hesped*: "Often," he said, "when we go to visit a *gadol b'Yisrael*, we shake and we shiver – there's a certain fear you have when you walk into the room. With Rav Nosson Tzvi it was different. You felt that he was on 'your side.' He was there to help you. He understood you."

When Rav Nosson Tzvi arrived in the Mir as a teenager, it was not common for *bachurim* from *chutz la'aretz* to come to Eretz Yisrael to learn. Girls certainly did not come; there were no seminaries for girls from abroad. And it was practically unheard of for a young couple from *chutz la'aretz* to settle in Eretz Yisrael.

But as the Torah world grew, so did the numbers of *bnei Torah* who flocked to Eretz Yisrael. First as *bachurim* and seminary girls, and then as married couples, intrepid young people would make the trip each year, leaving their families behind to bask in the special *kedushah* (holiness) of Eretz Yisrael, where the very atmosphere makes a person wise (*Bava Basra* 158b). Eventually, spending a year or two in Eretz Yisrael became de rigueur for children of Torah families, and living in Eretz Yisrael after marriage became a normal practice as well.

Even as their ranks swelled, however, most *chutznikim* remained just that: outsiders. Some adapted better to the Israeli culture, mentality, and language; some worse. As a general rule, though – once a *chutznik*, always a *chutznik*. Rav Chaim Shmuelevitz would joke that he was wiser than others, because others thought they could understand the Americans, and he realized that he couldn't.[2] To have an American-born *gadol* become the Rosh Yeshiva of the yeshiva in Eretz Yisrael with the largest contingent of Americans, as well as one of the leaders of the yeshiva world in general, was a great turn of *hashgachah*.

Rav Nosson Tzvi understood why Americans were bothered by certain things that Israelis considered normal – not only because he grew up in America, but mainly because he had such a giant heart.

Rav Yitzchak Berkowitz, who is the Rav of a large community of Americans in Yerushalayim – most of whom are Mirrer *talmidim* or alumni – relates that he would speak to Rav Nosson Tzvi about problems in his community. Rav Nosson Tzvi would listen to the problems, and he would cry along with those who felt wronged. Often, he couldn't solve the problem, but he knew how to listen in a way that made everyone feel better.

LESS THAN A YEAR AFTER BECOMING ROSH YESHIVA, RAV Nosson Tzvi had to deal with an extremely challenging dilemma. With **The Gulf War** the Gulf War looming, many parents asked their children to return home from Eretz Yisrael, afraid that Saddam Hussein would make good on his promise to bombard the country. Although Rav Nosson Tzvi felt that the Torah would protect those who remained in Eretz Yisrael, he understood the concerns of their parents. When *bachurim* came to ask him what to do, he would say, "Try to convince your parents to let you stay, and if not ..."

---

2. Rav Yitzchak Berkowitz.

Characteristically, he didn't finish his sentence by saying "and if not, *go home*," because he made a point of never issuing a directive to stop learning. But he made it clear to these *bachurim* that their parents' concern was valid and should not be ignored.

*Bachurim* preparing their sealed rooms for the impending scud attacks (above) and waiting in their gas masks for the all-clear sound

And Rav Nosson Tzvi took responsibility for the *bachurim* who did have parental consent to remain in Israel. At 2 a.m. on January 18, 1991, the first air-raid siren of the Gulf War sounded. Everyone in the yeshiva building ran up to the sealed rooms on the fourth floor. As they were settling in with their gas masks on, there was a knock at one of the doors.

The *bachur* who was in charge of instructing the *bachurim* how to use their masks was in that room, and he grew very agitated that someone wasn't taking the war seriously.

"Who's there?" he asked irately. "Why aren't you in your sealed room?"

"It's Nosson Tzvi Finkel," came a shaky voice.

While everyone else prepared for the war, Rav Nosson Tzvi had asked a *bachur* who had a car to pick him up from his home on Rechov Yisa Brachah as soon as a siren went off. He left his own family at home and rushed to be with the *bachurim*, who would certainly need a calming influence during the frightening hours in the sealed rooms.

The Rosh Yeshiva spent Shabbosos during the Gulf War in yeshiva, so that he could be with the *bachurim*. One Friday night, as he was giving a *shiur klali*, a siren went off in middle of the *shiur*. Everyone ran to their sealed rooms. When the all-clear siren sounded, they returned to the *beis midrash*, and the Rosh Yeshiva resumed his *shiur klali* from the very word he had left off!

The Gulf War ended shortly before Purim, and no *bachur* who was in yeshiva then can forget the celebrations that took place in the Mir that year.

AFTER RAV NOSSON TZVI'S *PETIRAH*, EVERYONE SPOKE ABOUT his "giant heart." Rav Tzvi Cheshin went a step further, examining the

**Noticing Everything** concept of a giant heart. "We tend to think of a big heart the way we think of a big living room," he remarked. "Just as a big living room can hold a lot of people, so can a big heart envelop thousands of people.

"But the truth is that Rav Nosson Tzvi didn't 'have room in his heart' for thousands; rather, he devoted his *entire* heart to each one of those thousands."

Because he devoted his entire heart to everyone, he would notice things that no one else would see. Immersed as he was in Torah, burdened as he was by the responsibility of running the yeshiva, and weakened as he was by Parkinson's, he nevertheless had an eagle eye for the tiniest details about people.

His son Rav Chaim recalled that Rav Nosson Tzvi was always the one to notice if someone at the table was missing a fork or anything else. "He saw everything because he *cared*," Chaim explains. "His perceptiveness was an outgrowth of his love and concern for every person."

On the first night of Rosh Hashanah, every member of the yeshiva would file past Rav Nosson Tzvi after davening to exchange *L'Shanah Tovah* greetings – a process that took several hours. He once told Rav Binyamin Carlebach that when a line of people filed past him – in any venue, at any time of the year – he would observe each face individually.

His brother Rav Gedalya related that one year Rav Nosson Tzvi suddenly pulled a *bachur* out of the line and began to converse with him, asking him his name and how he was doing. Later, someone asked why he had stopped the entire line to talk to this *bachur*. "His tie was askew, and he looked a little unkempt," he explained. "I figured that he must be going through a difficult time."

As always, he was on the mark – this *bachur* was actually experiencing a crisis. Who knows what those few moments with the Rosh Yeshiva did for him?

ONCE, A GROUP OF *BACHURIM* FROM A YESHIVA FOR BOYS FROM weaker backgrounds came to visit the Rosh Yeshiva on Shabbos, to hear

**The Extra Tag** words of *chizuk* and receive a *berachah*. The Rosh Yeshiva was very weak so he couldn't speak at length, but he gave each boy a *berachah*. As the boys filed by, he pulled one of them close and asked if there was an *eiruv* in his home city.

What was behind this odd question? Rav Nosson Tzvi noticed that the boy hadn't removed the manufacturer's label from the sleeve of his coat, which may have constituted a problem of *hotza'ah*[3] if the city did not have an *eiruv*.

NO MATTER HOW BUSY THINGS WERE, RAV NOSSON TZVI never lost sight of any individual. A daughter of a longtime Mirrer

**"Take for Your Sisters"** *talmid* had the honor of holding her engagement celebration in his home. When the guests were seated, Rav Nosson Tzvi noticed that two of the *kallah*'s siblings didn't have a place to sit, and he asked someone to bring them chairs.

When my son turned 3, we took him to Rav Nosson Tzvi for a *berachah* upon his *upsherin* (first haircut). A *maggid shiur* in yeshiva was about to make a *siyum* on all of *Seder Mo'ed* at that time, and Rav Nosson Tzvi's living room was already full of people participating in the *siyum*. But Rav Nosson Tzvi gave us his full attention, and after giving my son a *berachah*, he held out a bowl of taffies. My son misunder-

stood and tried to take the entire bowl. Rav Nosson Tzvi smiled broadly, and told him gently, "You can take two." Then, although the room was crowded, he noticed my wife standing outside the door with our two daughters. "Take two more," he told my son, "and give one to each of your sisters."

Nothing escaped his gaze.

My son receiving a *berachah* from Rav Nosson Tzvi upon his *upsherin*

---

3. I.e., carrying an object in a public domain.

ELI ARRIVED IN YESHIVA IN ELUL OF 5771, A YEAR BEFORE THE
Rosh Yeshiva passed away. Three weeks later, his father was *niftar*.

**Smiling for the Photographer** After the *shivah*, Eli returned to yeshiva, where he davened for the *amud* in the main *beis midrash*. Rav Nosson Tzvi developed a relationship with him, and took a particular liking to him.

In his later years, after kindling the menorah on the last night of Chanukah, Rav Nosson Tzvi would go down to the street in front of the Mir and dance with the *bachurim*. That year, approximately 300 boys were dancing with him – but Eli, who was in *aveilus*, couldn't participate in the festivities. He stood off to the side and captured the proceedings with his camera. As the *bachurim* danced around in a circle with the Rosh Yeshiva, Eli noticed that each time the Rosh Yeshiva passed him, he turned in his direction and smiled.

Eli was wondering whether the Rosh Yeshiva was trying to give him an opportunity to get a good picture. When the dancing ended, he escorted the Rosh Yeshiva back to his home, and when everyone else left, he said – a bit tentatively, because he wasn't sure whether he was correct in his assumption – "*Yasher koach*, Rosh Yeshiva."

Rav Nosson Tzvi looked up at him, smiled broadly, and patted his cheek – confirming that even amid the festivities, his heart was with this young *bachur*.


IT WASN'T ONLY FOR HIS OWN *TALMID* THAT HE WAS WILLING
to pose. On one trip to America, Rav Nosson Tzvi spent a Sunday in

**For Someone Else's Parnasah** Lakewood meeting with donors. His schedule was very tight, with little time between appointments. Somehow, a gentleman managed to sneak into the house, and after one of the donors left, he walked into the room and told the Rosh Yeshiva that he had no *parnasah*. One of the things he was doing to try to earn a living was to sell pictures of *gedolei Yisrael*. "Could the Rosh Yeshiva allow me to take some pictures of him?" the man asked.

The Rosh Yeshiva agreed.

This man didn't realize that it was inappropriate to order a Rosh Yeshiva around, however. He instructed the Rosh Yeshiva to sit this way and that; to take his hat off and put it back on; to look to the right and the left ... And the Rosh Yeshiva complied with each command, happy to do whatever he could to ease this man's financial woes.[4]

---

4. Heard from R' Mordechai Grunwald.

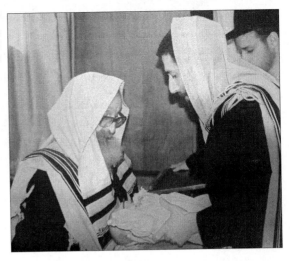

"I'm sorry for shaking." Rav Nosson Tzvi serves as *sandak* at a *bris* performed by R' Yehuda Baum

R' YEHUDA BAUM, AN AMERICAN *YUNGERMAN* IN YESHIVA who trained as a *mohel* in the early 1990's, relates that at his first *bris*

**Apologizing to the Mohel**

with Rav Nosson Tzvi as *sandak*, the Rosh Yeshiva motioned to him after the *bris*. He drew closer, but Rav Nosson Tzvi was too weak to make himself heard. R' Yehuda got even closer, and he was finally able to make out the words: "Sorry for shaking so much."

In his weakened state, Rav Nosson Tzvi was still thinking of how disconcerting it must have been for a young *mohel* to perform the *milah* while the *sandak* shook from Parkinson's.

RAV NOSSON TZVI HAD A SPECIAL LOVE FOR CHILDREN. After each *tefillah* on Shabbos, hundreds of people would file past him

**Love of Children**

to say *Gut Shabbos*. No matter how weak he was, he would always shake the hands of the children. The same held true in every event and venue around the world.

He understood the soul of a child. At an *upsherin*, he would give the child a candy or two. If the father then began talking to him, he would stop him and say, "Open the candy for your son, and then we'll talk."[5]

Moshe, a Mirrer *yungerman*, visited Rav Nosson Tzvi on Chol HaMoed, and brought along his young son, Boruch, to receive a *berachah*. They entered as the Rosh Yeshiva's family was finishing a *seudah*. The Rosh Yeshiva turned to Boruch and asked, "What would you like?"

---

5. R' Moshe Dov Fox.

Children always got a handshake.

Boruch, who had been primed before the visit, immediately replied, "A *berachah*."

"Which *berachah* would you like?" Rav Nosson Tzvi asked with a smile, pointing to the ice cream and fruit that had been served as dessert. "A *shehakol* or a *ha'eitz*?"[6]

Once Rav Nosson Tzvi asked, Boruch answered honestly, telling the Rosh Yeshiva that he wanted ice cream. "It's fine," Moshe stammered. "He doesn't need anything to eat. He just wants a *berachah* from the Rosh Yeshiva."

Rav Nosson Tzvi wouldn't listen to Moshe's protestations, and he asked one of his children to bring a portion of ice cream. "He is a child," explained the Rosh Yeshiva. "This is the type of *berachah* he is *supposed* to want."

R' YITZCHAK WAS RAV NOSSON TZVI'S SHABBOS *CHAVRUSA* for many years.[7] During the Rosh Yeshiva's last year, R' Yitzchak's old-

**A Toy Car for a Chavrusa's Son**

est child, who was 5 at the time, started accompanying his father to these learning sessions. This little boy was shy by nature, and although the Rosh Yeshiva's grandchildren invited him to play with them, he preferred to sit in a corner by himself playing with toys. The Rosh Yeshiva noticed that the boy liked a specific car, but there were times the

---

6. *Shehakol* is the blessing recited on ice cream, and *ha'eitz* is the blessing recited on fruit.
7. See pp. 279-281.

little boy would arrive and find that a grandchild of Rav Nosson Tzvi was playing with it. One week, when the father and son arrived, the Rosh Yeshiva reached down under the table and held out the car – he had saved it for the little boy!

On the Rosh Yeshiva's last Chanukah, the Rebbetzin bought another car exactly like that one, so their Shabbos guest would always have his favorite toy to play with in her house.

At the *shivah*, one of the Rosh Yeshiva's daughters told R' Yitzchak's wife that she had once remarked to her father that it was amazing that this little boy came week after week and played quietly while his father learned. *"Hu yodei'a eich lechanech, ve'eich lefanek,"* the Rosh Yeshiva replied. "[The father] knows how to educate him, and how to indulge him."

And when you hear his children and grandchildren recount their memories of Rav Nosson Tzvi, you cannot help but think that this description could have been said about himself.

A FEW YEARS BEFORE RAV NOSSON TZVI'S *PETIRAH*, A MAN who was nearing 70 came to seek the Rosh Yeshiva's advice. He had

**"Are You Sure It's Good for You?"** retired from a very successful fundraising career, and he had acquired many tricks of the trade that could serve other *mosdos* in their fundraising efforts. A certain organization offered him a job flying around the United States to teach a course on fundraising, but he really wanted to settle down to learn. "What should I do?" he asked Rav Nosson Tzvi. "Travel across the country giving the course, or sit and learn?"

When Rav Nosson Tzvi heard this question, the first thing he asked was, "Won't it be too taxing for you to fly around the country at your age?"

This man was only about two years older than Rav Nosson Tzvi, who was flying around the *world* on an almost monthly basis, racked by a debilitating disease, to try to fill the yeshiva's immense budgetary short-fall. He made no concessions to his own physical condition – but someone else's physical well-being was of paramount importance to him.

# CHAPTER TWENTY-THREE
# EXPANSION OF THE MIR

---

*"Thinking back to the soft-spoken American yungerman who sat and learned with singular devotion – and that was when he was healthy – who would have imagined that he would turn into the Rav Meir Shapiro, the Ponovezher Rav, the Rav Aron Kotler of our generation, building Torah as no one had ever built before, with a body that provided no energy."*
— Rav Yitzchak Berkowitz, in a hesped

---

WHEN RAV NOSSON TZVI BECAME ROSH Yeshiva of Mir Yerushalayim on 18 Shevat 5750/1990, no one could possibly have foretold the course he would chart for the yeshiva over the next two decades. Everyone knew that he was already weakened by Parkinson's disease. Just maintaining the yeshiva, with the approximately 1,200 *talmidim* who were enrolled at that point, would have been an accomplishment for a healthy person, all the more so for Rav Nosson Tzvi.

But then he began to build. And build. And build some more.

"The pace was dizzying," recalls Rav Binyamin Finkel. "People would see him strolling around the Beis Yisrael neighborhood and wonder what he was doing. They probably thought he was walking to get some fresh air. Little did they know that he was examining building after building, determining which ones could eventually be renovated to become parts of the yeshiva.

"And his imagination was vivid. He would look at a building and discern its full potential. He would note which additional buildings could eventually be annexed into the original building if there would be a need to expand."

DURING RAV BEINUSH'S DAYS, THE MIR'S STUDENT BODY WAS already expanding to the point in which it could no longer fit into its

**The Melohn Annex and the Fragin Extension**

original building.[1] During the 1980's, Rav Beinush added a fourth floor to the main building. The new floor

---

1. The bulk of the information in this chapter is based on interviews with Rabbi and Rebbetzin Binyamin Carlebach, who were Rav Nosson Tzvi's primary partners in planning and fundraising for the construction of the various buildings.

When people are learning on (and under!) the steps, it's time to build

included a *beis midrash* (called the Kollel) and what is now the *Otzar Hasefarim* (library), and accommodated another few hundred *talmidim* and several more dormitory rooms.

By the time Rav Beinush passed away, the main building could no longer hold all 1,200 *talmidim*. Rav Beinush had planned to encircle the entire main floor of the building with closed balconies and then annex them to the *beis midrash*, but he passed away before he could implement his plan.

When Rav Nosson Tzvi became Rosh Yeshiva, a new plan arose: to add an extension to all four floors on the left side of the building.

The Melohn Wing of the main building of Mir under construction

The work began almost immediately, but it took many years to complete. The foundation alone took over a year to finish, because the workers had to chip away at solid rock before pouring the cement.

Rav Nosson Tzvi's humility and his willingness to sacrifice his own comfort to make the yeshiva comfortable for the *talmidim* was such that when someone asked him how he would finance the construction, he said, "I'll go to America and knock on doors. I'll collect $5 at one house and $10 at the next, and eventually we'll have enough for the building."

Ultimately, that trip wasn't necessary. While the extension was being built, Mr. and Mrs. Yaakov Melohn of New York, urged on by Mr. Melohn's rebbi, Rabbi Yisrael Belsky *shlita*, Rosh Yeshiva of Torah Vodaath, decided to underwrite the extension of the structure. Mr. Melohn once related that when Rav Nosson Tzvi first visited him he didn't commit to anything, but the experience of meeting with the Rosh Yeshiva moved him to tears, and he thought to himself, "One day, I'll be a *shutaf* (partner) with him."

While this construction was going on, a *talmid* by the name of Michael Fragin enrolled in the yeshiva, followed a few years later by his brother Leib (Greg). Like almost all Mirrer *talmidim,* Michael and Leib were taken by the warmth of the *hanhalah.* Specifically, the two had a very close relationship with Rav Moshe Finkel.[2] The father of these two boys, Mr. Gary Fragin, also developed a relationship with Rav Moshe, who then introduced him to the Rosh Yeshiva. As the extension of the main building was nearing completion, Mr. Fragin stepped in and offered to dedicate the *beis midrash* portion of the new wing.

The friendship between Mr. Fragin and the Rosh Yeshiva would last until the last days of the Rosh Yeshiva's life. Mr. Fragin would come to Yerushalayim for the *Yamim Tovim*, and Rav Nosson Tzvi considered him and his children part of his own family. When talking to Mr. Fragin, he would refer to the Fragin children as, "our son ..."

All told, the additional wing of the building accommodated approximately 800 *talmidim,* in the annex to the main *beis midrash* and a large balcony built as an additional *ezras nashim*, but used as a *beis midrash* during the week. The kitchen and dining room were also expanded to enable the increased number of *talmidim* to eat in the yeshiva at the same time.

The Fragin Annex, filled to capacity

2. Rav Moshe Finkel was the son of Rav Chaim Zev Finkel, the son of Rav Leizer Yudel and the *mashgiach* for the first two decades of Mir Yerushalayim. Rav Moshe (whose name was pronounced with the emphasis on the second half of the name – Mo-SHE – to differentiate between him and his uncle Rav Moshe) was an extremely warm person who developed close bonds with his *talmidim*. He authored *Bnei Chayil* on several *masechtos* in *Shas*.

The Kramer Building

R' ARYEH LEIB KRAMER OF BROOKLYN HAD A LONGSTANDING
relationship with Rav Nosson Tzvi from the time that his son learned in

**The Kramer
Building**

the Mir. He wanted very much to immortalize the
name of his late wife, and he eventually did so by
sponsoring the Kramer Building, which houses a
beis midrash on the bottom floor and several stories of dormitory rooms
above it.

The *beis midrash* in the Kramer building was sponsored in memory
of Gavriel (Gabi) Wessel, a special *yungerman* who learned in the Mir
and tragically died of cancer just seven months after his wedding, on 29
*Sivan* 5758 (1998). His wife and friends joined to raise funds to dedicate
the *beis midrash* in his memory.

At the dedication ceremony for the *beis midrash*, Rav Nosson Tzvi
posed a question on the Mishnah (*Avos* 3:10) that states, "If the spirit
of one's fellows is pleased with him, the spirit of the Omnipresent is
pleased with him. But if the spirit of one's fellows is *not* pleased with
him, the spirit of the Omnipresent is not pleased with him."

*Chazal* tried to minimize the number of words in which they recorded their dictums, noted the Rosh Yeshiva. After reading the first half of
the Mishnah, we could have understood on our own that the reverse is
also true. Why did *Chazal* have to record the flip side of this dictum in
the second half of the Mishnah?

"Gabi was beloved to others."
The entrance to Ner Gavriel *beis midrash*,
named after Mir *talmid* Gabi Wessel

The answer, explained the Rosh Yeshiva, is that if *Chazal* would have recorded this principle only in the positive, we might have thought that finding favor in other people's eyes is merely one way of finding favor in Hashem's eyes, and that even those who don't find favor in other people's eyes can also be beloved by Hashem for other good qualities they possess.

The Mishnah therefore states the reverse as well: if one is not liked by others, Hashem doesn't favor him either – no matter how many other good qualities he has.

Rav Nosson Tzvi then went on to describe how beloved Gabi Wessel was to others, and how he would go out of his way to befriend people of all different stripes, even when he was terminally ill.

Rav Nosson Tzvi could have been speaking about himself.

RAV NOSSON TZVI THOUGHT BIG, BUT HE ALSO KNEW HOW TO make things happen one step at a time. Several Mir buildings started off

**Building Quickly – Step by Step** small, and then grew bigger and bigger as the Rosh Yeshiva would find adjoining properties to annex.

The Friedman building was an example of the Rosh Yeshiva's ability to anticipate the future, but not jump to build too quickly. Mr. Hershey Friedman of Montreal, Canada, had sons who learned in Mir, and his sons-in-law also learned in the yeshiva, both before and after their marriages. Taken by the special atmosphere in the yeshiva, he approached the Rosh Yeshiva and told him that he would like to do something for him. Rav Nosson Tzvi replied that he wanted to purchase a building, and perhaps Mr. Friedman could donate the *beis midrash* in that building. R' Hershey said he would think about it. A few days later, he informed the Rosh Yeshiva that he would sponsor the *entire* building, not only the *beis midrash*.

"The Rosh Yeshiva didn't want to spend money on frills."
The Hershey and Raisy Friedman building, built in three stages

The project got underway, and in 5757/1997, the Friedman building was ready. The building was assigned to the Israeli *bachurim* and *yungeleit*. Within months, however, it was clear that the building could not house the entire contingent for which it was intended.

Before long, Rav Nosson Tzvi set his sights on another building adjacent to the Friedman building, and the yeshiva was able to break through the walls and expand it to include another 200 seats.

A few years later, another section was added. Mr. Friedman financed the purchase and construction of the additional two parts of the *beis midrash* as well.

As was the case in each of his buildings, Rav Nosson Tzvi was deeply involved in the planning of the building – as Mr. Friedman says, "down to the last screw."

Although in general Rav Nosson Tzvi was not one to be overly concerned about details, when it came to the construction of the buildings, he was closely involved in every detail to ensure that the buildings would meet his personal objectives. "He told me," recalls Mr. Friedman, "that he has only two desires for his buildings: that the *talmidim* be comfortable so that they can learn better, and that the space be maximized to fit the greatest number of *lomdim*.

"He would not hear of wasting money on frills. Others might have built on the same space and used another half a million or a million dollars, but he wouldn't waste money on the esthetics of the building. He was only interested in it being comfortable, and no more."

EACH TIME THE YESHIVA WOULD ERECT OR RENOVATE A NEW building, Rav Nosson Tzvi would assign it to a segment of the yeshiva

**The Building Scraped Together Penny by Penny** or to specific *chaburos*. This was a very labor-intensive process, one that often involved measuring and re-measuring the *batei midrash* to ensure that each inch of space was going to be used. Although this might not be necessary in most yeshivos, in Mir, with people so desperate for seats that they would learn on the platform in front of the *Aron Kodesh* or under a set of steps, fitting in a few more benches was vital. Deciding who would sit where was difficult, and the Rosh Yeshiva confided in Rav Binyamin Carlebach that he spent many a sleepless night solving this puzzle each time they inaugurated a building.

Not long after the Friedman building was complete, the yeshiva was able to open yet another building, Shalmei Simchah, named after Rav Simcha Elberg. Rav Simcha was friendly with Rav Chaim Shmuelevitz from their days in Shanghai, and, when he passed away childless, his wife wanted to do something *le'ilui nishmaso* (as a merit for his soul). Her husband had been a Rav and she had worked all their married life, so they had accumulated enough money to sponsor this new building, which included a *beis midrash* and some dormitory rooms.

The building scraped together in memory of Rav Simcha Elberg,
author of *Shalmei Simcha*

The Rosh Yeshiva felt a great debt of gratitude toward Mrs. Elberg, and he would make a point of visiting her each time he was in New York. Once, he told her that he would visit her on a certain day. That day turned out to be extremely hectic, with the Rosh Yeshiva running constantly from one appointment to the next. When the day ended, he was thoroughly exhausted, and some members of his entourage suggested that he skip the visit with Mrs. Elberg. Rav Nosson Tzvi would not hear of it. Afraid that he might inadvertently cause pain to an *almanah*, he insisted on going to her house. Someone then suggested that they ask her to come down and visit the Rosh Yeshiva in the mobile home in which he was transported when he was in America, but Rav Nosson Tzvi wouldn't agree with that either. His energy spent, he forced himself to make his way up the steps to her house.

When the non-Jewish driver of the mobile home saw the incredible *mesirus nefesh* of the Rosh Yeshiva, he told Rav Nosson Tzvi's retinue that he wanted to come to Eretz Yisrael and tell the *bachurim* to what lengths their Rosh Yeshiva went for their benefit.

Shalmei Simcha was inaugurated in Elul of 5758/1998. For morning *seder*, it was assigned to *talmidim* who didn't attend regular *shiurim*, but learned in small *chaburos* with a *rosh chaburah* (leader of the group). In the afternoon, it housed the *bachurim* who learned an *amud* a day.

## A Yeshiva That Learns Kol HaTorah Kulah

ALTHOUGH THE QUICK ADDITION OF TWO NEW BUILDINGS did alleviate the shortage of seats to some extent, there were still many Mirrer *bachurim* and *yungeleit* learning in the shuls and *shtieblach* in the surrounding area. At that point, the Weinberg family of Slonim, which owned a building diagonally across from the main Mir building, offered to sell it to the Rosh Yeshiva.

In the case of the other buildings, the demolition and construction began almost immediately after the yeshiva purchased the property, but in the case of the Weinberg property, the *hanhalah* decided to convert part of it into a *beis midrash* for the interim, until they could finance the demolition and construction of a new building on that site. The *lomdim* in that *beis midrash* – which was dubbed the "Weinberg Beis Midrash" – had to navigate a steep set of iron stairs to get into the *beis midrash*. And yet, people clamored for those seats, quickly filling the *beis midrash* to capacity.

Beis Shalom, a building for a yeshiva where they learn the entire Torah simultaneously

Close to a year later, Mr. and Mrs. Moshe Kalter and Rabbi and Mrs. Aharon Fogel offered to sponsor the construction of another building. Although this family (Mrs. Kalter and Rabbi Fogel are siblings) did not have a personal connection to Mir, they chose to dedicate this building because they wanted to house a yeshiva that studied "*kol haTorah kulah* – the entire Torah."[3] The Mir Yeshiva, which had so many *chaburos* studying so many different parts of the Torah, was the natural choice.

In addition to the beautiful *batei midrash* on the upper floors of the building, Beis Shalom, named for the father of Mrs. Kalter and Rabbi Fogel, R' Shalom Fogel, contains many dorm rooms. For many years before Beis Shalom was built, lunch was served in two shifts in the Mir. One group would eat and leave, then the tables would be reset and another group would arrive. Eventually even the second shift wasn't enough to accommodate all the *talmidim,* and there was an era when the kitchen staff had to begin serving a third shift. The Rosh Yeshiva decided to add another dining room in Beis Shalom, with an underground tunnel from the kitchen in the main building to the new dining room.

Beis Shalom has been a bastion of learning ever since its inauguration in 5763/2003. It houses the 500+ *talmidim* of Rav Asher Arielli, as well as several prestigious *chaburos*, which use its *ezras nashim*.

For over a decade prior to the construction of Beis Shalom, Rav Asher delivered his *shiur* in the *miklat* (bomb shelter) in the main building.

---

3. The *Shach* in *Yoreh De'ah* extols the virtue of a yeshiva in which all of the Torah is studied concurrently.

Five people would squeeze onto a bench meant for four, and every inch of space in the *miklat* was occupied by *talmidim*, many of whom had to stand for lack of seats. Most of the attendees couldn't even see Rav Asher, because the *miklat* had a wall dividing it into two parts, and only a few hundred fit into the part where he sat. To accommodate those who couldn't fit into the *miklat* for the *shiur*, the yeshiva set up an audio system that broadcast the *shiur* into a dorm room on the fourth floor that had been home to Rav Asher's *shiur* in his earlier years. Even spots in that room were at a premium. The *bachurim* who slept in that room had to remove their bedding each day, because some *talmidim* had *chazakos* (first rights) to sit on the beds, and others would stand behind them on the bare mattress.

When Beis Shalom opened, Rav Nosson Tzvi assigned the new dining room to Rav Asher as a *shiur* room, and although the dining room is full to capacity during *shiur*, *talmidim* no longer have to sit cramped together in order to attend.

RAV NOSSON TZVI CONSIDERED THE EXPANSION OF THE yeshiva one of his primary forms of serving Hashem. One Rosh

**Never Stopped Dreaming**

Hashanah, Rav Nosson Tzvi turned to his brother Rav Gedalya after davening, and said, "You know what I was thinking about during davening? I was looking out the window at the plot of land across the street and thinking that one day I would build another building for the yeshiva there."

Today, the seven-story Beis Yeshayah stands on that spot.

The foundation is laid for Beis Yeshayah: "I was thinking that one day I would build another building for the yeshiva there."

Once again, the Rosh Yeshiva built this edifice in stages. He bought a small building that stood there, and converted it into a dormitory called the Noach Chodosh building. Then he purchased a large lot adjacent to that building, which housed a squat structure that served as a marble warehouse. That building, known as Shayish Beis Yisrael, was demolished, and large prefab caravans filled the lot, becoming a large *beis midrash* and dining room. This complex was affectionately called "Shayish," after its former inhabitants.

After Mr. and Mrs. Yossi Stern of Edison, New Jersey built the beautiful new building in Achuzat Brachfeld[1] and named it for his parents, they decided to immortalize Mrs. Stern's father, Mr. Yeshaya Weiss, by naming a building for him. This building was constructed in place of the prefab caravans, and thus was created one of the largest of all the Mir buildings, Beis Yeshayah, which holds more than a thousand *talmidim* and serves as the hub for many of the American *bachurim* in the yeshiva.

The relationship between the Rosh Yeshiva and the Stern family began when their son Moshe Dov learned in yeshiva, in Rav Binyamin Carlebach's *shiur*. The Rosh Yeshiva and Mr. Stern were extremely close

The seven-story Beis Yeshayah, upon its completion

1. See p. 347.

– so much so that from when their relationship began, no matter where in the world Mr. Stern would be on a Friday, he would call Rav Nosson Tzvi to say *Gut Shabbos*.

The Sterns, who are in the construction business in New Jersey, were also involved in every aspect of both their buildings, Brachfeld and Beis Yeshayah. They sat with the contractors, choosing the tiles, windows, and every other building material – down to the cement that was used! Mr. Stern even dealt personally with the painstaking process of getting a variance permit to add an additional floor onto the Beis Yeshayah building.

RAV NOSSON TZVI'S FINAL BUILDING WAS BEIS MENACHEM, sponsored by the Cohen Family from England. Mr. Jerry Cohen was a

## Beis Menachem

friend of the yeshiva for many years, and he served as Rav Nosson Tzvi's host when the latter visited England. While all other Mir buildings were bought by the yeshiva, Beis Menachem is a long-term lease, and both the lease and the renovation were underwritten by Mr. Cohen in memory of his brother Menachem.

Beis Menachem, a long-term lease underwritten by a long-time friend of the yeshiva

WITH EVERY ONE OF HIS BUILDING PROJECTS, BEGINNING
with the expansion of the main building, Rav Nosson Tzvi would not

## Kedushah in the Walls

only take an active role in every aspect of the construction, he would also go onsite many times to inspect the progress. He would often quote a *shmuess* from Rav Chaim Shmuelevitz in which the latter proves that a *domem* (inanimate object), such as a rock, can be infused with *kedushah*. Rav Nosson Tzvi would therefore insist on pressing the button on the cement truck that would start pouring cement for the foundation, explaining that he wanted the walls of the Mir to be filled with *kedushah*.

When witnessing the incredible level of *hasmadah* in each *beis midrash* of the Mir, when listening to the roar of Torah that can be heard even before one steps across the threshold, one might be struck by a question: How is it that in the Mir, even people who didn't succeed in learning elsewhere are suddenly able to learn with such diligence, alongside great *talmidei chachamim*?

Perhaps the answer lies in the walls – the walls that are soaked with the *kedushah* of the Rosh Yeshiva.

Pouring *kedushah* into a *domem*: Rav Nosson Tzvi greets Rav Yitzchok Ezrachi, as he waits onsite to press the button that would pour the foundations for a new building

# CHAPTER TWENTY-FOUR
# BUILDING BRACHFELD

*"I want a yeshiva for 2,000 talmidim in which each bachur will feel like a ben yachid (only child)."*
— *Rav Nosson Tzvi, while interviewing a candidate for the position of mashgiach in the newly established Mir Brachfeld*

OR YEARS, RAV NOSSON TZVI SPOKE OF HIS DREAM to open a separate *yeshiva gedolah*[1] for younger Israeli *bachurim*, in addition to the burgeoning Mir Yeshiva for older *bachurim* and *yungeleit* located in the Beis Yisrael neighborhood of Yerushalayim.

In the winter of 5760/2000, developer R' Meir Brachfeld, who built Achuzat Brachfeld, a community adjacent to Kiryat Sefer in the Modi'in Illit region, offered Rav Nosson Tzvi a tract of land on which to establish a yeshiva. At that point Mir Yerushalayim already had an enrollment of over 4,000, with the number growing each *zman*. It was also a period when the Rosh Yeshiva's Parkinson's was becoming increasingly debilitating. An ordinary person in Rav Nosson Tzvi's situation might have thanked R' Meir politely and declined the offer – but Rav Nosson Tzvi was not ordinary.

After considering the matter and consulting with *gedolei Yisrael*, he decided that he would start a *kollel* first. He asked his son Rav Yosef if he would be interested in establishing a *kollel* and then see whether a *yeshiva gedolah* could be added. Rav Yosef agreed and spent the next few months recruiting *yungeleit*. By the end of Shevat of that winter, sixty *yungeleit* had signed up. They convened for an inaugural gathering in the Rosh Yeshiva's home, and then started to learn in a prefab structure in Brachfeld.

At first, the other members of the *hanhalah* who were involved in establishing Mir Brachfeld thought that they would continue with the *kollel* for a few years, and then move on to establishing a *yeshiva gedolah*. Rav Yosef was shocked, therefore, when Rav Nosson Tzvi

---

1. A *yeshiva gedolah* in Eretz Yisrael is equivalent to what Americans call *"beis midrash"*; when a boy finishes *yeshiva ketanah* (which is equivalent to an American *mesivta*, but with three years instead of four) at the approximate age of 16, he enters *yeshiva gedolah*.

summoned him at the end of the summer *zman* (semester) of that first year and said, "What's with opening a yeshiva?"

"Isn't it a bit premature?" Rav Yosef asked.

"No," the Rosh Yeshiva replied. "It's time to start."[2]

The first step was to recruit a *"kibbutz"* – a group of serious older boys who would serve as the foundation upon which the rest of the yeshiva could be built. Rav Yosef went from one yeshiva to another to gather a group, but other Roshei Yeshiva were wary of sending their top *bachurim* to a yeshiva that had not yet developed a reputation.

At that point, there was a solid group of Israeli *bachurim* learning in the Friedman building in Yerushalayim, and Rav Nosson Tzvi chose some of the best *bachurim* in the group for the Brachfeld *kibbutz*. The yeshiva bought a prefab caravan, and the *yeshiva gedolah* opened with seventeen *bachurim*. The Rosh Yeshiva engaged Rav Aryeh Leib Auerbach, who led a *chaburah* in the Ner Gavriel *beis midrash* of Mir Yerushalayim, as the first *maggid shiur*, and the new yeshiva began to function.

That Elul, just a few months after the *kibbutz* in Brachfeld opened, the yeshiva began to accept *bachurim* into *"Shiur Aleph,"* the first year of *yeshiva gedolah*. Forty-five *bachurim*, the cream of the crop of Israeli *yeshivos ketanos*, were handpicked as the first group.

In the early years, Rav Aryeh Finkel would travel from Yerushalayim twice a week to deliver *shiurim*, as did Rav Refoel Shmuelevitz. Later, Rav Aryeh was formally named Rosh Yeshiva of Mir Brachfeld.

RAV NOSSON TZVI WOULD VISIT BRACHFELD TWICE A WEEK – Monday and Wednesday – and his visits caused much excitement among the *bachurim*. The Rosh Yeshiva

**The Biweekly Visits** would sit in the *beis midrash*, and *bachurim* who had prepared *shtiklach Torah* would line up to tell them to him. The Rosh Yeshiva loved these sessions, and he wouldn't miss them unless he absolutely couldn't be there.

Rav Nosson Tzvi knew every *bachur* in Brachfeld by name, and he was involved in the minutest details of the yeshiva. Not only was he there for the entrance exams, but in the unusual event that a *bachur* had

---

2. Rav Yosef notes that although it often took the Rosh Yeshiva some time to decide on a matter, and he would consult with many others before reaching a decision (see p. 415), once he made his decision he would follow through with alacrity, and he would never second guess himself or shift the responsibility to others.

to be asked to leave, he did that himself. Even when he had to do so, he managed to convey his love for the boy he was expelling.

Once, a *bachur* went to a place that the *hanhalah* had specifically forbidden. The next time Rav Nosson Tzvi was in Brachfeld, he summoned the *bachur*. Looking him in the eyes, Rav Nosson Tzvi raised his hand and patted the boy's cheek. "The place you went to is not so bad," he said softly, "but if you can't follow the rules, then I'm afraid this is not the yeshiva for you."

The boy had to pack his bags and leave, but he left with the knowledge that the Rosh Yeshiva still loved him and wanted the best for him.

A YEAR AFTER THE YESHIVA IN BRACHFELD WAS ESTABLISHED, Rav Nosson Tzvi decided that it was time to erect a proper building. He summoned the 26-year-old *yungerman* who served as the secretary of the yeshiva in Brachfeld to his home in Yerushalayim and said, "Go put up a building."

**The Stern Building**

"But Rosh Yeshiva," the secretary protested, "I don't know anything about construction."

"Don't be afraid," Rav Nosson Tzvi replied. "Just go ahead and start."

"How many *bachurim* should I plan for?" the secretary asked.

"2,000."

"2,000?" the secretary repeated incredulously. "There are only 50 *bachurim* in yeshiva."

The Rosh Yeshiva nodded and said, "Yes, for 2,000."

The secretary, who was not a Mirrer *talmid*, didn't know what to make of the Rosh Yeshiva's instructions. As he was driving back to Brachfeld, his cell phone rang. Rav Nosson Tzvi was on the line. "I was thinking that maybe a building for 2,000 is too much. Plan it for 1,000 *bachurim*."

A building for 1,000 *bachurim* still seemed excessive, considering the actual enrollment at that point, but the secretary accepted the new instructions and hung up.

As he was entering Achuzat Brachfeld, his cell phone rang yet again. "I was thinking that 1,000 is too little. Build for 1,500 *bachurim*."

Ultimately, when the time came to draw up final plans, the Rosh Yeshiva returned to his original figure, and the building was planned for 2,000 *talmidim*.

The construction was done in a way that allowed the building to fill up slowly. The *beis midrash* was built to accommodate 800 *bachurim*,

Built to expand: the *beis midrash* in Mir Brachfeld

but most of the walls were easily removable by unscrewing a few partitions, allowing for extensions on each side as they would become needed. Other parts of the yeshiva, such as the kitchen, had to be built large enough for the eventual enrollment of 2,000.

The sprawling, beautifully designed building was sponsored by Mr. and Mrs. Yossi Stern of Edison, New Jersey in memory of his parents, R' Eliyahu Yehoshua and Mrs. Frieda Stern.[3]

Twelve years later, when Rav Nosson Tzvi passed away, his vision for Brachfeld was well on its way to fruition. There were already 700 *talmidim,* and in his *zechus,* that figure will one day grow to the 2,000 he originally envisioned.

RAV NOSSON TZVI HAD A RARE ABILITY TO SIZE UP A PERSON within seconds. During the entrance exams for Mir Brachfeld, he would

**At First Glance**
sometimes decide on a potential *talmid* even before officially "meeting" him.

A boy entered the room where the *bechinos* were being held, and as he was walking from the door to the table, Rav Nosson Tzvi

---

3. As noted in regard to Beis Yeshayah, which was also sponsored by the Sterns, Mr. and Mrs. Stern were involved with planning every aspect of the Brachfeld building, from the tiles to the light fixtures.

leaned over to his son Rav Yosef and said, "*Zeh lo nir'ah li* (he doesn't look like he's for us)."

"But I checked into him very well!" Rav Yosef protested.

"Do whatever you want," the Rosh Yeshiva replied. "I'm just telling you what I think."

After the *bechinos* were over for that day, Rav Yosef reviewed all the information he had collected about this boy, and his credentials seemed perfect. He was accepted into the yeshiva – but it was not long before Rav Yosef discovered just how right Rav Nosson Tzvi had been. "Was this boy a challenge!" he recalls. "We never dealt with a boy like that before or after."

How did the Rosh Yeshiva know that this boy wasn't for Mir Brachfeld?

"It wasn't just that one boy," Rav Yosef stresses. "Similar stories would happen whenever we gave *bechinos*. He had an uncanny read on people. Just the way the boy walked, dressed, and carried himself spoke volumes to the Rosh Yeshiva – even when no one else saw anything amiss. And he was invariably right."

There were also times when the Rosh Yeshiva would see something positive that others had overlooked. He didn't have the energy to administer the *bechinos* himself, but he wanted to be present. Rav Aryeh Leib Auerbach, Mir Brachfeld's first *maggid shiur*, would sit at the side of the table and administer the tests, and the Rosh Yeshiva would sit at the head of the table and listen. Rav Aryeh Leib is a great *talmid chacham*, and he could ask each *bachur* questions on whichever *masechta* he was learning without preparing beforehand.

The 16- or 17-year-old boys who came for these exams were understandably nervous, and walking into the room and seeing Rav Nosson Tzvi quivering from Parkinson's would make them even more apprehensive.

Generally, upon finishing their *bechinos*, the boys would say "Shalom" to the Rosh Yeshiva and leave the room. One boy did not do particularly well on his *bechinah*, but as he was leaving the room, he said "Shalom" not only to the Rosh Yeshiva, but to Rav Aryeh Leib Auerbach as well.

The Rosh Yeshiva called him back. "This year, I can't accept you," he said. "But come back next year. If you have the presence of mind to take into account that there is another *maggid shiur* who deserves to receive 'Shalom,' you deserve to be in our yeshiva as soon as you advance a little more in your learning."

IN ADDITION TO HIS BIWEEKLY VISITS, RAV NOSSON TZVI would also spend five or six Shabbosos a year in Brachfeld. After each

**Shabbos in Brachfeld**

Shabbos with Rav Nosson Tzvi, the *bachurim* would be uplifted for weeks.

Rav Nosson Tzvi would spend many hours of those Shabbosos in the *beis midrash* listening to one boy after another telling him *shtiklach Torah*. On occasion, he would get up at *seudah shlishis* at the end of such a Shabbos and say, "This Shabbos, the following *bachurim* told me *shtiklach Torah*." He would then list each boy who had told him a *shtikel Torah* and what topic he had discussed – and there could be dozens of names each time! "Shloime had a good question on this *Tosafos*, Chaim said a wonderful *pshat* in the *Rambam* ..."

Every *bachur* would look forward to the final moment, when the Rosh Yeshiva would say, "But the best *shtikel Torah* this Shabbos was from ..."

In general, Rav Nosson Tzvi considered *kin'as sofrim* (competition among scholars – see *Bava Basra* 21a) a wonderful motivator, and he sought to utilize it when he felt that it would build *bachurim* without hurting others.

Rav Nosson Tzvi spent his last Shabbos, *Parashas Lech Lecha* 5772, in Mir Brachfeld. At the *levayah*, Rav Aryeh Finkel tearfully noted that although the Rosh Yeshiva hadn't left a written *tzava'ah* (will), he *had* delivered an impromptu Last Will and Testament for all of his *talmidim* during that Shabbos. When addressing the *bachurim* at *seudah shlishis*, he said, "*Achdus* has always been the hallmark of Mir. We must always make sure to remain united."

The light of Torah burns on in Mir Brachfeld, where the Rosh Yeshiva spent his last Shabbos.

# CHAPTER TWENTY-FIVE
# THE SELFLESS BUILDER

*"When Rav Nosson Tzvi would come into the Lakewood Yeshiva and see the amount of learning that was going on, he would cry tears of joy. His happiness was no less than when he saw the learning in his own yeshiva."*

*— Rav Aryeh Malkiel Kotler, Rosh Yeshiva of Beth Medrash Govoha, Lakewood, New Jersey, at a hesped the day after Rav Nosson Tzvi's levayah*

*T*HE STORY IS TOLD OF A RAV WHO CAME TO RAV Yisrael Salanter and related that he had visited a prominent Rosh Yeshiva who took him into his *beis midrash* at 2 a.m. to show him that his *talmidim* were still learning with incredible *hasmadah*. The Rosh Yeshiva literally cried tears of joy at this moving sight.

"I wonder," Rav Yisrael Salanter replied, "if he would have cried the same tears of joy if he had walked into someone *else's* yeshiva and seen that level of *hasmadah*."[1]

As many *gedolei Yisrael* bore witness, to Rav Nosson Tzvi it made not a whit of a difference where Torah was going to be studied. If there was a way to increase Torah study, he wanted to be a partner in it. Despite the overwhelming budget of his own yeshivos, he gladly undertook to fund other yeshivos and initiatives to increase Torah study beyond the walls of Mir.

RAV NOSSON TZVI'S ENCOURAGEMENT AND FUNDING OF increased Torah study in other institutions was by no means an innovation to the Finkel family. When Rav Leizer Yudel first moved to Eretz Yisrael, although he was living in a rented apartment and he desperately wanted to rebuild his own yeshiva, he partnered with the Chazon Ish by funding half of the first few months of expenses for a new yeshiva for Sefardi boys in Teveriah.[2]

**"I Already Promised ..."**

---

1 Heard from Rav Aharon Lopiansky, who noted that Rav Yisrael Salanter wasn't casting aspersions on the Rosh Yeshiva in question, who might very well have cried tears of joy in someone else's yeshiva. Rather, he was trying to educate his guest not to be impressed with outward displays of emotion without first identifying the underlying feelings that brought forth that emotion.

2 *Marbitzei Torah Umussar*, Vol. 3, p. 70 contains a letter dated at the beginning of 5702 (1942) – less than a year after Rav Leizer Yudel arrived in Eretz Yisrael – in which he explains that he has to

Rav Nosson Tzvi with Rav Malkiel Kotler, Rosh Yeshiva of Beth Medrash Govoha:
"Rav Nosson Tzvi's happiness was no less when he saw the amount of learning in
Lakewood than when he saw the learning in his own yeshiva."

And his approach didn't change once he had established his yeshiva
and was struggling to finance it.

Rav Yechezkel Abramsky, one of the *gedolim* of the time, related that
at a gathering of *gedolei Torah* to discuss the desperate plight of newly
arrived immigrants from Middle Eastern countries that had turned hos-
tile to Jews after Israel's War of Independence, the decision was made to
fund a new yeshiva for the children of these families. Rav Leizer Yudel
immediately declared, "I'll give a substantial sum."

When he returned home after the gathering, a family member asked
him how he could possibly commit to giving to another yeshiva when
his own yeshiva, which he had already established at that point, was in
desperate financial straits. "What can I do?" Rav Leizer Yudel replied
with a shrug. "I had already promised that I would take part in the
funding. How could I break my promise?"

"To whom did you promise that?" the family member persisted.

"I promised it to myself," retorted Rav Leizer Yudel. "A promise that
one makes in one's heart is also a promise that one must keep."

And he did just that.

---

pay his portion in installments, because he has no money. The lack of funds didn't deter him from
agreeing to assume a portion of the expenses, however.

NOT ONLY DIDN'T RAV LEIZER YUDEL DIFFERENTIATE BETWEEN his own yeshiva and other yeshivos, he expected all others involved in the Mir's finances to be equally unselfish.

## Torah Is Torah

Rav Shamshon Raphael Weiss was one of Rav Leizer Yudel's most devoted *talmidim*, and he was often called upon to raise money for the Mir Yeshiva.[3] All Rav Leizer Yudel had to do was call him on the telephone and say, "Shalom," and Rav Weiss instinctively knew that his beloved Rosh Yeshiva needed him to go on an emergency fundraising drive. On one such occasion, Rav Weiss raised a respectable sum and when he traveled to Eretz Yisrael, he personally delivered it to Rav Leizer Yudel. When he arrived, a Yerushalmi *yungerman* who was not a Mirrer *talmid* was in middle of telling Rav Leizer Yudel a *shtikel Torah*. When he finished, Rav Leizer Yudel reached into the envelope Rav Weiss had placed on the table, pulled out a bill of a large denomination, and handed it to the *yungerman*.

Rav Weiss was bothered by this scene. He had worked hard to collect funds to save the Mir from collapse, and Rav Leizer Yudel was just distributing that money freely? Turning to Rav Leizer Yudel, he said, "I thought I was collecting the money for the yeshiva, not for just anyone."

"Is this what I taught you all these years?" Rav Leizer Yudel replied sharply. "This is for ME? For MY yeshiva? There's no me, and there's no someone else. Torah is Torah. It doesn't make a difference if it goes to my yeshiva or elsewhere."

IF THERE WAS ONE PERSON WHO IMBIBED THIS MESSAGE FROM Rav Leizer Yudel, it was Rav Nosson Tzvi, whose willingness to put himself out for other yeshivos became the stuff of legends.

## Night Kollel in Beit Shemesh

When the Meah Shearim neighborhood grew to the point where housing was no longer available for the children of the local Yerushalmis, a satellite community was created in Ramat Beit Shemesh for young families. Shortly thereafter, a group of *askanim* from that community came to Rav Nosson Tzvi and told him that they felt that there would be an increase in Torah study if a night *kollel* were established in their new neighborhood, but they couldn't garner funding for the *kollel*. Rav Nosson Tzvi immediately agreed to underwrite the first year's worth of stipends for the members of the *kollel*.

---

3. See letter on p. 167 in which Rav Leizer Yudel appoints Rav Shamshon Raphael Weiss to the executive board of the Mir, together with R' Eliyahu Meir Finkel, Rav Nosson Tzvi's father.

IN MANY YESHIVOS, AS LONG AS THERE ARE MEMBERS OF THE Rosh Yeshiva's family who are capable of delivering *shiurim*, all posi-

**Talmidim Are Family**

tions in the yeshiva are reserved for family. Yet two years after becoming Rosh Yeshiva, Rav Nosson Tzvi made a crucial decision: *Talmidim* whose growth had taken place in the yeshiva were also "children," and they could therefore become *maggidei shiur* in the yeshiva. This decision led to the establishment of many popular *shiurim* in the Mir, which attracted many young American *bachurim*. They were able to relate to the new *maggidei shiur* – who were predominantly young Americans themselves – and these *shiurim* that were established over the years now fill a large majority of the seats in the Beis Yeshayah building.

A *YUNGERMAN* LEARNING IN A CERTAIN YESHIVA IN Yerushalayim wanted to bolster the level of learning in his yeshiva, so

**Rav Nosson Tzvi Covers the Costs**

he made a deal that anyone who would finish *Bava Kamma*, the *masechta* the yeshiva was learning at the time, would receive 700 *shekel*. He assumed that only a handful of *bachurim* would accept the challenge, and before embarking on his campaign he convinced a wealthy businessman to cover the costs.

To the pleasant surprise of this *yungerman*, over thirty *bachurim* finished the *masechta*! He called his sponsor, and feeling somewhat uncomfortable, he shared the news that he would need a lot more money than he had expected. The sponsor replied that he simply couldn't afford to furnish that large a sum.

The *yungerman* was in a panic. He owed some 21,000 *shekel*, and he had no way of obtaining the funds. When he shared his predicament with a friend, the friend suggested, "Why don't you go to Rav Nosson Tzvi?"

"How can I go to Rav Nosson Tzvi?" the *yungerman* wondered. "I never learned in the Mir, and he doesn't know me at all."

"Just go," his friend insisted.

The *yungerman* came to Rav Nosson Tzvi and told him about his problem. "Tell them to come to me this Friday," the Rosh Yeshiva said. "I'll test them, and if they know *Bava Kamma* well, I'll give them the money."

"But I can't take the Rosh Yeshiva's money!" the *yungerman* exclaimed.

"What do you care?" Rav Nosson Tzvi responded. "We're talking about Torah here!"

The *bachurim* came and took the *bechinah,* and Rav Nosson Tzvi gave each one 700 *shekel.*

## Too Good a Deal to Pass Up

LESS THAN A YEAR BEFORE HIS *PETIRAH,* WHEN THE MIR WAS suffering from staggering fiscal shortfalls, Rav Nosson Tzvi traveled to Baltimore to fundraise. During his trip, he visited the Ner Yisrael Yeshiva and addressed the *talmidim.* As he was speaking, he looked out at the crowd, and then he began to talk about the 12-hour learning program he discussed every so often in his own yeshiva. He concluded his address by offering a financial incentive to anyone in Ner Yisrael who would learn 12 hours each day through the end of the *zman.*

Someone in the Rosh Yeshiva's entourage was so shocked by this offer that he couldn't help but ask Rav Nosson Tzvi, "How can the Rosh Yeshiva promise these *yungeleit* money when he is here raising funds to prevent the Mir from collapsing?"

Rav Nosson Tzvi smiled and said, "I saw a group of people who love to learn, and they needed some *chizuk* to carry them to the end of the *zman.* It was just too good a deal to pass up."

## No American Branch

SEVERAL TIMES OVER THE YEARS, RUMORS CIRCULATED around the Mir that Rav Nosson Tzvi was going to open a branch of the yeshiva in America. Although those plans never did come to fruition, the rumors were not unfounded – as evidenced by the following story.

Sometime around the year 2000, the Rosh Yeshiva's brother-in-law, Rav Yisrael Glustein, contacted R' Aharon Yosef, a *yungerman* who had learned in Rav Zelik Epstein's Yeshiva Shaar HaTorah in Queens and was very close to both Rav Zelik and Rav Nosson Tzvi. "I heard that Rav Zelik is here in Yerushalayim," Rav Glustein began, "and the Rosh Yeshiva wants to visit him."

Rav Nosson Tzvi speaks in Baltimore.
"It was just too good a deal to pass up."

R' Aharon Yosef arranged the meeting, and he came to pick up the Rosh Yeshiva and drive him to the apartment in Rechavia where Rav Zelik was staying. When R' Aharon Yosef reached Rav Nosson Tzvi's house, however, the Rebbetzin informed him that the Rosh Yeshiva was extremely weak, and she didn't think that he could make the trip. But Rav Nosson Tzvi motioned to R' Aharon Yosef that he wanted to make the trip nonetheless.

"Rav Nosson Tzvi was so weak," R' Aharon Yosef recalls, "that Rav Yisrael and I practically had to lift him in order to get him into the car."

When they reached Rechavia, Rav Glustein and R' Aharon Yosef helped the Rosh Yeshiva climb laboriously up the steps to the apartment. Although Rav Zelik was decades Rav Nosson Tzvi's senior, when he saw how debilitated Rav Nosson Tzvi was, he felt terrible that the Mirrer Rosh Yeshiva had come to him. "Had I known," he told R' Aharon Yosef, "I would have come to him!"[4]

Seeing a Mirrer Rosh Yeshiva in such a weakened state jogged a memory. Rav Zelik, who had studied in the Mir in Europe, recounted that he had visited Mir Yerushalayim during the last year of Rav Leizer Yudel's life. Rav Leizer Yudel loved Rav Zelik and felt that he could have a wonderful influence on the *bachurim* in the yeshiva. He begged Rav Zelik to spend his vacation learning in the Mir Yeshiva and living in the Mir dormitory with his wife. When Rav Zelik demurred, Rav Leizer Yudel said, "Fine, you can stay somewhere else, but only on condition that you come to learn in yeshiva and spend time with the *bachurim* – and that you come visit me each day."

Rav Zelik agreed.

One day, when he arrived in Rav Leizer Yudel's house, Rav Zelik found the Rosh Yeshiva in a particularly weakened state. (Rav Leizer Yudel sustained a heart attack in his last year.) Rav Leizer Yudel sensed that Rav Zelik pitied him, and he said, "You feel bad for me? This is the best thing for me! When I am well, people come to visit me all day, and they don't allow me to learn. Now, everyone thinks that I am too weak to receive people, and I have hours upon hours to learn!"

After Rav Zelik told this story, Rav Nosson Tzvi revealed the reason for his visit. Rav Zelik was known as a great *pikei'ach*, an extremely wise person, and Rav Nosson Tzvi wanted to hear his opinion regarding

---

4. R' Aharon Yosef relates that for years after this meeting took place, each time he would meet Rav Zelik, he would lament again that R' Aharon Yosef brought Rav Nosson Tzvi to him rather than bring him to Rav Nosson Tzvi.

Rav Zelik Epstein welcomes Rav Nosson Tzvi into his apartment.
"Had I known how weak he was, I would have gone to him!"

whether he should open a branch of Mir Yerushalayim in America.

"Why do you want to branch out to America?" Rav Zelik probed. "So that you should have a yeshiva for your *talmidim* who return to America?"

"That's one reason," Rav Nosson Tzvi replied. "But I also want to spread Torah throughout the world, not just in Eretz Yisrael."

Rav Zelik mulled the matter over for a few minutes. Finally, he spoke. "If that's the case," he said, "then I would advise you not to open a yeshiva in America.

"The conditions for spreading Torah in America differ greatly from the conditions here," he explained. "If you want to spread more Torah, invest the same energy you would expend on branching out in America toward building here in Eretz Yisrael. Here, where you know the system, you will be able to use your energy more effectively than you could in America."

The two Roshei Yeshiva conversed for a while longer, and then Rav Nosson Tzvi went home. Though there may have been other factors that contributed to his decision not to open the branch in America, the Rosh Yeshiva certainly took Rav Zelik's opinion into account.

Just as Rav Nosson Tzvi was motivated purely by the desire to spread Torah, Rav Zelik, too, was purely motivated by the Rosh Yeshiva's best interests, as we can discern from R' Aharon Yosef's postscript to this story.

He relates that when rumors circulated that Mir Yerushalayim was planning to open a branch in Queens, someone asked Rav Zelik if he was concerned that the Mir might usurp Shaar HaTorah as one of the primary yeshivos in that borough.

"*Halevai* he would open on our block!" Rav Zelik replied.

ONE OF THE MOST ASTOUNDING MANIFESTATIONS OF RAV Nosson Tzvi's selflessness was the way he opened his yeshiva to

**Mir as a Way Station**

*bachurim* who had no intention of becoming Mirrer *talmidim*, but were quite openly using the Mir as a way station.

There are yeshivos in Yerushalayim that accept *bachurim* only at the beginning of certain *zmanim*, and it is often unclear before a *zman* whether enrollment will be open for that *zman* or not. Many *bachurim* have gone to Eretz Yisrael planning to enroll in one of those yeshivos, only to discover upon their arrival that enrollment was closed.

So what does an American *bachur* 6,000 miles and a $1,000 plane ticket away from home do when stranded without a yeshiva in Eretz Yisrael? Why, he comes to Rav Nosson Tzvi, of course.

Not only did Rav Nosson Tzvi allow these *bachurim* to enroll in the Mir, he even provided them with their own *maggid shiur* to help them prepare for the *masechtos* they would learn in the yeshiva of their choice when enrollment would open. This happened not once, but several times over the years!

Once, a group of *bachurim* came to the Rosh Yeshiva at the beginning of Elul and admitted, somewhat uncomfortably, that they wanted to join the Mir for just that one-month *zman*, because they had been promised that they would be allowed into a different yeshiva after Succos. Rav Nosson Tzvi welcomed them with open arms and provided them with seats for a *chaburah* of their own.

On Chol HaMoed Succos, these *bachurim* felt that they should visit Rav Nosson Tzvi to part with him before joining their new yeshiva. If the feeling that they were "using" the Mir had caused them discomfort at the beginning of Elul, they felt even more uneasy now that they had been hosted so graciously by the Mir for over a month.

Rav Nosson Tzvi welcomed them with his trademark warmth, waving off their attempts to thank him for his hospitality. "I don't deserve thanks," he said, "for providing a *bachur* who wants to learn with the opportunity to do it.

"But one favor I must request from you," the Rosh Yeshiva concluded. "If there's ever anything you need, *please* feel free to come back. My house is always open."

# CHAPTER TWENTY-SIX
## ON THE ROAD

*"Go home and kiss your children, and tell them that the kiss is from their grandfather. Because you are my children, and your children are my grandchildren."*
— *Rav Nosson Tzvi, at a breakfast for Mir Alumni in Toronto, Canada*

EVERYONE IN THE MIR UNDERSTOOD THAT THE ROSH Yeshiva traveled abroad on behalf of the current *talmidim*, to raise funds to maintain the yeshiva. While that was certainly true, it was only part of the story. Although the stated purpose of his trips was for the benefit of the *talmidim* in Eretz Yisrael, the trips were a lifeline for the thousands of alumni across the globe – alumni who had grown in the Mir, often as a direct result of their relationship with the Rosh Yeshiva.

On every trip, and in every city and town, Mirrer alumni and parents of current *talmidim* would rush to greet and reconnect with the Rosh Yeshiva. And they were always amazed to discover that every Mirrer *talmid* held a special place in his heart.

R' BEINISH MANDEL HAD THE PRIVILEGE OF PICKING UP THE Rosh Yeshiva from the airport every time he came to New York. R'

**At the Airport** Beinish was able to arrange a security detail so that he could park right near the entrance to the terminal and then walk directly to the plane.

Reconnecting with an alumnus during a trip abroad

Rav Nosson Tzvi with the Mandel children
at JFK airport in the early 1990's

R' Beinish would bring his sons along with him to greet the Rosh Yeshiva, and they would always emerge with another set of beautiful memories. One of R' Beinish's sons had a designated task: he would tell the Rosh Yeshiva the first *dvar Torah* on American soil, and every time, the Rosh Yeshiva found another way to express his appreciation. Once, after hearing the boy's *vort*, Rav Nosson Tzvi turned to R' Beinish and said, loud enough for his son to hear, "It would have been worth coming to America just to hear this *vort*." Another time, he told the boy, "As soon as your parents are ready to let you come, we have a bed waiting for you in the yeshiva."

When the Rosh Yeshiva and his entourage would deplane, some of his family members would go to the luggage carousel to retrieve their baggage, and the Rosh Yeshiva would sit down to wait for them. *Frum* Jews who were waiting for their luggage would take this opportunity to ask him for *berachos*, and some would even kiss his hand. After seeing this happen during a few of the Rosh Yeshiva's trips, the police officers in the airport took note of this phenomenon, and they started to ask R' Beinish Mandel if they could join his security detail. Sometimes they would even come over to ask the Rosh Yeshiva for a blessing!

Once, an officer asked for a *berachah* for something that was against halachah. The people standing around the Rosh Yeshiva blanched, but Rav Nosson Tzvi didn't miss a beat. "I hope everything works out for you," he said kindly.

The officer walked away thrilled with the warm wishes, not realizing that the Rosh Yeshiva had not compromised halachah while delivering the "blessing."

RAV BINYAMIN CARLEBACH, WHO TRAVELED WITH RAV Nosson Tzvi very frequently, recalls the Rosh Yeshiva's incredible alacrity on these trips. Often, as they would leave the airport after a flight in which Rav Nosson Tzvi hadn't been able to sleep, the Rosh

## Hitting the Ground Running

Yeshiva would ask, "Where is our first stop today?" Everyone else was tired from the flight, but Rav Nosson Tzvi had no time to rest: He wanted to maximize his time in the United States, both to fundraise and to meet alumni and other Yidden seeking *chizuk*.

Though people competed for the privilege of hosting Rav Nosson Tzvi, by and large he stayed with those who had hosted him during earlier trips.

R' Mendy Horowitz of Boro Park, who learned with Rav Nosson Tzvi for three years (1975-1978), served as his weekday host during most of his visits to New York. In his early years as Rosh Yeshiva, Rav Nosson Tzvi would spend Shabbosos in Boro Park at the home of R' Daniel Carlebach, Rav Binyamin's brother. In later years, he spent Shabbosos with R' Yossi Stern in the Edison community. In England, Rav Nosson Tzvi's trips were arranged by an alumnus and dear friend, R' Shia Ozer Halpern, who also hosted him at times. The Rosh Yeshiva's primary host in England was Mr. Jerry Cohen, who eventually sponsored the Beis Menachem building.

These families – and all other families who merited to host him – took great pleasure and pride in having him as their guest. They each have lasting memories of the visits – some touching and some humorous.

"Sarah," the daughter of one of his hosts, cherishes a memory of the time when the Rosh Yeshiva was getting ready to head back to the airport, and people were rushing into the house for one last chance to receive his *berachah*. As the people received a *berachah*, they would say "Amen."

Sarah was standing near Rav Nosson Tzvi, and he turned to her and said something. She didn't hear what he said, but following the pattern of everyone else, she replied with a loud "Amen."

Rav Nosson Tzvi began to laugh heartily. "What's so funny?" Sarah asked.

"I asked for another piece of *kugel*," the Rosh Yeshiva replied.

ONE THING THAT ALWAYS TOOK PEOPLE BY SURPRISE – NOT only in America, but even back home in Eretz Yisrael – was the Rosh Yeshiva's ability to remember each one of his *talmidim*.

## Friday Nights at the Carlebachs

Rav Chaim Kreiswirth *zt"l*, the legendary Rav of Antwerp, Belgium, would visit Rav Nosson Tzvi from time to time. Once, his grandson asked him why he goes to visit Rav Nosson

Tzvi rather than ask the Rosh Yeshiva to come to him. After all, Rav Kreiswirth was several decades older than Rav Nosson Tzvi, and, as his grandson reasoned, "You know *Bavli* and *Yerushalmi!*"[1]

"I may know *Bavli* and *Yerushalmi*," Rav Kreiswirth replied, "but he has 3,000 *talmidim* and he knows each one by name. He deserves to have me come to him."

This story was once retold by someone who introduced the Rosh Yeshiva at a fundraising event for the Mir. When the Rosh Yeshiva got up to speak, he said, "I don't know whether I know all 3,000 *talmidim* by name. But one thing I do know: I love every one of them."

Because of that love, he rarely forgot anyone – and he would person-ally deliver reports to parents about their sons, much to the delight of the mothers and fathers who missed their children.

R' Daniel Carlebach would call the parents of new *talmidim* in the yeshiva and invite them to his house for a Friday night *oneg Shabbos* with the Rosh Yeshiva. Sometimes a father would say, "Aah, he doesn't even know my son." "Come over," R' Daniel would say, "and we'll see if the Rosh Yeshiva knows him."

The father would say his son's name, and sure enough, from the Rosh Yeshiva's reply it would be quite evident that he knew the boy. Sometimes Rav Nosson Tzvi could tell the father on which *sugya* his son had said a *shtikel Torah*; other times he would tell the father where his son sat in yeshiva – little tidbits that showed that he knew the *bachur* and how he was progressing.

AT THE MIR DINNERS, WHEN HUNDREDS UPON HUNDREDS OF people would line up to say *Shalom Aleichem* to the Rosh Yeshiva, he would often take a moment to say something per-sonal about the son of the man greeting him.

**The Dinners**

A *bachur* named Mendel, who was a Kohen, would move to the front of the *beis midrash* for *Bircas Kohanim* every day.[2] When Mendel's father reached the front of the line at one of the Mir dinners and introduced himself, he said, "You probably don't know my son, but his name is …"

"Sure I know him," Rav Nosson Tzvi replied. "He comes to *duchan*[3] near me every day.

---

1. Rav Kreiswirth was renowned for his ability to quote the words of any passage in the Talmud by heart.
2. In Eretz Yisrael, *Bircas Kohanim* is recited every day.
3. In the vernacular, *Bircas Kohanim* is often referred to as *duchaning*, because the Kohanim ascend to a platform called a *duchan* to bless the congregation.

"By the way," he added, "your son could use a new hat." (He was absolutely right – Mendel's hat had seen better days.)

Mr. Gary Fragin, an early and frequent donor, relates that he was once on line waiting to greet the Rosh Yeshiva. Although he could easily have been pulled to the front of the line, he preferred to wait with the other parents. As he was waiting, a man turned around to him and said, "I don't even know why I'm waiting here. I can't imagine that the Rosh Yeshiva knows my son, out of the thousands of *talmidim* in the yeshiva. I only came because my son insisted that I had to meet the Rosh Yeshiva."

"I hear your logic," Mr. Fragin responded, "but I've known the Rosh Yeshiva for many years, and I think you might just be surprised."

When they reached the front of the line, this man leaned over the table, spoke to the Rosh Yeshiva for a few moments and then turned back around, a huge smile on his face. "The Rosh Yeshiva knows my son!" he exclaimed to Mr. Fragin. "He told me all about him!"

IT WASN'T ONLY PARENTS WHO WERE ASTOUNDED. ALUMNI were just as touched by the Rosh Yeshiva's ability to remember them

**Remembering the Talmidim** years after they had left the yeshiva. They would line up, either at dinners or at alumni breakfasts, to greet the Rosh Yeshiva. Some of them would feel sheepish, wondering if he would recognize them. Often, however, their discomfort would quickly be replaced by delight, as the Rosh Yeshiva greeted them by first name even before they managed to introduce themselves. Even when he didn't remember a name, he would remember some details about the alumnus, even years after he had left yeshiva: "I miss seeing you in your seat near the *mashgiach* at

"Will the Rosh Yeshiva remember me?" Alumni were delighted to find that he always did.

*Shacharis*," he would say, or "I hope to see you back in your *chaburah* on Tuesdays soon."

FOR MANY ALUMNI, THE ANNUAL OPPORTUNITY TO RECONNECT with the Rosh Yeshiva was a spiritual anchor, reminding them that they

**"What Are You Learning?"** were Mirrer *talmidim* for life. Leib, a *yungerman* who left the yeshiva in 1999, recalls that each time the Rosh Yeshiva saw him he would ask, "What are you learning?" His next question would be, "How's business going?"

"I always knew that he would ask about learning first," Leib relates, "and I realized that in his mind, I was still a *talmid* of the yeshiva even after I had entered the business world. That knowledge kept me connected to learning throughout the years."

IN THE LAST FEW YEARS OF HIS LIFE, THE ROSH YESHIVA AUG-mented his visits abroad with a special reverse invitation. The yeshiva

**Yarchei Kallah** would invite its alumni to attend a week-long winter *Yarchei Kallah* in the yeshiva, in which alumni would learn a *sugya* in depth and listen to *shiurim* and *shmuessen* from their past *maggidei shiur* and from *gedolei Yisrael*. For participants, it was an opportunity to relive the days they had spent immersed in Torah, invigorating themselves with spiritual energy to tide them over for many months.

The love that radiated between the alumni and the Rosh Yeshiva – as well as all other members of the *hanhalah* – was perhaps captured best

The Rosh Yeshiva delivering a *shiur* for the participants of the *Yarchei Kallah*

by the signs posted throughout the Mir buildings welcoming the guests: "Yeshivas Mir greets **her sons**, the participants in the *Yarchei Kallah*."

THE ROSH YESHIVA'S APPEARANCE IN ANY LOCALE – BE IT LOS Angeles or London, Montreal or Monsey, Buenos Aires or Baltimore –

**A Kiddush Hashem** caused a tremendous *kiddush Hashem* (Sanctification of Hashem's Name). Just seeing the frail man who was at the helm of the world's largest Torah empire – a man whose very being exuded holiness and love of Torah – was a profound inspiration to people, and they received him with obvious excitement and awe.

*Cheder* children would dress in their Shabbos finery in honor of the Rosh Yeshiva's visit to their schools, while teenage *bachurim* would sing and dance as the Rosh Yeshiva's mobile home[4] pulled up in their community. People were eager to hear an address directly from him, and he would be asked to speak almost everywhere he visited. If he was able to speak, he would oblige.

In these short visits, he touched thousands upon thousands of lives, and he considered this an important part of his trips abroad. For the people around the world who met him, every seemingly minor encounter turned into a treasured memory, and became yet another story to be recounted tearfully upon his *petirah*.

R' Shia Ozer Halpern related, for instance, that he once took the Rosh Yeshiva to visit a wealthy Chassidic Jew, who asked him to retell the famous story of Rav Chaim Shmuelevitz's visit to Kever Rochel. "You were the one who took him," the Rosh Yeshiva said to R' Shia Ozer, "so you tell the story."

R' Shia Ozer related that he had had the privilege of walking with Rav Chaim every morning at 6:00 a.m. One day, he asked if Rav Chaim wanted to visit Kever Rochel. He responded by asking if there was a public phone nearby, because he wanted to tell his wife that he would be home 45 minutes later than usual. The *talmidim* found a phone and told the Rebbetzin that Rav Chaim was planning to visit Kever Rochel. As soon as they told Rav Chaim that the Rebbetzin knew and they could

---

4. For the last decade or so of the Rosh Yeshiva's life, those organizing his trips to the New York area realized that they would be able to accomplish much more if he traveled in a mobile home, which would allow him to rest between stops. In addition, if he was too weak to enter the home or the office of the donor he was scheduled to meet, the donor would happily meet him in the mobile home. After a few years, the mobile home became so familiar that as it made its way through the streets of New York or Lakewood, people would line up to ask for *berachos*.

go, he began sobbing uncontrollably, as though some great calamity had struck. His wailing was so heartrending that when they arrived at Kever Rochel, the soldiers stationed there asked the *talmidim* what had happened.

Rav Chaim entered Kever Rochel and cried out, *"Mammeh, dein zun Chaim'ke iz gekumen* – Mother, your son Chaim'ke is here." He then davened for all the people he knew who were sick or in need of salvation. Before leaving, he famously declared, *"Mammeh,* Hashem tells you to stop crying – *Min'i koleich mibechi.*[5] But your son Chaim'ke says *Vein, Mammeh, vein* – keep crying for your children."

At an event in Toronto. People were eager to hear an address from the Rosh Yeshiva.

The Rosh Yeshiva being greeted by *cheder* children dressed in Shabbos finery, on a visit to Baltimore.

5. *Yirmiyah* 34:15.

Sensing that the Chassid was moved by the story, Rav Nosson Tzvi asked him, "What did you see in this story?"

"I see the feeling and heart that Rav Chaim had for *Klal Yisrael*," the man replied.

"While that is certainly true," the Rosh Yeshiva said, "I see something else: If you are going to come home late, call your wife and let her know."

In this brief encounter, the Rosh Yeshiva took the opportunity to impart an important lesson in *middos* that would remain with this donor forever.

The Rosh Yeshiva took the responsibility to make a *kiddush Hashem* very seriously. Before Rav Binyamin Carlebach would travel to the States by himself on behalf of the yeshiva, the Rosh Yeshiva would give him a standard *berachah*: "You should be *zocheh* to be *mekadesh Sheim Shamayim*."

ON THE FUNDRAISING FRONT, THE LEVEL OF *SIYATA D'SHMAYA* that accompanied the Rosh Yeshiva was incredible.

**Kefitzas Haderech?** "When we are taught about *kefitzas haderech* (the road being "shortened" miraculously) as kids," says R' Mendy Horowitz, "we try to imagine what it's like for the way to become shortened. Do you pass by some towns and not see them? Is it like flying?

"I still don't know what exactly *kefitzas haderech* is, but one thing I can tell you – when we would sit down at the end of the day and review the list of places we had visited with the Rosh Yeshiva in that one day, we knew that it was physically impossible for us to have accomplished as much as we did.

"Once, at a few minutes to 9, we got a call to be at a philanthropist's house in Flatbush by 9 a.m. I've done the drive from my home in Boro Park to that area of Flatbush many times, and I *know* that it takes close to 20 minutes to get there. But we got into the car in front of my house at a few minutes to 9, and we arrived at this man's house at 8:59."

Rav Binyamin Carlebach recalls a time when the Rosh Yeshiva was in Lower Manhattan at around 4 p.m., and the driver of the mobile home, who was a medic, sensed that something was wrong with the Rosh Yeshiva's breathing. He listened to the Rosh Yeshiva's lungs, and suspected that he had contracted pneumonia. "He needs to see a doctor right away," the driver said.

R' Beinish Mandel confers with the Rosh Yeshiva.

The problem was that there was a parlor meeting scheduled in an office in Battery Park City, in the southern tip of Manhattan, at 5:30, and the Rosh Yeshiva didn't want to miss it.

Thankfully, R' Beinish Mandel was in the vicinity, and he was able to schedule an appointment with a specialist in Columbia Presbyterian Hospital, who usually books appointments weeks in advance. R' Beinish picked up the Rosh Yeshiva and rushed him to the hospital, which is in Washington Heights, at the opposite end of Manhattan. The doctor examined the Rosh Yeshiva and wrote a prescription. R' Beinish then drove Rav Nosson Tzvi back to Battery Park City – arriving at 5:40, just 10 minutes late for the parlor meeting. The entire trip to the doctor, across Manhattan and back *during rush hour*, had taken about an hour and a half.

OFTEN, THE ROSH YESHIVA WOULD ASK DONORS FOR HEFTY sums. Many a potential donor would ask him for a specific *berachah*,

**For the Donor's Benefit**
and he would explain that a *berachah* needs something special upon which to attach itself, and that the merit of supporting Torah learning would allow the *berachah* to take effect.

Sometimes he would think for a while before asking for a specific amount, and then he would ask for an astronomical sum. Other times, a donor would offer a certain amount, and the Rosh Yeshiva would think and then ask him to double it.

"What do you think about during that time?" Rav Binyamin Carlebach once asked him.

"I don't ask for an amount," the Rosh Yeshiva revealed, "until I am sure that I am doing it for the donor's sake."

The Rosh Yeshiva would think about the merit he was offering the donor, and what that merit could accomplish for him. Not until he was certain that it was in the donor's best interest to give him the full amount would he make the request.

A CERTAIN WEALTHY INDIVIDUAL APPARENTLY WAS NOT convinced of the merit of becoming a partner with the Rosh Yeshiva.

**Why Do You Need So Much?** After listening to his appeal, he retorted, "I don't understand. Why does the Rosh Yeshiva need so many *talmidim*? Why do you have to keep expanding the yeshiva? If you would have fewer *talmidim*, you wouldn't need so much money!"

"And why do you need so much money?" the Rosh Yeshiva replied. "You could retire now and have plenty to live on. But you keep working because you love money, and you want more and more of it.

"I love Torah," he concluded, "so I want more and more of it."

This recalcitrant man later revealed that his businesses went into a tailspin after this encounter, and he sensed that it was because he had said something inappropriate to Rav Nosson Tzvi. He flew to Eretz Yisrael to ask for *mechilah*.[6]

DURING RAV NOSSON TZVI'S LAST YEARS, WHEN THE GLOBAL economy was sagging, the yeshiva's budgetary shortfall expanded

**Who's Shlepping Whom?** dangerously. The *yungeleit* weren't receiving their stipends on time, and although Rav Aron Leib Shteinman told him that it wasn't his direct responsibility, Rav Nosson Tzvi took the plight of these *talmidim* to heart, knowing that they relied on this money to live. He told people that he was embarrassed to look a *yungerman* in the eye when he owed him money.[7]

The Rosh Yeshiva made fundraising his primary pursuit, trying desperately to cover the shortfall. He started to travel with increasing frequency, sometimes flying abroad more than once a month. Rav Aron

---

6. Rav Binyamin Carlebach. Rav Gershon Meltzer also told this story, which he heard from a *yungerman* in yeshiva who is related to this wealthy man, and reported that his businesses recovered after he asked for *mechilah*.
7. R' Shia Ozer Halpern, in a *hesped*.

Leib Shteinman once traveled with him, and he couldn't take his eyes off Rav Nosson Tzvi during the entire flight. Afterward, he kept talking about Rav Nosson Tzvi's *mesirus nefesh* for Torah.

Perhaps the following exchange best captures Rav Nosson Tzvi's devotion to trying to solve the yeshiva's budget problems. On many occasions, people would see him in such discomfort and complain to Rav Binyamin Carlebach, "How can you shlep him around like this?"

"We don't shlep him," Rav Carlebach shrugged. "He shleps us!"

# CHAPTER TWENTY-SEVEN
# THE RIPPLE EFFECT

*"I learn an hour each day now because of my peripheral contact with the Rosh Yeshiva."*
— *Zion, a barber in the vicinity of the Mir, reveals Rav Nosson Tzvi's ripple effect.*

$\mathcal{R}$AV NOSSON TZVI'S ABILITY TO HAVE A LASTING effect on those who came into contact with him wasn't limited to *bnei Torah*; he also made a lasting impression on those from weaker religious backgrounds and even on secular Jews. Just witnessing his awe-inspiring *mesirus nefesh* and experiencing his sincere love for every Yid spurred many people to begin their growth process.

Alongside the Mirrer *talmidim* at Rav Nosson Tzvi's Friday *vaad*, one could often find an eclectic blend of boys from all walks of life, who would invariably walk out with a little more resolve to make strides in their spiritual growth.

"SHLOMO," THE SON OF A *TALMID* FROM RAV NOSSON TZVI'S first *chaburah* in the 1970's, bounced around from one yeshiva in the United States to the next, and eventually dropped out of yeshiva and started working. In due time, he began to hang out with a wilder crowd. His parents were extremely concerned about his spiritual well-being, but they didn't know what to do for him.

**"Welcome to the Family"**

One day, Shlomo told his father that his friend was getting married in Eretz Yisrael, and he was planning to go to the wedding. His father asked him for one favor – to attend the Rosh Yeshiva's *vaad* on Friday afternoon. Shlomo agreed.

Shlomo came to Eretz Yisrael, and he kept his end of the deal. After Shabbos, Shlomo called his father and, without explaining why, asked if he could stay another week. His father agreed, on condition that Shlomo would attend the Rosh Yeshiva's *vaad* again. To his father's surprise, Shlomo said that he certainly would. Little did the father realize that the *vaad* was precisely the reason Shlomo wanted to stay.

After the second *vaad*, Shlomo went to the Rosh Yeshiva and said, "I'm working, and I'm *baruch Hashem* successful. I want to come to Eretz Yisrael and learn for a *zman*, but only if the Rosh Yeshiva will guarantee me that when I go back to America, I'll have success with *parnasah* and with *shidduchim*."

When Shlomo's father heard this, he was aghast that his son had spoken in such a brazen manner. But as Shlomo related, the Rosh Yeshiva just smiled, closed his eyes and thought for a moment, and said, "You have a deal."

Shlomo enrolled in Mir for the summer *zman*, and returned for Elul *zman*. He returned to America a changed person. He dropped his old friends, and settled down into a solid routine.

As for the guarantees? Shlomo is very successful in business – and he did a wonderful *shidduch* as well. A while after his return to the States, he met a girl and was ready to get engaged. The day of the *l'chaim*, he heard that the Rosh Yeshiva was spending a few hours in Newark Airport on his way back from Panama to Eretz Yisrael. Shlomo asked his father to arrange a meeting with Rav Nosson Tzvi, adding that he wanted to bring along his prospective *kallah*. The Rosh Yeshiva gladly agreed.

Shlomo entered the Rosh Yeshiva's room, and saw that he was lying on the couch, very weak. But when he walked to the couch and leaned over, the Rosh Yeshiva gave him a big hug and kiss. After requesting permission from the Rosh Yeshiva, Shlomo went back outside and summoned his *kallah*.

As she walked in, the Rosh Yeshiva smiled broadly and said, "Welcome to the family."

Shlomo now devotes time to Torah study in a serious way, and he is one of the lay leaders of his community – and it all started with a 20-minute *vaad* at the Rosh Yeshiva's home.

FOR MANY YEARS, RAV YITZCHAK BERKOWITZ WAS THE *menahel ruchani* of Aish HaTorah, a yeshiva that specializes in drawing

**Aish HaTorah's Last Resort**

newcomers closer to Judaism. Rabbi Berkowitz recalls that on occasion, Aish HaTorah's dedicated staff and *yungeleit* would have trouble convincing a secular Jew to join their classes — and certainly to make real life changes — just based on their introductory seminars. Aish HaTorah searched for a formula to crack these difficult cases and they found it in Rav Nosson Tzvi and his yeshiva. First, they would take their

"He always knew the right words to say." Rabbi Berkowitz reciting *berachos* at a *bris* in which Rav Nosson Tzvi (foreground) served as *sandak*

not-yet-observant candidates to the *beis midrash* in Mir to watch hundreds of *bachurim* and *yungeleit* not just learning, but arguing as though their lives depended on it. These people had never seen anything like it – their mouths would hang open as they watched *talmidim* of the Mir debating the finer points of a *sugya*.

Then the visitors would be brought to Rav Nosson Tzvi. "The first thing they would notice was his physical state," Rabbi Berkowitz relates, "and they would start to feel very uncomfortable. But then they would see his smile, and they would feel his love for them.

"Finally, he would speak. And he always knew the right words to say. All the professional *kiruv* people couldn't do what a few minutes with the Rosh Yeshiva could do."

EVEN WHEN THE MEETING WASN'T SPECIFICALLY DESIGNED to influence the visitor, the sight of the Rosh Yeshiva would leave a last-

**With the Undersecretary of State**
ing impression. Once, during *Aseres Yemei Teshuvah*, the yeshiva was visited by Mr. Stuart Eisenstadt, the Undersecretary of State in the Clinton administration, whose son was learning

in the Mir. That year, the Israeli Justice Minister, Yaakov Ne'eman, had closed his office for *Aseres Yemei Teshuvah* and had come to learn in the

A state visit: Rav Nosson Tzvi with Undersecretary of State Stuart Eisenstadt (c) and Israel's Justice Minister, Yaakov Ne'eman (r)

Mir. The Rosh Yeshiva invited the two for lunch in his home. During the meal, the Rosh Yeshiva spoke about the concept of *teshuvah* and the meaning of the *Yamim Noraim* to the visibly moved Mr. Eisenstadt.

ONE HIGH-PROFILE INDIVIDUAL UPON WHOM RAV NOSSON Tzvi had a profound effect was Mr. Howard Schultz, the CEO of the Starbucks coffee chain.

**A Lasting Relationship**

The first time Mr. Schultz came to visit Rav Nosson Tzvi was when Aish HaTorah brought a group of prominent businessmen to the Rosh Yeshiva's home. Mr. Schultz himself was so taken by that meeting that he retold the story frequently at board meetings and other events, and his account of the meeting was printed in many secular newspapers:

> When I was in Israel, I went to Meah Shearim, the ultra-Orthodox area within Jerusalem. Along with a group of businessmen I was with, I had the opportunity to have an audience with Rabbi Nosson Tzvi Finkel, the head of a yeshiva there [Mir Yeshiva]. I had never heard of him and didn't know anything about him. We went into his study and waited 10 to 15 minutes for him. Finally, the doors opened.

*What we did not know was that Rabbi Finkel was severely afflicted with Parkinson's disease. He sat down at the head of the table, and, naturally, our inclination was to look away. We didn't want to embarrass him.*

*We were all looking away, and we heard this big bang on the table: "Gentlemen, look at me, and look at me right now." Now his speech affliction was worse than his physical shaking. It was really hard to listen to him and watch him. He said, "I have only a few minutes for you because I know you're all busy American businessmen." You know, just a little dig there.*

*Then he asked, "Who can tell me what the lesson of the Holocaust is?" He called on one guy, who didn't know what to do — it was like being called on in the fifth grade without the answer. And the guy says something benign like, "We will never, ever forget?" And the rabbi completely dismisses him. I felt terrible for the guy until I realized the rabbi was getting ready to call on someone else. All of us were sort of under the table, looking away — you know, please, not me. He did not call me. I was sweating. He called on another guy, who had such a fantastic answer: "We will never, ever again be a victim or bystander."*

*The rabbi said, "You guys just don't get it. Okay, gentlemen, let me tell you the essence of the human spirit.*

*"As you know, during the Holocaust, the people were transported in the worst possible, inhumane way — by railcar. They thought they were going to a work camp. We all know they were going to a death camp.*

*"After hours and hours in this inhumane corral with no light, no bathroom, cold, they arrived at the camps. The doors were swung wide open, and they were blinded by the light. Men were separated from women, mothers from daughters, fathers from sons. They went off to the bunkers to sleep.*

*"As they went into the area to sleep, only one person was given a blanket for every six. The person who received the blanket, when he went to bed, had to decide: 'Am I going to push the blanket to the five other people who did not get one, or am I going to pull it toward myself to stay warm?'"*

*And Rabbi Finkel says, "It was during this defining moment that we learned the power of the human spirit, because we pushed the blanket to five others."*

*And with that, he stood up and said, "Take your blanket. Take it back to America and push it to five other people."*

Chapter Twenty-seven: The Ripple Effect  □  381

The Mir maintained some contact with Mr. Schultz after he went back to America and publicized this story. Mr. Schultz eventually invited the Mir's *hanhalah* to Seattle to meet with him. Rav Binyamin Carlebach led the contingent, armed with a personal note from Rav Nosson Tzvi, written in longhand, stating that he was looking forward to a meaningful and lasting acquaintance with Mr. Schultz. The meeting went well – Mr. Schultz even invited them to dinner, understanding that they would have to bring their own kosher food – and he later sent the yeshiva a respectable donation.

The contact continued a few years later, when the Foreign Ministry was courting Mr. Schultz, hoping to partner with him on some venture. Before coming to Eretz Yisrael, he contacted the Finkel family to ask for a personal meeting with Rav Nosson Tzvi.

He arrived at Rav Nosson Tzvi's home with a friend, and they spent a while in the Rosh Yeshiva's company. When Mr. Schultz left, he asked if the Rosh Yeshiva could accompany him and his friend to the Kosel. The Rosh Yeshiva agreed to join them.

As they were leaving the Kosel, Mr. Schultz asked Rav Nosson Tzvi to give him one mitzvah to keep. Rav Nosson Tzvi asked him if he owned a pair of *tefillin*, and Mr. Schultz replied that he had received a pair at his bar mitzvah, but he wasn't sure whether they were kosher. Rav Nosson Tzvi told him that he would buy him a pair of *tefillin*, assuring Mr. Schultz that he wasn't going to ask him to commit to putting them on every day; he just asked that Mr. Schultz should keep them with him.

Mr. Schultz agreed, but pointed out that he was leaving for the airport at 5 o'clock. It was already 3 o'clock, and he was headed back to the Foreign Ministry for another meeting. Meanwhile, his friend asked if he could also have a pair of *tefillin*. Rav Nosson Tzvi asked Rav Binyamin Carlebach to please make sure that they would have two pairs of *tefillin* ready at 5. With *siyata d'Shmaya*, Rav Carlebach was able to track down R' Avraham Eisenbach, owner of a store for religious items on Rechov Meah Shearim. The store was closed for the midday break, but Rav Eisenbach agreed to open his store and furnish two pairs of excellent *tefillin* for the visitors. When they were ready, Rav Menachem Zaretsky delivered them to the Foreign Ministry, and presented them to Mr. Schultz and his friend.

Another couple of years passed, during which Rav Nosson Tzvi and Mr. Schultz were in contact by phone on occasion. One summer, about five years before Rav Nosson Tzvi's *petirah*, Mr. Schultz called to say that he would be in Eretz Yisrael over a Shabbos, and that he wanted to visit the Rosh Yeshiva on Shabbos. He assured the family that he would not come by car, but would walk from his hotel.

R' Yitzchak, who was the Rosh Yeshiva's *chavrusa* on Shabbos for close to 10 years, was privy to the rest of that story. He knew nothing of Rav Nosson Tzvi's relationship with Howard Schultz or of their imminent meeting, but by a twist of fate (we call it *Hashgachah!*), a relative of R' Yitzchak's came across Mr. Schultz's article and called R' Yitzchak to read it to him – on the Thursday night before Mr. Schultz was scheduled to meet with Rav Nosson Tzvi. R' Yitzchak wondered whether the article was true or was just another one of those "urban legends" that abound nowadays.

That Shabbos, when R' Yitzchak arrived at Rav Nosson Tzvi's home, he met two people standing outside. Although they were dressed in white shirts and slacks and had yarmulkas on their heads, they still looked slightly out of place. As R' Yitzchak walked up to the door, they asked, "Is this Rav Nosson Tzvi Finkel's house?"

R' Yitzchak answered in the affirmative. They thanked him and followed him into the house. They went straight to the kitchen, where the Rebbetzin greeted them warmly, and R' Yitzchak went to the dining room to begin learning with the Rosh Yeshiva. A few minutes later, the Rebbetzin came into the dining room with the two men – whose identities were still unclear to R' Yitzchak – and the Rosh Yeshiva became excited when he saw them. They sat down and started talking, and after a few minutes, one of the men turned to R' Yitzchak and said, "Those two are good friends, and they need some private time. Let's go out and let them talk."

R' Yitzchak walked out with this man, who asked him for a tour of the yeshiva. R' Yitzchak took a walk around the Mir with the man, and then headed back toward the Rosh Yeshiva's house. R' Yitzchak finally asked the visitor who the man sitting with the Rosh Yeshiva was, and he said, "That's Howard Schultz, CEO of Starbucks."

Yitzchak was amazed. Until that week, he had never even heard of Howard Schultz – and now, a mere two days after hearing about Mr. Schultz's famous meeting with Rav Nosson Tzvi, he had actually met him in the flesh.

When the two returned to the Rosh Yeshiva's house, the door to the dining room was still closed. R' Yitzchak went upstairs to learn in a room where the Rosh Yeshiva kept some *sefarim*, and asked the Rebbetzin to notify him when the meeting was over. A little while later, she called him down to continue learning with the Rosh Yeshiva. Mr. Schultz was still standing there, and R' Yitzchak asked him whether the story his relative had read to him was true. Mr. Schultz grew very animated, and he called the Rebbetzin and Mrs. Finkel, the Rosh Yeshiva's mother, into the room so he could repeat the story for them.

When he finished his tale, he asked Rav Nosson Tzvi what he was learning with R' Yitzchak. The Rosh Yeshiva asked R' Yitzchak to explain the Gemara to Mr. Schultz. When R' Yitzchak was finished, Mr. Schultz asked Rav Nosson Tzvi a question – which turned out to be the very question Rav Nosson Tzvi was discussing just before Mr. Schultz had entered the dining room. Rav Nosson Tzvi smiled broadly and said, "Howard, you're not too bad!"

They took leave of one another with Mr. Schultz beaming from that compliment.

The relationship continued until the Rosh Yeshiva's *petirah*. During the last summer of the Rosh Yeshiva's life, when Rav Binyamin Carlebach traveled to Seattle once again, he brought a gift from Rav Nosson Tzvi to Mr. Schultz: a *tallis* bag and *tefillin* bag, along with a *tallis*, to complete the gift of the *tefillin* he had given him several years earlier.

This story has two postscripts, which are perhaps more remarkable than the story of the development of this relationship between the titans of the Torah world and, *lehavdil*, the coffee industry.

After Mr. Schultz left Rav Nosson Tzvi's home that Shabbos, the Rosh Yeshiva told R' Yitzchak all about their relationship, revealing that in the course of their multiyear friendship, not once had he asked Mr. Schultz for a donation to the yeshiva! Mr. Schultz's donations were given strictly of his own volition, not because Rav Nosson Tzvi solicited them. In fact, on one occasion, Mr. Schultz pulled out his checkbook and told the Rosh Yeshiva, "I am ready to fill in any amount you request. Just tell me how much." Rav Nosson Tzvi replied, "Howard, our relationship is not about money. Put away your checkbook."

And Mr. Schultz clearly knew that the Rosh Yeshiva meant it sincerely. Rav Binyamin Carlebach was once on the phone with him and as they ended their conversation, Mr. Schultz said, "Please give Rabbi Finkel a kiss for me."

And finally, Rav Binyamin Carlebach heard from a Mir alumnus who became an extremely wealthy businessman after leaving the yeshiva that he was once at a convention for some of world's richest men in their

30's and 40's. Although he was wearing a cap, not a yarmulke, and had no outward signs identifying him as a Torah Jew, he was approached by a man who shook his hand and said, "Out of all the people in this room, it would appear to me that you would be the one who might know Rav Nosson Tzvi Finkel."

The man then introduced himself as Howard Schultz.

Even in a business setting, Mr. Schultz carried the image of Rav Nosson Tzvi in his heart – because theirs was a relationship of true friendship, not of money.

# CHAPTER TWENTY-EIGHT
# THE TZADDIK

Parkinson's disease will occasionally disable the throat muscles, and if the sufferer is eating while this happens, he can choke. This happened to Rav Nosson Tzvi a few times over the years. Once, several years before his passing, he was unable to breathe for a few minutes before someone managed to dislodge the food that was stuck in his throat. After he began breathing, the medics on the scene placed him on a stretcher to take him to the hospital for testing, to ensure that the minutes that ticked by without oxygen filling his lungs hadn't caused lasting damage. The family decided to summon Rav Nosson Tzvi's personal physician, Dr. Yitzchak Adler, to determine whether such observation was necessary. After examining the Rosh Yeshiva, Dr. Adler said that he felt that it would be worthwhile to go for testing.

As the medics were about to roll the stretcher out the door, Rav Nosson Tzvi motioned to the Rebbetzin and asked her to bring him a bentcher. The medics waited patiently while the Rosh Yeshiva, who had the presence of mind to think about Bircas HaMazon shortly after nearly losing his life, bentched word-for-word from the bentcher.

THE STORY IS TOLD THAT THE CHOFETZ CHAIM WAS once overheard praying that no one should remember him as a pious man. Someone once asked another *gadol* why the Chofetz Chaim had prayed only that his piety not be revealed, and not that people shouldn't realize what a great Torah scholar he was.

"There was no way anybody could miss the Chofetz Chaim's Torah scholarship," explained the *gadol*. "All you have to do is look into the *Bi'ur Halachah*[1] to see how great he was in learning. But he felt that his piety *could* be overlooked, and he prayed that it would happen."

Rav Nosson Tzvi's greatness in both learning and disseminating Torah was self-evident and well-documented. What is less known is his absolute devotion to Hashem and how much he cherished each mitzvah.

THE BASIS OF HIS DEVOTION WAS HIS PROFOUND *EMUNAH* (faith) in Hashem, which manifested itself most in matters related to

**Deep Faith**

Torah study. His firm faith that Torah study sustains the world[2] affected his every decision.

R' Yitzchak, Rav Nosson Tzvi's Shabbos *chavrusa*, was once in a bind. His brother's wedding was scheduled to take place in the United States on a Thursday night in the middle of a *zman*. After discussing it with the Rosh Yeshiva, he had booked a ticket for Tuesday night, so he would land on Wednesday with enough time to recover and tend to some errands before the wedding. About ten days before his flight, the

---

1. *Bi'ur Halachah* is a commentary printed in the *Mishnah Berurah* that examines the Talmudic background of many halachos. The depth and breadth of the Chofetz Chaim's Torah knowledge is self-evident from this commentary.
2. The Gemara (*Avodah Zarah* 5a) states that Hashem made Creation conditional on *Klal Yisrael* accepting the Torah; had they refused to accept it, Hashem would have returned the world to nothingness.

Histadrut (labor union) in Israel threatened to hold "the strike to end all strikes": everything in the country, from the airport to the sanitation department, would be closed. And the strike was scheduled to begin on Monday morning, 36 hours before R' Yitzchak's flight.

R' Yitzchak's friends and family urged him to fly to the States before Shabbos to ensure that he would be there for the wedding, but R' Yitzchak felt that the strike wouldn't actually take place, and he kept postponing his decision. Finally, on the Wednesday before the strike was planned, his friends told him that if he wouldn't leave on Thursday night, he would either have to take a boat to Cyprus and fly from there, or risk missing the wedding. They kept nagging him about it until he agreed to go to the Rosh Yeshiva.

R' Yitzchak explained the circumstances to Rav Nosson Tzvi, who answered that he should change his ticket and fly earlier than planned. "But the Rosh Yeshiva always says that *Torah meigin u'matzil*, the Torah protects and gives salvation," said R' Yitzchak.

The Rosh Yeshiva, who had been walking down the hall to hang up his hat, stopped in his tracks, turned to face R' Yitzchak, and said, "Don't change your ticket."

R' Yitzchak returned to his friends and recounted the exchange. "You didn't understand," they scoffed. "The Rosh Yeshiva didn't say you would make your flight. He meant that the Torah would protect you from your family's wrath when you miss the wedding!"

On Monday morning, the day before his flight, R' Yitzchak was walking from his home to yeshiva for *Shacharis*, and he was surprised to see that the Egged buses – whose drivers were supposed to be on strike from that morning – were running.

Immediately after davening, one of R' Yitzchak's friends approached him and said, "You won."

"What do you mean?" R' Yitzchak asked.

"At 11 o'clock last night, the court issued an injunction that the Histadrut can't strike."

R' Yitzchak went to tell the Rosh Yeshiva what happened. "Yitzchak," Rav Nosson Tzvi said, "you pushed off the strike."

"Me?" asked R' Yitzchak. "It was the Rosh Yeshiva's merit!"

But Rav Nosson Tzvi's faith in the power of Torah ran so deep that he was certain that the merit of this one *yungerman* who wanted to stay and learn a few more days could force a change in Israel's economic and political system. "No," he insisted. "**You** pushed off the strike."

Even with his deep *emunah*, the Rosh Yeshiva scrutinized himself every moment of his life, never feeling satisfied with his level of faith. In his last years, when the Mir's finances followed the world economy downhill, he remarked to R' Shia Ozer Halpern[3] that if he had been at the ultimate level of *emunah*, he would not have had to go the lengths he did to try to cover the shortfall.

RAV NOSSON TZVI DIDN'T OVERLOOK EVEN THE SMALLEST detail of halachah. His son Rav Shaya recalls that he would talk about

**The Small Things** the importance of following the order listed in halachah for putting on and tying one's shoes and not overlooking any of the daily halachos that are sometimes forgotten in one's haste to get on with his day. In fact, the Rosh Yeshiva devoted his last *shmuess* in the Friedman Building, delivered a month before he passed away, to the topic of the mitzvos that people often "trample,"[4] offering the examples of not biting one's nails on Shabbos and being careful to recite *Krias Shema* at the correct time.

There were certain halachos in which Rav Nosson Tzvi was extremely stringent. His father-in-law, Rav Beinush, was extremely careful with regard to *ribbis* (lending or borrowing on interest) – once even forfeiting an opportunity to add onto the main Mir building because he was concerned that it would require him to rely on a leniency in *Hilchos Ribbis*. Rav Nosson Tzvi accepted this extra measure of stringency upon himself as well. In his later years, when the yeshiva was in debt, he was still extremely careful not to allow the yeshiva's account to fall into overdraft, which would incur interest.

ALTHOUGH RAV NOSSON TZVI RARELY REVEALED WHY HE insisted on doing something a certain way, it sometimes emerged that

**So Others Don't Learn From Him** he was acting stringently out of fear that someone would learn from him to apply a leniency that he didn't consider proper.

Rav Nosson Tzvi did not rely on the general Yerushalayim *eiruv*, for instance, and the yeshiva erected a special *eiruv* so he could be taken from his home to the yeshiva in a wheelchair. One Shabbos, he was in the Sanhedria neighborhood for his grandson's *aufruf*, and the family

---

3. R' Shia Ozer organized the Rosh Yeshiva's trips to England, and sometimes hosted him as well.
4. See *Rashi* to *Devarim* 7:12.

constructed an *eiruv* so he could be wheeled from his host to shul. On Shabbos, however, he insisted on dragging himself from one place to the next. It emerged that he was concerned that someone might see him traveling in his wheelchair and, not realizing that the family had erected a special *eiruv* for that Shabbos, determine that the Mirrer Rosh Yeshiva relies on the general *eiruv*.

His fastidiousness applied to *minhagim* (customs) as well. His family's custom was to use chickens for *kapparos*. When his Parkinson's made it difficult for him to swing a chicken over his head, not only wouldn't he switch to another form of fulfilling this custom – such as giving money to *tzedakah* – he wouldn't allow someone else to swing the chicken for him. He had to fulfill the custom on his own.

EACH SEASONAL MITZVAH BROUGHT HIM GREAT EXCITEMENT. He wanted matzos baked with the best stringencies, and he would go to

### Out of Love, Not Anxiety

the bakery personally to supervise the process.

Before Succos, his children would bring him several *lulavim* and *esrogim* to choose from. "His *esrog* had to be perfectly clean," recalls his son Rav Shaya. "But his *dikduk* (meticulousness) in mitzvos did not stem from anxiety, as is often the case with people nowadays, but out of love for Hashem's mitzvos."

A story illustrates Rav Shaya's point. One year, Yom Kippur fell on a Thursday. Hudi, a *talmid* from America, went away for the Shabbos between Yom Kippur and Succos, leaving a *lulav* he had purchased near his bed in the dormitory. He returned to find his bedding askew – and that his *lulav* had become *passul*.

Rav Nosson Tzvi supervises the matzah-baking process.

"What happened to my bed?" Hudi asked his roommate, not wanting to confront him about the *lulav*.

"Oh, my friend came for Shabbos and needed a place to sleep," the roommate replied nonchalantly. "I figured you wouldn't mind ..."

Hudi was very perturbed, and he expressed his frustration to Rav Nosson Tzvi.

"Lots of people bring me *lulavim* because they want me to use their *lulav*," Rav Nosson Tzvi replied.

The Rosh Yeshiva's quest for perfect *arba minim* stemmed from love for mitzvos, not anxiety.

"Come to my house later and choose a *lulav* from my collection."

Later that day, Hudi came to Rav Nosson Tzvi's home and found several beautiful *lulavim* on the table. He chose one, and then asked Rav Nosson Tzvi how much it cost. Rav Nosson Tzvi wouldn't take the full price, insisting that Hudi pay him the price he had paid for his first *lulav* – which was less than half the value of this *lulav*!

"But I'm doing this on one condition," Rav Nosson Tzvi said. "You can't bear a grudge against your roommate." Hudi agreed, and went back to yeshiva elated at the thought of using this beautiful *lulav* on Succos. Only later did he find out that the Rosh Yeshiva had not had any extra *lulavim*. He had asked family members to put all their *lulavim* on the table, and then made sure that each one had a *lulav* – besides him.

He was punctilious in his mitzvah observance because he loved all mitzvos – and the mitzvah of promoting peace in the yeshiva was as important as the others.

EVEN WHEN RAV NOSSON TZVI COULD HAVE FULFILLED A mitzvah in a less-taxing fashion, if at all possible he made the effort to

**Enhancing a Simchah**

fulfill it in the most exemplary way. His brother Rav Gedalya describes how when Rav Nosson Tzvi would arrive at a *chasunah*, the entire hall would be filled

Even on the last *Motza'ei Shabbos* of his life, Rav Nosson Tzvi enhanced a *simchah*, dancing with the son of a *talmid*.

with an electric atmosphere. Just his appearance brought great joy to the *chassan* and the *baalei simchah*, but that level of gladdening the *chassan* wasn't enough. If he was up to it, he would go into the middle of the circle and dance with the *chassan* and the *mechutanim*.

"The entire *chasunah* would feel different if the Rosh Yeshiva would participate," recalls Rav Gedalya.

AFTER RAV NOSSON TZVI'S *PETIRAH*, STORIES EMERGED ABOUT how his blessings were fulfilled – sometimes in an astounding way.

**The Guarantee**     His son Rav Yitzchak related that he once traveled abroad with his father on a fundraising trip. One night they returned to their host's house after 11 p.m., and the Rosh Yeshiva was absolutely exhausted. No sooner did he lie down in bed then a donor called and said that he could meet right then with the Rosh Yeshiva.

"Bring me my frock," said the Rosh Yeshiva. "We're going."

"Abba," Rav Yitzchak replied, "How can we go? It's dangerous for you!"

"The yeshiva needs the money," Rav Nosson Tzvi replied. "We have to go."

They made their way to the donor's house, and when Rav Nosson Tzvi asked for a respectable sum, the donor said, "It's hard for me to give that much."

"It's hard for me too," said the Rosh Yeshiva.

The donor fell deep into thought. Finally, he confided to the Rosh Yeshiva that he needed a salvation in a certain area, and if Rav Nosson

Tzvi would *guarantee* him that he would see a salvation, he would give the amount the Rosh Yeshiva requested.

The Rosh Yeshiva thought for a long time, and finally agreed to the deal.

On the way out, Rav Yitzchak couldn't help but speak his heart. "Abba," he said, "How can you promise him a salvation? What if it doesn't come true?"

"Do you think I was relying on my own merit?" Rav Nosson Tzvi replied. "I was relying on the merit of the Torah he would be supporting with his donation."

RAV BINYAMIN CARLEBACH REVEALS THAT THE ROSH YESHIVA wasn't merely reasoning on his own that he could give blessings based on the merit of the Torah his donors were sup-

**Relying on the Nimukei Yosef** porting. Rather, he would rely on a *Nimukei Yosef* in *Maseches Bava Basra*.

A *yungerman* once came to the Rosh Yeshiva and related that he had gone to Rav Moshe Shapiro, a respected Torah genius and renowned master of Torah thought in Yerushalayim, and asked him for a *berachah*. Rav Shapiro told him that the *Nimukei Yosef* in Bava Basra[5] states that the custom in France was that a person who had a sick relative would go to a "*tofeis biyeshiva* – someone who maintains a yeshiva" for a blessing. He then gave this *yungerman* the names of two people whom he felt were worthy of the title "*tofeis biyeshiva*" – and one of them was Rav Nosson Tzvi.

From then on, when people would ask Rav Nosson Tzvi for a blessing, he would rely on this *Nimukei Yosef* – certain that it wasn't his own piety that might effect salvation, but that of the yeshiva he upheld.

His wife, Rebbetzin Leah Finkel, relates that he would also daven for those whom he had blessed, not relying merely on his initial blessing to that person.

WITH ALL THE EXPLANATIONS, THE STORIES OF THE SALVATIONS people experienced after receiving his blessings speak for themselves.

**The Rosh Yeshiva Repeats His Guarantee** About seven years before the Rosh Yeshiva's passing, a *talmid* who had been in his first *chaburah*

---

5. 53a in the Rif's pages, s.v. *Darash*.

in the 1970's was diagnosed on Chol HaMoed Pesach, without any prior warning, with a stage IV lymphoma – an advanced stage that few survive. Although it was already 11 o'clock at night in Eretz Yisrael, he called the Rosh Yeshiva directly from the hospital where he had received the terrible diagnosis. "I'm sorry for calling so late," he said, "but I've just been diagnosed with cancer."

The Rosh Yeshiva dropped the phone, and the *talmid* had to call back. When the Rosh Yeshiva picked up the phone the second time, his first words were, "*Who* was diagnosed with cancer?"

"*I* was diagnosed with cancer," the *talmid* replied.

"You're going to be okay," the Rosh Yeshiva said resolutely. "I don't want you to worry."

The *talmid* still had to undergo extensive chemotherapy, but ultimately, his cancer went into remission – no small miracle with a stage IV lymphoma.

Unfortunately, he relapsed a while later, which is not uncommon with lymphomas. He researched all the best cancer centers in the world and brought his findings to the Rosh Yeshiva to ask him what to do. The Rosh Yeshiva told him that he wanted to discuss it with R' Meilech Firer, a well-known medical-referral specialist in Bnei Brak. They traveled to Bnei Brak together, and the Rosh Yeshiva sat with Rabbi Firer for 45 minutes discussing the options. Ultimately, they decided that the *talmid* should go for a stem-cell transplant.

Before going for the transplant, the *talmid* came to Rav Nosson Tzvi again and said, "Rosh Yeshiva, I need another *havtachah* (guarantee) from you that I will be cured."

The Rosh Yeshiva was extremely weak; he could barely move. "I had a terrible week," he explained, excusing his lack of energy. "Today Rav Elya Baruch was *niftar*, and earlier this week a Yerushalmi *yungerman* in yeshiva passed away, leaving behind ten children."

"Please," the *talmid* begged. "I really, really need this *havtachah* that this second set of treatments should work."

The Rosh Yeshiva sat there for a long time, and then finally nodded his head.

Three years later, this *talmid* is completely clean, having survived cancer for a second time.

Whether from the merit of Torah or *tefillah*, the Rosh Yeshiva's *havtachah* came true once again.

## CHAPTER TWENTY-NINE
# JUST A FEW WORDS

*"The Rosh Yeshiva was able to accomplish so much in his life because he knew how to be silent when he didn't have to talk."*

*— Rav Menachem Zaretsky, Rav Nosson Tzvi's close confidant*

C HAZAL (*AVOS* 6:6) LIST FORTY-EIGHT QUALITIES through which one can acquire Torah. An entire series of books could be written with those forty-eight qualities as chapter titles, and stories of how Rav Nosson Tzvi embodied those qualities would fill thousands of pages: study, attentive listening, articulate speech, intuitive understanding, and so on.

One of those qualities is *mi'ut sichah* (limited conversation). Considering that Rav Nosson Tzvi met with thousands upon thousands of people each year and left an impression on each of them, one would not expect that quality to be among his attributes. Yet as friendly and down-to-earth as the Rosh Yeshiva was, he was not a man of many words. He didn't waste words even when he was young and healthy,[1] but in his later years, when every word was an effort, he used words even more sparingly.

RAV NOSSON TZVI DIDN'T HAVE TO TALK MUCH, BECAUSE HE was an excellent listener. He gave a person his full attention, maintain-

**A Hundred People an Hour** ing eye contact throughout the conversation. "It didn't matter who the person was," recalls Rav Menachem Zaretsky. "Young or old, the biggest *nebach* or the most important person – every single person received the Rosh Yeshiva's full attention.

"We would keep a log of how many people came in to speak to him during the hours when he received people," recalls Rav Zaretsky. "Close to a hundred people would pass through the room every hour! But because the Rosh Yeshiva gave each person his full attention, it took very little time to discuss a matter with him. He would answer in a few words,

---

1. See p. 209.

and the person would walk out knowing that the Rosh Yeshiva had understood his question or issue and had given him a satisfactory answer."

NOT EVERYONE WAS AWARE OF HOW LITTLE TIME IT TOOK TO receive guidance from Rav Nosson Tzvi. Someone once approached Rav

## The Shortest Half-Hour

Zaretsky and said, "I need to speak to the Rosh Yeshiva for a full half hour. When would be a good time?"

Rav Zaretsky instructed the *talmid* to come at 6:30 one evening, assuring him that Rav Nosson Tzvi would give him the time he needed.

"But I need a full half hour," the *talmid* repeated.

"No one else will be there," Rav Zaretsky pledged, "and he won't answer any phone calls then."

At 6:30 on the evening of the appointment, the *talmid* entered Rav Nosson Tzvi's living room and closed the door behind him. About seven minutes later he emerged with a big smile on his face. Rav Nosson Tzvi had given him his half hour in seven minutes.

PARTIALLY AS A RESULT OF HIS LOVE FOR PEOPLE AND HIS deep sensitivity toward their feelings, but no doubt with a heavy mea-

## The Right Words

sure of Divine inspiration, Rav Nosson Tzvi had the uncanny ability to say exactly what a person needed to hear at a given moment.

"Yossi" was a *bachur* in the yeshiva who didn't have much of a relationship with Rav Nosson Tzvi. His friends once shlepped him to a Friday *vaad*, and when it was over, Yossi's friend noticed that he was leaving without saying the customary *Gut Shabbos* to the Rosh Yeshiva. "Come say *Gut Shabbos*," the friend urged him.

"The Rosh Yeshiva doesn't care if I say *Gut Shabbos* to him," Yossi scoffed.

"Sure he cares," the friend answered.

"He doesn't care about me," Yossi contended. "He doesn't even know my name!"

"Of course he cares about you," his friend insisted.

The two had initially been standing near the end of the line of people waiting to wish Rav Nosson Tzvi *Gut Shabbos*, but while their exchange was taking place, they were unwittingly inching closer and closer to him as the line became shorter. Eventually, they were so close to the Rosh Yeshiva that Yossi had no choice but to remain on line.

The Rosh Yeshiva was very weak that Friday, and to each person who passed him he whispered the two-word *Gut Shabbos*. But when Yossi reached the front of the line, the Rosh Yeshiva looked him in the eye and said, *"Gut Shabbos,* **Yossi***"* – as if to say, "I know your name, I know who you are, and I care about you."

And there were dozens of such stories.

IN INTERACTING WITH *TALMIDIM* OR WITH FAMILY MEMBERS, Rav Nosson Tzvi could say more in two or three words than most people could express in a long conversation.

**"Chasarta Li"**

A member of his extended family davened diagonally across from him during *Yamim Noraim* for over a decade. The last Rosh Hashanah of Rav Nosson Tzvi's life, he noticed that the *yungerman* wasn't in yeshiva.

After Rosh Hashanah, the Rosh Yeshiva met him and said just two words: *"Chasarta li* – I missed you."

Rav Nosson Tzvi didn't ask him any questions ("Where were you? Is everything all right?"); he knew how to express his feelings in a way that opened a door for the *yungerman* to discuss an issue if he wanted to, but without prying or causing him discomfort if he preferred to keep the reason for his absence private.

EVEN WHEN DELIVERING A PUBLIC ADDRESS, RAV NOSSON Tzvi could accomplish a lot in very little time.

**A Deep Impact – in Minutes**

Rav Binyamin Carlebach recalls that during their numerous fundraising trips abroad, they would visit many different communities, and wherever they went, people asked the Rosh Yeshiva to speak. "Another person would have spoken for 20 or 30 minutes to convey the same message the Rosh Yeshiva could deliver in a few minutes," says Rav Carlebach, "In his short *derashah*, he always managed to find the words that would hit home with his audience."

IN GENERAL, RAV NOSSON TZVI'S *HESPEIDIM* AT *LEVAYAHS* were very short. One of his most memorable *hespeidim* was one that was

**"Ich Ken Nisht Redden"**

even shorter than usual.

Rav Elya Boruch Finkel[2] had been a *maggid*

---

2. Rav Elya Baruch was the son of Rav Moshe Finkel, who was a son of Rav Leizer Yudel and a

With Rav Elya Baruch Finkel *zt"l*, whose passing left Rav Nosson Tzvi unable to speak

*shiur* in Mir for over three decades, and when he passed away suddenly on 24 Adar 5768/2008 at the age of 60, the news sent shockwaves through the entire yeshiva. Rav Elya Baruch had a magnetic personality, and he had drawn many *talmidim* to him, *zman* after *zman*.

Rav Nosson Tzvi, who was a few years older than Rav Elya Baruch, began his *hesped* by speaking about Rav Elya Baruch's love of Torah. "The only way you can come to '*Mah ahavti sorasecha*' is through '*kol hayom hi sichasi*,'" he said in a tear-choked voice that was somehow heard clearly by the masses gathered throughout the yeshiva building and on the streets below. He continued to talk about Rav Elya Baruch's delight in Torah, when suddenly he stopped.

"*Ich ken nisht redden*," he cried out. "I can't speak."

That pronouncement sent shivers through the crowd of thousands, but the words that followed from Rav Aryeh Finkel *shlita* – the next *maspid* – evoked audible wailing. Rav Aryeh, who was several years older than both Rav Nosson Tzvi and Rav Elya Baruch, cried pitifully into the microphone, and then regained his composure just enough to say, "*Maran Rosh HaYeshiva shlita  ken nisht redden, un mir kennen yeh redden?*" he said. "The Rosh Yeshiva can't speak, and we can?"

---

brother of Rav Beinush. Recognized for his brilliance as a child, Rav Elya Baruch joined Rav Nachum Partzovitz's *shiur* at a young age and became one of his closest *talmidim*.

RAV AVRAHAM YITZCHAK BARZEL, ONE OF THE ROSHEI
Yeshiva of Mir Brachfeld, recounted that a few years prior to his *petirah*,

**Three-Word Speech**

Rav Nosson Tzvi spoke in Brachfeld before Shavuos. His speech consisted of just three words, which he repeated over and over: *"Torah iz zees, Torah iz zees"* (Torah is sweet). Those simple words penetrated the hearts of his audience, and remained etched indelibly on their hearts for years to come.

That wasn't the only three-word *derashah* that the Rosh Yeshiva gave. Toward the end of his life, he was asked to speak at a gathering for children on the subject of *shemiras halashon*, guarding one's speech. When he arrived at the hall, he had almost no energy, and he struggled to make his way to the podium. When he reached the microphone, he heaved out three words: *"Ve'ahavta ... lerei'acha ... kamocha* (love your fellow as yourself)." That was his whole speech, but the message came across louder than any lengthy *derashah*: If you love someone as much as you love yourself, how can you say something negative about him?

Rav Nosson Tzvi exemplified this message, as those close to him can attest. Rav Menachem Zaretsky, who spent many hours every day with the Rosh Yeshiva, said that in the two decades he spent at his side, not once did he hear the Rosh Yeshiva say – or even convey through body language – something negative about another person!

Rav Nosson Tzvi with Rav Menachem Zaretsky: "I never heard him express something negative about another person."

ANOTHER MANIFESTATION OF RAV NOSSON TZVI'S REMARKABLE power of *shtikah* (silence) was his absolute refusal to become involved in *machlokes*.

**Avoiding Machlokes**

"When people came to him to complain about others or to tell him about an ongoing dispute, he would turn into a stone," recalls a member of the *hanhalah*. "His facial expression would become frozen, and he would not utter a single word in support of either side. He refused to be dragged into the mud."

Even if there was a disagreement between *talmidim* or members of the yeshiva staff, the Rosh Yeshiva refused to become involved. He would listen to both parties, but would not react in any way. Once he grasped the issue, he would decide how to proceed, without expressing to either side that they were correct or incorrect. No one could ever brag to someone who disagreed with him, "The Rosh Yeshiva said I was right."

Yet everyone felt that the Rosh Yeshiva cared about them and their problems. He was able to empathize without taking sides, and to validate people's feelings without condemning anyone.

At times, Rav Nosson Tzvi's very presence was enough to quell a budding *machlokes*. One of the residents of the Beis Yisrael neighborhood strode toward the yeshiva one day, furious that some of the Mirrer *bachurim* were making noise at night and disturbing the peace. He met Rav Binyamin Carlebach outside the Mir building and began complaining to him loudly. Rav Nosson Tzvi was leaving the yeshiva building at that moment, and Rav Binyamin suggested that the man speak to the Rosh Yeshiva.

But rather than complain to the Rosh Yeshiva, the man ran over to him, bent his head, and said, "*Moshe ben Malkah* (his name); *Rabi barech oti* – Rebbi, bless me!"

Because Rav Nosson Tzvi remained untainted by any trace of *machlokes* in his lifetime, after his *petirah*, not a single person out of the thousands he came in contact with each year bore a grievance against him.

ALTHOUGH RAV NOSSON TZVI WAS A PUBLIC FIGURE, HE SHIED away from taking a public position on issues. He would give rulings for

**No Politics**

the *talmidim* of the yeshiva and put his name to proclamations directed at his own *bachurim* and *yungeleit*, but as a rule, he did not sign his name to *kol korei's* (public proclamations). Occasionally, people would urge him to add his name to a proclamation, saying, "All the other roshei yeshiva already signed."

"If you have so many other signatures," he would quip, "then why do you need mine?"

Nor did he agree to become involved in politics, unless he was specifically instructed by other *gedolei Yisrael* to do so. The first time he was invited to a meeting of the Moetzes Gedolei HaTorah – which was an implicit invitation to join the Moetzes – he dispatched a messenger to ask Rav Elyashiv if he really wanted him to attend the meeting, or if he was just inviting him as a courtesy.

When Rav Elyashiv sent back a message that he was inviting him as a courtesy, Rav Nosson Tzvi said that in that case, he would prefer to stay home. (Later in life, he did attend several Moetzes meetings.)

## Getting the Message Across

DESPITE HIS DEEP-SEATED AVERSION TO *MACHLOKES*, RAV Nosson Tzvi found ways to get his message across when he was displeased with something a person had done or said.

On September 11, 2001, Rav Nosson Tzvi was at home with a visitor from America, when the news arrived of the World Trade Center attacks.

The visitor immediately telephoned his family in America to assure himself that they were safe. "*Baruch Hashem*, nothing happened to anyone in my family," he declared happily when he hung up.

The Rosh Yeshiva did not respond, but he immediately went to the *beis midrash* and took the unusual step of delivering an impromptu *shmuess*.

"I don't understand how a person could be happy during such a tragedy because he finds out that his family was spared," the Rosh Yeshiva exclaimed with obvious distress. "How can you be happy after hearing that so many people are suffering?"

## Gentle Humor

EVEN IF RAV NOSSON TZVI DIDN'T SPEAK MUCH, NO ONE EVER found him to be severe or terse. On the contrary, it was pleasant – even fun – to be around him.

His sons Rav Shaya and Rav Yosef Shmaryahu independently recalled the Finkel home as a relaxed, enjoyable place to be. "The atmosphere was light, and things just flowed easily," they related.

Rav Nosson Tzvi had a great sense of humor, which he used to put people at ease and dispel tension. Yet even his jokes were only a few words – quips, one-liners, and bon mots.

The Rosh Yeshiva's humor often emerged when he was trying to make people feel comfortable around him despite his Parkinson's disease.

R' Beinish Mandel and two *bachurim* were once his guests at a Shabbos *seudah*. The Rosh Yeshiva was trying to cut into a grapefruit, but it kept slipping away from him. He pushed the grapefruit toward a *bachur* who had offered to cut it open for him. The *bachur* took the knife and sliced into the grapefruit, causing it to spray juice all over the Rosh Yeshiva.

The boy's face turned as red as the grapefruit in front of him – but the Rosh Yeshiva turned to him and said, "You see – that's why I wanted *you* to do it!"

RAV NOSSON TZVI WOULD OFTEN SLIP A WITTY REMARK INTO his casual conversation. Once, when R' Beinish Mandel and his sons met him at JFK Airport in New York, one of the Mandel boys was walking with crutches, his leg in a cast.

A year later, Rav Nosson Tzvi traveled to America and was met by R' Beinish and his sons. He turned to the boy whose leg had been in the cast the last time and struck up a friendly conversation with him. "How are you?" he asked. "What are you learning? *Keitzad Haregel?*"[3]

Not only did Rav Nosson Tzvi remember that Beinish's son's leg had been broken a year earlier, he even remembered which son was the one with the broken leg.

RAV NOSSON TZVI WAS ONCE HONORED WITH *SIDDUR Kiddushin* at the wedding of a *talmid*, and when the time came for the *kesubah* to be completed under the *chuppah*, as is the custom in Jerusalem, there was no surface on which the witnesses could place the *kesubah* to sign their names. One witness asked the other if he could rest the *kesubah* on his back and sign it that way. Without missing a beat, the Rosh Yeshiva quipped, "Oh, a *kinyan agav!*"[4]

---

3. *Keitzad haregel* literally means, "How is the leg?" But this question was a play on words, because *Keitzad Haregel* is also the name of the second *perek* of *Bava Kamma*.

4. A *kinyan agav* is a method of acquisition by which one can acquire an object together with a field even though the *kinyan* (act of acquiring ownership) for a field is not normally valid for the object; since the *kinyan* is valid for the field, the object can "piggyback" on that *kinyan*. *Kinyan agav* literally means "acquisition on the back" – which is, in a sense, what was happening when the witness signed the *kesubah* on the other one's back.

MOSHE, AN AMERICAN *BACHUR*, LEARNED IN THE MIR DURING the early 1990's, and remained in Eretz Yisrael for Pesach, which was

**The Siman Berachah** relatively unusual. When the Rosh Yeshiva heard that he was not going home, he invited Moshe to his Seder. At first Moshe was uncomfortable with the idea of sitting at the Rosh Yeshiva's table, but Rav Nosson Tzvi assured him that he would feel comfortable because another two *bachurim* would also be there.

Moshe's comfort at the Seder lasted for a few minutes – until he accidently knocked over his *Kiddush* cup, spilling wine all over the table and sending the family scrambling to remove all the matzos from the table before they became wet. Moshe was mortified. He apologized profusely to the Rosh Yeshiva, who tried to soothe him. "I couldn't calm down," recalls Moshe. "As we went on to the next sections of the Haggadah, I kept thinking about how I had ruined the Seder for the family."

Finally, as the family went to wash for *Rachtzah*, Moshe approached the Rosh Yeshiva to apologize once again. "I don't understand," the Rosh Yeshiva replied. "The Gemara states that any house in which wine isn't spilled like water does not see *siman berachah*. Spilled wine is a sign of blessing. You gave me a blessing, and now you're apologizing to me?"

Moshe was mollified, and he was able to enjoy the rest of the Seder.

---

WHEN *BACHURIM* WOULD GO HOME AT THE END OF A *ZMAN*, Rav Nosson Tzvi would often tell them, "I'll be waiting for you to come

**"How Are We Going to Do It Without You?"** back!" or "I can't wait to see you back here!" From anyone else, these words might have sounded trite, but from Rav Nosson Tzvi, they were completely sincere. As his son Rav Yosef Shmaryahu says, "Shlomo HaMelech tells us *kamayim hapanim lapanim, kein lev ha'adam la'adam* – just as water reflects a face, so does a heart reflect another heart. [5] The fact that everyone felt in his heart that the Rosh Yeshiva wanted him to come back means that he really meant it for each individual that he said it to."

But sometimes the Rosh Yeshiva would add just a few words to his standard parting words – with everlasting results.

---

5. *Mishlei* 27:19.

"Shlomo" was an American who came to the Mir after floundering in his previous yeshivos. Back home he had associated with a tough crowd, but like so many others, he found his niche in the Mir. He remained there for three years, and advanced immeasurably in his learning and other spiritual pursuits. But then it came time to return to America and begin *shidduchim*, and he was afraid that the spiritual growth would dissipate once he returned home and rejoined his old *chevrah*.

Shlomo's flight home was on Motza'ei Yom Kippur, and he spent the entire *Yomim Noraim* with a pit in his stomach in anxious anticipation of his return home.

On Motza'ei Yom Kippur he decided to visit Rav Nosson Tzvi one last time to say goodbye and receive a *berachah*. "The Rosh Yeshiva is very weak," he was told. "Come back later."

When Shlomo returned later than night, he found Rav Nosson Tzvi lying down, still weak. Rav Nosson Tzvi motioned to him to come closer, and then even closer. Finally, he wished Shlomo goodbye.

Shlomo turned to leave, but as he was walking out the door, someone in the room called to him, "The Rosh Yeshiva wants you to come back."

He walked back to where Rav Nosson Tzvi was lying, and Rav Nosson Tzvi whispered in his ear, "How are we going to do it without you?"

Years later, Shlomo still feels that the Rosh Yeshiva was giving him a message that his place was in the Mir – and that message gave him the strength to continue his spiritual ascent upon his return home.

Rav Nosson Tzvi's parting message to Shlomo was paraphrased – at least subconsciously, if not overtly – by thousands of orphaned *talmidim* after his shocking *petirah*: "Rosh Yeshiva, how are we going to do it without you?"

# CHAPTER THIRTY
# HUMILITY

One Chol HaMoed, a yungerman learning in Mir came to visit the Rosh Yeshiva and brought along his young son for a berachah. The Rosh Yeshiva blessed the child and then told him, "I gave you a berachah, now it's your turn to give me a berachah!"

The boy hesitated, but Rav Nosson Tzvi insisted that he wanted a berachah. Finally the boy said, in all sincerity, "The Rosh Yeshiva should be a big talmid chacham."

The Rosh Yeshiva responded with a resounding, "Amen!" For the rest of the day, he was smiling from that simple exchange.

*T*O SAY THAT HUMILITY IS A TRAIT THAT RUNS IN THE Finkel family – in all its branches, through all its generations – would be an understatement. Every Mirrer *talmid* can tell you stories of the simple, heartening ways in which members of the family respect every individual. While this trait has been in the Finkels' genetic stock for generations, it was particularly remarkable in Rav Nosson Tzvi's case, considering how much he accomplished in his life, both in terms of his personal spiritual achievements and his success as a Rosh Yeshiva and visionary builder.

Speaking at Rav Nosson Tzvi's *kever* at the end of the *shivah*, Rav Avraham Shmuelevitz quoted the Gemara (*Sanhedrin* 88b) that says, "*Eizehu ben Olam HaBa? Anvisan ushfal berech, shayif ayil, veshayif nafik, velo machzik tivusa lenafshei* – Who is destined for World to Come? One who is modest and humble, who enters [the *beis midrash*] bowing and leaves bowing, and who learns Torah constantly but does not take credit for himself."

Rav Avraham recalled that his father, Rav Chaim Shmuelevitz, would describe how difficult it is for a person to leave the *beis midrash* the same way he entered, especially if he has just delivered a *shiur* that he knows was powerful and appreciated by his audience. Yet the Gemara's words are a perfect description of Rav Nosson Tzvi, said Rav Avraham. Rav Nosson Tzvi entered the yeshiva an extremely humble person, and he left this world the very same way – never considering that his accomplishments in both learning and building Torah should allow him a moment of personal pride.

Another relative, Rav Tzvi Partzovitz, noted the incredible humility it took for Rav Nosson Tzvi to begin his ascent in learning when he returned to the Mir at 17. At the time, he had younger cousins who were far more advanced than he, and were able to argue in learning with the greatest minds in yeshiva – while he was studying with paid *chavrusas*. "Imagine," said Rav Partzovitz, "how much humility it would take for one of us to sit in the *beis midrash*, for even one *seder*, with *chavrusas* who had obviously been hired to 'tutor' us in learning, while *bachurim* younger than us are able to learn with regular *chavrusas*. Now imagine how hard it would be to learn with tutors for all the *sedarim*! Yet Rav Nosson Tzvi had no qualms about this learning regimen. He sat and learned with those *chavrusas*, and perhaps because of his humility, within a few short years, he became one of the top *bachurim* in yeshiva."

Rav Moshe Meir Heizler relates that even after Rav Nosson Tzvi had advanced in his learning and was already recognized in yeshiva as being *mekurav* (close) to the Rosh Yeshiva, Rav Leizer Yudel, he never let his success go to his head. He would still approach anyone who he felt could help him grow and request a *chavrusashaft*, never thinking that they should be the ones approaching him.

BY THE 1970'S, RAV NOSSON TZVI HAD ADVANCED SO FAR IN HIS learning that he could easily have given a *shiur* of his own *chiddushim*.

## Beginning to Disseminate Torah

Yet his first foray into teaching Torah was not giving his own *shiur*, but delivering a review of Rav Nochum Partzovitz's *shiur*. He learned with Rav Nochum during night *seder* so he would know what Rav Nochum was planning to say during *shiur*, and although he was already known as a phenomenal *masmid* and a great *lamdan*, he was happy to give a review of someone else's *shiur*.

Years later, as a Rosh Yeshiva, he still displayed interest in hearing *shiurim* given by others. Two *talmidim* of Rav Asher Arielli

Rav Nosson Tzvi with Rav Asher Arielli, whose Torah he heard every Friday night

Everyone's Torah is precious.
Rav Nosson Tzvi in a Torah discussion with a group of young boys in Baltimore

(Rav Nochum's son-in-law) would repeat Rav Asher's Torah to him each Shabbos, and he would make a point of attending Rav Refoel Shmuelevitz's *shiur klali*.

It wasn't only illustrious *talmidei chachamim* whose *chiddushei Torah* earned Rav Nosson Tzvi's rapt attention. When *bachurim* would deliver *chaburos* to Rav Nosson Tzvi, he would listen intently, never removing his gaze from the person speaking. No person's Torah was unworthy of his attention.

AT THE FIRST MEETING OF *GEDOLEI YISRAEL* THAT HE ATTENDED in the capacity of Rosh Yeshiva, shortly after the passing of his father-in-

**The First Meeting as Rosh Yeshiva** law, Rav Beinush, Rav Nosson Tzvi sat quietly as the *gedolim* present offered their opinions on a certain matter. Suddenly, Rav Baruch Mordechai Ezrachi, Rosh Yeshiva of Ateres Yisrael, rose to his feet and called out, "*Un vus zugt der Mirrer Rosh Yeshiva* – what does the Mirrer Rosh Yeshiva say?"

Rav Nosson Tzvi later told his brother, Rav Gedalya, that he nearly fainted at hearing himself described as the Mirrer Rosh Yeshiva – especially in front of the great leaders of *Klal Yisrael*.

In those early years of Rav Nosson Tzvi's tenure as Rosh Yeshiva, R' Beinish Mandel – who had been a member of Rav Nosson Tzvi's first *chaburah* and had maintained a connection with him ever since – once apologized to the Rosh Yeshiva for not remembering to address him in third person. He explained that since their relationship went so far back, he was used to addressing Rav Nosson Tzvi as "you," rather than as "the Rosh Yeshiva," and he had a hard time adjusting to the third person.

"You think *you're* not used to it?" the Rosh Yeshiva said ruefully. "I can't get used to having people stand up for me when I walk into the room."

EVEN IN RECENT YEARS, AFTER HAVING SUCCESSFULLY BUILT the Mir into the colossal Torah citadel it is today, Rav Nosson Tzvi

### Hisbatlus to Gedolim

would still consult with others at every step of the way. His *hisbatlus* (self-abnegation) to *gedolei Yisrael* – and specifically to Rav Shach and Rav Chaim Kamiel in earlier years, and to Rav Aharon Leib Shteinman in his later years – was legendary. He would not make any significant policy change in the yeshiva without consulting them, and he would follow their directives faithfully.

Even Rav Nosson Tzvi's basic duties as a Rosh Yeshiva were dictated by Rav Shach. When he first took control of the yeshiva, he asked Rav Shach whether he was required to travel overseas to fundraise. Rav Shach told him that he should.

"But how will I have energy for it?" he asked. (He had already been suffering from Parkinson's for approximately six years at the time.)

"*Hanosen laya'ef koach* – He who gives energy to the weary [will give you the energy]," Rav Shach replied.

For more than a decade thereafter, Rav Nosson Tzvi never gave a second thought to whether he should continue fundraising abroad; he

Rav Nosson Tzvi consults with Rav Schach. "Hashem will give you strength."

did not hesitate to travel to any continent or country in the world to raise funds to keep building Torah.

Several years before his passing, when the Parkinson's became more severe, he asked his rebbi, Rav Chaim Kamiel, whether he had to continue traveling. Rav Chaim told him that he didn't have to. A few days later, however, Rav Chaim called him and related that Rav Leizer Yudel had appeared to him in a dream and had admonished him, saying, "Why are you getting involved in the business of the Mirrer Yeshiva?"

Rav Chaim took this as a sign that Rav Nosson Tzvi should continue traveling, and he rescinded his initial advice.[1]

In Rav Nosson Tzvi's final months on earth, Rav Aharon Leib Shteinman asked him if he still had energy to travel. "I go without energy," Rav Nosson Tzvi replied.

ON CERTAIN MATTERS, RAV NOSSON TZVI WOULDN'T CONSULT only *gedolei Yisrael* – he would seek advice from many, many others.

**Advice From Anyone**

Whether it was regarding the purchase or construction of a new building, or about some other matter, he sought the opinion and advice of any person knowledgeable in that particular area. In his deep humility, explains his son Rav Yosef Shmaryahu, he was always concerned that his own *negios* (personal motives) would cloud his decision-making process. Only after hearing from several others that his plans seemed correct did he feel comfortable going ahead with them.

---

1. Rav Refoel Katz, who confirmed with Rav Nosson Tzvi both parts of the story (the part about Rav Shach and the part about Rav Chaim Kamiel).

DUE TO HIS DEEP HUMILITY, RAV NOSSON TZVI WAS A BEACON
of light to everyone in the Beis Yisrael neighborhood – from the neigh-
**A Friendly Neighbor** borhood's Yerushalmi residents and laborers to the
sanitation workers who passed through each morning,
and everyone in between.

R' Zalman Rosental, whose *D'fus Bitachon* printing press was located next door to Rav Nosson Tzvi's home on Rechov Ha'ameilim, relates
that each time they met, the Rosh Yeshiva would greet him and engage
in small talk. If Rav Nosson Tzvi was already in his car, when he would
see R' Zalman coming down the street he would tell his driver to wait so
he could wish R' Zalman, "Good morning." And he didn't do this only
for R' Zalman – he did the same for R' Zalman's son, R' Yisrael, who is
a young man.

Many storekeepers and vendors who provide services for the Mirrer
*talmidim* were in deep mourning in the weeks after Rav Nosson Tzvi's
passing. Each day, several dry cleaners park their vans outside the Mir
and accept laundry and dry-cleaning items, which they return the same
day. Each one thought that he was special to the Rosh Yeshiva, because
Rav Nosson Tzvi would make a point of greeting him each morning.
They were all shocked to learn after his *petirah* that he had greeted
every one of them as he passed them on his way home.

One of the dry cleaners related that before one of Rav Nosson Tzvi's
last trips to the United States, as he was being wheeled past this cleaner's van, he asked his attendant to stop. Turning to the cleaner from his
wheelchair, he said, "I'm not going to be here for a few days, because

I'm traveling abroad to fundraise. Please give me a *berachah* that I should be successful."

"*I* should give the Rosh Yeshiva a *berachah*?" the dry cleaner asked incredulously.

"Yes," insisted the Rosh Yeshiva. "Give me a *berachah*."


EVEN PEOPLE WITH WHOM RAV NOSSON TZVI HAD ONLY A casual acquaintance were treated like cherished friends. The manager of

**Everyone's Friend**

the Tamir wedding hall, in which Rav Nosson Tzvi made several of his children's weddings, was once walking in Bnei Brak when a car pulled up alongside him. There, in the front seat, sat the Rosh Yeshiva, waving and smiling at him. The manager walked over to the car, and the two conversed for a few minutes.

A few months later, a member of the manager's family married a Finkel relative. A while later, he was walking on the street once again when Rav Nosson Tzvi's car pulled up alongside him. The window rolled down, and Rav Nosson Tzvi called out to him, "Now we're not only friends, we're also *mechutanim*!"


ONE OF THE *MIDDOS* THAT MADE THE ROSH YESHIVA SO beloved to his *talmidim* was his lack of pretension. This was perhaps

**The Small Kabbalah**

most apparent during his Friday *vaadim*, when he would talk openly about whatever was in his heart or on his mind.

He once revealed, for instance, that he had made a *kabbalah* (resolution) not to eat taffies. He explained that people tend to make resolutions on a grand scale, accepting things that are hard to keep. A few months after making such a *kabbalah*, a person may become despondent when he realizes that he didn't keep his resolution. When this process repeats itself many times, the person will begin to feel like a failure and give up entirely on making resolutions to improve his behavior. "I accepted this *kabbalah* of not eating taffies," explained the Rosh Yeshiva, "because I knew that it was easy for me to keep. This way, I prove to myself that I can keep my *kabbalos,* and that gives me the confidence to accept bigger *kabbalos* upon myself."

Few in his position would admit to having had a desire for candies altogether, much less to having difficulty keeping a resolution.

One can only imagine how many *bnei Torah* were encouraged to make *kabbalos* to grow in their own *ruchniyus* because of this little nugget of personal information!

**No Shows**

THOSE WHO WERE CLOSE TO RAV NOSSON TZVI FROM WHEN he first became Rosh Yeshiva recall his discomfort at having been handed the mantle of leadership.[2] He never changed his *levush* (manner of dress) to don a Rosh Yeshiva's high yarmulke or distinctive hat, and his unchanged outer appearance was a reflection of how unaffected his inner self was by his new title. He would still talk to everyone with the same respect – and he continued doing that until his very last day in this world.

He didn't put on a show for anyone. Family, *talmidim,* and *meshamshim* who spent many hours at his side each day related that it was clear from the way he acted that not once did he think of adopting a certain mannerism because that is how a typical Rosh Yeshiva is expected to act. He was comfortable with who he was, and he saw no need to act like someone he wasn't.

His comfort with who he was manifested itself in many ways. One minor example is the way he would talk to people. He would use common, everyday phrases to express himself. At the first Friday *vaad* after returning from a fundraising trip abroad, for instance, he would often tell the *bachurim,* "I missed you," never switching to language that would be perceived as more "Rosh Yeshivish."

**Posing for Pictures**

ALTHOUGH RAV NOSSON TZVI DID NOT SEEK HONOR AND HAD no airs about him, he understood how to utilize his position in a way that brought honor to others.

When he would come to family *simchos*, he would sit at the side of the head table, not in the middle. But when attending the wedding of a *talmid*, he knew that the family would feel honored if the Mirrer Rosh Yeshiva would sit at the center of the head table, so he would take a seat there.

Similarly, Rav Nosson Tzvi would graciously allow people to take pictures of him, and would even help them get good shots.

About five years before his *petirah*, a young *bachur* learning in a yeshiva for boys from non-yeshiva communities was reading a book on

---

2. See p. 229.

*Bachurim* file past the Rosh Yeshiva after a Friday *vaad* to wish *Gut Shabbos.*

*gedolim* of prewar Europe, and he kept reading amazing stories about Rav Nosson Tzvi Finkel, the Alter of Slabodka. Knowing little of the history of the yeshiva world, the *bachur* naively thought that Rav Nosson Tzvi, the Rosh Yeshiva of Mir – whose *vaad* some of his friends attended on Fridays – was the Alter of Slabodka. *I **must** go listen to a vaad from this gadol*, he thought.

That Friday, the boy came to Rav Nosson Tzvi's *vaad*. After the *vaad*, everyone present would file past Rav Nosson Tzvi and shake his hand and exchange *Gut Shabbos* greetings. This boy gave his friend a disposable camera and asked him to snap a picture as he shook hands with Rav Nosson Tzvi.

As the boy walked away from Rav Nosson Tzvi, he realized that his friend had become engrossed in conversation with someone else and had forgotten to take the picture. "Listen," he said to his friend, "I'll go to the end of the line and shake the Rosh Yeshiva's hand again. I'm sure he won't remember that I already shook his hand. But this time, remember to take the picture!"

Little did he know that Rav Nosson Tzvi never forgot a face. As he shook Rav Nosson Tzvi's hand for a second time, the Rosh Yeshiva looked at him quizzically, as if to ask, "Didn't you say *Gut Shabbos* already?" But a split second later, a look of understanding crossed Rav Nosson Tzvi's face, and he turned to see the boy's friend holding the camera. He grasped the *bachur's* hand, faced the camera, and his face lit up with his trademark smile. Only later did this *bachur* — who joined the Mir a few years later and even merited a *chavrusashaft* with Rav Nosson Tzvi — realize that the person who had posed for him was not the Alter of Slabodka, but a giant of the spirit nonetheless.

THE TALMUD (*MEGILLAH* 31) STATES, "WHEREVER YOU FIND THE greatness of *Hakadosh Baruch Hu*, there you find His humility. This

**Wherever You Find His Greatness ...**

phenomenon is written in the Torah, repeated in the *Neviim*, and stated a third time in *Kesuvim*."

The Gemara goes on to cite proof verses from each of the three sections of Tanach. Interestingly, all three verses that demonstrate Hashem's humility refer to Him as caring for the downtrodden: "He performs justice for orphan and widow, and loves the stranger, to give him food and clothing" (*Devarim* 10:18); "But [I] am with the contrite and lowly of spirit, to revive the spirit of the lowly and to revive the heart of the contrite" (*Yeshayah* 57:15); and "Father of the orphans and Judge of the widows, God in the habitation of his Holiness" (*Tehillim* 68:6).

In keeping with the principle that one should emulate Hashem by following in his ways (*Shabbos* 153b), a key aspect of Rav Nosson Tzvi's humility was the immense concern and mercy he had for downtrodden people – and especially widows and orphans.

When "Shimon," a *talmid* who had lost his father right before Pesach, was sitting *shivah* in America, he received a phone call from none other than Rav Nosson Tzvi Finkel. The Rosh Yeshiva had one message for him: "I need you to be strong and take care of your mother."

The Rosh Yeshiva didn't know Shimon's mother, but he knew that a widow needed a strong shoulder to cry on, and he felt that Shimon was capable of comforting his mother.

EVEN WHEN HE WAS EXTREMELY BUSY, RAV NOSSON TZVI found the presence of mind to put himself in the shoes of a widow.

The *bechinos* (entrance exams) for Mir Brachfeld are extremely intense.[3] Generally, the *hanhalah* waits until the end of a day of *bechinos*, reviews the rosters, and then informs those who were tested whether they were accepted into the yeshiva. One day, while testing

---

3. See pp. 348-349.

dozens of applicants, Rav Nosson Tzvi learned that one of the boys was an orphan. He called aside a *hanhalah* member and said, "Go call this boy's mother and tell her that her son was accepted."

When the *hanhalah* member expressed surprise at this departure from the standard operating procedure, Rav Nosson Tzvi explained, "She is a widow. I have no doubt that when her son left for his *bechinah* this morning, she took a *Tehillim* in her hands and has not put it down since. She probably hasn't even eaten anything today. Go call her and inform her that her son is accepted so she doesn't have to fast any longer."

The *hanhalah* member followed Rav Nosson Tzvi's instructions and called the mother to pass on the good news. "Oh, thank you," she exclaimed. "Now I can go make myself a coffee and eat something. I haven't eaten yet today!"


RAV NOSSON TZVI DIDN'T HAVE TO KNOW A FAMILY IN ORDER to feel for them. A close *talmid* who consulted him on many issues had a friend who lost his father. This *bachur* knew that he should call to be *menachem avel*, but he wasn't sure what he should say. He asked the Rosh Yeshiva for advice.

For a few moments, the Rosh Yeshiva didn't respond. Thinking that perhaps his question hadn't been clear, he started to repeat it, when he suddenly realized why the Rosh Yeshiva hadn't answered: tears – hot, wet tears – were slowly trickling down his cheek, as he thought about the young orphan's plight.


RAV NOSSON TZVI DIDN'T SUFFICE WITH EMPATHIZING WITH orphans and widows. When a Mirrer *talmid* passed away, leaving behind a large family, Rav Nosson Tzvi called his widow and promised her that he was now her children's "father." He told the children that any time they had anything to discuss, they should write to him, and he would write back.

Sure enough, the children wrote letters to the Rosh Yeshiva, and he wrote back to them in longhand.

After a few of the boys in the family received his letters, Rav Nosson Tzvi received a complaint from a 6-year-old girl in the family, who felt left out at not having received a letter. Rav Nosson Tzvi took a piece of paper and wrote her a short note, adding a picture of a heart to show that his heart was with the family. This girl, who is now married with a family of her own, still cherishes the note that carried her through many a difficult moment.[4]

---

4. Heard from R' Mordechai Grunwald.

# CHAPTER THIRTY-ONE
# CHAKARAS CHATOV

*In 1974, Rav Nosson Tzvi learned that a friend who had studied with him when he had first arrived in Mir – more than a decade earlier – was in bed with a severe case of gout, and it was so painful that he could not even put his feet on the floor.*

*So deep was Rav Nosson Tzvi's appreciation for this friend that one night he borrowed his father's car and drove to the friend's home with two bachurim in tow. He walked into the apartment, and with the help of the two bachurim, he lifted the yungerman, sat him on a chair, and carried him out to the car. Rav Nosson Tzvi drove to the office of one of the biggest specialists in the country, they carried the patient inside, and paid some $200 to have him examined. The doctor prescribed some medication, and told him to come back in a few weeks.*

*A few weeks later Rav Nosson Tzvi went through the entire process once again, paying full price for the second visit as well, until the gout was healed.*

LTHOUGH RAV NOSSON TZVI MADE HIMSELF AVAIL-able to everyone and gave every *talmid* as much time as he needed, he would extend himself even further for those who had helped him at any point.

He retained friendships forever. Even his childhood friends from Chicago were never forgotten, and he would capitalize on any opportunity to reignite the friendship, because he truly appreciated their influence on his life.

Rav Moshe Meir Heizler, who had learned with Rav Nosson Tzvi during his third year in the Mir, recounted that Rav Nosson Tzvi wouldn't suffice with sending him an invitation to a family *simchah*; he would also call to invite him personally.

In 5748/1988, Rav Heizler wanted to help a certain *yungerman* get accepted into the Mir Yeshiva's *kollel*. Money was tight, and not everyone could be accepted into the *kollel* and receive a stipend. Rav Heizler made the request of Rav Beinush, who told him to speak to Rav Nosson Tzvi. [Apparently, Rav Beinush had handed certain responsibilities to Rav Nosson Tzvi by that point.] At first Rav Nosson Tzvi said, "I just turned down a similar request from one of the *gedolei hador* to whom I owe a certain measure of *hakaras hatov*." He then paused, thought for a moment, and said, "But we are friends ...

"I'll tell you what: let him learn in yeshiva for two months, and then I'll add him to the payroll." So great was he feeling of indebtedness to someone who had once helped him.

EVEN WHEN A PERSON WHO HELPED RAV NOSSON TZVI HAD A personal stake in doing the favor, the Rosh Yeshiva would be appreciative nonetheless.

R' Zalman Rosental, whose printing press is next door to the Rosh Yeshiva's home on Rechov Ha'ameilim, eventually became one of the **Thanks for a** landlords of Beis Menachem when he leased the **Business Deal** space above his shop to the yeshiva. His space didn't suffice, however, and he went through the effort of convincing the owners of the neighboring shops to rent their adjoining spaces so the yeshiva could break through the walls and enlarge the *beis midrash*.

At the *Chanukas Habayis* for Beis Menachem, the Rosh Yeshiva thanked R' Zalman publicly for helping the yeshiva. "For me, it was a business deal," recalls R' Zalman, "but the Rosh Yeshiva had *hakaras hatov* to me nonetheless!"

RAV NOSSON TZVI LOOKED FOR OPPORTUNITIES TO HELP those who helped him. Because he appreciated all that R' Yehuda Neuhaus, **Seeking** his trusted helper, did for him, Rav Nosson Tzvi **Hakaras Hatov** would ask R' Yehuda why he never spoke to him **Opportunities** about issues that cropped up in his life. When R' Yehuda explained that he didn't want to waste the Rosh Yeshiva's time and energy, and that he preferred to free him up to learn, Rav Nosson Tzvi protested, "My time is your time!"

ONE OF THE DONORS OF A MIR BUILDING WAS PLANNING TO daven in the yeshiva one Yom Kippur, and Rav Nosson Tzvi told a member of the *hanhalah* that he wanted to give this man an *aliyah*. The *hanhalah* member, who had an extremely close relationship with this philanthropist, conveyed the message to him, and asked him whether he knew how to recite the *berachos* on the Torah with the traditional Yom Kippur *nusach*. When the man said that he didn't, the *hanhalah* member spent an hour and a half with him, repeating the *berachos* with the man countless times until he knew the *nusach*, just so the Rosh Yeshiva could express his appreciation for this donor's largesse.

ON THE LAST HOSHANA RABBAH OF THE ROSH YESHIVA'S life, someone brought him very tall and beautiful *hoshanos*. The Rosh Yeshiva tried to give these *hoshanos* to R' Yehuda Neuhaus as a token of his *hakaras hatov*, but R' Yehuda refused to accept them. Rav Nosson Tzvi then looked around the *beis midrash* and noticed that R' Meir

Feiler, an alumnus who is a close friend of the yeshiva and helped a lot with fundraising in Montreal, was visiting Eretz Yisrael for Yom Tov and had joined the yeshiva for the Hoshana Rabbah davening. He asked R' Yehuda to bring the *hoshanos* to him. Befuddled, R' Meir came to ask the Rosh Yeshiva why he had sent the *hoshanos*.

"It's a *segulah*," the Rosh Yeshiva quipped, but he pressed him to take them as a sign of his appreciation for all that he had done on behalf of the Mir.

RAV NOSSON TZVI HAD A CLOSE RELATIONSHIP WITH RAV Aharon Schechter, Rosh Yeshiva of Yeshiva Mesivta Rabbeinu Chaim

### Appreciation for Decades

Berlin, which began when a Finkel learned in Chaim Berlin for a year. Rav Nosson Tzvi was eternally grateful for Rav Schechter's personal attention to his relative. To show his *hakaras hatov*, he would make a concerted effort to daven *Shacharis* in Chaim Berlin during each visit to America.

He had overwhelming *hakaras hatov* for those involved in his children's *chinuch* – even for the *melamdim* who taught them as youngsters. He would remember them decades after his children had been in their classes, and would thank them again each time he met them. Whenever one of them was sitting *shivah*, he would be *menachem avel* to show his appreciation.

THE FAMILIES OF THOSE who had donated buildings or *batei midrash* to the

### The Two-Hour Trek

Mir were extremely dear to Rav Nosson Tzvi. He considered them his *"shutfim"* (partners) in *harbatzas Torah*, and he would go out of his way to show his appreciation – sometimes against the donor's own instructions.

Rav Nosson Tzvi spent

Rav Nosson Tzvi greets Rav Aharon Shechter, to whom he was extremely grateful, at a Mir dinner

a Shabbos in Edison, New Jersey, with Mr. and Mrs. Yossi Stern, who had donated both the Mir building in Brachfeld and the Beis Yeshayah building in Yerushalayim. That Motza'ei Shabbos, Mr. Gary Fragin, who had sponsored the annex to the main *beis midrash* in 1994, was celebrating the inauguration of a building he had sponsored for a yeshiva in Far Rockaway, New York.

Concerned that the Rosh Yeshiva might hear about the ceremony and travel from Edison to Far Rockaway — a 2-hour ride each way — to join in the celebration, Mr. Fragin called Rav Nosson Tzvi on Friday to ask him not to make the trip. "I was always concerned for his health," Mr. Fragin explains, "and I thought the trip would be too much for him."

His protestations fell on deaf ears. "During the ceremony," Mr. Fragin recounts, "everyone was silent, listening to a speaker. Suddenly, there was an excited murmur in the room, and people craned their necks to see which dignitary was entering. I looked up at the door, and there was Rav Nosson Tzvi, shuffling in to join in the inauguration."

He didn't wait for monumental occasions to show his appreciation, however. Many of Mr. Fragin's grandsons traveled to Eretz Yisrael to put on *tefillin* for the first time in the Mir, and after *Shacharis*, the Rosh Yeshiva would hold a *seudah* in his home in honor of the occasion.

ALTHOUGH PEOPLE CONSIDERED IT A PRIVILEGE TO HOST RAV Nosson Tzvi — and many vied for the honor of doing so — he would

**Leaving a Gift**

bring a gift to every host. R' Daniel Carlebach, a brother of Rav Binyamin Carlebach, hosted Rav Nosson Tzvi for most of his Shabbosos in New York. R' Daniel cherishes a *siddur* that Rav Nosson Tzvi personally inscribed with simple, but touching, words, thanking him for his hospitality and friendship.

The inscription in a siddur Rav Nosson Tzvi gave R' Daniel Carlebach, who hosted him on Shabbosos·in New York

ALTHOUGH RAV NOSSON TZVI WAS CAREFUL TO EXPRESS HIS gratitude to everyone, he himself never expected to be thanked, and he

**No Expectations in Return** tried to teach those close to him that they should to do things for others without being thanked. He once told R' Yehuda Neuhaus that the reason Dovid HaMelech and Moshe Rabbeinu were chosen as leaders only after demonstrating their concern for the sheep they tended is that a leader must exert himself for the public without expecting thanks, much as a caring shepherd deals kindly with his sheep even though they are unable to thank him.

AS MUCH AS RAV NOSSON TZVI VALUED AND APPRECIATED everything that was done for him personally or for the yeshiva, he didn't

**No Pandering** allow his appreciation to affect his objectivity when he had to make a decision.

Once, a man who had helped the yeshiva over the course of a decade was seen in the United States searching for a *lulav* to match an exquisite *esrog*. When someone asked him where he had found such a beautiful *esrog*, he replied that he had received it from Rav Nosson Tzvi. He went on to reveal an incredible story.

Among other things, this philanthropist had been instrumental in funding a specific program in the Mir. Because the program was reserved for top *talmidim*, each entrant had to be approved by the Rosh Yeshiva himself. This donor's nephew wanted to join the program, but had not passed the screening process. Confident that he could rely on "protektzia" (connections), he asked his uncle to intercede on his behalf. When the Rosh Yeshiva heard the philanthropist's request, he smiled warmly, but explained that he could not accept the man's nephew into the program.

A short while later, the philanthropist traveled to Eretz Yisrael to join the yeshiva for *tefillos* on Yom Kippur. After Yom Kippur, he went to part with the Rosh Yeshiva before returning to America. Before leaving the Rosh Yeshiva's home, he repeated his request for his nephew. "I'll do anything else you want," Rav Nosson Tzvi replied. "I'll even give you my own *esrog*![1] But I'm sorry, I can't let your nephew join the program."

And the Rosh Yeshiva made good on his words. He handed over his *esrog*, but did not allow his appreciation toward the philanthropist to sway his decisions in regard to the yeshiva.

---

1. Out of his love for mitzvos, Rav Nosson Tzvi would be careful to select only the most exquisite *arba minim*. See p. 392.

WHEN ONE OF THE MIR BUILDINGS WAS CLOSE TO COMPLETION,

**No English** the donor who had sponsored the construction made a request. In his years of spending *Yamim Tovim* in Eretz Yisrael with the same families at the same hotels, he had amassed a large group of friends from *chutz la'aretz* who planned to attend the inauguration for the building. Many of them didn't understand Yiddish, and the donor requested that the Rosh Yeshiva speak in English at the inauguration ceremony.

"Let me think about it," Rav Nosson Tzvi replied. A day later, he called the sponsor and said, "I thought about it, and I realized that the language of the yeshiva is Yiddish, and it would be inappropriate for me to switch to English."

To this day, many years later, the donor still marvels at that decision – a decision, he says, that boosted his appreciation for the Rosh Yeshiva immensely. "I've heard from people on the *hanhalah* that the amount I donated for the construction was the single largest donation the yeshiva had received at that point. Yet he didn't pander to me – he felt that he had a *mesorah* (tradition) to protect, and he wasn't going to abandon a yeshiva tradition to please a donor."

A family member of this donor explains that it is *because* of the Rosh Yeshiva's insistence on sticking to tradition – not despite it – that this donor has remained a friend of the Mir throughout the years, donating large sums to the yeshiva many times since that incident.

# CHAPTER THIRTY-TWO
# PERSEVERANCE OVER PARKINSON'S

*The Vilna Gaon passed away on Chol HaMoed Succos. That Simchas Torah, his talmidim couldn't bring themselves to dance. How could one rejoice with the Torah only days after losing their beloved rebbi, one of the greatest Torah giants in many, many generations?*

*Suddenly, one of them started singing a song with lyrics that he composed on the spot, which has since become a Simchas Torah classic: "Olam Haba iz a gutte zach, lernen Torah is ah bessere zach, varf avek yedden yuch, lernen Torah nuch un nuch, nuch un nuch un nuch ..." The intent of these words was that Olam Haba, where our dear rebbi the Gaon is right now, is a good thing, but learning Torah, which we can do here in Olam Hazeh, is even better. Cast away every burden, learn Torah more and more ...*

*Rav Nosson Tzvi had many burdens — most significantly, the burden of the Parkinson's disease that riddled his body. Yet he threw away every burden and learned and built Torah — nuch un nuch, more and more.*

*— Rav Avraham Shmuelevitz, at the kever at the end of shivah*

ONE OF THE FIRST THINGS — OFTEN THE FIRST THING — that anyone noticed about Rav Nosson Tzvi during the last 28 years of his life was the Parkinson's disease that afflicted him. At good times, his body would merely shake; at harder times, he would thrash about spastically.

Parkinson's is a degenerative disease that robs a person of the ability to control his muscles. In addition, Parkinson's sufferers experience extreme weakness and emotional pain, and most people diagnosed with later-stage Parkinson's end up bedridden for the rest of their lives.

At the *shivah* for Rav Nosson Tzvi, a man who arrived in a wheelchair said that he has had Parkinson's for several years, and although he was a *talmid chacham*, he had not opened a Gemara from the time he was afflicted. He often didn't even make it to shul to daven.

That statement alone would have been an eye-opener to those at the *shivah*. After all, Rav Nosson Tzvi had not only davened regularly in the yeshiva and learned for many, many hours each day while suffering for *28 years*, but he had also built the biggest Torah empire in the world during that time, taking the massive financial responsibility for the yeshiva's growth on his weary shoulders – while finding the time and patience to impart warmth and love to every one of his *talmidim*. To hear that a Parkinson's victim who had the disease for a few years couldn't go to shul or open a Gemara suddenly cast Rav Nosson Tzvi in a greater light than anyone had fathomed.

But the visitor in the wheelchair topped his initial revelation when he informed the family that he shared the same doctor as Rav Nosson Tzvi, and the doctor had told him that the severity of his case was approximately *one-tenth* of Rav Nosson Tzvi's.

The story of his leadership of the Mir goes far beyond his triumph over a dreadful disease. He would have been remembered for generations as one of the great Torah giants and Torah builders of modern times even if he had been healthy. That he achieved what he did despite his debilitating illness is a remarkable lesson and *chizuk* for everyone,[1] and the stories of how he transcended his physical limitations are an indelible part of his legacy.

IN APPROXIMATELY 5744/1984, RAV NOSSON TZVI BEGAN TO show the first signs of Parkinson's disease. The symptoms were barely

**Early Signs**

noticeable at first – *talmidim* from the earlier years didn't even notice that he was ill – but it was clear to the people close to him that it was only a matter of time until his condition would deteriorate. Many people in his situation would have tried to hide the disease for as long as possible, but Rav Nosson Tzvi quietly informed those who were close to him so they wouldn't be hurt later when they found out that he hadn't told them.

Not long after he was first diagnosed, he began to develop noticeable symptoms. Rav Gershon Meltzer,[2] who was in the Rosh Yeshiva's Daily

Whatever Rav Nosson Tzvi could do himself, he did.
Escorting Rav Nosson Wachtfogel out of his house at Rechov Ha'ameilim 33

---

1. Rav Gedalya Finkel relates that one of Rav Nosson Tzvi's doctors once remarked that everyone thinks that he came to the house to help Rav Nosson Tzvi, but in reality, he gained more from those visits than Rav Nosson Tzvi did, because he would leave the house so inspired by the Rosh Yeshiva.
2. See p. 170, fn. 17.

*Daf chaburah* in the Mir, recalls that one day, 27 years before his *petirah*, Rav Nosson Tzvi brought a bag of money to distribute to the *yungeleit* in the *chaburah*. His hands were already shaking so badly that he could barely open the bag. Nevertheless, he refused people's offers for help, preferring to keep trying himself.

From that early phase of his illness until his last day, he continued to insist on doing whatever he could for himself. Although he would eventually require help even with basic functions, whatever he could do himself, he did.[3]

## Not His Sugya

"MY FEELING WAS ALWAYS THAT HE SIMPLY DIDN'T CONSIDER the illness his '*sugya*,' " says Rav Binyamin Carlebach, Rav Nosson Tzvi's brother-in-law and closest partner in maintaining and building the yeshiva. "It was a part of his life that he had to contend with, but he would invest as little effort as possible into dealing with it."

A *talmid* recalls a moment during a *vaad* that illustrates Rav Carlebach's suggestion.

Rav Nosson Tzvi held a weekly *vaad* in *Ohr Yisrael*, Rav Yisrael Salanter's writings. Once, a member of the *vaad* read a selection in which Rav Yisrael Salanter compares *cholei haguf*, physical maladies, to *cholei henefesh*, spiritual maladies. The reader paused and pointed out that there is an inherent difference between the two: physical maladies have clear symptoms, and spiritual maladies don't. How then, asked the *talmid*, can one determine if he has a spiritual malady? Rav Nosson Tzvi answered that there *are* symptoms that come along with a spiritual malady, and he explained how one can diagnose a *choli hanefesh*. But then he added a sentence that left those around the table in shock.

"*Choli haguf* isn't so serious," Rav Nosson Tzvi added, "because it passes. *Choli hanefesh* is much more serious."

Apparently, Rav Nosson Tzvi considered his Parkinson's disease a passing affliction; in the World of Truth it would no longer affect him. He considered spiritual maladies far more dangerous, on the other hand, since those maladies last for all eternity, if the person doesn't work to cure them.

---

3. He once told R' Ari Gottesman, a longtime close *talmid*, that Rav Beinush had told him not to accept help when he could do things by himself.

"Physical disability isn't serious, because it passes. Spiritual maladies are much more serious."

ALTHOUGH RAV NOSSON TZVI DIDN'T CONSIDER PARKINSON'S to be a central issue in his life, he did adjust his lifestyle now and then

**Reserving His Strength**
to conserve his energy for when he would need it.

For many years, Rav Nosson Tzvi avoided using a wheelchair. The first time he actually agreed to sit in a wheelchair was when he and his entourage were rushing to catch a flight, and they realized that they had a better chance of making it to the gate on time if he went in a wheelchair. After that incident, he was more amenable to being wheeled from place to place in America, but he still resisted being seen in a wheelchair by his *talmidim* in Eretz Yisrael.

At some point, however, he decided that forcing himself to walk everywhere was depleting his energy and preventing him from delivering his *shiurim* and functioning properly, so he agreed to use a wheelchair when necessary. In fact, there were times when he could have walked somewhere, but he nevertheless asked to be wheeled so that he would have energy to deliver a *shiur* later on.[4]

---

4. R' Yehuda Neuhaus.

WHEN RAV NOSSON TZVI FIRST BECAME ROSH YESHIVA, *talmidim* were accustomed to see their rosh yeshiva sitting during *shiur*

**Standing Up for the Torah's Honor**

*klali*, because Rav Beinush and Rav Chaim Shmuelevitz had done so in their later years. Rav Nosson Tzvi, who already suffered from serious tremors at that point, also sat for his first *shiur klalis*.

Once, however, he was asked to deliver a *shiur* in Lakewood, where the Roshei Yeshiva stood during *shiur klali* – so he stood as well. After seeing that he was able to deliver a *shiur* while standing, he felt that it would be greater *kavod haTorah* to stand in Eretz Yisrael as well.

For many years thereafter, Rav Nosson Tzvi made a point of standing during *shiur klali*, in honor of the Torah. There were times when he could walk up to the podium energetically, but other times, his trek to the front of the *beis midrash* was a painstaking process that required at least one, and sometimes two, assistants.

Once at the podium, he would grip two *shtenders*, one on each side, and start speaking. His voice would sometimes come out in a hoarse whisper; sometimes it was louder. But even those who could not make out the words he was saying gained immensely from witnessing his overwhelming love of Torah.

About ten years before his *petirah*, Rav Nosson Tzvi realized that the effort he was expending on standing at his *shtender* during *shiur klali* might be compromising the quality of the *shiur*, so he decided to sit instead. Nevertheless, he would begin each *shiur* standing up, and only

Struggling to stand for the Torah's honor: Rav Nosson Tzvi delivering a *shiur klali* surrounded by *shtenders* to grip if necessary

then would he sit down. At some point toward the end of the *shiur* he would struggle to a standing position again – all in an effort to honor the Torah.

Only in his final years, when it was physically impossible to continue this practice, did he sit throughout his *shiur*.

PARKINSON'S GRADUALLY ROBS ITS VICTIMS OF THE ABILITY to perform even the most basic daily tasks, such as cutting food and eat-

**No Complaints** ing it. Aside from the frustration of not being able to care for themselves, Parkinson's sufferers experience significant embarrassment when they are seen in public shaking violently or when their bodies are wracked with spastic, uncontrollable movements.

It would have been understandable, even expected, for someone in Rav Nosson Tzvi's position to shy away from public appearances, and certainly to remain out of the view of *talmidim* at times when

"I don't learn *mitoch yissurim*; I learn *mitoch simchah*."

he was extremely weak. But as Rav Binyamin Carlebach once heard Rav Nosson Tzvi relate to a fellow who was stricken with a different muscular disease, "I decided that I can't let it stop me from doing what I have to do."

He would encourage other people with disabilities to make a similar resolution, so that they could lead fulfilling lives.

Rav Nissan Kaplan[5] related that after the Rosh Yeshiva passed away, he heard that a relative of the Rosh Yeshiva had testified that he never heard him complain about his disease. Rav Nissan was so surprised by this claim

---

5. Rav Nissan Kaplan is one of the beloved *maggidei shiur* in Beis Yeshayah.

that he decided to verify it. When he visited Rav Nosson Tzvi's children during the *shivah*, he asked each one whether they had ever heard Rav Nosson Tzvi complain – and each one said no!

Not only didn't he complain, he didn't even consider himself unfortunate. A *talmid* who had been struck by several tragedies in the span of a few months came to the Rosh Yeshiva for *chizuk*. "How does the Rosh Yeshiva learn *mitoch yissurim* (amidst suffering)?" he asked.

"I *don't* learn *mitoch yissurim*," the Rosh Yeshiva replied. "I learn *mitoch simchah* (amidst joy)!"

RAV NOSSON TZVI'S PRIORITY SCALE WAS CLEAR: ANY YESHIVA obligation overrode the need to take care of his Parkinson's.

## Torah Comes First

Before leaving to America with the Rosh Yeshiva, the Rebbetzin would sometimes schedule an appointment with a specialist there, hoping that he might be able to suggest a new treatment plan. But if the Rosh Yeshiva would learn that a philanthropist was available to meet him at the time of the doctor's appointment, he would immediately cancel the appointment and meet with the potential donor.

Rav Nosson Tzvi was also adamant about not sacrificing his mental acuity for the sake of alleviating his physical symptoms. He refused to take any medicine that would impair his ability to concentrate on learning or was liable to affect his memory. Nor was he willing to undergo any invasive procedures – even those that had excellent success rates – for fear that they would inflict lasting damage on his brain or cause him to forget his learning.[6] The only medications he took were those that provided temporary relief from his symptoms, allowing him to function at some level, but no more than that.

There were certain forms of physical therapy that could have helped him, but even when he did agree to receive those therapies, says Rav Binyamin Carlebach, "His mind wasn't in it."

Interestingly, however, his attitude toward therapy changed shortly before his *petirah* – but only because he wanted to do a *chessed* for someone else: his new physical therapist, Mendy.

Mendy had learned in the Mir as a *bachur*, and had then trained as a physical therapist in Eretz Yisrael. When Rav Nosson Tzvi realized that it would be a favor for Mendy if he would take the therapy seriously,

---

6. R' Mendy Horowitz, Rav Nosson Tzvi's primary host in New York.

he started investing more effort into his therapy session. (Typical of the Rosh Yeshiva, he would ask Mendy to tell him a *vort* at the beginning of each therapy session; only afterward could they begin the therapy session.)

IN A *HESPED* ON RAV NOSSON TZVI, RAV MECHEL ZILBER – whose absolute mastery of all sections of Torah has earned him renown

## No Excuses Left

throughout the world – posed the following question:

The first *al cheit* for which we beat our chests in the *vidui* of Yom Kippur is "*Al cheit shechatanu lifanecha be'oness u'veratzon* – For the sin that we have sinned before you under duress and willingly."

There is an axiom that *oness rachmana patrei* – one who was coerced to sin is exempted from liability. Why, then, do we have to beg Hashem's forgiveness for sins that we did under duress?

"When we think about Rav Nosson Tzvi, we have the answer to our question," said Rav Zilber. "If ever a person was exempt, it was he. Considering what he accomplished, however, no one else can claim to be exempted from his obligations because he is an *oness*."

Rav Nosson Tzvi was at his kitchen table and he mapped out an approach to a *sugya* in his mind. Too weak to walk to the dining room, and with no one around to bring him paper, he used an envelope from an invitation that was on his table to record it.

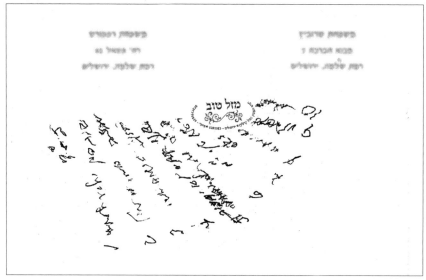

Rav Nosson Tzvi pushed himself until he couldn't get a word out of his mouth.

IN THE LATE 1980'S AND EARLY 1990'S, RAV NOSSON TZVI USED TO give his Daily *Daf shiur* in a room that is now the library in the yeshiva's

**"I Tried, I'm Sorry ..."**
main building. Often, he had to struggle mightily to drag his body up the two flights of stairs, and when he finally did reach the *shiur* room he would take a few minutes to gather his strength.

Many times, he would start delivering the *shiur*, but after a while he would stop and whisper, "I'm sorry, but I just can't." He would wait a few minutes and try to regain some strength before continuing. Sometimes he succeeded in finishing the *shiur* after taking a break, but sometimes he was forced to end the *shiur* early. His mind was perfectly clear, and he remembered all the intricate logical arguments he had prepared, but his body simply wouldn't cooperate.

"The *shiurim* when he stopped in the middle actually left a deeper impression on us than some of his regular *shiurim*," recalls Dovid, a *talmid* from those years. "Seeing him push himself to the point where he absolutely could not get a word out of his mouth was an unbelievable lesson in *ahavas haTorah* and *mesirus nefesh* for Torah. That lesson remained with us long after we forgot the actual *shtiklach Torah* he had composed."

Likewise, in the years closer to his *petirah,* even on days when he was too weak to give one of his myriad weekly *chaburos,* he wouldn't cancel them. They would come, and he would try to give the *chaburah.* If he couldn't continue, he would say, "I can't." Once, he reached a point where he couldn't even move his lips to mouth the words "I can't." Instead, he asked someone to pass him a piece of paper, and he wrote, "*Nisiti, selichah* — I tried, I'm sorry."

The Rosh Yeshiva was never self-conscious about his flailing, feeble body, even when he had a roomful of people waiting for him to find his voice and continue speaking. Often, he would crack a joke to assuage the discomfort of the *talmidim.*

Sometimes, when a *bachur* was delivering a *chaburah* to a group in his house, the Rosh Yeshiva would be too weak to sit in a chair. Rather than cancel the *chaburah,* he would lie on the couch, and urge the *bachur* to begin his discourse. On some occasions he would quip, "*Ich vell liggen, uhn ihr vet lernen. Tzuzamen vet men liggen in lernen!* (I'll lie, and you'll learn. Together, we'll 'lie in learning' " — an expression that means delving into Torah).

ON A PHILOSOPHICAL LEVEL, RAV NOSSON TZVI SEEMED TO have two different approaches to understanding his illness.

**The Illness —** One approach emerged in conversa-
**for Everyone Else** tion with a certain rosh yeshiva, when Rav Nosson Tzvi admitted that he had absolutely no *yetzer hara* for *bitul Torah* (neglecting his learning); so strong was his love for Torah that he simply had no interest in wasting time with idle pursuits. "Perhaps Hashem gave me this illness," he mused, "because He wanted to make it harder for me to learn so that I could get *s'char* (reward) for learning despite the difficulty."

The second approach was even more sobering.

R' Nochum Stilerman once visited Rav Nosson Tzvi's home shortly after the latter became Rosh Yeshiva. There was a bottle of soda on the table, and Rav Nosson Tzvi wanted to honor his guest by pouring him a cup of soda. When R' Nochum saw the Rosh Yeshiva trying to pour him a drink, he said that he wasn't thirsty. "I have to pour my guest a drink," said Rav Nosson Tzvi. "If you don't want to drink it, that's your business."

He tried to lift the bottle and pour the drink, but his hands refused to cooperate. R' Nochum was so disturbed by the sight of the Rosh Yeshiva struggling to pour a cup of soda that he blurted out, "Rosh Yeshiva, why do you deserve this?"

As soon as those words left his mouth, R' Nochum wished he could somehow retract them. But it was too late.

"I was wondering the same thing," replied Rav Nosson Tzvi. "And I think I know the reason.

"I *love* learning. In fact, I love learning so much that I think there's no way I can learn Torah *lishmah* (for its own sake), because I enjoy it too much.[7] Maybe I was stricken with this disease as a punishment for not learning Torah *lishmah*."

R' Nochum left the Rosh Yeshiva's house deeply saddened, and stunned at the possibility that the Rosh Yeshiva's Parkinson's could be a punishment.

Twenty years passed, and the Rosh Yeshiva's condition continued to deteriorate. During the last year of Rav Nosson Tzvi's life, around Pesach time, R' Nochum came across a Gemara in *Talmud Yerushalmi*, and was so excited by what he saw that he hurried to show it to the Rosh Yeshiva.

The *Talmud Yerushalmi* (*Horayos* 3:5) teaches that when Moshe Rabbeinu ascended to the Heavens and learned Torah there for forty days and nights, he kept forgetting everything Hashem taught him. At the end of the forty days, he received the entire Torah as a gift.

"Why?" asks the *Talmud Yerushalmi*. "*Bishvil lehachzir es hatipshim* — so there will be a response to the fools."

"Imagine Moshe Rabbeinu's plight," R' Nochum said to the Rosh Yeshiva. "He's in Heaven learning from Hashem Himself, and each time he walks away for a moment and says, 'What did I just learn?' he draws a total blank. It must have been so frustrating.

"Why did Hashem do that to him? So that some unwise people who feel that they can't learn because they keep forgetting the material will take heart and say, 'If Moshe Rabbeinu could forget what he learned and still continue studying Torah, so can we.' "

R' Nochum then reminded Rav Nosson Tzvi that 20 years earlier, the Rosh Yeshiva had suggested that his Parkinson's was a punishment for not learning *lishmah*. "Maybe there's a different reason," suggested R'

---

7. R' Nochum discussed the Rosh Yeshiva's suggestion with two *gedolim*, Rav Avraham Pam and Rav Avigdor Miller, both of whom said that an ordinary person should learn Torah for *any* reason – as long as he isn't learning *only* for ulterior motives – and not strive for the level of purity that Rav Nosson Tzvi demanded of himself.

Nochum. "Maybe the Rosh Yeshiva had to suffer from this illness so that in case any of us would say that we can't learn because we aren't feeling up to it, we would have the Rosh Yeshiva to look to as proof that one *can* learn even with a debilitating disease."

The Rosh Yeshiva kissed R' Nochum and said, *"Akiva nichamtani, Akiva nichamtani."*[8]

---

8. The Rosh Yeshiva was paraphrasing a Gemara (*Rosh Hashanah* 25a) that states that Rabbi Akiva once offered consolation to another Tanna, who responded, *"Akiva nichamtani* – Akiva, you have comforted me."

# CHAPTER THIRTY-THREE
# ORPHANS THROUGHOUT THE WORLD

*"The way of the world is that people tend to wither before they pass away. Despite his debilitating illness, the Rosh Yeshiva didn't wither. He was plucked from this world between night seder and first seder."*
— *Rav Aharon Lopiansky, a brother-in-law of Rav Nosson Tzvi, in a hesped*

*g*UDGING BY RAV NOSSON TZVI'S SCHEDULE ON 10 Marcheshvan, 5772, no one would have imagined that the next day he would no longer be with us.

On that day he was in Brachfeld, as he was every Monday and Wednesday, and then he returned to Yerushalayim to deliver a *shiur klali*. Later that day he participated in the *levayah* of Rav Dov Schwartzman *zt"l*, and he still found time in the evening to be *menachem avel* a family in Bnei Brak. Late into the night, he was still trying to arrange an appointment with a donor in Los Angeles to discuss the desperate financial straits of the yeshiva.

11 Marcheshvan, 5772 started off as a sunny Tuesday, but an hour or two into the day, the world went black for multitudes around the world.

The news of Rav Nosson Tzvi's sudden *petirah* spread through the world in minutes. In America, *talmidim* received phone calls in the middle of the night and cried until morning, when they were able to follow a live hookup to the *levayah*. In Eretz Yisrael, the thousands of *talmidim* who converged on the Beis Yisrael neighborhood each morning arrived in the yeshiva as they always did, but with aching hearts. Wherever you turned when you reached Yeshivas Mir, you saw people crying. Some people tried valiantly to follow the signs posted in yeshiva asking that everyone should continue learning until the *levayah*, but many others were just too dazed. Some put their heads down on *shtenders* and cried, while others recited *Tehillim* on behalf of the Rosh Yeshiva.

At noon, the *beis midrash* filled up, and when the *mittah* bearing the Rosh Yeshiva was carried into the room, the wailing reached a crescendo.

After *Tehillim* was recited, Rav Aharon Leib Shteinman *shlita*, who loved Rav Nosson Tzvi dearly, delivered a *hesped*, announcing that Rav Nosson Tzvi's eldest son, Rav Eliezer Yehuda *shlita*, would be his successor as the Rosh Yeshiva of Mir.

As placards were posted notifying the public of the Rosh Yeshiva's passing, a sign in the Mir requested that the *talmidim* continue to learn until the *levayah*.

Each *hesped* drew more tears, until the *mittah* was finally escorted outside. As would behoove the Rosh Yeshiva, who had been so careful not to hurt others, an announcement was made asking, on behalf of the family, that no one push to hold onto the *mittah*.

OVER 100,000 PEOPLE FILLED THE STREETS OF YERUSHALAYIM, slowly making their way, on foot, from the Mir to Har Hamenuchos. One could see everyone contemplating the great loss, with many sharing their own memories and reflections of the Rosh Yeshiva with those around them.

A small drama had played itself out that morning as the family was trying to decide where to bury the Rosh Yeshiva; he had not left instructions specifying where he wanted to be interred.

Upon hearing the terrible news, Rav Avraham Shmuelevitz recalled that there was an open spot on Har Hamenuchos several graves over from the *kevarim* of Rav Leizer Yudel and Rav Beinush, which belonged to a family named Broyde. Most of the Broydes had already passed on and been buried elsewhere, but the *chevrah kaddisha* couldn't release the grave without written consent from a family member. Rav Binyamin Carlebach was able to reach one of the Broydes, who issued the consent.

Only after securing that letter could the Mir announce that Rav Nosson Tzvi would be buried on Har Hamenuchos.

In the end, the consent proved to have been unnecessary. The leader of the *chevrah kaddisha* went back to the original records of that area on Har Hamenuchos, and found that the gravesite had been paid for by none other than Rav Leizer Yudel himself.

IN THE WEEKS FOLLOWING THE *LEVAYAH,* MANY PEOPLE FOUND it difficult to return to their normal lives. Members of the *hanhalah*

**Mourning Throughout the World**

related that wherever they went, people would share their memories of the Rosh Yeshiva and talk about how profound the loss was for them. His influence had been so vast that he was mourned on five continents, as roshei yeshiva, *rabbanim,* and educators – many of them Mirrer alumni – held public *hespedim* (eulogies) to share their grief. All told, in the first month alone, over 200 *hespedim* were delivered throughout the world, with most audiences numbering in the hundreds.

Even months after the shocking *petirah,* as this book goes to print, many people still haven't come to terms with the loss. During interviews conducted for this book three months after the Rosh Yeshiva's

A small section of the 100,000 who escorted
Rav Nosson Tzvi to Har Hamenuchos

*petirah*, I often found myself joining the interviewees in shedding a tear over yet another heartwarming story.

The collective feeling of loss felt by Jews around the world may have been expressed best by the wife of a *yungerman* who was close to the Rosh Yeshiva. This *yungerman* related that one night a few months after the Rosh Yeshiva's passing, his wife suddenly began to cry. "Who is going to take care of us now?" she moaned. "The Rosh Yeshiva loved us. Who else is going to love us like that?"

Indeed, Rosh Yeshiva. You loved each one of us.

Who is going to take care of us now?

# CHAPTER THIRTY-FOUR
# ECHOES OF THE ALTER

*In Slabodka, hundreds of bachurim learned with great diligence, day and night — during the regularly scheduled sedarim and in additional sedarim that they established for themselves — each person according to his ability. But the overall image of the yeshiva was etched by that wondrous Jew, Rav Nosson Tzvi, who would say, "I don't have a yeshiva of hundreds of talmidim. Rather, I have a yeshiva of individuals, and when you add them together, the number happens to total in the hundreds. Each talmid is a world of his own."*

*— A talmid recalls the first Rav Nosson Tzvi Finkel, the Alter of Slabodka*

T HE *GEMARA (BERACHOS* 7B) TEACHES THAT *"SHMA garim"* — a person's name can play a role in enabling him to attain greatness. While it was common knowledge that Rav Nosson Tzvi Finkel was the exact namesake of his great-grandfather the Alter of Slabodka,[1] until his *petirah* we could have seen the similarity between the two Rav Nosson Tzvi Finkels only in a general way. We knew, for instance, that the Alter of Slabodka had been responsible for the dissemination of Torah throughout the world — in fact, Rav Eliezer Menachem Man Shach *zt"l* remarked that "most of the Torah in the [post-War] world should be credited to the Alter";[2] we also knew that "our" Rav Nosson Tzvi was responsible for the dissemination of Torah throughout the world in the late 20th and early 21st centuries, as Mir alumni filled rabbinic, educational, *kiruv*, and *kollel* positions throughout the world.

What we didn't know before Rav Nosson Tzvi's *petirah* is that he actually shared a much deeper connection with the Alter. The Alter's genius was his ability to tailor an educational approach for each *talmid* as an individual, utilizing his personal strengths and helping him repair his weak areas.

---

1. See p. 38.
2. Recounted by Rav Aviezer Piltz, Rosh Yeshiva of Tifrach – who heard it from Rav Shach – at a *hesped* for Rav Nosson Tzvi in Mir Brachfeld. A simple calculation substantiates Rav Shach's statement: Mir in Eretz Yisrael was established by the Alter's son, Rav Leizer Yudel Finkel. Beth Midrash Govoha Lakewood was established by his *talmid*, Rav Aron Kotler. Together with Torah Vodaath, Chaim Berlin, and Ner Yisrael, which were led by Rav Reuven Grozovsky, Rav Yaakov Kamenetsky, Rav Yitzchok Hutner, and Rav Yaakov Yitzchak Ruderman – all *talmidim* of the Alter – they account for a major share of Torah in the yeshiva world today.

With each additional week after Rav Nosson Tzvi's *petirah,* more and more people from around the globe shared their stories. And where we might once have thought that his approach to *chinuch* was monochromatic, the many stories focusing on how he built *talmidim* through love and warmth made it obvious that the second Rav Nosson Tzvi shared the gift of the first: he could tailor his messages according to the needs of an individual *talmid,* just as the Alter did nearly a century earlier.

FOR THE MOST PART, RAV NOSSON TZVI'S APPROACH WAS TO shower his *talmidim* with his overflowing warmth and love. In many

## Cultivating People

cases, the Rosh Yeshiva's love was like life-giving rain on arid land. *Bachurim* who had never shown any interest in learning, or who had significant obstacles to growth in Torah, suddenly found that not only *could* they learn, they *loved* to learn.

"Avrumi," a *talmid* from the late 1990's, came to the Mir in a last-ditch effort to find his place in a yeshiva. He had meandered from yeshiva to yeshiva in America, never seeing much success in his learning. Avrumi wasn't a troublemaker who would be expelled — he was always the one who made the decision to move on, hoping that he would somehow connect with his next rebbi or rosh yeshiva.

When Avrumi arrived for his entrance exam into the Mir, Rav Nosson Tzvi asked to hear a *shtikel Torah* from him. Avrumi admitted, quite bluntly, that he hadn't succeeded in his learning in years. "But I really want to learn," he said earnestly. "And if I don't succeed now, I'm going to go to work."

Rav Nosson Tzvi, who could discern a person's inner character at a glance,[3] sensed that Avrumi was sincere. Not only did he accept Avrumi into the yeshiva, he offered to learn with him for a full *seder* each day during Avrumi's first *zman* in yeshiva — at a time when the yeshiva already had 4,000 *talmidim.* Slowly, patiently, Rav Nosson Tzvi built Avrumi from the ground up, teaching him to read a Gemara on his own, then to analyze and expound a *Rishon,* then to develop *chiddushim* in a *sugya.*

Today, Avrumi is a beloved rebbi in North America. And he has just one *chinuch* motto, which he learned from his own rebbi, Rav Nosson Tzvi: Love every *talmid,* and treat him like a son.

---

3. See p. 348.

The message Rav Nosson Tzvi imparted to his *talmidim* who went into *chinuch*:
Love each of your students and treat him like a son.

Avrumi's story is one that hundreds of other Mirrer *talmidim* echoed, both before and after Rav Nosson Tzvi's *petirah*. In the months after his passing, however, many stories came to light that paint a broader, more nuanced picture of Rav Nosson Tzvi's approach to *chinuch* – an approach that was far more individualized than we may have thought.

ONE OF THE WAYS THAT RAV NOSSON TZVI DEVELOPED A CON-nection with *talmidim* was through the weekly *chaburos* he held with different groups of *bachurim*. These groups were usually split up according to the yeshivos the *bachurim* had attended before joining the Mir: There was a *chaburah* with Long Beach alumni, Montreal alumni, Torah Vodaath alumni, and so on.

In most cases, the *bachurim* would each take a turn saying a *chaburah* as Rav Nosson Tzvi listened. Sometimes he would comment or ask a question during the *chaburah*, and he would invariably compliment the presenter when he finished.

"Ephraim," was once presenting a *chaburah* when his mind suddenly went blank. Try as he might, he simply couldn't remember the next part of his *chaburah*.

In what could only be explained as a combination of sheer brilliance and deep feeling for another person, Rav Nosson Tzvi determined what the next logical step would be, and whispered a few words to Ephraim. The reminder was all Ephraim needed, and he was able to finish the rest of the *chaburah* smoothly.

BUT RAV NOSSON TZVI ALSO KNEW HOW TO USE THOSE *CHAburos* to help *talmidim* advance – sometimes in an extremely surprising fashion.

Sruli was once delivering a *chaburah*, and he placed a small note on his Gemara outlining the key points that he wanted to mention. As he was speaking, he noticed Rav Nosson Tzvi's hand creeping across the table. Suddenly, the Rosh Yeshiva's hand shot forward, snatched the note, and put it into his pocket. "It's not a *kuntz* to say a *chaburah* out of a paper," he said with a twinkle in his eye. "Let's see you say it without the paper."

Fifteen years later, Sruli remembers how empowered he felt after giving that *chaburah* by heart. "The Rosh Yeshiva knew that I could say a *chaburah* without notes," he explains, "and he was determined to reveal my own hidden ability to me!"

Amazingly, the Rosh Yeshiva was able to differentiate between the Ephraims and the Srulis among his thousands of *talmidim*, and he used the weekly *chaburos* to build each *talmid* according to his ability.

TO RAV NOSSON TZVI, BUILDING AN INDIVIDUAL *TALMID* WAS

**Quoting From the Source**

so important that he would even devote a portion of a public *shiur* to it on occasion.

"Leizer" wanted to have a *kesher* (connection) with Rav Nosson Tzvi, but he didn't want to burden the Rosh Yeshiva. When he enrolled in Mir, Leizer asked Rav Nosson Tzvi if he could walk the Rosh Yeshiva home from davening one day a week and tell the Rosh Yeshiva a *vort* on the *parashah* as they walked. Naturally, the Rosh Yeshiva agreed.

Each Tuesday morning after *Shacharis*, Leizer would wait in the *beis midrash* until the line of people who wanted a short audience with Rav Nosson Tzvi ended, and he would then walk the Rosh Yeshiva home and tell him a *vort*. Each week, as they reached the door at Rechov Ha'ameilim 33, Rav Nosson Tzvi would thank him for the *vort*, and Leizer would go on with his day.

In his heart, Leizer wondered whether the Rosh Yeshiva even heard the *vort*, because his only reaction was a polite thank you. One week, after escorting the Rosh Yeshiva home, he began to consider giving up this Tuesday morning custom.

Just three days later, at the Friday *vaad*, his thoughts of quitting were cut short by the Rosh Yeshiva. The Rosh Yeshiva paused suddenly in middle of the *vaad*, and scanned the room until his eyes locked with Leizer's. Then he began speaking again. "A *bachur* told me a *vort* this week," he said, and he then proceeded to retell the *dvar Torah* exactly as Leizer had told it to him. Years later, Leizer still recalls the thrill he felt upon learning that the Rosh Yeshiva had indeed listened – and remembered – his *divrei Torah* each week.

Similarly, in the last year of his life, Rav Nosson Tzvi had a *chavrusashaft* with Shlomo, a young *bachur* learning in Beis Yeshayah. The Rosh Yeshiva was once preparing his *shiur klali* with Shlomo, who posed a difficult question on the Gemara they were learning. The Rosh Yeshiva thought for a few minutes, but didn't have a solution.

The next day, Shlomo happened to attend *shiur klali* in the main *beis midrash*, which he rarely did because he didn't understand Yiddish. When the Rosh Yeshiva reached the Gemara they had learned the day before, he said, "A *bachur* asked me a question yesterday," and proceeded to repeat Shlomo's question to the entire audience.

A small gesture, but one that filled Shlomo with renewed confidence in his learning.

TWO BROTHERS WHO ARE AMONG THE TOP *TALMIDEI CHACHA-mim* in Yeshivas Mir spent 30 years learning all of *Shas* together *b'iyun*.

**A Tale of Two Siyumim**

When they were ready to complete the last *masechta*, Rav Nosson Tzvi insisted – characteristically – that they celebrate their monumental achievement in his house and invite all their friends and relatives to the *siyum*.

The Rebbetzin arranged for a full meat meal, and the two brothers and their families arrived to find a table bedecked in the finest tableware

As they were waiting to begin, one of the two brothers saw a young Israeli *bachur* wandering around the room. Wondering what the boy was doing there, he walked over to the *bachur* and greeted him. They struck up a conversation, and the boy mentioned that Rav Nosson Tzvi had told him to come to his house at this hour to make a *siyum*.

"What are you completing?" the *talmid chacham* asked.

"*Kiddushin*," the boy answered.

All *siyumim* were valued by the Rosh Yeshiva; many were held in his home –
and at his expense.

This *talmid chacham* relates that he learned an invaluable lesson from
Rav Nosson Tzvi that day. *Siyumim* were a weekly – if not daily – event
in Rav Nosson Tzvi's house.[4] The Rosh Yeshiva could have told this boy
to come the next afternoon, and he could have made a modest *siyum* for
him and his friends. But Rav Nosson Tzvi wanted to show this boy that he
valued the hard work he had invested into learning *Kiddushin* as much
as he valued the effort these two brothers had put into learning *Shas*.

JUST AS THE ROSH YESHIVA WAS ABLE TO CONVEY THE CORRECT
message to every *bachur*, *yungerman*, and *talmid chacham* in the Mir,

**"Now THAT'S
a Plan"**

he was able to leave a lasting impression on those
whom one wouldn't necessarily consider his
*talmidim*.

R' Nochum Stilerman is a professional who worked for close to half a
century. When he was nearing 70, he decided to settle in Eretz Yisrael for
about ten months of the year. His son is a *rosh chaburah* in Mir, and R'
Nochum wanted to learn in the yeshiva. A methodical person by nature,
after completing *Maseches Shabbos* in honor of his 70th birthday, R'
Nochum drew up a study program that would enable him to complete a

---

4. See p. 264.

*masechta* and also *Sefer Tehillim* by his next birthday. When he showed his plan to Rav Nosson Tzvi around Pesach of 5771, the Rosh Yeshiva looked up at him and said, "But what about the rest of the Torah? Draw up a plan to finish *kol haTorah kulah!*"

R' Nochum went home and drew up a five-year plan that would enable him to finish another few *masechtos*, all of *Tanach*, and a *mussar sefer*. He brought the detailed printout to Rav Nosson Tzvi, who reviewed it and said, "But you're not finishing *Shas!*"

"Rosh Yeshiva," R' Nochum protested, "to finish *Shas* according to this program I'll need many, many years."

"Go print out a learning program for the whole *Shas*," Rav Nosson Tzvi insisted.

R' Nochum went home and printed out the plan. Some 2,500 pages later, he had a program to present to the Rosh Yeshiva – a program that would take 23½ years to complete!

When Rav Nosson Tzvi saw the two-volume printout, he exclaimed, "Now THAT'S a plan! THAT'S a plan!"

"But Rosh Yeshiva," R' Nochum objected, "I can't do this! I'm already 70, and it would take me until I'm over 93 to finish this – at a pace of 10 hours of learning a day! I hope to live to 120, but how can I undertake a plan that I can't possibly complete?"

The Rosh Yeshiva struggled mightily to stand up, and while quivering in his place he said, "And do you think I can do what I'm doing? Look at *me!*"

Rav Nosson Tzvi then reached under his tablecloth and pulled out his plans for the Mir, which included adding more buildings to the yeshiva and making space for even more *talmidim*. "Do you think I can do this?" he asked R' Nochum. "Of course I can't.

"But you and I have a great advantage," Rav Nosson Tzvi continued. "We both realize that we can't possibly do what we would like to do. Everyone else fools themselves into thinking that they *can* do what they want to do. You and I realize that we are in the hands of the *Ribbono shel Olam*, and that we can't do more than try."

The Rosh Yeshiva then pointed out that at the beginning of *Parashas Va'eira*, even before Moshe and Aharon actually followed Hashem's directives to go to Pharaoh, the Torah states, "Moshe and Aharon did as Hashem commanded them; so they did" (*Shemos* 7:6).

"How could the Torah state, in past tense, that they *did* what Hashem commanded them to do?" asked the Rosh Yeshiva.

"We see from here," he answered, "that when you accept upon yourself to do something – even if it is beyond your natural capabilities – Hashem considers it as if you already did it.

"Accept upon yourself to learn according to your program, and leave the rest to Hashem."

R' Nochum took the leap, and will finish *Shas* at 93, with Hashem's help.


"ESTHER," THE DAUGHTER OF A *YUNGERMAN* WHO HAS BEEN learning in the Mir for close to two decades, was becoming bas mitzvah.

**Bas Mitzvah Lesson**

In honor of the occasion, she visited several prominent rebbetzins – Rebbetzin Leah Finkel among them – and asked them for *berachos*.

The Rebbetzin welcomed Esther warmly, and after they conversed for some time, she ushered Esther into the dining room to receive a *berachah* from Rav Nosson Tzvi, who was learning at the table. Before giving a *berachah*, the Rosh Yeshiva said, "You're becoming a bas mitzvah. Do you know how to separate *challah* from dough?"

Esther shook her head no.

"Do you know how to separate *terumos* and *maasros* (the tithes that one must take from produce grown in Eretz Yisrael)?"

Esther shook her head once again.

"Do you know how to *kasher* a chicken?"

The answer was no yet again.

The Rosh Yeshiva gave her his trademark smile and said, "So now that you are a bas mitzvah, it's time to learn how to do these mitzvos." He then gave her a *berachah* and resumed learning.

Several years have passed since Esther took leave of the Rosh Yeshiva, but the moments he spent teaching her about her value and obligations as a Jewish woman have remained with her ever since.


THE ALTER OF NOVARADOK, WHOSE APPROACH TO *MUSSAR* was the polar opposite of that of the Alter of Slabodka,[5] nevertheless

**The Softest Rebuke**

referred to the latter as a "*gaon* in *savlanus* – a genius in patience." The Alter of Slabodka could wait weeks, sometimes even months or a year, before issuing a

---

5. Slabodka stressed the grandeur of man, while Novaradok stressed the lowliness of man as compared to the greatness of Hashem.

rebuke to a *bachur* in his yeshiva. He would wait – to see if the *bachur* would get the message by himself without the Alter having to say something; or to determine whether the infraction was due to a momentary lapse of judgment that the *bachur* wouldn't repeat, thus obviating the need for rebuke. Only when he was absolutely certain that the *bachur* needed to be admonished did he begin to think of the words with which to admonish him. Even then, he would carefully scrutinize his own motives: Was he personally invested in the story? Did he have any ulterior motive, or was he thinking only of the *bachur*'s best interests? When he was finally certain that he had to rebuke a boy, he would choose each word carefully to ensure that he would be building the boy, not destroying him.

The Alter's great-grandson and namesake, Rav Nosson Tzvi, rarely had to rebuke anyone directly. Just knowing that the Rosh Yeshiva loved you was powerful *mussar*, enough to keep a *talmid* in line and guide him to make the proper decisions in life.[6]

In instances when the Rosh Yeshiva did have to rebuke someone, however, he did it in the fashion of his great-grandfather, choosing his words carefully – and sometimes not even using words at all.

Once, when Rav Nosson Tzvi was walking from yeshiva to his home on Rechov Ha'ameilim, he passed by two *bachurim* who were laughing uproariously, attracting the attention of passersby. He approached them with a big smile and asked, "Which one of you asked the *kushya* and which one said the *teirutz*?"

The boys understood his implied message: The only valid reason for such a conspicuous display of mirth is the joy of Torah.

THE BUILDING NEAR THE YESHIVA THAT RAV NOSSON TZVI moved into in 1997, when his physical condition made it difficult for

**Good Neighbors** him to walk to and from his apartment on Yisa Brachah, had two entrances – a private entrance to his house on Rechov Ha'ameilim, and an entrance to a dormitory and a *shiur* room in an alleyway behind the house. The layout of the building was such that some of the dorm rooms were situated directly under the Finkel apartment.

At one point, a rowdy crowd moved into a dorm room beneath the Finkels. These *bachurim* would play music at deafening decibel levels at

---

6. See p. 299.

all hours of the day and night, and the Finkels were having a hard time living over them. Though anyone else in his position would probably have evicted these raucous "tenants," the Rosh Yeshiva opted to send someone to respectfully ask them to please tone things down – but to no avail. The boys continued to disturb the peace, with no concern for the Rosh Yeshiva and his family, or anyone else.

At this point, even the most tolerant of "landlords" would have lost patience and had the *bachurim* thrown out. But not Rav Nosson Tzvi.

One day, he asked his family to buy a very nice cake from the bakery. When the cake arrived, he donned his frock and hat and headed around the corner to the building's other entrance. He knocked on the door of the dorm room beneath his apartment, and when the *bachurim* opened the door, he handed them the cake. "Good neighbors treat their neighbors well," he said with a smile.

The *bachurim* accepted the cake sheepishly, and the loud music stopped.

SOMETIMES THE ROSH YESHIVA DIDN'T NEED TO OPEN HIS mouth at all in order to admonish someone. When a relative arrived in

**With No Words at All**

his house for Shabbos wearing a tie that Rav Nosson Tzvi deemed inappropriate for a *ben Torah*, he motioned to that *bachur* to come over. When the *bachur* reached his seat, Rav Nosson Tzvi held onto his tie, looked up into the boy's eyes, and smiled.

The boy got the message.

THE ROSH YESHIVA'S APPROACHES TO SPECIFIC INDIVIDUALS or groups within the yeshiva could differ so starkly from one another

**Choosing the Questions**

that the approaches seemed almost contradictory. Only when the broader picture came into view after his *petirah*, and we were able to truly grasp the wisdom of his tailor-made approach to each *talmid*, could we appreciate the depth of the following two stories.

In a Friday *vaad* during his last full winter *zman*, Rav Nosson Tzvi related that his first rebbi in Mir, Rav Yosef Stern, had joined him in a car ride home from a wedding that week. Rav Yosef had shared several stories regarding Rav Leizer Yudel at that time, mentioning, for instance, that Rav Leizer Yudel had insisted that the *bachurim* finish a *masechta* each *zman* and submit to an oral *bechinah* on the material they had learned.

"Wouldn't it be wonderful," Rav Nosson Tzvi remarked to the *bachurim*, "if we could undertake to finish *Bava Metzia* this *zman*?"

He paused for a moment, and then said, "I'll make you a deal." The *bachurim*, who had heard about Rav Nosson Tzvi's monetary incentives for learning,[7] were expecting him to say that they would get a certain sum for excelling on the *bechinah*. Rav Nosson Tzvi surprised them, however, by saying, "If a large enough group finishes the *masechta*, you'll be *mechayev* (obligate) me to finish the *masechta* too, because I'll have to test you. That's the deal!"

The unique "deal" caught the interest of many of the *bachurim* at the *vaad,* and one *bachur* undertook to draw up a list of those who were committing to take the *bechinah* at the end of the *zman*. True to his word, Rav Nosson Tzvi informed R' Yehuda Neuhaus, his trusted helper, that they would be learning the later parts of *Maseches Bava Metzia* together to prepare for the *bechinah*.

When the *zman* wound down, the *bachurim* came to the Rosh Yeshiva for the *bechinah*. Rav Nosson Tzvi started testing them from the beginning of the *masechta*, going around the table and asking each boy a question. After posing several questions and receiving less-than-perfect answers, he realized that the *bachurim* had spent the recent months learning the last few *perakim* (chapters) of *Bava Metzia*, and their memories of the first sections of the *masechta* were growing fuzzy.

"It was astounding to watch how quickly the Rosh Yeshiva was able to switch gears," recalls R' Yehuda Neuhaus. "He found a way to determine the portions of the *masechta* each boy *did* remember, and he deliberately asked them questions that they could answer!"

BUT THEN THERE'S THE OPPOSITE BOOKEND TO THIS STORY, IN which Rav Nosson Tzvi chose a similar venue to deliver a powerful message to an individual *talmid* who he felt could strive for true *gadlus*.

Ephraim, one of Rav Nosson Tzvi's closest *talmidim*, merited a long-term *chavrusashaft* with Rav Nosson Tzvi every Motza'ei Shabbos, and he was one of the *talmidim* of Rav Asher Arielli who would take a *bechinah* several times each *zman* on the material they learned in Rav Asher's *shiur*. Ephraim was considered one of the top prospects in the yeshiva;

---

7. See pp. 258-260.

many *bachurim* viewed him as a role model, and everyone expected him to become a great *marbitz Torah* in the future.

One week, Ephraim was in bed with pneumonia during the second half of the week, and he was still so sick on Shabbos that he sent a message to the Rosh Yeshiva that he would miss his *chavrusashaft* that Motza'ei Shabbos. On Sunday morning after *Shacharis*, the Rosh Yeshiva greeted Ephraim, asking, "How are you feeling?" When Ephraim said that he was feeling better, the Rosh Yeshiva asked him whether he was planning to come to the *bechinah* that night. Ephraim explained that he didn't know the *sugya* of *meishiv aveidah* (*Kesubos* 18), because he had been bedridden when Rav Asher learned it, but he was ready to be tested on the sixteen *blatt* that preceded it. "In that case," the Rosh Yeshiva said, "you should come to the *bechinah*."

That night, the group arrived for the *bechinah*, and Rav Nosson Tzvi started making his way around the table, asking each *talmid* a question. When it was Ephraim's turn, Rav Nosson Tzvi asked "Ephraim, what are five points of *machlokes* (dispute) between *Rashi* and *Tosafos* in the *sugya* of *meishiv aveidah*?"

Ephraim blanched. The Rosh Yeshiva knew that he didn't know that *sugya*! Why was he asking him about it?

Thinking quickly, Ephraim remembered that he had learned a parallel *sugya* in *Bava Metzia*, and he managed to recall two disputes between *Rashi* and *Tosafos* from that *sugya*. After stammering out those two, he could recall no more.

Rav Nosson Tzvi moved onto the next participant, leaving Ephraim bewildered for the rest of the *bechinah*. Had the Rosh Yeshiva forgotten that he didn't know that *sugya*?

When the exam ended, Ephraim waited until all the other *bachurim* had left, and then approached the Rosh Yeshiva. Before he could get a word out of his mouth, Rav Nosson Tzvi turned to him with a heart-warming smile and said, "Ephraim, I know that you were an *oness* (coerced), that you couldn't know that *sugya* for reasons beyond your control. But you should know one thing for the rest of your life: *fun onsin vakst nisht ois kein gadlus*. (Roughly: no greatness can grow out of being excused for being unable to do something for reasons beyond your control)."

Fast-forward a decade: R' Ephraim is now a popular *rosh chaburah* in the Mir, having lived up to everyone's expectations of him.

And he will forever be fueled, at least subconsciously, by the message

Rav Nosson Tzvi's individual *talmidim* happen to number in the thousands.

Rav Nosson Tzvi imparted to him on that Sunday night: "From excuses, you don't become a *gadol*."

IN DEALING WITH AN ASTONISHING RANGE OF PEOPLE — whether it was a new *bachur* who had never succeeded in his learning or two *talmidim* who could gain from two different approaches while delivering a *chaburah*; a 70-year-old retiree who was settling into serious learning for the first time in many decades, or a bas-mitzvah girl who wanted a *berachah*; a group of *talmidim* who had worked hard to complete a *masechta* or a top prospect who could grow into a *gadol* — Rav Nosson Tzvi, like his great-grandfather, the Alter of Slabodka, did not open his home to thousands each year. He opened the door to individuals — each one, a world of his or her own — who happened to number in the thousands.

# THE DANCE OF TORAH

ROSH YESHIVA, WHO CAN FORGET SIMCHAS TORAH IN Mir Yerushalayim? Some years, you would come into the beis midrash so weak that you had to be wheeled in, yet as soon as the dancing would reach your favorite song, "Ashrei mi she'amalo baTorah – praised is he whose toil is in Torah," you would jump out of your seat like a young child and dance with us as if you had suddenly been cured of the disease that robbed your body of energy.

But in truth, we didn't have to wait for Simchas Torah to see you dance, for every moment of your life was a dance. Etched into the minds of every Mir talmid are images of you shuffling into the beis midrash for a shiur klali, barely able to make your way to the podium. But once there, you would grip the two shtenders at your side and begin speaking.

And your body would dance.

How your body would dance!

Your muscles would move you involuntarily from side to side, to and fro – but you just kept on speaking, weaving yet another intricate shiur. We sat spellbound, watching the dance of Torah, and we would leave after the shiur not only wiser in Torah, but uplifted at the incredible dance we had just witnessed.

Rosh Yeshiva, one memory will remain with me forever.

On 11 Cheshvan, 5772, that Tuesday that began like any other but ended with thousands around the world shedding rivers of tears, the yeshiva's workers turned off the lights and barricaded the doors to the beis midrash – the beis midrash in which you had learned thousands of hours and in which you enabled others to learn millions of hours – to clear the furniture for your levayah.

When the doors finally opened, the lights were still off as hundreds filed in, trying to digest the harsh reality. On your shtender stood a candle that had been lit that morning before Shacharis.

Ner Hashem nishmas adam (Mishlei 20:27). The soul of every Jew is a flame of G-dliness.

Even the most dormant Jewish soul contains a spark of Hashem. In your soul, Rosh Yeshiva, the Ner Hashem was a bonfire that was so powerful that it kindled hundreds of thousands of souls across the globe. But on that Tuesday morning, all that we found at your place in the beis midrash was this small candle.

When your holy body was finally at rest, having danced its last dance of Torah several hours earlier, that candle took its place. That little flame danced as the multitudes converged onto the streets of Yerushalayim to accompany you to your final resting place.

Rosh Yeshiva, the dance of Torah hasn't ended.

The flames you lit in our souls will continue to dance until we are able to join with you in the ultimate dance, with the arrival of Moshiach Tzidkeinu, bim'heirah v'yameinu.

# APPENDIX

# FAMILY TREE GLOSSARY

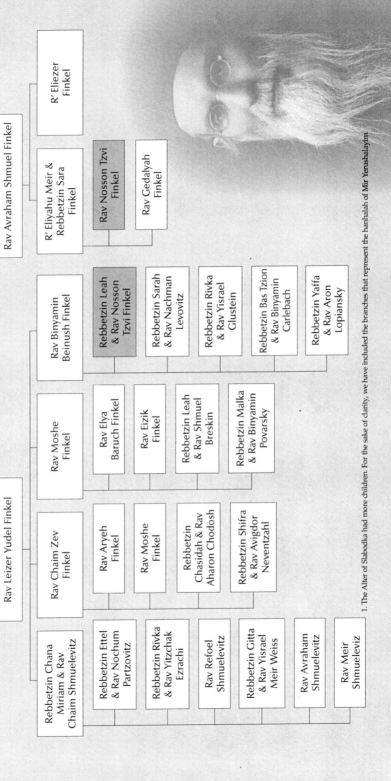

# RAV NOSSON TZVI FINKEL, ALTER OF SLABODKA[1]

**Rav Avraham Shmuel Finkel**
- R' Eliezer Finkel
- R' Eliyahu Meir & Rebbetzin Sara Finkel
  - Rav Nosson Tzvi Finkel
  - Rav Gedalyah Finkel

**Rav Binyamin Beinush Finkel**
- Rebbetzin Leah & Rav Nosson Tzvi Finkel
- Rebbetzin Sarah & Rav Nachman Levovitz
- Rebbetzin Rivka & Rav Yisrael Glustein
- Rebbetzin Bas Tzion & Rav Binyamin Carlebach
- Rebbetzin Yaffa & Rav Aron Lopiansky

**Rav Moshe Finkel**
- Rav Elya Baruch Finkel
- Rav Eizik Finkel
- Rebbetzin Leah & Rav Shmuel Breskin
- Rebbetzin Malka & Rav Binyamin Povarsky

**Rav Leizer Yudel Finkel**

**Rav Chaim Zev Finkel**
- Rav Aryeh Finkel
- Rav Moshe Finkel
- Rebbetzin Chasidah & Rav Aharon Chodosh
- Rebbetzin Shifra & Rav Avigdor Neventzahl

**Rebbetzin Chana Miriam & Rav Chaim Shmuelevitz**
- Rebbetzin Ettel & Rav Nochum Partzovitz
- Rebbetzin Rivka & Rav Yitzchak Ezrachi
- Rav Refoel Shmuelevitz
- Rebbetzin Gitta & Rav Yisrael Meir Weiss
- Rav Avraham Shmuelevitz
- Rav Meir Shmuelevitz

1. The Alter of Slabodka had more children. For the sake of clarity, we have included the branches that represent the hanhalah of Mir Yerushalayim.

# GLOSSARY

*Acharonim* — authoritative commentators on the Talmud, 16th century to the present

*achdus* — unity

*Aggadah, Aggadata* — the homiletical, non-halachic teachings of the Sages

*ahavas Torah* — love of Torah

*Akeidah* — tying of the patriarch Isaac on the altar

*al cheit* — "For the sin ..."; confessional recited on Yom Kippur and before death

*al kiddush Hashem* — in sanctification of G-d's Name

*aliyah* — growth, in a spiritual sense; being called to the Torah; moving to Israel

*ameilus* — toiling in the study of Torah

*Amoraim* — Sages cited in the Gemara

*amud* — one folio of the Talmud; podium or lectern

*aron kodesh* — holy ark

*Aseres Yemei Teshuvah* — Ten Days of Repentance between Rosh Hashanah and Yom Kippur

*aufruf* — celebration on the Shabbos before a man's wedding

*av beis din* — chief judge of a rabbinical court

*Avinu* — our father, usually used in reference to the Patriarchs

*aveil*, pl. *aveilim* — mourner

*aveilus* — mourning period

*avodas Hashem* — the service of Hashem

*baal chessed* — person who performs acts of kindness

*baal korei* — person who reads aloud from the Torah on behalf of the congregation

*baal mussar*, pl. *baalei mussar* — master of ethical conduct

*baal simchah*, pl. *baalei simchah* — person who makes a celebration

*baalebos*, pl. *baalebatim* — householder

*bachur*, pl. *bachurim* — unmarried young man

*bar mitzva* — the occasion at which, at 13 years of age, a boy becomes responsible for observing the commandments of the Torah

*Baruch Dayan Emes* — Blessed is the True Judge (Blessing recited upon hearing bad news)

*Baruch Hashem* — thank G-d

*bas mitzvah* — the occasion at which, at 12 years of age, a girl becomes responsible for observing the commandments of the Torah

*bayis* — house

*bechinah*, pl. *bechinos* — test

*bein adam la'chaveiro* — between man and his fellow

*bein hasedarim* — break between daily learning sessions

*bein hazmanim* — vacation time between semesters in a yeshiva

*beis din* — rabbinic court

*Beis HaMikdash* — the Holy Temple

*beis midrash*, pl. *batei midrash* — study hall

*bekiyus* — expertise; proficiency; erudition; wide-ranging knowledge in a given subject

*ben bayis* — member of a household

*ben Torah*, pl. *bnei Torah* — one who studies and observes the teachings of the Torah

*ben yachid* — only child

*ben yeshiva*, pl. *bnei hayeshiva* — yeshiva student

*bentch* — recite Grace After Meals

*bentch licht* — light candles

*bentcher* — booklet containing the text of Grace After Meals

*berachah*, pl. *berachos* — blessing

*bimah* — table or platform in the synagogue from which the Torah scroll is read

*Bircas Kohanim* — Priestly Blessing

*Bircas HaMazon* — Grace After Meals

*bitachon* — trust in G-d

*bitul Torah* — idle use of time that could be used for Torah study

*blatt* — folio page of Talmud

*bris, bris milah* — circumcision

*chaburah*, pl. *chaburos* — group learning together; a lecture or discourse delivered to a group

*chachamim* — Sages; wise men

*chalat* — long coat

*challah* — tithe separated from dough

*chanukas habayis* — celebration of the dedication of a building or home

*chareidi*, pl. *chareidim* — one who is strictly observant of Jewish law

*chas v'shalom* — Heaven forbid

*chashuv* — important

*chassan* — bridegroom

*Chassid*, pl. *Chassidim* — followers of the Chassidic movement founded by Rabbi Yisrael Baal Shem Tov

*chasunah*, pl. *chasunos* — wedding

*chavrusa*, pl. *chavrusas* — study partner

*chavrusashaft* — study partnership

*Chazal* — Our Sages, of blessed memory

*chazarah* — review

*chelek*, pl. *chalakim* — portion

*chessed* — lovingkindness; acts of beneficence

*chevrah kaddisha* — burial society

*chiddush,* pl. *chiddushim;* alt. *chiddushei Torah* — original Torah insight

*chinuch* — education

*chizuk* — encouragement

*Chol HaMoed* — the intermediate days of Pesach and Succos

*Chumash* — the Five Books of Moses

*chuppah* — canopy under which the marriage ceremony takes place

*chutz la'aretz* — outside of the land of Israel

*chutznik* — person from outside Israel

*dvar Torah,* pl. *divrei Torah* — a Torah thought

*daf,* pl. *dafim* — page, usually of the Talmud

*Daf Yomi* — Talmud study project in which one folio is learned every day

*daven, davening* — praying

*derech eretz* — proper conduct; respect; politeness

*derech halimud* — an approach to learning; study plan

*din* — law; justice

*diyuk,* pl. *diyukim* — a Torah insight in which a word or even an extra letter is noted, analyzed, and explained

*domem* — inanimate object

*derashah,* pl. *derashos* — discourse

*einikel,* pl. *einiklach* — grandchild

*eiruv* — structure that encloses an area to permit carrying within that area on Shabbos

*eishes chayil* — woman of valor

*emes* — truth

*emunah* — faith

*Eretz Yisrael* — the land of Israel

*erev* — the eve of

*esrog* — citron; one of the Four Species taken on Succos

*ezras nashim* — women's section

*fargin* — to be glad at another's success

*farher* — oral test or examination

*frum* — religious; Torah observant

*gabbai* — synagogue sexton; attendant of a *tzaddik*

*gadlus* — greatness

*gadol hador,* pl. *gedolei hador* — leaders of the generation

*gadol,* pl. *gedolim* — outstanding Torah scholar

*galus* — exile; Diaspora

*Gan Eden* — the Garden of Eden

*gaon,* pl. *geonim* — brilliant Torah scholars

*gashmiyus* — materialism

*gedolei Torah* — Torah giants

*gedolei Yisrael* — leaders of Israel

*gemach* — fund providing interest-free loans or services

*Gemara* — Talmudic passage

*geshmak* — zest

*gevaldig* — outstanding; wonderful

*Goral HaGra* — a type of lot innovated by the Vilna Gaon

*guf* — body

*gut Shabbos* — "have a good Shabbos"

*hafganah,* pl. *hafganos* — protest or demonstration

*Haggadah* — Liturgy recited at the Pesach Seder

*hakaras hatov* — gratitude

*Hakadosh Baruch Hu* — the Holy One, Blessed is He

*hakafos* — the ceremony on Simchas

Torah marking the completion of the reading of the Torah

*halachah* — Jewish law

*halachic* — pertaining to Jewish law

*halevai* — if only

*hanhalah* — administration

*harbatzas Torah* — disseminating Torah

*hashgachah* — Divine providence

*hashkafah*, pl. *hashkafos* — outlook; ideology; worldview

*Haskalah* — Reform movement

*haskamah*, pl. *haskamos* — agreement; approbation

*hasmadah* — diligence in learning

*Havdalah* — ceremony marking the conclusion of the Shabbos and holidays

*havtachah* — guarantee

*hesped*, pl. *hespedim* — eulogy

*hisbatlus* — self-abnegation

*hoshanos* — willow branches used on Hoshana Rabbah

*hotza'ah* — prohibition of carrying an object in a public domain on Shabbos

*Imeinu* — our mother, usually used in reference to the Matriarchs

*iyun* — in-depth (study)

*kabbalah*, pl. *kabbalos* — resolution

*kabbalas haTorah* — receiving the Torah

*kabbalas Malchus Shamayim* — accepting the Yoke of Heaven

*kallah* — a bride

*kapitel*, pl. *kapitlach* — chapters (usually of Psalms)

*kapparos* — atonement ceremony

*kashrus* — Jewish dietary laws

*kasher* — make kosher

*kavanah*, pl. *kavanos* — concentration or intent in prayer and religious observance

*kavod* — honor

*kedushah* — holiness

*kefitzas haderech* — miraculous shortening of the way

*kesubah* — marriage contract

*Kesuvim* — Holy Writings

*kever*, pl. *kevarim* — grave

*Kever Rachel* — the burial place of the matriarch Rachel

*kibbutz* — group of diligent Torah students

*Kiddush* — mandatory blessing expressing the sanctity of Shabbos or festivals; festive gathering at which Kiddush is recited

*kiddush Hashem* — sanctification of G-d's Name

*kin'as sofrim* — competition among scholars

*kiruv* — outreach

*Klal Yisrael* — the community of Israel

*Kohen*, pl. *Kohanim* — members of the Priestly family of the tribe of Levi

*kol Torah* — the sound of Torah learning

*kol korei* — public proclamation

*kollel* — academy of higher Jewish study, whose students are usually married men

*korban* — sacrifice

*Kosel* — the Western Wall, remnant of the Holy Temple

*krias haTorah* — the reading of the Torah

*Krias Shema* — recitation of the Shema

*kushya* — a question on a Torah topic

*kuntz* — feat

*l'chaim* — celebratory toast

*lamdan*, pl. *lamdanim* — Talmudic scholar

*lashon hakodesh* — the holy tongue; i.e., Hebrew

*lashon hara* — gossip; slanderous talk

*le'ilui nishmaso* — as a merit for his soul

*lehavdil* — to differentiate between; generally used for holy and secular items

*L'Shanah Tovah* — have a good year

*leshitaso* — in line with a position expressed by the same person elsewhere

*levayah* — funeral

*levush* — manner of dress

*licht bentching* — candle-lighting

*limud haTorah* — learning of Torah

*lishmah* — for its own sake

*lomdus* — erudition; method of Talmud study

*lomeid*, pl. *lomdim* — person who studies Torah

*lulav* — palm branch; one of the Four Species taken on Succos

*ma'arachah*, pl. *ma'arachos* — comprehensive analysis of a Talmudic topic

*maamin* — one who believes (in G-d)

*Maariv* — the evening prayer

*machlokes* — dispute

*maggid shiur*, pl. *maggidei shiur* — teacher of Torah to students on an advanced level

*malach* — angel; Divine messenger

*mammeh* — mother

*marbitz Torah* — one who disseminates Torah

*masechta*, pl. *masechtos* — a tractate of Talmud

*mashgiach* — spiritual guide in a yeshiva

*mashpia ruchani* — spiritual mentor

*maskil* — adherent of the Haskalah movement

*masmid*, pl. *masmidim* — an exceptionally diligent student

*mechanech* — educator

*mechilah* — forgiveness

*mechutan*, pl. *mechutanim* — parents of one's in-law children

*meilitz yosher* — advocate

*mekadesh Sheim Shamayim* — sanctify G-d's Name

*mekurav* — close

*Melaveh Malkah* — meal eaten after Shabbos in honor of the departed Sabbath

*melech* — king

*menachem avel* — comforting a mourner

*menahel* — supervisor; principal

*mentchlichkeit* — decency

*menuchah* — rest

*mesader kiddushin* — one who conducts the marriage ceremony

*mesibah*, pl. *mesibos* — party

*mesirus nefesh* — self-sacrifice

*mesorah* — tradition

*mevater* — to concede to someone else; to forgo in favor of another

*mezuman* — quorum of three for Grace After Meals

*mezuzos* — parchment scrolls affixed to the doorpost

midbar — desert

middah, pl. middos — character trait

Midrash — the Sages' homiletical teachings

miklat — bomb shelter

Minchah — the afternoon prayer

minhag, pl. minhagim — custom

minyan — quorum of 10 men necessary for conducting a prayer service

Mishkan — Tabernacle, the Temple used by the Jews during their sojourn in the wilderness

mishloach manos — gifts of food sent on Purim

Mishnah — teachings of the Tannaim that form the basis of the Talmud

mittah — bier

mitzvah, pl. mitzvos — Torah commandment; good deed

mi'ut sichah — limited conversation

mivtza — project

Modeh Ani — prayer recited upon awakening in the morning, expressing gratitude for life

moed — festival

Moetzes Gedolei HaTorah — Association of Torah Sages

mohel — one who performs a circumcision

mossad, pl. mosdos — institution

Motza'ei Shabbos — Saturday night, after nightfall

Mussaf — additional prayers recited on Shabbos and festivals

mussar — ethical teachings, aimed at self-refinement

Mussar Movement — a movement founded by R' Yisrael of Salant that encourages the study of mussar and the pursuit of self-refinement

mussar shmuess — a lecture on self-improvement

navi, pl. nevi'im — prophet

nebach — piteous person

nefesh — soul

negios — personal prejudices or interests

Ne'ilah — the concluding prayer of Yom Kippur

neitz — sunrise

neshamah, pl. neshamos — soul

niftar — deceased

niggun — tune, melody

Olam Haba — the World to Come

Olam Hazeh — this world

Omer — refers to the 49-day period between Pesach and Shavuos

oness — one who was coerced to sin

p'shat — basic explanation

parashah — weekly Torah portion

parnasah — livelihood

passul — invalid

pasuk, pl. pesukim — verse

perek — chapter

petirah — passing on (death)

petur — exemption

pikei'ach — wise person

pikuach nefesh — danger to life

pilpul — analytical method of Talmud study

posek, pl. poskim — halachic authorities

Rabbeinu — our teacher

Rachtzah — ritual hand-washing during the Pesach Seder

Rashi — Rabbi Shlomo Yitzchaki, 11th-Century scholar who wrote the basic commentaries on the

Bible and Talmud; a commentary written by Rabbi Shlomo Yitzchaki

*rav*, pl. *rabbanim* — rabbi

*rebbi*, pl. *rebbeim* — Torah teacher

*ribbis* — borrowing or lending with interest

*Ribono shel Olam* — Master of the World

*Rishon*, pl. *Rishonim* — early commentators on the Talmud, 11th-15th centuries

*rosh chaburah*, pl. *roshei chaburah* — leader of a *chaburah*

rosh yeshiva — dean of a Torah institution; senior lecturer in a yeshiva

*ruach* — spirit, enthusiasm

*ruchniyus* — spirituality

*sandak* — person honored to hold the baby at a *bris*

*s'char* — reward

*seder*, pl. *sedarim* — study session; Pesach traditional festive meal commemorating the Exodus from Egypt

*Sefer Torah* — Torah Scroll

*sefer*, pl. *sefarim* — book

*Sefirah* — period between Pesach and Shavuos during which certain mourning customs are observed

*segulah* — spiritual remedy

*Sephardi*, pl. *Sephardim* — Jew of Spanish, Oriental, or Middle Eastern ancestry

*seudah*, pl. *seudos* — meal, especially a festive meal

*seudah shlishis* — the third meal of the Sabbath

*Shacharis* — the morning prayer

*shakla vetarya* — dialogue of the Gemara

*shaliach tzibbur* — emissary of the community

*Shalom Aleichem* — traditional greeting; "peace be on you"

*shalom bayis* — harmony in the home; peaceful relationship between husband and wife

*Shamayim* — Heaven

*Shas* — the Talmud as a whole

*Shechinah* — Divine Presence

*Shemoneh Esrei* (lit. *Eighteen*) — a prayer, originally 18 blessings but now 19, that forms the central core of each weekday prayer service

*sheva berachos* — festive meals held for a bride and groom during the week after their wedding, so named for the seven blessings recited after the meal

*shutaf*, pl. *shutfim* — partner

*shidduch* — marriage match

*shiur*, pl. *shiurim* — Torah lecture

*shiur klali* — a lecture given to the entire student body in a yeshiva

*shiur*, pl. *shiurim* — lecture

*shivah* — seven-day mourning period for a deceased person

*shmuess*, pl. *shmuessen*; alt. *mussar shmuess* — lecture on Torah topics; ethical discourse

*shofar* — ram's horn, blown on Rosh Hashanah

*shtikel Torah*, pl. *shtiklach Torah* — a complex examination of a Torah topic that usually includes a novel interpretation

*shtiebel*, pl. *shtieblach* — small synagogue

*shtikah* — silence

*shemiras halashon* — guarding one's speech

*Shulchan Aruch* — Code of Jewish Law

siddur, pl. siddurim — prayer book

sifrei mussar — books on ethical topics

siman berachah — an omen of blessing

simchah — joy, happiness; celebration

siyum haShas — completion of the entire Talmud

siyum, pl. siyumim — completion of a portion of Torah or Talmud

siyata d'Shmaya — Heavenly (Divine) assistance

succah — booth in which Jews dwell during Succos

sugya, pl. sugyos — conceptual unit in Talmud study; topic in Talmud

tallis, pl. talleisim — prayer shawl

talmid chacham, pl. talmidei chachamim — Torah scholar

talmid, pl. talmidim — student

Tanach — acronym for Torah, Neviim, Kesuvim; the Written Torah

Tannaim — Sages of the Mishnah

terumos and maasros — tithes

tatteh — father

tefillah, pl. tefillos — prayer

tefillin — phylacteries

Tehillim — Psalms

teirutz — explanation; answer; excuse

tekias shofar, pl. tekios — blowing of the shofar

teshuvah — answer; repentance

tochachah — rebuke

Tosafos — explanatory notes on the Talmud by scholars of the 12th-14th centuries

tzaddik, pl. tzaddikim — righteous person

tzavaah — last will and testament

tzedakah — charity

tzibbur — congregation

Tzion; Zion — Jerusalem

tzitzis — four-cornered garment containing fringes, worn by Jewish men and boys

upsherin — a boy's first haircut, usually at the age of three

vaad, pl. vaadim — a group symposium on a Torah topic, usually a mussar topic

vasikin — prayer at sunrise

vidui — the confession recited on Yom Kippur and before death

vort — a Torah thought; celebration of an engagement

yahrtzeit — anniversary of the death of a person

Yamim Noraim — the high holy days

Yasher koach — thank you

Yarchei Kallah — lit. Months of Gathering, i.e., a time when large numbers of people come together for Torah study and lectures

yedios — general Torah knowledge

yerei Shamayim — person who fears Heaven

Yerushalayim — Jerusalem

yeshiva — a school where Torah is studied

yetzer hara — evil inclination; connotes desire to violate the Torah

Yetzias Mitzrayim — Exodus from Egypt

Yid — Jew

Yiddishkeit — the Jewish way of life

yiras Shamayim — fear of Heaven

Yom Tov, pl. Yamim Tovim — holiday; festival

*yungerman,* pl. *yungeleit* — married man, usually referring to one studying in a yeshiva or *kollel*

*zechus* — merit; privilege

*zees (Yid.)* — sweet

*zemiros* — songs sung at Sabbath and festive meals

*zimun* — quorum of three for Grace After Meals

*zocheh* — to merit

*zman,* pl. *zmanim* — semester; time